TAROT
AND THE
GATES OF LIGHT

"Mark Horn's brilliant new book opened up a new world for me. I was familiar with both fields of tarot and Kabbalah, but I had never viewed them through the larger lens Mark provides. This unique synergy offers rich psycho-spiritual insights and provides practical processes anyone can apply. May it change the lives of millions of readers."

NEW YORK TIMES BESTSELLING AUTHOR
GAY HENDRICKS, PH.D., AUTHOR OF *THE BIG LEAP*

"Mark Horn has distilled decades of study and practice into a journey of archetypes and images that is powerful, healing, and transformative. *Tarot and the Gates of Light* is a road map for anyone of any background to follow. So sit, read, study, and follow this step-by-step path from bondage to liberation, and you will find yourself growing into the wise, embodied soul you really are."

ANDREW RAMER, AUTHOR OF
FRAGMENTS OF THE BROOKLYN TALMUD AND
COAUTHOR OF *ASK YOUR ANGELS*

"Perfect for those who want to follow a spiritual practice that combines tarot, Hebrew Kabbalah, and personal meditation. It is also a great way to explore the deeper meanings of the Minor Arcana."

MARY K. GREER, AUTHOR OF *TAROT FOR YOUR SELF* AND
21 WAYS TO READ A TAROT CARD

"Spiritual disciplines are like prisms, refracting the ineffable light into radiant diversities of human imagination. This makes *Tarot and the Gates of Light* a prism within a prism, glittering with Mark Horn's insights, histories, wit, and wisdom."

RABBI JAY MICHAELSON, AUTHOR OF
GOD VS. GAY? AND *THE GATE OF TEARS*

"By using a traditional Jewish devotional system, the 49-day spiritual exercise known as Counting the Omer, and then matching each day with the appropriate tarot images, Mark Horn gives tarot readers a way into both Jewish Kabbalah and the contemporary Jewish Renewal movement and gives concrete form to some of the more abstract ideas about the Tree of Life. This book is rich in both information and practice. A valuable and innovative contribution."

RACHEL POLLACK, AUTHOR OF
SEVENTY-EIGHT DEGREES OF WISDOM AND *TAROT WISDOM*

"Mark has given a profound gift and 'technology' to the serious seeker: an erudite, yet highly accessible and engaging, compendium of knowledge and wisdom teachings and, most importantly, a dedicated path of transformation—one self, one soul, one day at a time."

PROFESSOR KATHERINE KURS, M.DIV., PH.D.,
EDITOR OF *SEARCHING FOR YOUR SOUL*

"Offers a spiritual practice for self-transformation, based on the tarot and the mystical practice of counting the 49 days prior to the revelation holiday of Shavuot/Pentecost. For each of the 49 days, Horn offers a combination of tarot cards as a meditative opening to growth and self-knowledge. Horn's work displays a deep appreciation of tarot as a language for the soul and applies that language to a mystical technology for daily transformation. His book will appeal to diviners and spiritual seekers, Kabbalists and New Age practitioners. The practice laid out in this book is openhearted and challenging, ecumenical and ethically astute. It has the potential to set us on the path to enlightenment."

RABBI JILL HAMMER, PH.D., AUTHOR OF
THE JEWISH BOOK OF DAYS AND
OMER CALENDAR OF BIBLICAL WOMEN

"Mark Horn courageously provides an autobiographical approach to teaching the Kabbalistic practice of Counting the Omer. *Tarot and the Gates of Light* gives Jews and Christians alike a powerful, accessible tool for advancing personal spiritual growth and development."

RABBI GOLDIE MILGRAM, AUTHOR OF
RECLAIMING JUDAISM AS A SPIRITUAL PRACTICE

"Horn has shattered the old saying 'there's nothing new under the sun' with this unorthodox and ambitious work. *Tarot and the Gates of Light* presents the rare opportunity to find liberation through a serious and meaningful ancient practice refined over the centuries. Tarot and Kabbalah are wedded together as never before—in perfect harmony and beauty."

ANGELO NASIOS, AUTHOR OF *TAROT: UNLOCKING THE ARCANA*

TAROT
AND THE
GATES OF LIGHT

A Kabbalistic
Path to Liberation

MARK HORN

Destiny Books
Rochester, Vermont

Destiny Books
One Park Street
Rochester, Vermont 05767
www.DestinyBooks.com

Text stock is SFI certified

Destiny Books is a division of Inner Traditions International.

Unless otherwise noted, the New Testament Scripture quotations contained herein are from the New Revised Standard Version Bible, copyright © 1989 by the Division of Christian Education of the National Council of Churches of Christ in the U.S.A. and are used by permission. All rights reserved.

Quotes from *Man's Search for Meaning* by Viktor E. Frankl, copyright © 1959, 1962, 1984, 1992 by Viktor E. Frankl. Reprinted by permission of Beacon Press, Boston, Massachusetts.

Image on page 110 created by Brendan Dowling.

Cataloging-in-Publication Data for this title is available from the Library of Congress

ISBN 978-1-62055-930-7 (print)
ISBN 978-1-62055-931-4 (ebook)

Printed and bound in the United States by Lake Book Manufacturing, Inc. The text stock is SFI certified. The Sustainable Forestry Initiative® program promotes sustainable forest management.

10 9 8 7 6 5 4 3 2 1

Text design by Virginia Scott Bowman and layout by Priscilla Baker
This book was typeset in Garamond Premier Pro with Heirloom Artcraft, Gill Sans, and Legacy Sans used as display typefaces

To send correspondence to the author of this book, mail a first-class letter to the author c/o Inner Traditions • Bear & Company, One Park Street, Rochester, VT 05767, and we will forward the communication, or contact the author directly at **www.GatesOfLightTarot.com**.

Contents

A Personal Introduction   xi

Kabbalah, Tarot Cards, and Counting the Omer—
What's This All About?   1

    The Forty-Nine Steps of Spiritual Refinement   2

    How a Biblical Commandment Turned into a
        Kabbalistic Meditation   3

    The Adoption and Adaptation of Pentecost by the Early Christians   5

    The Tikkun Prayer Vigil   8

    Kabbalah, Cabala, and Qabalah   9

The Tree of Life   12

    The Sephirot   16

    The Four Worlds   26

    The Tarot Connection   31

    Putting It All Together   36

How to Follow the Daily Practice   38

    The Ritual   38

    Using the Cards   38

    How to Use the Key Words to Help Interpret the Cards   40

The Meditation   43

The Blessing: A Nontraditional Version   43

The Prayer: A Nontraditional Version   43

Looking Ahead to the 50th Day   43

Week 1   Chesed   46

Day 1: Chesed of Chesed. Starting the Journey with Love   46

Day 2: Gevurah of Chesed. Structure and Struggle Held
in Loving-kindness   54

Day 3: Tiferet of Chesed. Holding Hurt and Pain with
Love and Compassion   61

Day 4: Netzach of Chesed. Defending Yourself without
Falling Prey to Your Defenses   68

Day 5: Hod of Chesed. Finding the Victory in Love
by Surrendering the Ego   74

Day 6: Yesod of Chesed. Shining the Light of Love into
Our Darkest Places   82

Day 7: Malchut of Chesed. Accepting Love and Being True
to Who You Fully Are in Relationship   92

Week 2   Gevurah   100

Day 8: Chesed of Gevurah. Creating Structure without
Stricture   101

Day 9: Gevurah of Gevurah. Learning Restraint
in Judgment   108

Day 10: Tiferet of Gevurah. Seeing the Beauty in Structure   112

Day 11: Netzach of Gevurah. Perseverance Furthers   121

Day 12: Hod of Gevurah. Getting Yourself Out of the
Way of Your Self   128

Day 13: Yesod of Gevurah. Intimacy Can Blossom
in a Strong Container   138

Day 14: Malchut of Gevurah. Healthy Boundaries Make
Healthy Relationships   147

Week 3   Tiferet   156

Day 15: Chesed of Tiferet. Finding Joy in Harmony 156

Day 16: Gevurah of Tiferet. The Role of Judgment
in Compassion 166

Day 17: Tiferet of Tiferet. The Heart of the Matter 174

Day 18: Netzach of Tiferet. Finding the Victory in Truth 178

Day 19: Hod of Tiferet. Witness and Withness—
Humility in Compassion 187

Day 20: Yesod of Tiferet. Harnessing the Passion
in Compassion 196

Day 21: Malchut of Tiferet. The Dignity in
Compassionate Action 206

Week 4   Netzach   215

Day 22: Chesed of Netzach. Love Endures All Things 216

Day 23: Gevurah of Netzach. Endurance Requires Discipline 227

Day 24: Tiferet of Netzach. Finding Compassion in Victory 237

Day 25: Netzach of Netzach. Passive Endurance
vs. Active Endurance 246

Day 26: Hod of Netzach. The Victory That Comes
from Surrender 249

Day 27: Yesod of Netzach. The Connection That Fuels
Commitment 260

Day 28: Malchut of Netzach. Nobility in Endurance 271

Week 5   Hod   282

Day 29: Chesed of Hod. Overflowing with Gratitude 283

Day 30: Gevurah of Hod. Living in Awe of the
Splendor of Creation 294

Day 31: Tiferet of Hod. An Open Heart Is Always Full,
but Never Full of Itself 302

Day 32: Netzach of Hod. Finding Endurance in Humility
Is Finding Victory in Humility 312

Day 33: Hod of Hod. Glory, Glory Hallelujah 321

Day 34: Yesod of Hod. The Connection of I-Thou Begins in Humility 327

Day 35: Malchut of Hod. When You're Secure in Your Dignity, Humility Comes Naturally 335

Week 6   Yesod 345

Day 36: Chesed of Yesod. The Secret Love Binding the World Together 346

Day 37: Gevurah of Yesod. Setting Boundaries in Intimacy 358

Day 38: Tiferet of Yesod. Truth Is the Foundation of Intimacy 369

Day 39: Netzach of Yesod. The Ongoing Commitment to Intimacy 381

Day 40: Hod of Yesod. Humility Creates the Space for Intimacy 391

Day 41: Yesod of Yesod. Desire as the Foundation for All Spiritual Pursuits 402

Day 42: Malchut of Yesod. Being Fully Present for Relationship 413

Week 7   Malchut 425

Day 43: Chesed of Malchut. Directing the Flow with Nobility 426

Day 44: Gevurah of Malchut. Self-Discipline and Restraint Define Sovereignty 434

Day 45: Tiferet of Malchut. Leadership Sets an Example through Compassion 442

Day 46: Netzach of Malchut. The World in a Grain of Sand, Eternity in an Hour 450

Day 47: Hod of Malchut. Balancing the Openness of Humility with Sovereignty 459

Day 48: Yesod of Malchut. The Foundation of Nobility 469

Day 49: Malchut of Malchut. Living in Integrity Is True Sovereignty 478

Pentecost
Day 50: The Gates Are Always Open   481

◆ ◆ ◆

Meditation Instructions   486

Glossary   488

A Note about God Language   499

Notes   502

Bibliography   507

Acknowledgments   515

Index   518

When you begin the practice of focusing your mind to hear the voice of God in everything, you soon come up against the issue of the human intellect. The intellect conceals the Divine by imagining it is separate from God; believing itself to be the source of imagination. But it is by developing a rigorous practice of deep listening for the voice of God in everything, including in the intellect, that God's voice is also revealed within the intellect. Then it is precisely in your mind that you will encounter true Divine revelation.

RAV ABRAHAM ISAAC KOOK

The first and most essential service of a mythology is this one, of opening the mind and heart to the utter wonder of all being.

JOSEPH CAMPBELL

Teach us to count our days rightly, that we may gain a heart of wisdom.

PSALMS 90:12

You shall count seven full weeks . . . count fifty days to the day after the seventh full week.

LEVITICUS 23:15–16

A Personal Introduction

And you may ask yourself, "Well, how did I get here?"
FROM "ONCE IN A LIFETIME,"
LYRICS BY DAVID BYRNE

I WALKED AWAY FROM JUDAISM on October 3, 1965. It was the day after my bar mitzvah, and I was done with all organized religion. I wasn't going back to a synagogue (or any house of worship) ever again. So how did I end up writing a book about Kabbalah, Jewish meditation, and tarot?

Even though I was just thirteen years old, I knew I was gay. I knew what Judaism (and Christianity) had to say about homosexuality, and I wasn't buying it. But even though I was out the door (if not entirely out of the closet), I had a deep spiritual hunger. I believed my (yet to be experienced) love could be an expression of my spirituality. In many ways, I was walking a very traditional Jewish path—that of exile. So I became a seeker in and out of many traditions, looking for a community that shared my sense of the sacred and a path that enabled me to be my authentic self and experience a connection to the Divine.

I first encountered tarot cards when I was sixteen years old. At the time, I was a member of the Society for Creative Anachronism—you know, that group of folks who hold medieval tournaments in period clothing. One of the group's founders, author Marion Zimmer Bradley, gave me a tarot reading just before I borrowed her tent to go up to the Woodstock festival. Based on that reading, she recommended I get my own deck and give readings myself. She could see that the images and symbols on the cards called to me, and indeed, I followed her advice. I have been studying the tarot ever since. I still have and use the first deck I bought in 1969.

At that point, I'd heard of Kabbalah. The second book I read about the cards (way too advanced for me at the time) was Paul Foster Case's *The Tarot: A Key to the Wisdom of the Ages.* It was filled with Kabbalah stuff that seemed abstract and convoluted to me, so for many years, I just ignored the whole Kabbalah thing. After all, I'd pretty much cut Judaism out of my life anyway.

For a lower-middle-class kid from Brooklyn, I was following some pretty exotic paths. Because my heart longed for a spiritual community, I searched for one in all the options that seemed to pop up in the sixties. I read Ram Dass, dropped acid, crashed with a commune that was squatting in a tenement in the East Village, backpacked across Europe (my cards always with me), tried astral projection, and chanted with Guru Maharaj Ji cultists, all the while participating in the early gay activist movement. Meanwhile, I got my B.A. in English, writing papers that almost always included references to tarot.

Eventually, I made my way to Japan, where I first encountered Vipassana meditation. Practicing this meditation was one of the most profound experiences of my life. In those first ten days of deep work in rural Japan, I faced a lot of inner demons. And I experienced the joy and light that's the underpinning of all reality.

The Vipassana people don't push the Buddhist origin of the meditation. They emphasize that the practice is nonsectarian, that it's simply breath and observation and that this is shared by all humans regardless of religion. So when I first tried to learn more about the Buddhist background from them, they put me off. The teachers' position was: if this practice works for you, use it to be a better person, whatever your religion. But I was persistent, and eventually I got in so deep that I was going to retreats where students would learn Pali so we could read sutras in the original language of the Buddha. I loved it, but I had to laugh. I had balked at learning Biblical Hebrew as a child, and now I was learning another "dead" language. Then something strange happened. The deeper my meditation went, the more I felt a longing to reconnect with Judaism—that deep down in my soul (which of course the Buddhists don't believe in), my Judaism was important.

When I returned home to the United States, I shared this experience with an old friend of mine. She asked me what I had learned and received from Buddhism. When I explained, she pulled down Jewish texts from her shelf to show me analogous teachings—including texts that I recognized as meditation instruction. I was stunned. Of course, I wouldn't have understood these texts as a child, but I'd never met a rabbi or Jewish teacher who ever spoke about meditation. I didn't think such rabbis existed. My friend, who lived in North Carolina, said that if she could find a teacher there, then there certainly had to be rabbis in New York who taught with this understanding. So my spiritual search sent me back to the tradition I'd left years ago.

Just as I had grown, so had Judaism: I found a synagogue that was LGBTQ-positive and dived in to learn teachings I was never taught as a child. Soon I was going to Jewish spiritual retreat centers such as Elat Chayyim, where I studied Kabbalistic texts with Reb Zalman Schachter-Shalomi, z"l, and chanting meditations with Rabbi Shefa Gold. I took classes in the Zohar taught by Professor Eliot Wolfson at New York University. Before I knew it, I was invited to teach a class in Jewish storytelling at the Prozdor program of the Jewish Theological Seminary. This was kind of dizzying to me; after all those years away, I found myself deeply involved in Jewish life. I wrote a liturgy for a Queer Pride Seder, which became an annual event at my synagogue for a decade and was adapted by other synagogues around the world. And I learned about a Kabbalistic meditation tied to an obscure Jewish custom I'd never learned about in my youth that would be the next step in my spiritual journey: Counting the Omer.

As I deepened my Jewish studies and my learning in Kabbalah, I realized it was time to go back and finally begin to look at the correspondences with the tarot cards. I realized that I could use tarot cards to do the special Kabbalistic meditations practiced during the period of Counting the Omer.

I started sharing my experience of Counting the Omer online each year, on a blog I called Another Queer Jewish Buddhist. I wrote about using the cards with the Omer count as a kind of a spiritual MRI for inner exploration. Doing this revealed issues I tried to hide, even from myself, and it uncovered gifts I didn't even know I had. Working with the cards in this way brought me to new depths of understanding in the tarot, in Judaism, and, of course, in myself. And because I shared my personal struggles in this practice publicly, many people who read my posts online felt a connection and wrote me with questions about how to use the cards in their own Omer practice. Which is, of course, what led me to write this book.

Counting the Omer using tarot and Kabbalistic meditation is a journey that you can take too, whether you're Jewish or not. This book will serve as a guide, whether you do it during the traditional period between Passover and Pentecost or for any forty-nine-day period you choose. Because this has been part of my path, as I give examples of how to use the cards in the daily practice, I reveal many of my own struggles and triumphs. I hope this inspires you to follow suit and use this practice as an opportunity to explore deeply within. My wish is that it brings you deep peace, a heart of compassion, spiritual strength, and the blessing of experiencing the Divine light that always surrounds and supports us.

MARK HORN
NEW YORK CITY
GATESOFLIGHTTAROT.COM

Kabbalah, Tarot Cards, and Counting the Omer— What's This All About?

THIS BOOK IS AN UNORTHODOX GUIDE through the forty-nine-day mystical practice known as Counting the Omer—an ancient Jewish ritual that is observed between the holidays of Passover and Shavuot (also known as Pentecost). As practiced by Kabbalists, the ritual is designed to refine the soul in preparation for spiritual revelation. It creates a psycho-spiritual inner journey that follows the path of the ancient Israelites from the moment of their physical freedom from slavery in Egypt to the moment of their spiritual freedom when they received the revelation of the Torah at Mt. Sinai. You can take this inner journey yourself; it's a powerful practice that can help you change your life for the better and open you to a closer relationship with the Divine.

This book will guide you along the path, drawing on teachings in the Torah, the Talmud, and other Jewish sources, including concepts and meditations from traditional Kabbalistic texts. What makes it unorthodox is that it uses correspondences between these concepts and the underlying structure of the tarot deck to deepen your experience of this mystical practice through reflection, contemplation, and specific meditations. We'll also be making stops along the way for insights from Christianity, Buddhism, and other wisdom traditions, both Eastern and Western, to help open our minds and hearts to the wonder of all being.

While Counting the Omer is an age-old practice, it is also a living tradition. Today many Jews continue to use the period between Passover and Shavuot for study and meditation as a way of finding their spiritual center—learning to hear and align their will with Divine will. So can anyone do this? The answer is a resounding yes. As the old advertising campaign for Levy's Rye Bread proclaimed, "You don't have to be Jewish." In fact, the early Christians adapted and transformed this practice to follow the arc of the spiritual journey as they experienced it from Easter to Pentecost.

Whether you identify as Jewish or Christian (or even, like me, as Jewish-Buddhist), you can indeed experience the benefits of this path. You just have to be willing to take the steps of this forty-nine-day spiritual journey. But before you start, you'll need a map of the territory:

- The origins and meaning of the original Omer practice and how it has evolved over time into a Kabbalistic meditation,
- An essential explanation of the Kabbalistic concepts at the heart of the meditation,
- An exploration of how those concepts correspond to the structure of the tarot deck, and
- A guide on how to work with the cards and the Sephirot over the course of forty-nine days in preparation for an experience of personal revelation on the fiftieth day.

If you do the work, at the end of this period, you can experience profound changes in all your relationships, and you will find a stronger, deeper connection to the Divine in your life. After counting the forty-nine days of the Omer, you'll know how to make every day count for the rest of your life.

THE FORTY-NINE STEPS OF
SPIRITUAL REFINEMENT

How long does it take to make an important change in life? Sure, some of us are capable of overnight change, but for most of us, making a major change to the direction and compass of our lives takes time and practice. You might want to change a bad habit or build up the discipline to start a daily spiritual practice. You may want to break free of an addiction or overcome negative thinking. You might need time to consider a new direction in life or to heal from a personal tragedy. Whatever your motivation, the many wisdom traditions of humanity offer a wide range of effective practices for personal and spiritual growth. One that has resonated for me personally is the forty-nine-day period known in the Jewish tradition as Counting the Omer, culminating on the Jewish holiday of Shavuot, also known as Pentecost, the fiftieth day.

Pentecost is the Greek word that Hellenized Jews used to name this period of observance because it simply means "fifty days." If you're Christian, you may know Pentecost as the first time the Holy Spirit descended on a group of Jesus's disciples, including the apostles. What both traditions share is the connection between Pentecost and revelation. Whatever tradition you come from, this forty-nine-day period of reflection and meditation is a spiritual discipline that can bring great benefit.

HOW A BIBLICAL COMMANDMENT
TURNED INTO A KABBALISTIC MEDITATION

Originally, this forty-nine-day period was part of the liturgical calendar of sacrifice at the Temple in Jerusalem three thousand years ago. In Judaism, the Counting of the Omer is one of the 613 Biblical commandments:

And you shall count from the day after the sabbath, from the day that you brought the sheaf offering; seven weeks shall there be complete; to the day after the seventh week shall you shall count fifty days; and you shall present a new offering of grain to YHVH.[1]

During this period, the ancient Israelites were commanded to bring an *omer* (a unit of measure approximately 3.5 liters that is sometimes translated as a "sheaf") of the new barley harvest to the Temple every day as an offering. It was an agricultural holiday, giving thanks for the first harvest and offering a portion of it as a sacrifice in the hope that the next harvest (of wheat) would be a good one.

Today most of us aren't growing any barley, and there hasn't been a temple in Jerusalem since the Romans destroyed it in 70 CE. Without a temple, it's impossible to carry out any commandments focused on temple practice. This is where the oral Torah and the Jewish mystical tradition come in. Besides the written Torah with its many commandments, there was also an oral tradition that was passed down from teacher to teacher, generation to generation. According to the Mishnah*, this tradition of transmission began with Moses: "Moses received the Torah on Sinai, and handed it down to Joshua; Joshua to the elders; the elders to the prophets; and the prophets handed it down to the men of the Great Assembly."[2]

The oral tradition included accounts of mystical practices that, over time, developed into the Jewish mystical tradition of Kabbalah. Kabbalah simply means "received," and it is used to mean the knowledge of Jewish esoteric teachings and meditation practices that were transmitted orally from teacher to student. Sometimes it also refers to knowledge that was received through direct revelation and then passed down. The earliest writing that is considered to be a Kabbalistic text is the Sefer Yetzirah; the date of its origin is disputed, but it has been narrowed down to somewhere between the second century BCE and the second century CE.

The Sefer Yetzirah is the first written reference to one of the essential concepts in Kabbalah: the ten Sephirot, which are central to the practice of Counting the Omer:

> *In two and thirty most occult and wonderful paths of*
> *wisdom*
> *did YHVH the Lord of Hosts engrave his name. . . .*
> *Ten . . . are the Sephiroth, and twenty-two the letters,*
> *these are the Foundation of all things.*[3]

---

*The Mishnah was the first time in history that the "oral tradition" in Judaism was written down, sometime in the third century CE.

When you practice Counting the Omer, you will work to draw down the Divine energies known as the Sephirot in a practice of purification and meditation designed to strengthen your spiritual container. This will gradually open any spiritual blockages so you can feel the Divine flow that is always available to us. The forty-nine steps work in a graduated order, in a kind of spiritual workout regimen, day by day. It is designed to prepare you for a more direct experience of the Divine on the fiftieth day.

The oral tradition of Judaism also teaches that it was not only Moses who received the Torah on the mountaintop. Every Israelite standing at the foot of the mountain also received their own revelation, making the event at Sinai both a uniquely individual and a communal encounter with the Divine. The oral tradition also teaches that the soul of every Jew—past and future—was also present at the foot of Mt. Sinai. And because the fiftieth day is the day the Torah was given to the people, the holiday of Shavuot is also known as the birthday of the Torah.

So for the Jewish mystics, even though there was no longer a temple where the people could offer their omer of barley in sacrifice, it was meaningful (and, as a commandment, essential) for Jews to continue Counting the Omer symbolically as a practice of spiritually reexperiencing the journey of Exodus from the first moment of freedom in Egypt to the revelation at Sinai. Today there are several books that observant Jews use to guide them through the practice.

The main part of this book is also a guide through this forty-nine-day practice, with the difference of using tarot cards to deepen your experience of the Sephirotic energies of each day and as an aid for your daily reflection and contemplation.

THE ADOPTION AND ADAPTATION OF PENTECOST BY THE EARLY CHRISTIANS

For Christians, the genesis of their observance of Pentecost finds its origin in the New Testament, Acts 2:1–6, which recounts the story of the first Pentecost prayer gathering after the Crucifixion in the same "upper room" where the Last Supper was held. It was fifty days after Passover.

Present were the apostles, Mary, and Jesus's brothers, along with several women whose names aren't given. While the names of those women, like so many other women in the Bible, remain unknown, the message that the Holy Spirit can come to anyone regardless of gender comes through loud and clear, because the Holy Spirit descended on all of them, and everyone began speaking in a language they didn't know.

> When the day of Pentecost had come, they were all together in one place. And suddenly from heaven there came a sound like the rush of a violent wind, and it filled the entire house where they were sitting. Divided tongues, as of fire, appeared among them, and a tongue rested on each of them. All of them were filled with the Holy Spirit and began to speak in other languages, as the Spirit gave them ability. Now there were devout Jews from every nation under heaven living in Jerusalem. And at the sound the crowd gathered and was bewildered, because each one heard them speaking in the native language of each.[4]

Just as Jesus had been proclaimed the fulfillment of Jewish prophecies of a messiah, the Apostle Peter proclaimed this event to be the fulfillment of the words of prophecy in Joel:

> I will pour out My spirit on all flesh; and your sons and daughters shall prophesy, your old men shall dream dreams, your young men shall see visions.[5]

The apostles and their followers were engaged in a traditional Pentecost eve prayer vigil. After all, they still identified as Jews, and their experience of personal and communal revelation was simply a renewal and reinterpretation of the Jewish tradition.

Following their experience of the descent of the Holy Spirit, Peter used Joel's prophecy as evidence that from this point on, revelation was not only available on Shavuot, but on every day continuously. In fact, Jews believe that God is pouring forth Sephirotic energies into existence continuously, so that creation is renewed and revelation is available to us every second. By attuning yourself to this energy and strengthening your container, you can have a deeper and more direct experience of it. Peter took this further to proclaim this revelation is available to everyone, Jew and Gentile, man and woman.[6] This first celebration of Pentecost after the Crucifixion, with its own distinct experience of revelation, has come to be known in some Christian traditions as the birthday of the Church, because those who began speaking "in tongues" went out to spread the Gospel on the streets of Jerusalem to Jews from other countries in their native language.

In the early Church, the period between Easter Sunday and Pentecost was known as Eastertide, and the entire fifty-day period was celebrated as a single feast. In medieval and Renaissance Italy, it was the custom to drop red rose petals from the ceiling of the church to reenact the "tongues of flame" that descended on the apostles with the Holy Spirit.* To this day in the Roman Catholic Church, each Sunday between Easter and Pentecost has its own title and theme connecting to the Resurrection.

In recent years, Roman Catholics have taken on the practice of the Via Lucis, the Stations of the Resurrection. This fifty-day practice of meditation and devotional prayer is based on the scripturally recorded appearances of Jesus after the Resurrection and before the Ascension through to the Descent of the Holy Spirit at Pentecost. The tradition of all-night prayer vigils the night before Pentecost continues to this day in the Eastern Orthodox and Eastern Catholic Churches, where a liturgical book known as the Pentecostarion has been in use for centuries and continues to be the focus of communal worship during this fifty-day period.

While most modern Christians are unaware of the spiritual dimension of this fifty-day period, leaders in some Protestant denominations have been working to reinvigorate the customs of this ancient practice.[7] In Western denominations such as the Anglicans and Lutherans, only the Night Prayer is recited on Pentecost eve.

---

*This custom actually survives to this day; you can see it enacted in the online YouTube video titled "A Shower of Rose Petals for Pentecost at St. John Cantius Church."

THE TIKKUN PRAYER VIGIL

In Jewish communities, the ritual of a prayer vigil the night before Pentecost evolved into what is known today as a Tikkun Leil Shavuot. As it has evolved from its origins among Jewish mystics, the ritual goes from sunset throughout the night until sunrise. Today many congregations continue to observe this ritual, studying the Torah and Kabbalistic texts that celebrate Divine union: the marriage of the people of Israel to God with the Torah serving as the *ketubah* (wedding contract). The morning service that follows has a wedding canopy (called a *chuppah*) over the altar.

One example of such a vigil is the story of Rabbi Joseph Caro, one of the most respected rabbis and Kabbalists of the mid-1500s. He had invited Rabbi Shlomo Alkabetz to his home for a Tikkun Leil Shavuot, and in the course of study that evening Rabbi Caro spoke in the voice of the Angel of the Mishnah.[8] Clearly, speaking in tongues on this holy day was not just a Christian experience. This angel was Caro's mentor, and Caro credited the wisdom in his writings to what he learned from it. Caro said that his most famous work, the Shulchan Aruch, a manual of observance for the Orthodox Jew that is still used today, was written while he was channeling the Angel of the Mishnah and was not really his work at all.

Today millions of believers in these two Abrahamic traditions across millennia share a faith that this forty-nine-day period is important in preparation for personal revelation and Divine connection. Jews continue to Count the Omer and celebrate a Tikkun Leil Shavuot prayer vigil of study and meditation before Pentecost services the next morning, and many Christians use devotionals for special prayers between Easter and Pentecost, with some denominations still observing the all-night prayer vigil. This shared belief creates a morphic field with a vibratory resonance that helps to unlock our inner pathways to the Divine. When you use this period of seven weeks plus one day following Passover or Easter for inner work, you tap into this energy.

Of course, the Jewish celebration of Counting the Omer and

Shavuot do not exactly line up with the Christian celebration of the Eastertide season. Since the Jewish calendar is lunar, the dates that Passover and Shavuot are celebrated rarely align with the Christian calendar, even though Easter and Pentecost are also movable feasts. But often there is enough of an overlap to make this time in spring most auspicious to begin your practice.

That doesn't mean you couldn't start this practice at any time, since tradition holds that revelation is available and the Torah is given at every moment. However, I believe that if you choose to do it when so many millions of others on the planet are doing similar work in different ways, you'll get a booster shot of spiritual energy to help you on the way.

KABBALAH, CABALA, AND QABALAH

The Kabbalah is not a book; it's one strand of the Jewish mystical tradition that encompasses many books, the most famous of which is the Zohar (The Book of Splendor). Kabbalah also includes oral teachings that have never been written down. The word Kabbalah is best translated as "received tradition." Kabbalistic writings and practices were secret, reserved for initiates only, and one of those practices was the esoteric meditation during the Counting of the Omer.

The reason we know about the Sephirotic "drawing-down" (*meshikhah*) meditations that were practiced during the forty-nine-day period is because a well-known member of the circle of Spanish Kabbalists living in the thirteenth century, Rabbi Azriel of Girona, wrote about them.[9] Azriel was one of the most influential Kabbalists of his day, but he was reprimanded by his own teacher, Rabbi Isaac the Blind, who sent a letter to the Kabbalists in Girona demanding that their teachings be kept secret and not written down.[10] We don't know how Azriel felt about this, but we do know he obeyed his teacher, because from that point on he stopped writing down any of these teachings.

The Zohar is a pseudepigraphon, written by Rabbi Moses de León, another Spanish Kabbalist of the thirteenth century. He claimed he was merely copying a text written by Rabbi Shimon Bar Yohai, a great sage of the first century CE. This claim gave the Zohar an ancient authenticity that conferred authority to its teachings. However, from the very start, there were people who did not believe the text was ancient, as it was filled with linguistic anachronisms. Nevertheless, de Léon's contemporaries did believe that the content—the teachings—were ancient and that they represented authentic wisdom from the oral tradition. But there were, and still are, people who believed the Zohar was an ancient text.

Almost from the beginning, Christians were interested in the teachings in the Zohar. While it was written in Hebrew and Aramaic, many learned Renaissance scholars had studied these languages, and there were also apostate Jews who were willing to help in the translation. Passages of the Zohar were first translated into Latin in the fifteenth century.[11] This led to the development of a Christian Cabala tradition that, while its origin was in Judaism, grew into a tradition of its own that diverged in a very important way from the original Jewish tradition. Just as Christians had reinterpreted the Torah as evidence that Christ was the messiah, so too the Zohar was appropriated to provide evidence of Christ's divinity. By the late sixteenth century, the Christian tradition of Cabala gave birth to another offshoot when occultists, of what is now known as the Western Hermetic tradition, integrated Qabalah into a system of Western mystical traditions, including alchemy, magic, and astrology.

What's up with all these different spellings? Because these teachings diverged in three different traditions, some people have come to adopt a unique spelling for each so it's clear which tradition the writer is referring to. Generally speaking, the original Jewish tradition is Kabbalah with a *K;* Christian Cabala is spelled differently and starts with a *C,* while the Western Hermetic tradition spells Qabalah with a *Q.* Confused? Don't worry about it; I'm sticking to the traditional Jewish spelling, since most of my orientation is from the Jewish tradition, though I do make some adjustments for the Western Hermetic tradition.[12]

By the nineteenth century, European occultists included tarot cards in this integrated Western Hermetic tradition, even though there is no evidence that there was a direct connection between the creation of the tarot and the original Jewish tradition of Kabbalah.[13] Nevertheless, there is a surprising convergence between the structure of the tarot deck, early interpretations of the cards, and Kabbalist teachings about the Tree of Life and the Sephirot. Applying knowledge of these Kabbalistic concepts to the tarot reveals deep layers of meaning. Similarly, the cards throw new light on the interactions of the Sephirot.

Of course, historically the daily Sephirotic meditations used in the Counting of the Omer were completely unknown outside of a small group of Jewish Kabbalists, so Western occultists knew nothing of this practice. However, in recent years, as Kabbalah has been popularized, some of its key concepts and practices have become more widely known. In the last decade, books that serve as guides to the Omer practice have become available in English for the first time, though the intended readership is observant Jews.

Before you can do the Omer practice or work with the tarot deck to experience the Sephirotic energies available on each of the forty-nine days, you need a grounded and practical understanding of Sephirot. Obviously, there are people who have devoted their lives to the study of Kabbalah. This brief introduction can only scratch the surface of the teachings in this tradition, but it will give you enough of an understanding of these concepts to use them in your own practice.

The Tree of Life

THE TREE OF LIFE IS THE CENTRAL SYMBOL in Kabbalah study. In fact, the very name is a symbol, since there's no real tree anywhere. This "Tree" is made up of ten Sephirot—emanations from the Source, vessels that create a channel through which the Divine can pour Its energy into creation. As you can see in figure 1, the ten Sephirot are arranged in three pillars with twenty-two pathways between them. Together, these are the thirty-two mystical pathways mentioned in the Sefer Yetzirah.

The Kabbalistic creation story of Rabbi Isaac Luria explains that the first time the Source emanated these energies, the Sephirot were arranged in a straight line that was too rigid to hold the Divine energy. The vessels shattered, and sparks of Divine light were scattered throughout all creation. (Some people connect this myth to the theory of the big bang.) After the sparks were scattered, the Source began the creation process again, but this time with the Sephirot in the relationships you see in the diagram of the Tree, enabling the Sephirot to exist in a relationship of dynamic balance that is capable of holding and directing the Divine flow. Because these scattered sparks of Divine light exist throughout the entirety of creation, Judaism does not see the world as an illusion to be transcended; rather, the world is of profound importance. The goal of each individual's spiritual journey in Kabbalistic Judaism is to make oneself a pure vessel that can see, raise, and return these sparks to the Source (as if they were ever really separate). Or as Rav Abraham Isaac Kook described it, "Hear the voice of God in everything."

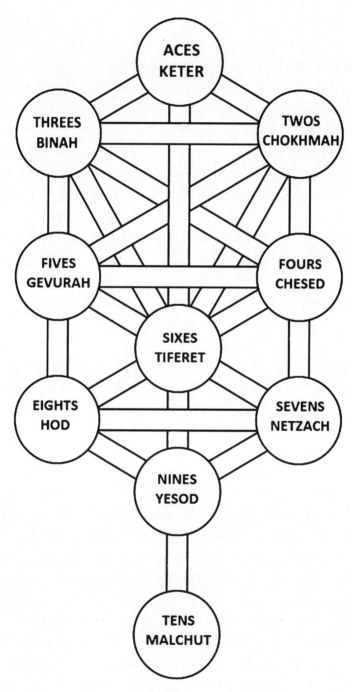

Figure 1. The ten Sephirot and their corresponding numeric Minor Arcana cards in the four tarot suits

The Sephirot are not the Source; they serve as intermediaries between the Source and the world. Think of each Sephira as a container of the Source's light (remember, it's all metaphor), each a bounded infinity of a particular quality of God essence.* Each Sephira veils this light, with successively greater veiling as we move down the Tree. To use a concrete metaphor within our experience to describe this abstract spiritual metaphor, it's as though a series of filters are placed over a spotlight, so that the intensity and color of the light changes. When we encounter this light, these filters guarantee it doesn't blind or overwhelm us. The Sephirot are ubiquitous and always accessible, so that we can access them as a channel to consciously connect to the Source without being overwhelmed.

Like a holographic piece of the Source, each Sephira contains an entire Tree within it, so that to access any one of them is to access all of them on multiple levels—and in multiple worlds.

In the Omer meditation, you will always work with a pair of Sephirot, never one by itself. This work is about reestablishing a full relationship and connection between the Sephirot within you (because you're not separate from any of this; it all exists in you) so that any spiritual blockages are removed. Think of this work as a sacred workout, making you strong enough to feel the outpouring of Divine energy throughout your entire being.

Anxiety is intrinsic to this process, but to be in this process, you will learn to observe and hold your anxiety, surrounding it with Divine light so that you will be able to let the small cup of your ego rest in the larger cup of the Source. Remember, the ego fears the inability to be in control, and there's nothing more uncontrollable than Divine energy.

While descriptions of each of the individual Sephirot follow, they really don't exist separately; they exist only in relationship. Just as none of us really exist separately—that is an illusion—we only exist in relationship. And because this is a path of nonduality (which includes

---

Sephirot is plural; *Sephira* is singular.

duality), the Sephirot are always in a dynamic process and are always unchanging.

The emanation of the Sephirot is described as being created in an order, but they were created outside of time, so descriptions of such an order don't really apply. From my "heretical" Buddhist point of view, they are mutually co-arising in nonlinear causality. However, because we are limited beings living within the dimension of time and using the limited tool of language, we are only capable of describing them separately and in an order.*

Of these ten emanations, the top three are considered by some to be beyond the experience of our embodied sensorium. This leaves the lower seven Sephirotic energies that we can encounter and experience as living human beings. And this is where the Omer meditations begin. Because, as it happens, the forty-nine-day period of Counting the Omer is seven weeks of seven days each. So the Kabbalists created a practice where each week represented an opportunity to work with one of the lower seven Sephirot. And because each individual Sephira contains an entire Tree within it in a kind of holographic reality, each day was an opportunity to meditate on how that week's Sephira was expressed in relationship to the energy of each day's Sephira. This gives us forty-nine permutations that explore every possible relationship between these Sephirot, one relationship per day.

Thus, the first day of the first week, the Omer count's Sephirotic meditation is "Chesed of Chesed," the second day is "Gevurah of Chesed," the third day is "Tiferet of Chesed," and so on until the last day of the first week, "Malchut of Chesed." You can use the Omer calendar in figure 2 to keep track of the combinations each day. Each of these forty-nine combinations provides an opportunity to reflect deeply on these energies and feel how they are at work in your life, and how best to be in a conscious relationship with them so that every moment is a chance to open to the Source.

---

*If you study Kabbalah on your own, you will encounter different opinions and teachings about the order of the emanations, their names, and so on. The beauty of the story of the revelation at Sinai is that there is a unique revelation for each of us.

	DAYS						
WEEKS	Chesed	Gevurah	Tiferet	Netzach	Hod	Yesod	Malchut
I. Chesed	I	2	3	4	5	6	7
2. Gevurah	8	9	10	11	12	13	14
3. Tiferet	15	16	17	18	19	20	21
4. Netzach	22	23	24	25	26	27	28
5. Hod	29	30	31	32	33 Lag B'Omer	34	35
6. Yesod	36	37	38	39	40	41	42
7. Malchut	43	44	45	46	47	48	49

Figure 2. The Omer calendar

THE SEPHIROT

To do the Omer practice, you need an understanding of the meaning of each of the Sephirot, including the top three, even though you won't be working with these three directly. Traditionally, Jews work with the Sephirot without the mediation of an image (since of course that would be in violation of the Second Commandment). But because we'll be using tarot cards, with the description of each Sephira below I will note the corresponding cards. Don't feel that you must memorize the full descriptions of the Sephirot, since each day there will be some discussion of the meanings. Following the descriptions of each of the lower seven Sephirot, there will also be a list of key words associated with that Sephira. You can use those key words to understand and consider the different shades of meaning for each day's pairing and determine which combination of key words speaks most directly to you and where you are now.

Because the Sephirot are bounded infinities, trying to describe each one of them is a challenge, to say the least. But based on how they've been explained over the centuries (and how I have experienced them in my own study and practice), what follows is my attempt to capture the constellation of meanings that orbit these essential energies.

1. Keter: Translated as "Crown," it is the Sephira that is considered closest to the Unknowable. Because it's described as the first emanation, it is often considered to be the first expression of Divine Will, and thus connected to the first expression of that will in the Torah: "Let there be light." As humans, we experience light as devoid of materiality, so Keter is also connected to the concept of emptiness. Keter is only the slightest separation from Ein Sof, the Kabbalists' nondescriptive description of God as that which is beyond language, thought, concept;* that which can only be described negatively—as in, It's not that. Thus, the concept of Ein Sof in some ways resembles the Buddhist description of Nirvana or what the Christians refer to as the Via Negativa. This isn't such a farfetched comparison when you consider Keter has been called "the annihilation of thought," where human consciousness dissolves into infinity. Keter is barely differentiated from Ein Sof—it's just enough to be different, but not enough of something to be a thing other than Will and light. Because the Kabbalists also believed that humans were embodiments of the Sephirot (since, after all, we were created in the image of the Divine), each Sephira is associated with a part of the body. And no surprise, Keter is at the Crown of the head. As you might imagine, some people also find correspondences between the Sephirot and the chakras of the Hindu tradition, although the two systems are not entirely congruent. However, if you find linking them helpful when appropriate, I am certainly not one to turn up my nose at that kind of unorthodox exploration! They are simply different maps of the same territory.

Correspondences:
Minor Arcana: The aces of each suit.
Body Map: The crown of the head.
Divine Name: Ehyeh Asher Ehyeh
Keter Key Words: Crown, Will.

---

*Ein Sof can be translated as meaning "without end" or "infinite."

2. Chokhmah: Translated as "Wisdom," it is the transitional state from nothingness to something. As Keter is too close to Ein Sof to even be a location, Chokhmah is the primordial point of beginning. Because it is the wisdom that permeates all Creation, it is associated with the primordial Torah, the blueprint of all the universes and all they contain. As a blueprint, it is still just an idea, a plan not of any material reality.

Correspondences:
Minor Arcana: The twos of each suit.
Body Map: The right eye and/or right brain.
Divine Name: YHVH.
Chokhmah Key Words: Wisdom, Potential, Inspiration, Fear, Selflessness.

3. Binah: Most often translated as "Understanding," it is the uppermost level of discernment and insight. Rabbi Jay Michaelson refers to Binah as the "ground of space and time—not yet expanded, not yet contracted, but the principle of spatiality and temporality itself, ready to give birth to the world."[1] And in this way, I think about Binah as the Divine manifesting itself as the quantum foam, the foundational fabric of the universe(s) that is space-time at the most infinitesimal scale, yet the place at which materiality at its smallest subatomic level winks into (and out of) existence. Binah is the place from which all else is born. Binah is also called the "Divine Womb" or Illa Ima'ah, the Supernal or Higher Mother.

Correspondences:
Minor Arcana: The threes in each suit.
Body Map: The left eye and/or left brain.
Divine Name: YHVH Elohim.
Binah Key Words: Understanding, Divine Womb, Reason.

4. Chesed: This is the first (and the "highest") of the Sephirot that we have direct access to experientially. Some words used to define its qualities include Loving-kindness, Love, Mercy, and Flow. This is not transactional love with give and take, but an endless outpouring without expectation of return. It is the nonstop showering of blessings on all Creation without measure or limit. Other words that capture its qualities include "boundary-lessness," unconditional giving, and expansion. Because there is a negative, shadow side to each of the Sephirot, here we can understand the negative in terms of human experience; for example, someone with a lack of boundaries, someone with an inability to say no, or someone whose messiness seems to be uncontrollable. These are people whose expression of Chesed is out of alignment or relationship with the other Sephirot. Another of its negative manifestations is in smother-love that doesn't allow for separation—because Chesed doesn't allow for differences. Think of it as the hot lava of love pouring out of the Divine Source: nothing can stand in its way. It flows over everything, unimpeded without end. Feeling a scintilla of pure Chesed anywhere in your body calls forth a response of love for the Creator and for all Creation that will flood through your entire body, if only for a millisecond. A gentler version of the lava metaphor associates Chesed with water. Another name for Chesed is Gedulah, meaning "Greatness."

Correspondences:
Minor Arcana: The fours of each suit.
Body Map: The right shoulder and arm.
Divine Name: El.

Chesed Key Words: Love, Loving-kindness, Endless Flow, Unconditional Love, Giving, Mercy, Grace, Nurturance, Boundless Love, Benevolence, Expansion, Goodness, Kindness, Generosity, Greatness.

5. Gevurah: Because it acts as the balance, the container for the limitless outpouring of Chesed, Gevurah is associated with Strength, Constriction, Structure, Boundaries, Law, Justice, Judgment, Focus, Restraint, Discipline, Severity, Discernment, and Limitation. When you consider the relationship of Chesed and Gevurah, another metaphor for understanding the Sephirot comes to mind: imagine a series of dams containing the flow of water and then directing it so that it doesn't cause a flood. Because Gevurah is the container that holds judgment and sets limits, the experience of this Sephirot includes awe—the fear of

God as opposed to love. In fact, other names for Gevurah are Pachad, meaning "Fear," and Din, meaning "Judgment." Gevurah gets a bad rap because of this. In some New Age thinking, Gevurah comes off as negative. But without the container of Gevurah, there is no separate existence from the Divine: we are all subsumed by Chesed. A good way to think of Gevurah is as the mother who restrains her child when it wants to put its hand in the fire; this is setting boundaries out of love.

Of course, as with all the Sephirot, there is a negative side to Gevurah. When it is out of relationship with Chesed, it is judgment that isn't tempered by love. And that's severity. It can become the setting of limits for the sake of power. On the human side, we can see the negative side of Gevurah at work in people who are overly self-critical or judgmental, or in those who are power-hungry authoritarians or strict disciplinarians. When Chesed is in harmony with Gevurah, love has a location, giving it both boundaries and a direction. When Gevurah is in harmony with Chesed, judgment is expressed with compassion.

Correspondences:

Minor Arcana: The fives in each suit.

Body Map: The left shoulder and arm.

Divine Name: Elohim Gibor.

Gevurah Key Words: Strength, Constriction, Structure, Boundaries, Limits, Law, Justice, Restraint, Discipline, Severity, Discernment, Limitation, Awe, Judgment, Constraint, Might, Power, Organization, Harshness, Courage, Power, Control.

6. Tiferet: I think the poet John Keats best expresses the meaning of this Sephira: "Beauty is truth, truth beauty." Both Beauty and Truth are synonymous in Tiferet. It is Harmony and Balance—an aesthetic balance you resonate with. In the Tree, it is placed between Chesed and Gevurah, balancing both energies in a way that creates harmony to reveal the higher truth. It is the first Sephira on the central pillar that we can encounter, which means it is a place that holds all the higher energies and directs them, so it is a place of great strength, and in the physical body it is associated with one of our strongest muscles: the Heart.

And like the heart, Tiferet is able to hold love and pain together. Traditionally in Jewish belief, this is the Sephira that represents the messiah, because it is a transition point between the upper and lower worlds, between the Divine and the human. So it should be no surprise that in the Christian tradition, this Sephira is often associated with the Sacred Heart of Jesus—the open wound that bears all pain and pours forth love. I like to think of Tiferet as the realm of the bodhisattvas in the Buddhist tradition. A bodhisattva is an enlightened being who takes a vow to remain in the world of Samsara to help all other beings on the path to enlightenment.

Correspondences:
Minor Arcana: The sixes in each suit.
Body Map: The heart.
Divine Name: Elohim.
Tiferet Key Words: Compassion, Beauty, Truth, Harmony, Balance, Heart, Openheartedness, Dynamic Equilibrium.

7. Netzach: Concepts associated with this Sephira include Mastery, Victory, Mission, and Eternity. On the human level, this means channeling power with intention and direction. Other qualities of this Sephira include Dominance and Triumph, Endurance and Ambition, Fortitude and Physical Energy. This is expressed in human terms as defining oneself through mastery, showing Drive and Determination and moving forward. Within this Sephira is the power to choose—to say yes or no to a situation. In the Zohar, Netzach and its partner Hod are connected to prophecy. Netzach has the outward movement of Chesed, but in the service of establishing personal identity. And because we're speaking of the outer world, it's not only identity but also persona. The image I have when thinking of Netzach (in balance with Hod) is Neil Armstrong stepping out of the capsule and onto the lunar surface. His words, "That's one small step for [a] man, one giant leap for mankind," and then his planting the U.S. flag on the moon, capture for me the active victory principle expressed in Netzach, while at the same time his words express the humility of Hod in his relationship with all humanity.

Correspondences:

Minor Arcana: The sevens in each suit.

Body Map: The right hip and leg.

Divine Name: YHVH Tzevaot.

Netzach Key Words: Mastery, Victory, Mission, Eternity, Endurance, Ambition, Willpower, Fortitude, Dominance, Triumph, Drive, Focused Energy, Determination, Perseverance, Persistence, Commitment, Achievement, Tenacity, Resolve, Resilience.

8. Hod: Often translated as "Splendor," it is also called "Glory." This Sephira carries the energies of Gratitude and Humility, Submission and Surrender. When you consider the pair of Chesed and Gevurah above, the pairing of Netzach and Hod is also a balancing of energies. The surrender we speak of here is the surrender of the ego in humility—when we are able to listen to and truly hear others wiser than ourselves. The wisdom in the balance of Netzach and Hod is expressed in a section of the Mishnah known as the Pirkei Avot.

> *Who is wise? One who learns from all . . .*
> *Who is strong? One who subdues their passions.*[2]*

This stands in direct opposition to the energy of Netzach by itself, which is all about establishing the ego in dominance of all outside. But this doesn't mean Hod is about being a milquetoast; it's on the side of Gevurah, so it takes in the strength of Gevurah. This is surrender from the place of a healthy, strong ego. So in opposition to Netzach, Hod is inner-directed.

In some ways, Glory (Hod) is a greater realization of Victory (Netzach). If Victory isn't internalized, integrated, and nurturing of the self, it is an empty experience. Glory includes the experience of internalized Victory. Victory without this internalization can feel the need for constant reassurance, an unquenched thirst for continual wins.

---

*All following quotes from the Pirkei Avot (Ethics of the Fathers) are from *The Standard Prayer Book*. Some words have been changed to remove gender bias; for example, "He" has been changed to read "One."

The negative side of Hod can be seen in the holding back of taking action due to constant second-guessing, discussion, and preparation that doesn't end. If you've ever been in a long meeting where the discussion feels endless and no action steps are decided, you've been in the presence of negative Hod. The ability to stand strong and yet surrender the ego is what opens one's consciousness to the possibility of prophecy in the balance of Netzach and Hod.

Correspondences:

Minor Arcana: The eights in each suit.

Body Map: The left hip and leg.

Divine Name: Elohim Tzevaot.

Hod Key Words: Splendor, Glory, Humility, Submission, Surrender, Gratitude, Inspiration, Majesty, Sincerity, Devotion, Elegance, Flexibility, Diversity, Appreciation.

9. Yesod: This is the Sephira through which all the upper Sephirotic energies come together again to be channeled into Malchut. The holding and channeling of these energies is one of the reasons Yesod is traditionally associated with the male sexual organ (from a twenty-first-century point of view, this is simplistic, but as I never tire of saying, "Remember, it's all metaphor"). Recently, I've heard teachers also connect Yesod to the birth canal, which also makes sense, since as it's the ninth Sephira, it calls to mind the nine months of gestation to birth. Yesod is all about the desire to connect. This connection is way more than just sexual, but sexual energy and desire certainly play a powerful part in the energy of Yesod. However, while I have started the discussion of Yesod's sexual energy right at the start, I don't want to give the impression that this is the first quality to consider in this Sephira.

Words that are associated with Yesod are Bonding, Connection, Attachment, and Foundation. A true and deep emotional bond demands fearless intimacy and radical integrity that enable both closeness and separateness at the same time. All humans have their feeling of safety and security in the world formed by their first bond with the mother. When an infant can completely trust the mother to be there, provide, and protect, the result is a child and adult who feels at home in the world—someone who has a strong foundation. When you are bonded with another you are seen completely and you see the other completely with acceptance and trust.

However, the Yesodic desire to connect or bond can be indiscriminate, and some results of Yesodic energy that is out of balance are addiction, obsession, and attachment disorders. Yesod that is unable to connect to the energy of Tiferet is distorted and can lead to substance addiction or compulsive behaviors such as gambling or sex addiction. Just as I noted earlier that as each Sephira is associated with a part of the body, each Sephira is also associated with a Biblical personage. Yesod is identified with the biblical embodiment of male chastity and sexual purity, Joseph, because of his ability to withstand the sexual advances of Potiphar's wife (and in some tellings of the story, Potiphar as well).

Just as Tiferet is both a balance and a synthesis of Chesed and Gevurah, Yesod is both a balance and synthesis of Netzach and Hod. This combination includes the outward-facing sense of determination and mission in Netzach with the vulnerability and humility of Hod to create a connection of true intimacy. It's where the self and other are in a balanced relationship.

The negative side of Yesod is what the Buddhists call the Realm of the Hungry Ghosts, where animalistic desire drives everything and where nothing can satisfy this desire: it is endless. But when Yesod is in relationship with Tiferet, it creates the possibility of connecting with the Divine through connection with the world, including the experience of that connection in sexual union. This is where the Kabbalists' practice of heterosexual sex in a marriage on Erev Shabbat* was considered a way of reuniting the Divine with the Shekinah, the feminine presence of God, which is identified with the next Sephira, Malchut. It unifies all four levels of the soul within each person. This sexual union is meant to heal the split in creation and to unify the masculine and

---

*In Judaism, the day begins at sunset, so the Sabbath begins on Friday night, known as Erev Shabbat.

feminine energies within the practitioner. As you can see, this could easily be misunderstood or misinterpreted. In fact, there are other relationships and sexual energies between the Sephirot I've not mentioned. These teachings were only transmitted by the Kabbalists to chosen students who could fully understand them without the danger of their acting out relationships prohibited by biblical law. Obviously, for queer people like me there are other ways to unify the Divine Masculine and Feminine energies. More about that later as we get into the practice.

The power of Yesod is best expressed in E. M. Forster's novel *Howards End,* which captures how Yesod holds the possibility of healing the duality of the Divine and the demonic.

> Only connect! That was the whole of her sermon. Only connect the prose and the passion, and both will be exalted, and human love will be seen at its height. Live in fragments no longer. Only connect, and the beast and the monk, robbed of the isolation that is life to either, will die.[3]

When Yesod is connected to Tiferet, one feels the connection to the Divine in all relationships. And in the ecstasy of sexual and spiritual connection, not only does isolation die, but also all separation is revealed as an illusion.

Correspondences:

Minor Arcana: The nines in each suit.

Body Map: Traditionally, the male genitals, the phallus. Recently, also the birth canal.

Divine Name: El Chai Shaddai.

Yesod Key Words: Foundation, Connection, Generativity, Bonding, Attachment, Basis, Channel, Creativity, Intimacy, Base, Yearning, Desire, Relationship.

10. Malchut: Sometimes called "Kingdom" or "Kingship," which could be confusing since the first suggests a location in space and the second is more about a quality or character trait. And that's a good thing, since Malchut encompasses both definitions and more. As a location, Malchut is the physical world we live in, which receives Divine energy every second: it receives the combined energies of all the upper Sephirot that create the reality that surrounds (and includes) us. In fact, Malchut has neither energy nor light of its own, but only receives and reflects the light of heaven as filtered through all the higher Sephirot. It is also called "Majesty"; when one receives all the higher energies in balance in Malchut, one sees all creation as majestic.

As a quality or character trait, Malchut was translated historically as "Kingship" but is better described as "Sovereignty" because when one receives all the higher energies in a balanced relationship, the result is a human being who is fully Grounded, self-assured, and Self-possessed. This confers a level of dignity that isn't about being haughty or stuffy but is the dignity of the human spirit at its purest. And when we have reached the forty-ninth day, Malchut of Malchut, you should have greater access to this pure spirit, which can now serve as a stronger container for Divine revelation.

Correspondences:

Minor Arcana: The tens in each suit.

Body Map: The feet; in some systems, the mouth, the womb, the digestive system.

Divine Name: Adonai.

Malchut Key Words: Kingdom, Kingship, Sovereignty, Nobility, Shekinah, Manifestation, Service, Divine Presence, Immanence, Royalty, Authority, Responsibility, Dignity, Self-Possession, Presence, Groundedness.

THE FOUR WORLDS

In addition to the ten Sephirot, there are also four worlds (the Hebrew word for world is *olam* and is singular; *olamim* is plural), and not surprisingly, just as the Sephirot correspond to the numbered cards in each suit, the four worlds correspond with the four suits. Just as the Sephirot hold Divine energy in ever-deepening concealment, the olamim hold the structure of reality in ever-deepening concealment.

A good way of thinking about this is through the lens of complexity theory and the ideas of implicate and explicate order. Theoretical physicist David Bohm posited that implicate order and explicate order are two frameworks for understanding the same phenomenon. The implicate or "enfolded" order is a deeper and more fundamental order of reality, while the explicate or "unfolded" order includes phenomena that humans normally perceive. He developed this concept to explain the behavior of subatomic particles.

When we scale up the phenomena we're looking at from the subatomic realm to look at a living human being, we see that human as a discrete and individual organism. That's how we normally perceive things. We don't see an amalgamation of separate organs or, getting down to an even lower level, the billions of cells that make up a person. In fact, we also don't see the billions of nonhuman organisms that live on us and in us that make the complex system we perceive as a discrete person possible. If you look under a microscope at any of these cells, you see that each of them is also a complex system that can be broken down further and further. We get down to complex biomolecules and DNA until we get back down to the subatomic level that Bohm was writing about. It's all a matter of scale and what we're able to perceive. Except that you can't see the explicate and implicate orders at the same time. You can't look at a human and see a discrete individual and a mass of cells at the same time. Each level or order conceals the ones below it.[4]

This is a way of looking at the idea of the olamim, or the worlds or multiverses. Only the Divine can perceive these levels of reality simultaneously, because the Divine is the Source of all these levels of reality. These worlds, like the Sephirot, follow an order and interpenetrate each other. The first world, Atzilut, is the world closest to the Divine, so it is associated with our spiritual aspirations. Just as Keter is the Sephira that is closest to the Divine, Atzilut is the world that is closest to the Source. Which means that within Atzilut is a whole Tree—ten Sephirot that are closer to the Divine than the ten Sephirot in the next Tree below it. Atzilut is the world of emanation. Looking at Atzilut through the lens of complexity theory, you could think of it as the world of the quantum foam—the first manifestations of reality, where matter and antimatter wink in and out of existence, giving space-time and the universe a "foamy" character. This is the most enfolded, or implicate, order there is.

While I have no idea if the great Jewish philosopher Rabbi Abraham Joshua Heschel knew about this theory or quantum foam, these words of his from *God in Search of Man* speak to this mysterious moment: "The very structure of matter is made possible by the way in which the endless crystallizes in the smallest."[5]

Some Kabbalists will say that Atzilut comes before even the existence of space-time. However, I use the example of quantum foam because it is the deepest order science has been able to reach . . . so far. I don't mean to suggest that the world of Atzilut is the actual world of quantum foam (or that there is actually foam). Once again, this is a metaphoric correspondence to enable you to understand the many enfolded and concealed levels of reality. Because it is associated with the will to create, the tarot suit that corresponds with Atzilut is Wands.

Moving up (or down, or in, depending on the metaphor you prefer) from Atzilut is the next level of implicate order, B'riah, and coming forth from B'riah is Yetzirah. Finally, there is the world of Assiyah: the world of matter as we can ordinarily perceive it—the explicate order. But before we look at the two "middle" worlds of B'riah and Yetzirah, let's consider the world of Assiyah.

Assiyah is sometimes called the world of action and physical manifestation. It's the material universe we live in and can perceive with our sensorium and with the tools we have created that enable us to see further down into that material universe. It's important to note again here that Judaism is a nondual path. The physical world of Assiyah is not meant to be transcended because ultimately there is no separation between it and the other worlds. The path of Tikkun Olam*— the healing, the making whole of the world—is to see the Divine, the

---

*Tikkun Olam means "healing or repairing the world," and as taught by Rabbi Isaac Luria, it was about the path of raising the scattered sparks. Today most Jews use the phrase to mean the pursuit of social justice.

hidden sparks of God energy, in the material world of Assiyah and thus return them to the Divine. Some Jewish meditation traditions focus on training the mind to be able to apprehend the simultaneous interpenetration of these multiple worlds. This is one of the esoteric meanings of the interpenetrating triangles of the Star of David: the upper and lower are not really separate. The tarot suit that corresponds to Assiyah is Pentacles. While we are not able to physically see the implicate order of biomolecules or atoms with our eyes, we are able to apprehend the implicate order of the multiple universes with our souls.

Before we get to the "middle" two worlds, it's time to note once again that traditional Jewish Kabbalah and the Hermetic (Western tradition) Qabalah are different, and one of the places these differences are clear is in the definition and mapping of correspondences to the "middle" worlds. In the Jewish Kabbalist tradition, the world of B'riah is the world of creation and of conceptual thought—the world of the intellect, while the world of Yetzirah is the world of formation and of the emotions. In the Qabalah of the Western Hermetic tradition, this is completely reversed: the emotions are assigned to B'riah and the intellect is assigned to Yetzirah.

Why am I bringing this up? Because the Western Hermetic tradition assigned the correspondences between Kabbalah or Qabalah and the tarot deck. They aligned the suit of Wands with Atzilut and spirit, and the suit of Pentacles was aligned with Assiyah and action. This makes sense symbolically. But in the middle, the suit of Cups was aligned with emotion (which makes sense to me metaphorically) and with the Kabbalistic world of B'riah. This tradition also aligned the suit of Swords to intellect—which also makes sense to me metaphorically— and with the world of Yetzirah. For a traditional Jewish Kabbalist, these reversals would be a mistake. Of course, the traditional Jewish point of view doesn't recognize the value of tarot to begin with. So while my own studies in Kabbalah have all been deeply within the Jewish tradition, at least when it comes to the four Kabbalistic worlds in the tarot deck, I work with the Western Hermetic set of correspondences. The three decks that trace their origin to the Hermetic Order of the Golden Dawn are organized in this way, and that is the organization this book follows.

Don't let this puzzle or disturb you: consider these differences as simply different maps to the same territory. The Jewish Kabbalists themselves disagreed on how the Sephirot and the olamim correspond with each other, and there are many traditions within mystical Judaism that take different approaches to all this. Azriel of Girona even had very different names for some of the Sephirot. The diagram of the Tree of Life and its paths differ between Rabbi Isaac Luria and Rabbi Elijah ben Solomon (the Vilna Gaon). Everyone is trying to describe what ultimately goes beyond language. Remember, the purpose of these metaphorical maps of the inner journey is to help you to connect with the Source. But as Alfred Korzybski said, "The map is not the territory." Your experience doing the practice will be different from mine. We all come up against different challenges. Welcome these challenges as the teachers they are.

Besides the four worlds, the Jewish tradition also recognizes four levels of the soul, and of course, they also correspond to the four worlds. So when you work with the Sephirot in each world, you're purifying your soul at each of these levels. These four worlds and four levels of the soul also correspond to the Tetragrammaton—the unpronounceable four-letter name of the Divine: YHVH. There are some who say that these four letters come from the Hebrew verb "to be" and that by taking out the vowels that indicate whether the verb is future, past, or present tense, the letters create a word that roughly translates as "is-was-will be." That is to say, eternal and beyond time. Rabbi Mark Sameth gives a midrashic interpretation of the secret meaning of the letters, explaining that the name "was probably not pronounced 'Jehovah' or 'Yahweh,' as some have guessed. The Israelite priests would have read the letters in reverse as Hu/Hi—in other words, the hidden name of God was Hebrew for 'He/She.'" So that the deity "was understood by its earliest worshipers to be a dual-gendered deity."[6]

I don't believe that the Deity is dual-gendered so much as to say that It includes all genders (of which there are six in classical Judaism[7]) and is also beyond all gender. This may seem tangential, but I bring in this mind-blowing consideration of gender because amid this discussion of Kabbalistic concepts, along with structures and diagrams of correspondences, I want to be mindful that our ability to describe reality is filtered by our bodies, our sensorium, and our culture. And we are using these concepts to enable us to apprehend, if only for a second, much that is beyond our experience. So it bears repeating: the map is not the territory.

THE TAROT CONNECTION

Tarot and Kabbalah do share a history—just not the history described by the occultists of the eighteenth and nineteenth centuries. Scholarship finds no evidence for the existence of tarot cards much before the fifteenth century. Now, I know that just because academics can't find any trace of something in history doesn't mean it wasn't there. After all, we have no scripts of the secular plays put on by traveling actors in the fifteenth century, but we know they existed because we have the written condemnation of these plays by the Church.

Cards are ephemera, and the earliest examples we have are only a small number of cards from Renaissance Europe held in museum collections that survive for us to examine and study today. Upon examination, we can see competing systems and deck designs, some of which were used for games and gambling and some used for divination.[8]

Nevertheless, Court de Gébelin, a French occultist of the eighteenth century, made the claim that the tarot was of ancient Egyptian heritage. His contemporary and a rival French occultist, Etteila, did him one better and claimed that individual tarot cards were actually pages from the Egyptian Book of Thoth, a collection of writings from the pre-Christian Egyptian religion. Etteila also claimed that this book was written by the god Thoth himself. So what the Zohar and the tarot both share are pseudepigraphal claims for a heritage of antiquity as an appeal to the authenticity of the secret wisdom found in them.

Court de Gébelin claimed that the Major Arcana were numbered to correspond to the twenty-two letters in both the Egyptian and Hebrew alphabets. It didn't seem to trouble him that at the time different versions of the deck that were in circulation sometimes had more and sometimes fewer than twenty-two cards or that ancient Egyptian didn't use an alphabet. But to prove the correspondence, Etteila issued a "rectified" deck with twenty-two Major Arcana cards so that they matched up with the Hebrew letters.* Another French occultist of the time, Comte de Mellet, suggested that the tarot suits might possibly also be a Kabbalistic reference, with Cups assigned to Joseph (since he was Potiphar's cupbearer), the Wands to Moses (since his staff plays an important role), Swords to David (since he was a warrior-king, though one could say he was just as much a poet), and Coins to Laban (here de Mellet gets pretty twisted in his reasoning).[9] And while there really isn't a connection between the suits and these Biblical figures, it works for at least three of the suits. In today's decks, where Coins are replaced with Pentacles, a better correspondence would be to King Solomon, who was known as a master magician in folklore and who created amulets and talismans of great power.[†]

By the time we get to the early nineteenth century, Eliphas Levi (yet another French occultist who changed his name) had syncretized tarot, Kabbalah, Hermeticism, and other esoteric traditions. His writing deeply influenced the members of the Hermetic Order of the Golden Dawn, an organization that is the source of the tarot decks in most widespread use today.

In fact, the Golden Dawn used its own version of the Major Arcana as part of a ritual of initiation for all its members. As members moved up

---

*Arthur Edward Waite considered his version of the deck "rectified"—that is to say, a return to the original order and meaning of the cards. A number of deck creators make similar claims. Recently, Yoav Ben-Dov, working with the numerous versions of the Marseilles deck, poked fun at the idea of a rectified deck and then created his own "rectified" version of the Marseilles deck as designed by Nicholas Conver in 1760 that I like.

†In the Raziel Tarot, a new deck inspired by Judaic myth and legend created by Rachel Pollack and Robert Place, the connection between Solomon and amulets (Pentacles) is made directly. When the Minor Arcana for the Raziel deck becomes available, it would be interesting to try this practice with that deck.

in the organization, they learned the mysteries of the twenty-two paths between the ten Sephirot as coded in the Major Arcana cards, since each path on the Tree corresponds to one of the Hebrew letters and each Major Arcana card was assigned a Hebrew letter. Each Sephira corresponded to a graded rank within the organization, attained once a member had mastered the esoteric spiritual teachings from the cards on the paths to that Sephirot.[10] This initiatory guide map thus explicitly connected the tarot deck to the thirty-two mystical paths of the Sefer Yetzirah and Kabbalistic tradition. I can't get the image of all of this as a kind of nineteenth-century British board game out of my head.

At least three decks came out of the Golden Dawn membership. The deck created by Arthur Edward Waite and Pamela Colman Smith is the most popular deck today, and you can find many images within it that refer to teachings of the Kabbalists as understood by these British occultists through their Hermetic lens. Here's where the scholarship of Ronald Decker, who was the curator of antique cards at the United States Playing Card Company, has provided an extraordinary theory. While he believes there is no direct connection between Kabbalah and the Major Arcana, he suggests there is a link between the meanings of the Sephirot and the divinatory meanings of the Minor Arcana cards. In his book *The Esoteric Tarot: Ancient Sources Rediscovered in Hermeticism and Cabala,* he notes that the meanings of the numeral cards in the tarot deck as recorded by Etteilla align systematically with explanations of the Sephirot in one of the most widely known Kabbalistic works, *The Gates of Light* by Joseph Gikatilla.

Rabbi Joseph Ibn Gikatilla was a contemporary of Rabbi Moses de León, the author of the Zohar. However, while it took a long time for the entire Zohar to be translated into Latin, Gikatilla's masterpiece, *The Gates of Light,* was translated into Latin in 1516. Just as there are no scripts of the medieval plays condemned by the Church, there is no smoking gun that shows whether Etteilla was aware that the key phrases he used as the meanings of the Minor Arcana correspond to phrases used by Gikatilla in *The Gates of Light.*

Decker surmised that there must have been a deck that someone wrote on to create Kabbalistic flash cards to learn from, so the definitions for the Sephirot were written on the Minor Arcana cards that correspond numerically. Then Decker provided a side-by-side comparison of Etteilla's interpretations of the cards with descriptions of each of the Sephirot from Gikatilla, showing what appears to be a clear influence of Gikatilla's descriptions on Etteilla's interpretations— whether Etteilla was aware of their origin or not—and these interpretations have influenced all subsequent interpretations of the cards.

Some of the imagery and the meanings in Waite's deck were heavily influenced by Papus (yet another Frenchman who took an esoteric nom de plume), whose understanding of tarot came directly from his study of Etteilla. Waite used this information in his own explanations of the cards in his book *The Pictorial Key to the Tarot*.

While several decks can claim their origin in members of the Golden Dawn, and all have Kabbalistic correspondences, my first deck was a Waite-Smith deck. It is the deck I have worked with the longest and the deck that is probably the easiest for people of European heritage to relate to. I like to think of this deck as a warehouse of Western symbolism (or a Renaissance Rorschach test). Learn all the symbols in this deck and you'll have a key to the mythology, art, and literature of Western civilization.

The interesting thing is that Waite knew there was no "ancient" connection between Kabbalah and tarot. He understood that claims for the antiquity of the cards were spurious, and he rejected any correspondence between the Hebrew alphabet and the Major Arcana.[11] Nevertheless, as an adept of the Golden Dawn, he seems to have understood that the systems reflected each other in ways that create constellations of deep meaning. The innovation that set the Waite-Smith deck apart from almost everything that came before is that the cards of the Minor Arcana depicted situational scenes with people and not just the objects of the suit. And because he gave Smith more latitude in her designs for the Minor Arcana, it's no surprise that some Kabbalistic references appear in those cards.

Rachel Pollack notes that despite Waite's deep knowledge of

Kabbalistic teachings, the meanings he assigned to the Minor Arcana and the images created by Smith for the Minors don't always match with the Sephirot.[12] This is true, since, of course, Waite was drawing from several traditions for his meanings, including alchemy. That said, Smith was an adept in the Golden Dawn, so she was certainly aware of some of the correspondences between the Sephirot and the numeric cards of the Minor Arcana. So while it might not be immediately apparent, I've found in my work with the cards for Omer meditation that there is always a relationship between each of the Sephirot and the situations in their corresponding cards, though sometimes the card image illustrates a negative meaning of a Sephira.

For example, the Four of Wands would correspond with Chesed in Atzilut. Decker points out that Etteilla includes "covenant" as a meaning for this card and that in *The Gates of Light,* Gikatilla associated Chesed with a covenant. The image on the Four of Wands is of a chuppah—a traditional wedding canopy. In Judaism, marriage is a covenantal relationship of love. But there are other important connections between the image on the Four of Wands and the concept of a covenant.

One of the stories about Abraham was that he kept his tent open on all four sides so he would be sure not to miss an opportunity to welcome a guest—an expression of Chesed—which is why he is the biblical personage associated with Chesed.* We can consider the image of the four wands as a tent open on four sides. Abraham, as the founding patriarch of the Jewish people, was also the first to undergo the B'rit Milah, the covenant of circumcision.

Let's circle back now to the image of the wedding canopy on the Four of Wands, which would be the very first card to consider on the first day of Counting the Omer. This symbol looks ahead to the very last day of the Omer, when we arrive at Pentecost—the symbolic marriage of the Israelites to the Divine Source, with the Torah serving as the wedding contract and Mt. Sinai as the wedding canopy.

---

*Traditionally, the Sephirot also correspond to what I will call characters in the Hebrew Bible. Male and female characters are assigned to each.

Moses betook himself to the encampment and awakened them [the Israelites] with these words: "Arise from your sleep, the bridegroom is at hand, and is waiting to lead his bride under the marriage canopy."[13]

It is doubtful that Pamela Colman Smith was aware of all of this, but she may have known some of it. And for me, it's clear that when you approach each Minor Arcana image and its corresponding Sephira, you will always find a relationship that gives greater depth to the meaning of each.

PUTTING IT ALL TOGETHER

With this understanding that each numbered Minor Arcana card corresponds to one of the Sephirot and that each suit corresponds to one of the four worlds, you can see how combining the matching cards each day during the Counting of the Omer can be used to deepen meditation and reflection. Using the cards in this way can be a powerful tool that can help take you to great psychological depths and spiritual heights.

Following the schema of pairing the week's Sephira with the day's Sephira, the third day of the first week of Counting the Omer is Tiferet within Chesed. Translating this to the tarot, these Sephirot would be represented in the world of Atzilut as the Six of Wands (Tiferet) as channeled through the Four of Wands (Chesed). Each day, you have a choice of four pairs of cards to work with, aligning with the four worlds. Putting pairs of cards together in this way can open you to experiencing the Sephirotic energies of each day in unexpected ways. If you're an experienced card reader, even if this practice isn't one you wish to follow, reading the cards with these Sephirotic relationships in mind will add depth and meaning to your readings.

Of course, as I've noted previously, from a traditional Jewish point of view this is heretical. Not only is it a commandment not to make a graven image of the Divine, the Sephirot (which are not to be identified with the Deity Itself) also are never depicted through figurative representation. In fact, from a traditional Kabbalistic point of view, the tarot deck itself (which also employs Christian and pagan symbols) is *to'e'vah,* or taboo. As a Jewish-Buddhist, though, I've found much that is precious in many traditions and that wisdom from one can shine a light that deepens the experience of the other. I hope that your experience using the cards as an aid to Count the Omer gives you similar gifts.

In fact, the Buddhist in me wants to point out a completely different kind of correspondence. It is said that before Gautama Buddha became enlightened, he sat for forty-nine days under the Bodhi tree and experienced Nirvana on the fiftieth day. Similarly, in the Tibetan Buddhist tradition, after death, the "soul" of a human spends forty-nine days in the bardo before taking rebirth. Why should these very different religious traditions settle on forty-nine days as the period it takes for transformation? I don't pretend to know the answer to this question—or even whether there is an answer to this question. But it's interesting to note, and I suspect there is some deep hidden wisdom at work in this correspondence with the forty-nine day Omer practice.

As you read through this guide, you will learn interpretations for each of the cards, even though this book is not a conventional guide to tarot card interpretations. In fact, because the same cards appear and reappear in different combinations, you'll learn how these combinations change the meanings of each card. So if you haven't already studied the cards before, this book will provide a more nuanced interpretation of the cards than you'll find in many guides. Still, it's always good to read other books on the subject. Similarly, if you are already a student of tarot but you haven't studied Kabbalah, I hope this book inspires you to learn more about this Jewish wisdom tradition, as opposed to the occult version. You'll find a number of good books on both these subjects and more in the bibliography.

Now that you have a basic understanding of the Omer practice and basic Kabbalistic concepts and their correspondences with the organization of the tarot deck, you're ready to begin a new way to practice this ancient spiritual discipline.

How to Follow the Daily Practice

THE RITUAL

The ritual of Counting the Omer, as practiced by Jews for centuries, requires actually counting each day and week. And because Judaism observes the start of the day at sunset, the Omer is counted at night, while standing, in a ritual that includes a blessing and a prayer said before counting the day. I like this ritual. It sets the *kavvanah,* the Jewish practice of creating mindful and heartfelt intention. I make it a part of my practice, and I include a modified, nonsectarian version of the blessing and prayer below for those who wish to bring this intention to their practice as well.

If you prefer to count in the morning, that's okay too. But like any practice, it's best to set aside a specific, regular time of the day that you know is only for this practice.

USING THE CARDS

The heart of this book is based on the forty-nine paired combinations of the Sephirot that occur during the Counting of the Omer. Each day of the count there are paired combinations of corresponding tarot cards. Because the four suits correspond to the four worlds, there are at least four possible pairings for each day, so that each day you can explore how the Sephirotic combinations affect the energy of that day in each world: spiritually, emotionally, intellectually, and physically.

With four pairs a day, there are probably too many pairings for most people to work with in one day, unless you're living the life of a cloistered contemplative. So here are five different suggestions for ways to work with these card pairings to Count the Omer plus one advanced practice for when you have already worked with all four suits. Of the suggested ways to work, choose the one that makes the most sense to you and follow it through to the end.

1. Follow One Suit
Choose one suit and only follow that suit through the forty-nine days of the count. Choose the suit that best matches with the focus of the inner work you want to do this year. Next year, choose one of the other suits. Continue each year until you have done all four suits.

2. Start at the Top of the Worlds
Start with Wands and do the count with that suit only. Next year, do the same with Cups. Then go through the following suits, one per year, in order of the four worlds so that you finish in the fourth year with Assiyah and Pentacles.

3. Around the Worlds in Two Hundred Days
Do all four suits in one year, one suit at a time in order of the four worlds. Between each suit, on the fiftieth day, follow the practice for the fiftieth day recommended at the end of this book. In this way, you'll finish the full work in two hundred days. You could start doing the count at the start of the traditional counting period and then just continue over the course of the year. Or start whenever it feels right to you.

4. Around the Worlds in Fifty Weeks
Do all four suits for the day—one week at a time—so that you complete the full work in forty-nine weeks, with the fiftieth week set aside for special meditations. As above, you could start at the beginning of the traditional counting period or at any time that seems right to you. Since this practice takes two weeks less than one year, it might be a good thing to start the first week of January.

5. Follow Your Calling

Choose one pair from any one suit each day—either the pair that calls to you or the pair you feel most resistant to.

6. Interpenetrating Worlds: Advanced Practice

Once you have followed this practice within each of the four suits, in whatever order works for you, you can start mixing the suits. For example, on the second day, Gevurah of Chesed, you could work with the Five of Pentacles and the Four of Wands, paying attention to how the worlds of the physical and the spiritual interact and influence each other. You can consciously choose which suits to mix or have it decided by shuffling the four cards for each Sephira and seeing what the universe presents you with.

Each day, read the interpretation for the pair(s) you're working with that day. In these interpretative essays, I share my own experience with this practice. After each pair you'll find several questions associated with that pairing. Use those questions for either reflection or your own Pentecost journaling exercise.

You'll probably want to write your own interpretations, questions, and journal entries based on your own life experience. You may wish to focus on a different facet of the day's pairing than I have. Go for it! Each Sephira can be approached from a variety of angles. To help you consider the many facets of each pair, use the Sephirot key words as described below.

HOW TO USE THE KEY WORDS TO
HELP INTERPRET THE CARDS

In the section on the Sephirot, there is a list of key words for each of the lower seven we'll be working with. When you substitute different key words for each Sephira, a different facet of the day's energy will be revealed for you to work with. By considering these key words in combination to create a theme for each day and by looking at the cards that correspond to the Sephirot, you'll find that the cards point to deeper meanings of these concepts and that the key words reveal deeper meanings in the cards. Be alert to the combinations that speak to possible issues or blocks that you face and keep an awareness of the shadow side of these combinations. As you do this, you'll discover the combination of key words that best fits your experience of the cards and the subject of the Sephirotic healing you should work on that day.

As an example of how this works, let's look at one pair for the twenty-second day: Chesed of Netzach in Atzilut. This Sephirotic combination corresponds to the Four of Wands as the card of the day's Sephira and the Seven of Wands as the card of the week's Sephira. So some of the key word combinations you could make include:

Chesed within Netzach

Key Word for Day's Sephira	within	Key Word for Week's Sephira
Love	within	Endurance
Flow	within	Fortitude
Nurturance	within	Mission
Love	within	Mastery
Flow	within	Ambition
Mercy	within	Triumph
Grace	within	Determination
Expansion	within	Dominance
Benevolence	within	Perseverance

In the chapters ahead, you'll see that I have chosen key words that worked for me as I've interpreted the cards to work the count over the years. Sometimes I'll look at more than one combination of key words and concepts as part of a deeper dive into the meaning of the cards and my own self-examination. My choices might change next year, since the issues I might be facing next year might well change. My choices might resonate for you, but try the key word substitutions for yourself each day—you might be surprised at the personal insights that arise. This will help you truly make this your own inner journey, giving you much to contemplate and journal about. In each daily section, I sometimes include several key word combinations to explore an issue. In these sections, when a key word appears, the first letter of that key word will always be capitalized, so you can more quickly recognize and become familiar with them.

If the pairings bring up questions of your own that are different from those I suggest, accept them as the teachers they are and seek out the answers within. As you work with the cards, you should use your own experience and history to help you find the interpretations and questions that mean the most to you at this moment on your path. And each day, find a few minutes to do the meditation for that day's Sephirotic pairing.

If you do the count at the time it's traditionally done, at night, you might simply use the reading, images, and questions to set your dream intentions to see what messages you receive.

While this book includes illustrations of each card pairing, I recommend having your own deck and carrying the pairings for each day with you to look at over the course of the day when you have some time to just immerse yourself in the images. Underneath the illustration of each day's card pairs there is a space for you to fill in the key words that are most meaningful for you. Or you may prefer to do this in a journal. When you have a record of your key word choices, you'll be able to look back next time you work with that pair to see if your choice is different.

THE MEDITATION

After the reading and reflection, consider experimenting with Sephirotic meditation. You'll find instructions for opening up to the Sephirotic energies of each day at the end of this book.

THE BLESSING:
A NONTRADITIONAL VERSION

Stand and speak this blessing, then the prayer, and then do the count aloud:

> Blessed is the One, Sovereign of All Universes and Creator of Time and Space, which has given us the sacred task of learning to make every day count by Counting the Omer.

> Today is the ___ day of the Omer. Which makes ____ week(s) and ____ day(s) of the Omer.

THE PRAYER:
A NONTRADITIONAL VERSION

Holy One, may it be Your will that by completing the sacred task of Counting the Omer today, any ways I have created separation or division of the Sephirot within me or in my relationships will be healed, made whole and holy. May my counting help to purify and unify my soul at each level, in *nefesh*, *ruach*, *neshamah*, and *chaya*, so that I may experience Your Divinity throughout and live in harmony with all Creation. Amen.

LOOKING AHEAD TO THE 50TH DAY

Because the practice of Counting the Omer is the preparation for the reenacting of a mythic event—receiving the revelation of the Torah at

Mt. Sinai—and because this revelation was experienced by the entire gathering of people at the foot of the mountain at the same time, both Hebrews and members of the "mixed multitude" among them, the practice, which has been solitary up to this point, now becomes a community event.

If you're following this practice at the same time as other Jews around the world, you may be able to find a community where you would be welcome to join a traditional Tikkun Leil Shavuot. In major cities, there are many such events, and in New York City there are several that are deliciously untraditional and open to all.

If you're not following this practice at the traditional time or if you prefer to observe the fiftieth day in a different way, let me make two suggestions based on two specific Jewish customs, that of *hevruta* and *minyan*.

Hevruta is studying in a pair with a companion on the path who will challenge you and whom you will challenge with questions about your experience to help you go deeper. Obviously, this is something you do with someone you know and trust and who wishes to do this practice as well. This practice builds spiritual intimacy, and as both the Pirkei Avot and the Zohar state, when two people study together, the Divine Presence hovers between them.

The custom of the minyan is praying and studying with a minimum of ten adults. I suggest this for the Tikkun on the fiftieth day. With ten people, each person embodies and holds the energy of one of the Sephirot, and the energy created in this space helps each of you go deeper than you might be able to do otherwise. And as with the custom of hevruta, it recognizes that revelation and enlightenment must be integrated into your life and your relationships. If you have ten companions who are willing to do this work with you at the same time and then come together for a Tikkun on the fiftieth day, your experience can be both revelatory and grounded. There will be more on how to follow this custom in the section on the fiftieth day at the end of this book.

If this is not something you can do, though, for whatever reason, don't be discouraged, and don't let it stop you from proceeding. Because doing this work over time will connect you to a community of seekers you didn't know before. You'll better recognize others who are also doing this work by themselves or in other groups. So if you're looking for a spiritual home, this practice may be your Divine GPS.

And so we begin. I wish you well on this journey over the next fifty days and on every day after that.

WEEK 1

Chesed

THE FIRST DAY OF THE COUNTING OF THE OMER is the second day of Passover—the first full day of freedom for the ancient Israelites escaping the bondage of Egypt. What better place to begin the count than from a place of freedom and gratitude for the Loving-kindness (Chesed) that pours forth from the Divine and sustains the world in every moment. This love colors the experience of each day and the subsequent Sephirot of the first week.

Day 1: Chesed of Chesed

Starting the Journey with Love

Today is the first day of the Omer.

While each day of the count has four pairs of cards showing that day's Sephirot in relationship, each week there is one day where the Sephira of the week and the Sephira of the day are the same. On these days, we will look at all four cards that correspond to that one Sephira, so that we can look at how this energy penetrates the four worlds. And today, the very first day, is just such a day. What better way to begin this inner journey than with a double dose of love?

Day 1: Chesed of Chesed

The Four of Wands, Cups, Swords, and Pentacles

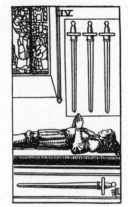

_____ *within* _____

The first day of the count is Chesed of Chesed—to remind us that on this path it is essential to start with a heart of Loving-kindness for ourselves. This is a journey that will take us through all the dark places in our hearts, and we need to remember that, just like the Jews in the desert, we're going to slip sometimes. We're going to forget to count some days. We're going to go unconscious in response to the issues the Sephirotic energies can bring up. I've done this many times. That's human nature, and nothing is more in need of Loving-kindness than that.

On the second night of Passover, we are figuratively free of Egypt. This was the first day our ancestors were no longer slaves, and since one of the Passover commandments is that we tell the story as though we ourselves were freed this day, we too are no longer slaves. The question is, What are we free from, and what were we enslaved to?

The ritual of counting days is not new to anyone in a twelve-step program, where you get a chip after your first thirty days of continuous sobriety—freedom from addiction. Sometimes it takes people many months, or even years, to reach that first thirty days. As our ancestors went through the desert, they slipped many times back into their "addiction": they wanted to go back to Egypt, they worshipped idols, they complained endlessly. Addicts know from experience that spiritual transformation, because that is what a twelve-step program really is about, often takes time. It comes with practice.

It took a forty-nine-day process for the ancient Israelites to learn how to be free from slavery before they could take on the spiritual responsibility of the Torah. In the next forty-nine days, another of the questions to ask might very well be, What am I enslaved to that I am not yet aware of?

In the tarot suits, the cards that correspond to Chesed are the fours, and the first card to look at on this, the first day, is the Four of Wands, or Chesed in Atzilut. It's appropriate that the image on this card captures the outpouring of Loving-kindness into the world.

The four wands, with a garland of fruit and flowers, look like a chuppah. Thus, this image looks forward to the marriage of Israel and the Divine on Shavuot, the ultimate expression of Love and Mercy. It also is reminiscent of Abraham's tent, which was described in the *midrash** as open on all four sides so he could see any and all visitors as they approached, the better to be able to welcome them. This is not wishy-washy Loving-kindness, but rather it is about being active in the world. Today is a day to meditate on the energy that is released when we go from bondage to freedom. And it's a day to bring our expression of Love into the world in ever more creative ways as we join with the Divine as partners in the ongoing act of Creation. Of course, I'm not always feeling so expansive, so when I consider this card I often ask myself what side of my tent is closed off; where am I reflexively unwelcoming in my life, and how is that keeping me enslaved?

The next Minor Arcana card to consider in looking at Chesed of Chesed is the Four of Cups, for Chesed in B'riah. Here we see someone

---

*The midrash is a genre of rabbinic literature that includes stories created to resolve contradictions or explain gaps in the biblical narrative. For example, there is no account in Genesis of what Abraham's father did for a living, but any Jewish child can tell you he made idols; the story of Abraham smashing idols in his father's shop is a midrash. Historically, the Midrash refers to a specific collection of these interpretive stories composed between 400 and 1200 CE, but people have continued to write midrashim (the plural form) up to today.

in what could be a meditative pose, and the image on the card can be interpreted as a warning against distraction. There are some interpretations of this card that suggest the person is not satisfied with what he has and keeps imagining more or that he is desirous of more. But in the context of Chesed in B'riah, the card shows an example of Chesed that just keeps giving—Divine Flow that doesn't stop Flowing. There isn't anything required other than a receptive mind for the next cup to appear. Here on this first day of the count, this card serves as a warning sign not to be distracted and miss the ever-present Flow of Lovingkindness available to us.

Chesed is Love, Mercy, and Bounty that Flows without boundary. The suit of Cups, connected to the element of water, feels deeply connected to Chesed and Flow. You'll recognize this in the famous line from Psalm 23 that expresses gratitude for this quality of Chesed: "My cup runneth over."[1] However, some people shut down in the face of Love that has no boundaries. I know this from my own personal history, and it leads me to consider whether the seated figure has experienced boundary violations and wounding that prevents him from letting Love wash over and through him. An experience like this can be genuinely terrifying for many people because it feels like an obliteration of the self. The ego isn't strong enough to withstand what can feel like an assault rather than Love. One can only transcend the ego when one's ego is healthy and secure to start off. So an experience like this in the Four of Cups is a sign of elemental wounding that needs gentle Love, balanced with the Restraint of Gevurah. When someone suffers from this elemental wounding, we need to recognize that starting a journey with a blast of Chesed can indeed be terrifying. A remedy for this is found in the very next card.

In the Four of Swords, Chesed in Yetzirah, we are given a clue as to how to approach the Omer counting practice, because the Four of Swords, like that of Cups, can also be read as a card of meditation. The card image shows a knight lying on a sepulcher as though he were dead. But this is not a card of death; it's a card of initiation into starting the inward journey. The knight is in a chapel, and the stained-glass window shows an image of a saint healing a supplicant, with *pax,* the Latin word for "peace," in the halo around the saint's head. It calls to mind the following words of St. Augustine on the subject of meditation. I particularly like the phrase "splendor of eternity" in this quote, since it pairs concepts that are associated with Hod and Netzach.

> Who shall lay hold upon his mind and hold it still, that it may stand
> a little while, and a little while glimpse the splendor of eternity,
> which stands forever: compare it with time, whose moments never
> stand, and see it is not comparable.[2]

The image on the card is a reference to the Night Vigil, the ritual initiation into knighthood. The evening before the title of knight is bestowed on a squire, he prepares himself with a ritual bath of purification. He wears a white robe and enters the chapel with his sword and shield. In some places, the sword and shield are placed on a coffin. In some versions of the ritual, the knight-to-be actually lies down in the open coffin, or rests atop it, and there he spends the night in prayer and meditation.[3]

The suit of Swords (and in Hermetic Qabalah, the world of Yetzirah) corresponds to the intellectual and mental faculties—the ability to distinguish reality from illusion. The knight-to-be in the Four of Swords is not dead or sleeping. He is ever vigilant—Swords being the suit of the mind that makes distinctions. He is ready to face the awe and terror that an experience of Chesed can bring to the unstable ego. This is the test of the knight-to-be: not unlike the temptation of Christ in the desert or the temptation of Gautama Buddha by Mara, he must face his fears in order to undergo a spiritual transformation. Of course, when we look at this card, the first thought is that the fear is of death. And this is true, since the job of a knight, a warrior for Christ, is to face death: it's just not the whole truth.

Remember that Chesed is both Boundless and "Boundary-less" and that to face this is to face the obliteration of the ego, a kind of death, which is a pretty terrifying prospect. The task of the knight-to-be is to face this fear and come away with an experience that is beyond duality—that he is both a separate being and an egoless expression of Divine Love.

The best expression of this idea that I know of comes from outside the Judeo-Christian tradition. It is in the words of Krishna to Arjuna in the Bhagavad Gita. In this story, Arjuna hesitates before battle; he does not want to kill anyone (least of all his cousins with whom he is at war). But Krishna tells him that the Spirit that pervades the universe cannot kill or be killed:

That by which all this is pervaded—that know for certain to be indestructible. None has the power to destroy this Immutable.

Of this indwelling Self, the ever-changeless, the indestructible, the illimitable—these bodies are said to have an end. Fight therefore, O descendant of Bharata.

He who takes the Self to be the slayer, he who takes It to be the slain, neither of these knows. It does not slay, nor is It slain.

This was never born, nor does It die. It is not that not having been It again comes into being. This is unborn, eternal, changeless, ever-Itself. It is not killed when the body is killed.

He that knows This to be indestructible, changeless, without birth, and immutable, how is he, O son of Prithâ, to slay or cause another to slay?[4]

In both the Hindu tradition and the Zen tradition in Japan, this was the philosophy of the warrior's path. Only once you have purified your mind with this understanding are you fit to enter battle. And as you can guess, the misappropriation of the warrior's path has been used to justify a lot of bloodshed by every religion. Remember, the image on the card is of a medieval knight—a warrior for Christ. Many such knights were Crusaders, which means some of my Jewish ancestors likely died at their hands.

Just because the historical reality of knighthood isn't very pretty doesn't mean the ideal of knighthood is any less spiritual. The ideal knight was a protector of the poor and weak. He was a protector of the faith by embodying its values. For when one is attuned to the Flow of Chesed within, it naturally flows out in ways that lead one to help everyone. When Chesed is experienced within, by turning inward and using your powers of the discriminating mind (as represented by the suit of Swords and the world of Yetzirah) to face your fears of the universal Flow, you can start this journey of forty-nine days with a sense of Loving-kindness for oneself and for all beings. This is one lesson of the Four of Swords.

As we move to Chesed in Assiyah, we come to the Four of Pentacles. On this first day of the count, remember that we are symbolically on the first day of freedom from Egypt. In Hebrew, Egypt is called Mitzrayim, which means "a narrow place"—the place where we feel constricted. And in the Four of Pentacles, Chesed in Assiyah, that freedom is frozen. The Flow has been stopped up. The way in which the person in the card is holding the Pentacles—one covering the crown, one in front of the heart, and with two other disks held down solidly underfoot—suggests a quality of defensiveness to this expression of Chesed. This is the shadow side of this Sephira. When confronted with a threat or a shock, there are four responses that are possible: fight, flight, freeze, or faint. Here, when faced with the shock of the new—in this case, freedom—the man (or woman) in this card has frozen. It's as though the person in the card doesn't trust this new freedom, doesn't trust himself to go with the Flow. In twelve-step language, while the man in the card has made the decision to take the path to freedom, he is "white-knuckling it"; that is, holding on so hard because opening up to the Flow may feel dangerous.

Because one of the qualities of Chesed is "Boundary-lessness," we can see the person in the Four of Pentacles as desperately trying to keep things under control. A lack of boundaries is threatening for someone who has been violated or is in recovery from addiction. The slavery in Egypt led to a mind-set of subservience—a kind of addiction. Any addict will tell you, whether it's alcohol or gambling, opioids or sex, addiction is like being enslaved to a substance or behavior that also soothes. For many of the enslaved ancient Israelites, it was terrifying to leave Egypt. Even though they were slaves, they had homes, beds, food, and family.

It was all they knew. One of the warnings of the Four of Pentacles is to beware of being enslaved by the seeming comfort of the material world.

The man in the Four of Pentacles has the freedom that material wealth can bring but is terrified due to some trauma, and he holds on as though still in need. He doesn't trust the Flow, so he is also enslaved by the fear of losing the material comfort he has, so much so that he can't let go and enjoy what he has. For him, Mitzrayim, the narrow place, his spiritual Egypt, feels comforting and secure in the face of such terrifying freedom.

This card gives us an example of someone who is enslaved to the world of Assiyah, who sees only the material and misses the spiritual. The figure grasps a Pentacle without an awareness of the star in the center of it—the Divine that is at the root of all material existence. Rather than participate in the Flow and contribute to it with Generosity and kindness or altruism, the man in this card appears stingy and miserly. The Pentacles in this card block the man's head, so that new ideas or thinking can't get in. They block his heart, so he won't be emotionally vulnerable. And with his feet on two of these disks, they block him from moving: he has become a physical prisoner, blind to the Divine at the center of each Pentacle and unaware of the freedom he holds in his hands.

Questions for reflection and contemplation: Day 1

1. (Wands) How open are you to receive Love? What side of your tent is closed? Where are you reflexively unwelcoming to others? Why?

2. (Cups) In what ways do you distract yourself from the Flow of blessings? How do you shut down when you feel overwhelmed by Love, and how can you open yourself to feel safe enough to receive more? Are you pulling inward or feeling defensive in some way?

3. (Swords) How can you show compassion for yourself when you need to withdraw or look within? What beliefs do you hold that prevent you from fully experiencing the Flow of Divine Love?

4. (Pentacles) In what ways are you Generous or stingy with your love?

Day 2: Gevurah of Chesed

Structure and Struggle Held in Loving-kindness

Today is the second day of the Omer.

Gevurah gets a bad rap. Structure. Discipline. Law. Severity. Awe. If you're a child of the sixties like me, you may bristle at these words. But love requires Discipline, Structure, Boundaries. I can't tell you how many New Age meetings I've had to sit through where no one paid attention to time Boundaries. That's Chesed with no Structure or Discipline (or negative Hod, as we'll see later). Balanced Loving-kindness is expressed with Discipline, regularly and appropriately.

It's like going to the gym and working out. Going to the gym is an act of love for oneself, taking care of one's body and health. But you gotta have a regimen, a Structure. Like the thousands who join a gym on New Year's Day and stop after a couple of workouts (I'm talking to myself here!), we need to realize that the process of Counting the Omer is a Discipline, and already on day two, one can hear the small voice of resistance inside. Discipline is working through that resistance. Structure provides the Organizing principle of Counting the Omer; it is a container of safety that enables each of us to experience the transformation from spiritual slavery to spiritual maturity through love.

Day 2: Gevurah of Chesed in Atzilut

The Five and Four of Wands

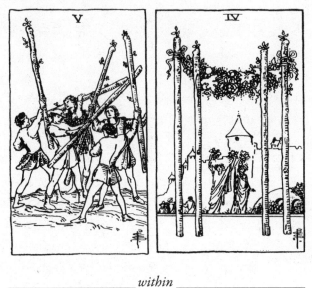

_____ *within* _____

So we're two days into the journey out of Egypt, and in the Five of Wands it looks as though the Israelites are already fighting among themselves—complaining, competing, kvetching. Discipline has yet to take hold. Discipline and Structure are precisely what's missing in the Five of Wands, and here is an example of a card that shows the negative or shadow side of the Sephira. Everyone has a wand, everyone wants to be the leader, so everyone is at cross-purposes, rebelling against the Discipline needed to reach the (metaphorical) Promised Land. When everyone wants to establish his own Structure, when everyone wants to lead, the result is chaos. Focus on the man on the left: he is not holding that wand in a gesture of attack. He looks as though he's trying to get the attention of all the other people: he is standing in a position of leadership, yet those around him are too busy arguing among themselves to really see him or follow his direction. The image of this man reminds me of so many paintings and filmic images of Moses standing at the edge of the sea, raising his rod to part the waters. And what was happening just before he parted those waters? The Hebrews were arguing and complaining and were not happy about his leadership.

> And they said to Moses, "Is it because there were no graves in Egypt that you brought us here to die in the wilderness? Why did you bring us out of Egypt anyway?
>   Didn't we tell you to leave us alone? Didn't we tell you we'd rather serve the Egyptians than die in the wilderness?"[5]

They're barely out of Egypt, and the people have already forgotten the pain of their slavery. They're fearful of the way forward. How are we any different when we make a vow to change? I can't go a few minutes after making a decision without hearing the voices of my inner "stiff-necked" Israelites complaining and trying to change my direction.

Perhaps you know these voices. That's when to focus on the energy of Chesed as expressed through the Structure of Gevurah. This is the example of the Loving leadership of your inner Moses. He is ready to help guide you through the wilderness over the next forty-eight days to a new freedom. Of course, you'll have your inner Israelites too, complaining and looking to backslide almost every step of the way. This pairing is a warning not to let them distract you. Hold them with the Love of Chesed and keep them in line with the Discipline of Gevurah.

Day 2: Gevurah of Chesed in B'riah

The Five and Four of Cups

_____ *within* _____

The protagonist in the Four of Cups is the recipient of the Divine Flow. As he sits there, it keeps coming to him, and he doesn't yet have the spiritual strength or Discipline to hold it all.

So in the Five of Cups, three of the cups have been overturned and their contents lost, much in the way the first Sephirot shattered. Some describe the protagonist in this card as someone in mourning because the person is wearing a black robe. However, a black robe is also the uniform of the judge, and Judgment is one of the names or qualities of Gevurah. Gevurah as Structure or Discipline directs the energy of Chesed positively. But when the Structure isn't strong enough to hold that energy, or if the Structure is too rigid, the energy breaks the container.

In the Five of Cups, I see a judge who has been too rigid and who suffers the unfortunate results of that rigidity. This could be a warning against the negative face of Gevurah: self-Judgment and criticism. It's a warning not only against the inner critic but also against the inner pessimist who says, "Oh, I'll never be able to do this; I missed a day, did it wrong, and now all is lost." Remember, not everything is lost since we see the remaining two cups in the card are still standing. Yes, we live in a broken world, and there is loss that must be mourned. But the brokenness is holy. The loss is holy. The mourning is holy. Sacred.

All is not lost. You just pick yourself up and, in the words of my meditation teacher, the late S. N. Goenka, "start again."

Day 2: Gevurah of Chesed in Yetzirah

The Five and Four of Swords

_____ *within* _____

When we first looked at the Four of Swords, I referred to the Night Vigil—the test of a man about to be knighted, who must stand watch through the night in a church. He is meditating. In the image in the Waite-Smith Tarot, and bringing some of our contemporary experience of meditation to the card, we can think of him of as lying in the yoga pose of *savasana,* the corpse pose. Of course, if you've ever done savasana, you know the danger the pose, uh, poses. You're supposed to remain alert, and one of the first things to happen to many people who get into this position is that they fall asleep. The Discipline of meditation is to be watchful. It's not enough to say you're going to watch: you've got to stay awake and focused; otherwise the mind drifts. You can see the result of this lack of Discipline in the Five of Swords. We've let our guard down, and our unhealthy mental habit patterns are ever watchful for that opportunity. They pick up our dropped sword of Discriminating intelligence, and we get lost in a fantasy; our unconscious habits take over . . . or worse, our addictions.

It's the nature of our mind to drop its attention and lose focus when meditating. And one unhealthy mental habit pattern that stands ready to attack us when this happens is self-criticism designed to undermine (one of the meanings of the Five of Swords when applied to one's inner landscape, and one of the negative faces of Gevurah).

This pairing on day two is a reminder to pay attention. Don't get lost in the clouds. Divine Love is serious business that requires Discipline to be balanced, and you can't hold and direct that Love if you can't hold your attention.

Day 2: Gevurah of Chesed in Assiyah

The Five and Four of Pentacles

_____ *within* _____

In the last pairing of the day, we see the result of Severity, another reading of Gevurah. In the Four of Pentacles, we have a man who cannot let go, who is restricting the Flow of Chesed. And in the Five of Pentacles, the poor and the sick are outside in the snow. Some interpret this card metaphorically; these people could enter the church at any time and what keeps them outside is their own spiritual poverty. But in this pairing, I see the result of any institution or any organized religion whose role in the world is to manifest Chesed, Mercy, but has forgotten this role and turned its back on the poor and sick. They are unwelcome in the church. The light shines out of the stained-glass window, but there is no door leading inside. This is Severity at work in Gevurah that is out of balance.

Of course, it's easy to point a critical finger at organized religion. So the question to ask of ourselves on our inner journey is, Where are we punishing ourselves, being too Severe and restrictive in ways that hold us back from our birthright of Love? Most importantly, what parts of ourselves do we see as unacceptable to the Compassionate One?

If you believe that the Divine doesn't accept you in all your imperfections, you are closing the door on the poor woman and lame man within you. Not only does the Source of All Being Love you in all your imperfection, but it is also by loving your imperfections and offering them up to Ein Sof with consciousness that you heal yourself and make yourself whole. This is the inner work of Tikkun Olam and perhaps the most profound lesson of this day; remember, you were set free just yesterday on the second day of Passover. As you set out on this journey to revelation at Sinai, don't leave any part of yourself behind.

Questions for reflection and contemplation: Day 2

1. (Wands) Do you lead with Love or do you Love to lead? What can you do to find a balance between them?

2. (Cups) In what ways are you rigid in expressing or expecting to receive Love? What is your experience of Judging how much love your beloved can hold? In what ways are you afraid of your capacity to accept the Flow of Love; what are your thoughts when you Judge yourself or others when that acceptance reaches a Limit? How can you show Restraint and gauge the appropriate expression of Love?

3. (Swords) How do you bring the Discipline of mindfulness to your Love? How can you bring an awareness to your Love so that it is supportive rather than undermining? What are the ways in which you rebel against Love?

4. (Pentacles) What parts of yourself do you feel are unacceptable to the Source of All Compassion? What ways are you punishing yourself that hold you back from feeling your birthright of Love? What can you do to let go of this thinking? Consider your close relationships: where have you been so rigid that you've lost the heart of something?

Day 3: Tiferet of Chesed

Holding Hurt and Pain with Love and Compassion

Today is the third day of the Omer.

Beauty, Harmony, Truth, Balance. Tiferet is the place on the Tree that is connected to everything, like the Heart that it is. It holds the conflicting energies of Chesed and Gevurah in Dynamic Balance. This means that in order to feel the energy of Tiferet we must simultaneously be open to the Severity and Judgment that sometimes fuel our anger, as well as the Love that just wants to Flow out of us. We have to allow ourselves to feel deep into the Stricture of our pain and into the expansive nature of our Compassion.

Tiferet of Chesed is about feeling all this Love and Stricture at the same time and going ahead to do the work that needs to be done. Sometimes that requires more of an expression of Chesed. Sometimes it requires more of the Severe expression of Gevurah. Commitment to change within ourselves, within our community, and in the wider world requires both Love and Discipline meeting in the Harmony of Tiferet.

Day 3: Tiferet of Chesed in Atzilut

The Six and Four of Wands

_____ *within* _____

Tiferet is the Sephira of the open Heart, and this seems at odds with the image in the Six of Wands, an image of triumph, which usually means success in battle. While it is tempting to see the laurel wreath on the head of the rider as a celebration not only of peace but also of the arts, I focus on the two central staffs in the image, noting that they appear to be crossed just at the point where the rider is holding his staff. This makes the wreath on the staff the rider is carrying also a crown at the top of a cross! So hidden in the Six of Wands is the central Christian image referring to the Crucifixion. Tiferet, in Christian Cabala, is associated with the Sacred Heart of Jesus and the sacrifice of the open Heart. So today is the day to do open-Heart surgery on ourselves, without fear of spilling some blood in the process. But whose blood? Ours? Those we see as enemies?

A few years ago at a Passover Seder I attended, there was a discussion of the issues raised by the Rwandan government's mandated forgiveness of participants in the genocide of 1994, as opposed to the process of forgiveness practiced in South Africa for their period of apartheid with their establishment of a Truth and Reconciliation Commission. This was not an academic discussion, since one of the Seder guests was also a friend of the family of Captain Richard Phillips, who was then currently being held hostage by pirates off the Somali coast.

Can we bear the pain the Phillips family felt in that situation? And are we Openhearted enough to feel the unconscious pain and anger at injustice felt by people who act it out in the world as pirates? Do we have enough Gevurah to respond with Discipline and measured strength used with Compassionate Chesed for all? Do we truly understand what sacrifices must be called for? Meditating on the Omer is not divorced from what is happening right here right now in the world and in our own lives. It is a practice and process of clarification and purification so that hopefully we can act consciously in the world and not act out our unconscious patterns.

Perhaps the victory of the Six of Wands is having an open Heart with the ability to feel all these complexities without being overwhelmed or unbalanced. (It takes Balance to ride a horse!) Having an open Heart of Tiferet includes both clarity of purpose and Compassion for all. I can't even pretend to be close to attaining this Balance, but it's important to keep working to reach this goal.

Day 3: Tiferet of Chesed in B'riah

The Six and Four of Cups

_____ *within* _____

In the world of B'riah, we see the Four of Cups paired with the Six of Cups. The Six of Cups is often read as nostalgia, but I see it as the memory of innocence lost, because in the Six of Cups we see a child being given a gift from someone older. An older child? The author Isabel Radow Kliegman suggests the possibility that the figure on the left is an adult leaving the situation and the child unguarded—and that this can refer to sexual abuse of a child.[6] But children are betrayed in so many ways. We all lose our innocence. Can we have the open Heart of a child even after the pain of betrayal, after the loss of innocence and loss of safety in the world? Can we live in the world with the Heart of a child and the wisdom of an adult?

This interpretation made me consider my own life experience. When I was a young child, I ate everything that was put in front of me and loved to try new foods. Then suddenly, around the time I was five years old, like the figure in the Four of Cups, who seems to be refusing what's offered, I began refusing to eat anything new. In fact, I started to refuse many foods that I had loved. Previously, if you had asked me about this time in my life, I would have looked back on my childhood through a golden haze of nostalgia. It was only as an adult, and after I'd been in therapy, that I understood my refusal to eat as a response to an experience of abuse that I had repressed and that left me feeling unprotected and unnourished by the adults in my life. So I acted out this feeling with food.

On this day, some questions to consider are: What painful emotions must we feel to restore the Flow and move on? Can we open our own wounded child's Heart and comfort it with the loving Chesed and secure Gevurah of the adult that we now are? And after our childhood wounding, as adults are we able to let down our guard to accept or give Love Generously?

Day 3: Tiferet of Chesed in Yetzirah

The Six and Four of Swords

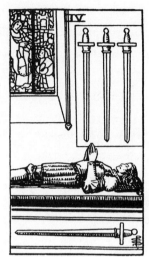

_____ *within* _____

Here we see the relationship of the knight starting his inward journey in the Four of Swords and the people in the Six of Swords on an outward journey across the water. Once again, a six card is showing us a Balancing act—this time in a boat. The water is not choppy, but it's a small craft, and without the right balance it could tip over. The boatman stands at the rear, and his passengers sit in the middle. This means the swords that are standing upright in the front could well be balancing the boat. But it's an odd image, since of course if a sword were piercing the bottom of a boat, it would be sinking.

A popular interpretation of this card is as a passage away from difficulty. But with the swords in the boat, it feels to me like a visual expression of the idea that you can't run away from your problems. Considered with the meditating knight on an inner journey, it feels to me that this pairing is about coming to a place of emotional pain and slowly, carefully, making one's way across and through. To use a phrase from the twelve-step world, "The only way out is through."

The passengers seem depressed, sad, in mourning. And indeed, when going into the open Heart, one will experience pain and sadness. But there is another side, another shore. And because you're taking the swords with you, well, there may be a new life awaiting you, but to live that life fully, you need clear-minded access to the pain in order to feel Compassion and empathy for others. So the pain comes with you, and the pairing of these cards promises that with careful awareness and Balance, being open to this pain won't sink you.

Day 3: Tiferet of Chesed in Assiyah
The Six and Four of Pentacles

———————— *within* ————————

In the world of Assiyah, the world of action and materiality, we look at the relationship of the Six and Four of Pentacles. Moving from the four, where the Flow of Chesed is stuck, to the six, we seem now to have struck a Balance. In fact, an old-fashioned Balance scale is pictured on the card. Yet the arrangement of Pentacles on the card itself is out of Balance. We see a man, possibly a merchant or banker, giving coins to a person in the position of a supplicant. Giving appropriate charity is certainly a Balanced expression of Chesed and Gevurah in the world of Assiyah. However, something is out of Balance in this image. It feels as though the way charity is being given is being used as a way to feel separate and superior. So one question to ask of ourselves in Tiferet of Chesed is, How does our giving of charity or lending a hand to another serve as a defense, and what is it a defense against?

Many of us may not feel so far from the supplicants in the card. One catastrophic illness, a job loss, or a death in the family, and we might find ourselves homeless or without resources to help ourselves recover. Is this fear real? Do we give with stinginess because we're afraid we will run out of resources ourselves? Or is it that we're afraid of opening up to the pain and vulnerability of being in this position?

Tiferet is the place of the open Heart, and the best way to examine your Heart is when faced with other people and their suffering directly. The ability to be with that suffering, to try to help without being either overwhelmed or shutting down is the task of the day. This means being able to face one's own suffering as well.

Questions for reflection and contemplation: Day 3

1. (Wands) Consider your capacity for empathy. Can you recall any times when, knowing how empathetic you were in a situation, you found yourself feeling superior?

2. (Cups) What painful emotions must you feel to restore the Flow and move on? How can you open your wounded child's Heart and comfort it with the loving Chesed and secure Gevurah of the adult that you now are? While holding your childhood wounds with Chesed and protecting them with Gevurah, examine where in your life you might be able to let down your guard a little more to accept or give Love Generously.

3. (Swords) Remember a painful experience in your life that you feel helps keep you in touch with your Compassion. What do you do to connect with that pain without feeling overwhelmed? Think of people who have hurt you in some way and consider the pain that made them act out in this way. See if you can feel Compassion for them without losing your boundary of protection.

4. (Pentacles) Think about a time when you gave charity to someone directly—and if so, what feelings did it bring up? Do you have any beliefs about money and Flow that approach magical thinking?

Day 4: Netzach of Chesed

Defending Yourself without Falling Prey to Your Defenses

Today is the fourth day of the Omer.

As we descend the Tree, Netzach is the first of the more physical Sephirot. While it is most often known as Victory, one of its more important characteristics is that of Endurance. Love is a feeling, but the ability for that Love to Endure requires both mental and physical stamina.

We're still only in the first week. It's just the fourth day of the count. Yet my own experience is that the fourth day is a test of Endurance: Can I really keep doing this? Can my Love Endure the challenges I face day after day?

Day 4: Netzach of Chesed in Atzilut

The Seven and Four of Wands

_____ *within* _____

One meaning of the Seven of Wands is defending what you believe in, and that includes standing up for yourself and any of the ways you don't conform to society's expectations of who you should be. Paired with the Four of Wands, which can be seen as the openness of Abraham's tent, the energy of these Sephirot moves forward with the willingness to defend what needs defending (without being defensive about it). I see this Sephirotic pairing as the energy of openness, self-love, and compassion for others, joined to the courageous Endurance to fully express who you are in the world, knowing that there will always be some who will attack you for it. Netzach of Chesed gives you the ability to be ready to withstand such an attack without shutting down or losing your ability to Love (which includes compassion for the attacker). As a gay man who seeks to live from the place of an open heart and, of course, as an out gay man who thus must on a regular basis declare or announce his identity, this is a day in the count that has great meaning for me.

It's interesting to note the natural movement between opening and closing that happens between Chesed and Netzach in the suit of Wands on this the fourth day of the Omer. Remember that a flower opens and closes naturally every day. It opens to take in the energy of the sun and then closes to conserve energy and use it to grow from within in the dark (as do we all). So what does all of this have to do with today's Sephirotic energies? It's a day to examine whether you're feeling open or closed. Do you notice times and places during this day where you feel yourself open to deeper places or where your defenses kick up so you start to close down? This is a good day to pay attention to this movement and inquire into it.

This pairing suggests that storms and attacks from the world outside are inevitable and warns that while it's important to be ready for them, an attitude of defensiveness will undermine one's Chesed. As a queer JuBu (Jewish Buddhist), I try to remain conscious of the attitude of defensiveness I can sometimes carry. Sometimes I expect to be attacked by communities of faith for my expression of Love for another man. And there are times I expect to be attacked in queer communities for identifying with a faith community or for expressing Love for the Divine and the world. Can I hold on to the dynamic tension of both without feeling tense? Am I able to see the chip that's sometimes on my shoulder or the wound I carry and not react in blind anger or pain? Am I able to learn how to live with an open heart and still know how to stand my ground and keep good boundaries? These are some of the questions I consider on this day. How does this pairing speak to you?

Day 4: Netzach of Chesed in B'riah

The Seven and Four of Cups

_____ *within* _____

In the pairing of the Four and Seven of Cups, it's almost as if we're seeing the fourth cup being offered in the Chesed card from the point of view of the figure in the Seven of Cups, so that he's not seeing just one cup in the air, but seven. Here the distraction we see in the Four of Cups is multiplied. This is a warning. On the first day of counting, you could imagine a better future at the end of the count. But while imagination is a good incentive to help you get started, imagination in meditation (that isn't a guided visualization) isn't a good thing. It's a distraction, and the deeper you go, the more powerful the distractions will become—and the more of them will appear.

This is where the energy of Netzach, Endurance, is essential. To endure in this practice, you must be focused on exactly where you are right now and the next step you are taking to move forward, without getting caught up in distractions and fantasies.

Day 4: Netzach of Chesed in Yetzirah
The Seven and Four of Swords

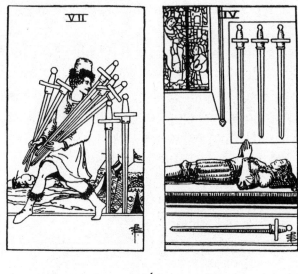

_____ *within* _____

In this pair, we find that while the knight is on his watch, on the meditation retreat that is the Night Vigil, someone is making off with the goods in the Seven of Swords. Once, when I was on a Buddhist meditation retreat in Yangon, the teacher asked me, "Who are your enemies?" This was a simple question, which, if I'd been more awake, I would have answered immediately. But I was so drowsy from the heat (and from my inner defenses kicking up to keep me from being awake) that I couldn't answer. The classic answer in Buddhist meditation is that drowsiness, anger, desire, aversion, and ignorance are your enemies. So let's consider for a moment that, like me on that retreat in Yangon, the knight is not really awake. He has fallen asleep on the job because he is lost in a fantasy meditation that all is Chesed and there's nothing to worry about. It's the mushy-minded thinking you'll sometimes encounter in people who define themselves as "spiritual."

There are people who use meditation as a defense against the world rather than a way to be fully in it. They close their eyes and (for example) repeat a mantra: all is love, all is love. They create a psychic vibrational wall in themselves that blinds them to real dangers from outside as well as the danger of their own trickster energy within that is sapping the strength of their insight. This is one warning of this pair: staying awake calls for the Endurance of discriminating intelligence.

Certainly, besides inner tricksters, there are con artists of all kinds in this world waiting for the moment you fall asleep. I've met any number of people who call themselves religious and/or who have a spiritual practice yet nevertheless are quite happy to steal something from you—whether it's monetary or psychological resources.

As the Buddha said, "Arise! Pay attention!"

Day 4: Netzach of Chesed in Assiyah

The Seven and Four of Pentacles

_____ *within* _____

In this pair, I see the relationship between an employer and employee. In the Four of Pentacles, we see a man who wears a crown, while the man in the Seven of Pentacles is clearly a worker: he has a spade or hoe in the ground that he is tilling (quite successfully).

For the man in the Seven of Pentacles, his Endurance in his work has led to the creation of abundance. But does he have his full share in it? Not if his boss is the man in the Four of Pentacles—a man who is stopping up the Flow of Chesed. But the true power of gold is in the Flow of energy and Love it represents.

Don't sit on the gold you have inside you. This only stops up the Flow. And don't use it in the service of someone or something that doesn't understand that it's essential to participate in the Flow; that denies its true value, which is beyond valuation. That is one message in this pairing. What other messages do you receive?

Questions for reflection and contemplation: Day 4

1. (Wands) In what ways does opening up to Love make you feel vulnerable to attack? Have you ever felt that you had to fight to win your Love? Were you able to Endure and be Victorious? How did that affect your Love?

2. (Cups) What are the temptations that distract you from your Love? How can you stay Focused in your Love? In what ways has Love clouded your judgment?

3. (Swords) What is the defense that has consistently undermined you in your relationships? How did it serve a positive purpose at one point? What can you do to weaken its hold on you now?

4. (Pentacles) How would you characterize your willingness to do the hard work it takes for a relationship to Endure?

Day 5: Hod of Chesed

Finding the Victory in Love by Surrendering the Ego

Today is the fifth day of the Omer.

You've got to win a little, lose a little,
Yes, and always have the blues a little.
That's the story of, that's the glory of love.
"The Glory of Love," lyrics by Billy Hill

One of the characteristics of Hod is Glory. Another is Surrender. And this lovely old song recognizes the truth that you've got to lose to win. You've got to Surrender to let Love in. Surrender to one's lover and to the Divine lover. "That's the story of, that's the glory of love."

Five days into the count, and while I often continue to experience the resistance of the second day, the energy of Hod enables me to begin to Surrender more deeply to the process. Just as an addict Surrenders in a twelve-step program, admitting powerlessness, there is a moment when the ego Surrenders and the experience of the greater Glory and Splendor of creation is revealed for just a moment. The ego is a small cup, held with Love in a much greater cup.

Day 5: Hod of Chesed in Atzilut

The Eight and Four of Wands

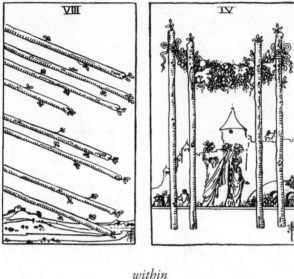

_____ *within* _____

In this pairing, we really have the Glory of Love. One of the visual references in the Four of Wands is the chuppah under which the Divine Marriage takes place on Shavuot. Some of the images that have been associated with the Eight of Wands are Cupid's arrows and the explosive energy of the male orgasm! After all, not only are the wands phallic, but they are also budding with green shoots. Pairing this card with the Four of Wands in the context of the upcoming holiday of Shavuot, it's almost as though we're looking forward to the consummation of the Divine Marriage and the Surrender to revelation. But besides looking forward to the fiftieth day, we're also looking at the energy of this, the fifth day of the count, in Atzilut. And the cards suggest that if you're receptive to the energy of this day, if you Surrender to the process, you can receive a burst of joy and inspiration.

Another thing to point out about the Eight of Wands is that it's one of only two cards in the Minor Arcana with no human being in the image. One reason might be the connection of Hod to the Surrender of the ego. Another might be because at the moment of orgasm, our ego, and the sense of separateness that comes with ego, often dissolves. There is only an outpouring of Love that is a momentary reflection of the eternal Divine outpouring. So while meditating today, if your ego can get out of the way, you just might experience a moment of the Divine outpouring that feels orgasmic.

Day 5: Hod of Chesed in B'riah

The Eight and Four of Cups

_____ *within* _____

When these cards are paired, the figure in the Four of Cups seems more dissatisfied than distracted. By the time we get to the Eight of Cups, even though the Flow of Chesed has continued and the cups just keep stacking up, the figure has decided to turn his back on it all. This is a different kind of Surrender. This is renunciation and letting go of attachments.

While we're in the suit of Cups and the world of B'riah, where emotions hold sway, Hod is the Sephira of the intellect, so this renunciation may come from a desire for greater balance. Indeed, this is a card that can be seen as the beginning of the inner journey, turning away from outward expression toward inner examination.

Hod also carries the quality of Humility. Consider this in combination with the esoteric title of the Eight of Cups: The Lord of Abandoned Success. So here is where we can look at one of the shadow sides of this Sephirotic pair. The power of Chesed can be overwhelming, and for some people, the shadow side of Humility is not a feeling of modesty but an expression of low self-esteem and a feeling of unworthiness. If you're feeling unworthy yet love, abundance, and success keep coming at you, it wouldn't be a surprise if you feel as if you want to flee. Perhaps that's what the figure in the Eight of Cups is doing.

That makes this a day to consider whether any feelings like that are hiding inside you. After all, metaphorically speaking, you were just set free from slavery a few days ago. Psychologists Gay and Kathlyn Hendricks refer to this kind of situation as the Upper Limits Problem: when you find yourself in a place of success or happiness, but because it's an unfamiliar experience, you're uncomfortable, so you do something to bring yourself down to a more familiar level of misery. When you look at the Eight of Cups in this pairing, it's good to ask whether you're turning away from Love or success because you're uncomfortable with it, or whether you're turning toward something deeper.

Day 5: Hod of Chesed in Yetzirah
The Eight and Four of Swords

 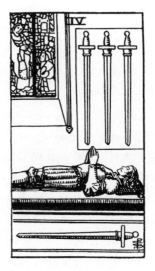

within

Hod of Chesed in Yetzirah does not look so Glorious at first glance in this pair. Yet clearly, both of these images are a Surrender of a kind. We've already considered the meditative retreat of the Four of Swords. How is that mediated by the Eight of Swords, which looks and feels coercive?

In the Eight of Swords, a woman's arms are bound and her eyes are blindfolded. She stands on ground that is treacherous, since it is neither level nor solid. On this not-entirely-solid ground, the swords and the woman are in danger of falling over at any time. There is the danger of losing one's balance and falling into something dangerously sharp or onto the ground. With the ground being not entirely solid and the woman's arms being bound, it would be extremely difficult (though not impossible) to stand up again.

Compare this with the knight in the Four of Swords, who in his position of rest on top of a sarcophagus is completely stable. Here, Chesed is in fact providing a solid ground of compassion that enables the woman in the Eight of Swords to make her way through this hazardous landscape. This interpretation suggests that the woman is being guided from within, from a place of deep Love for herself in this situation. At the same time, both of the people are figures in solitude. They are alone, and certainly the woman in the Eight of Swords could use some assistance.

One of the meanings given to Hod is Humility. An act of Love for oneself in this situation would mean having the Humility to ask for assistance. After all, on a meditation retreat, unless you're shut up in a cave by yourself, when one encounters difficulties there is always a teacher or guide to consult or seek assistance from.

Because both Hod and the suit of Swords correspond to the world of intellect, there is the possibility that the Eight of Swords shows someone who is a prisoner of her thoughts and perhaps her unconsciously held ideas. Maybe one such idea is that she is alone and there is no one she can seek help from. Perhaps she thinks that this is an ordeal that must be gone through alone, just as the knight in the Four of Swords must go through his vigil on his own.

With this double focus on the intellect, this card pairing can stand as a warning of the arrogance of the intellect that it can solve a problem alone, without the help of intuition. Certainly, an overreliance on the intellect can blind and bind. Yet the only way the woman can move forward without falling is by dropping the total reliance on the intellect (since she is bound and blindfolded) and Surrendering to her intuition (and thus keeping her balance). For someone who sees the world through the lens of the intellect, giving up its primacy to the power of intuition can feel like a terrifying surrender. This card suggests that without such a Surrender, there is no way forward.

Are we really alone in our trials? Often one's partner or a family member is right there pointing out something you don't want to see. Or you're trapped in a behavior pattern or an argument that has left you feeling isolated or unwilling to ask for assistance from a loved one. Your pride in your intellect tells you that you are right about something, yet an insistence on this leaves you alone.

I know this particular trap fairly well, since I am one of those people who puts a premium on intellect. And in an argument with someone who is a more intuitive and emotional person, my reliance on logic only makes things worse because I am often blind(folded) to their way of seeing things. Intellect and logic are important, but they aren't everything. Reliance on intellect alone results in a world out of balance.

As the saying goes, Would you rather be right or would you rather be happy? Being happy requires Humility in Loving-kindness, Hod in Chesed.

Day 5: Hod of Chesed in Assiyah

The Eight and Four of Pentacles

_____ *within* _____

In the Eight of Pentacles, we have a man at a workbench carefully engraving the pentagrams into these golden disks. When I look at him, I am reminded of when I lived in Japan and would go up to visit traditional potters in the town of Mashiko. I got to know many potters personally and was lucky enough to stay as a guest in their homes. Every potter had apprentices.

The path of the apprentice potter is not an easy one in Japan. They get up before sunrise and roll the cold clay by hand for throwing, often in an unheated studio. It can be months before they get to make something themselves—not something original, mind you, but a copy of one of the master's pieces. When they finally throw this form, if the master doesn't like it, he simply breaks it. If he approves, he stamps it as his own. To be an apprentice is to understand the path of Surrender.

In the Eight of Pentacles, I see an apprentice who is just at the moment of becoming a master. And as a master, he makes the same thing again and again, as perfectly similar as any human can. Before the era of mass production, this was the sign of a master. He is a master who has Surrendered to the practice; thus, Chesed Flows into his work unimpeded. That's what puts the spirit of the five-pointed star into each gold disk. His work (matter) is infused with his Love and his spirit.

In the relationship of these two cards, I see the master and the former apprentice. Here I see the man in the Four of Pentacles as a master holding the space, the form for others: he holds on to the practice, the artistry, with Love and in the spirit of Generosity. The coins that he holds are points in the three pillars of the Tree of Life—at the points of Keter, Tiferet, Netzach, and Hod. His holding of the Pentacles in this way is a sign to the apprentice of the path he must follow.

Now you may be thinking, wait a minute here, the Four of Pentacles is not about Generosity, it's about the opposite: miserliness. But the cards are not signs; they are symbols with a constellation of meanings that sometimes invert based on the cards that surround them. One of the earliest writers on tarot, Etteilla (whose work you'll remember may have been influenced by Gikatilla's description of the Sephirot), described the meaning of this card as Generosity. I've heard some tarot experts describe the man in the card as not clinging to the disk in front of his torso so much as presenting it, offering it.

Because the man in the Four of Pentacles is holding the central pillar of the Tree, he has great power. This pillar is where the dynamic tension of the Sephirot is at its greatest. In this pairing, I see the man in the Four of Pentacles as the Magician King and the man in the Eight of Pentacles as the Apprentice at the very moment of his becoming a master himself because he has totally Surrendered.

When you look at Japanese pottery, when you hold it, you can feel the energy of the person who made it—a potter who sensed the Divine Love that wanted to be revealed in the form of a clay body (not unlike the love we seek to express with our own bodies of clay) and who Surrendered his ego to allow that expression of Divine Love to manifest in the material world. This is the Glory of Hod of Chesed in Assiyah, and if we're diligent in our spiritual work—and our work in the world— we can share in the Glory by letting this Love shine through our work in the material world.

Questions for reflection and contemplation: Day 5

1. (Wands) How does your love help you feel connected to Divine love—love that's bigger than you are?

2. (Cups) In what ways do you experience a split between spiritual and physical love? Is there a relationship that has suffered because of your pride? What can you do to repair that relationship?

3. (Swords) When people you love criticize you, how do you respond? Do you feel self-righteous in any of your relationships?

4. (Pentacles) Does what you do give you an opportunity to express Loving-kindness?

Day 6: Yesod of Chesed

Shining the Light of Love
into Our Darkest Places

Today is the sixth day of the Omer.

The energy of Yesod is about the Desire for Connection. This Connection can go in any direction. This statement is not a judgment but is simply a recognition that the energy of Yesod is a strong rush to Connect anywhere. When a person's relationship to this Sephirotic energy isn't in balance, the desire for Connection can be expressed, as the Buddhists say, unskillfully. And so it should be no surprise that this Sephira can be associated with addiction. This includes the addiction of consumerism, which can make hungry ghosts of us all.

The dark side of Yesod is particularly associated with sex addiction because Yesod corresponds in the human body with the genitals. When the Yesodic desire for outer Connection isn't balanced by inner Connection with Tiferet, there is the danger of the misuse of Yesodic energy in sexual encounters that denigrates the humanity and divinity of the other.

It's hard to hold the energy of Yesod: this is the place on the Tree where all the energies of the "higher" Sephirot come together once again before pouring into Malchut. That's one reason Yesod is known as Foundation: it has to be strong enough to hold all this energy that wants to go somewhere right now—and to direct it with Love. When Yesod is in a balanced relationship with these other energies, sexual Intimacy is a channel to express and share spiritual Intimacy in the deep connection of physical Intimacy. Or it can be the channel for Generative energy to create and share something (art, ideas, a child!) with the world.

Ultimately, Yesod of Chesed is about the desire for Connection that is born of boundless Love. It gives those who can hold this energy the ability to Connect with the suffering of another on the deepest level, even the suffering of those who project their unhappiness onto us and make us the enemy. It is Love and understanding for the suffering and delusion that leads those people to spread their misery. That doesn't mean we don't oppose the actions of such people; we just don't fall victim to their delusion of demonizing the other because we know that, in fact, we are all Intimately Connected.

Nobody said this was an easy path.

Day 6: Yesod of Chesed in Atzilut
The Nine and Four of Wands

_____ *within* _____

Yesod is the Sephira of Connection and emotional Bonding. Yet in the Nine of Wands, we have an image that is very defended and closed off. Notice that there is an opening in the defense, the line of staves, so it's not a total shutdown. It can be seen as an ingathering of energy, a psychic regrouping before the movement of all the energy stored in Yesod rushes into Malchut tomorrow. So let us look at the stockade image of the Nine of Wands in juxtaposition with the very open image in the Chesed card, the Four of Wands. Love requires the vulnerability we can see in the openness of the Four of Wands, and the man in the Nine of Wands has been open; he made himself vulnerable in the past, but he has been wounded. However, he hasn't fully closed himself off. He may be defended, but he has left his defenses somewhat open because, while hurt and wary, he still wants to trust and hope. These two cards together capture the issues we all face in relationships: open idealism and wary defensiveness. We need both, but we can't let ourselves be completely ruled by either. True Intimacy that lasts is accepting of the hurts that we know will inevitably come. Even in the best Relationships, sometimes we get hurt and need to retreat, but it's essential to always leave a door open and eventually relax, return, and reaffirm our commitment.

The Four of Wands is a vision of total trust—the trust of Abraham with his tent flaps open on all sides. Chesed is an outpouring of the energy of Loving-kindness. Yesod takes that energy and channels it with Generative, Creative, and/or sexual energy to Connect. With this understanding, you can see that even though the man in the Nine of Wands is in a defensive position, his very nature is outgoing.

Looking at these two cards through the darker lens of addiction, we can interpret the man in the Nine of Wands as someone in recovery, possibly from sexual wounding or addiction. He may be defending himself against the energy of Yesod of Chesed, which can be indiscriminate. Flowing in all directions equally, Yesod of Chesed in Atzilut can be a dangerous energy pairing for those not skillful in handling it. Let's also remember that the word Kabbalah literally means "receiving." The problem of the man in the Nine of Wands might be that because of wounding, addiction, or both, he finds himself unable to receive Love.

When we overlay the mythic journey of the Hebrew slaves just freed from slavery in Egypt, the sixth day is the day when they came to the Red Sea. On one side, they are being pursued by Pharaoh and his army. Before them is the sea. And just as there is an opening in the wall before the man in the Nine of Wands, the sea is parted and God's Chesed Flows to hold two walls of water for the Hebrews to pass through. You can see the man in this card as one of these Hebrews at the shore, looking at the newly parted sea. His headband is a symbol of the psychic toll slavery has taken; he remains wary and uncertain about taking the next step through the waters to freedom.

So we can also read this pairing of cards as the passage out of slavery (whether addiction or even working for an abusive company) that requires us to step through the wall of Wands to be reborn and free on the other side. There is a way out, and it is through. Divine Chesed is holding those wands apart so that you may escape "the narrow place" and open to a deeper Connection.

Day 6: Yesod of Chesed in B'riah

The Nine and Four of Cups

_____ *within* _____

In both the cards for Yesod of Chesed in B'riah, we see solitary figures, each seated with arms crossed, guarding the heart and separating the energy of the upper Sephirot from the lower. With Chesed not in relationship with Yesod, it's no surprise these figures are solitary. In the Nine of Cups, it's almost as if the seated man is blocking our way at a banquet. He has been gifted with plenty and has much to share, but his position, with his thighs "manspreading," suggests a veiled aggressive energy. Though dressed like a merchant or minor noble, he displays an attitude best expressed by a great Mel Brooks song: "It's Good to Be the King." Yet he is not seated on a throne, but on a bench. And indeed, the bench is clearly long enough for two people to sit closely together, except for the fact that the man has spread out to take all the room.

The cups on the table could signify the past Creative achievements of this man; they are behind him, and he is resting on his laurels, no longer using his Creative energy and not sharing his gifts with others. Still, he smiles as he faces us because he's happy to show off all his cups; he just isn't going to share their benefits. On the table under the nine cups, there is a tablecloth that's so long it reaches the ground. It functions more like a curtain, hiding what's underneath it. What's being hidden? Because this is Yesod of Chesed, I see one meaning for this card as an expression of the loneliness that can't be filled by material possessions and outer success. The cups behind the man are empty and arrayed like trophies. I think of a man who collects lovers like objects, a man who wants one trophy Relationship after another. So while the seated man looks satisfied with himself at having won one cup after another, he is at his core very lonely and Disconnected (the shadow side of Yesod) from others and himself.

The Nine of Cups also raises the possibility of another addiction— alcoholism. At the root of many addictions is a wounded ability to express or receive Intimacy. Or he could be a "social loner." That is, someone who is happy to throw lots of parties and who uses the crowds as a way of avoiding direct and deeper Connection with any one person.

All these images suggest that this would be a good day to shine a Loving light of Chesed on where we use substances or behaviors to avoid Intimacy. We all have ways of refusing the Flow of Love. We all have ways of avoiding Intimacy, some of which, while not at the level of addiction, can keep us cut off from a deep Relationship with ourselves and others.

Day 6: Yesod of Chesed in Yetzirah
The Nine and Four of Swords

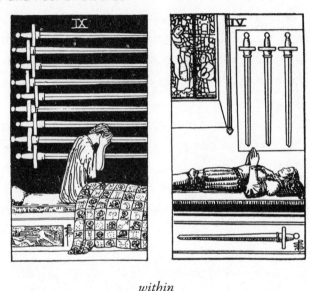

within

Our unconscious energy in Relationship is also part of the story when we look at Yesod of Chesed in Yetzirah. In the Nine of Swords, a solitary figure sits up in bed in the middle of the night, perhaps in deep grief, anxiety, or awakening from a nightmare. Nine swords are arrayed against the dark, as though hanging on a wall, and all are pointing in one direction—the same direction that the figure in bed is facing. In a reading, the Nine of Swords can indicate depression. Psychologists say depression is the result of anger toward others that feels too dangerous to express in Relationship and too dangerous even to admit to conscious awareness, so that it gets turned inward toward the self. I see the swords arrayed above the figure in bed as unexpressed anger, floating there in the dark because this anger has not even been admitted into consciousness; hence, the depression. But this withheld anger means one's inner Relationship is damaged and one's outer Relationships are not whole. From another point of view, the unexpressed emotion may not be anger. It can be anything unexpressed (or unowned) because it's considered unacceptable; hence, a shadow trait, which in fact could be a positive trait that is considered unacceptable by the person who has it. If we see the figure in this card as a woman and take into consideration the interpretation of the suit of Swords as representing discriminating intelligence, this could be the depression of an extremely intelligent woman who lives in a social situation where her intelligence is not only not valued but is actively discouraged.

The inner gifts that we find unacceptable become shadow traits that fuel our nightmares, so perhaps the nightmare the figure is awakening from is in fact this unowned gift reappearing as shadow. There is also the possibility that what is unconscious has been expressed, but because it's not fully conscious, the expression has been unskillful—hurtful. This could be a picture of the grief of someone who has hurt another with sharp words that seemed to come out of nowhere (at least to the speaker).

Because this is Yesod, we also have to explore the sexual element to the image and its symbols. Swords, like wands, are phallic, and this is a figure alone in bed. Are these the "notches" in the bedpost of sexual conquest without real Connection? This visual could signify the deep emptiness of compulsive sexual Connection. And because there is an addictive quality to Yesodic energy, one can see this image as what is referred to in twelve-step programs as "hitting bottom," when it feels as though one is as far as possible from the Divine light.

When considering the interplay between the images of the Four and Nine of Swords, we come to a spiritual truth that many meditation teachers don't share with students at the beginning of their journey. As you open yourself up to the Sephirotic energies, the chakra energies, or however you characterize the Divine Flow that is tapped into in meditation, over time the blockages within will be revealed. Meditation may feel peaceful and relaxing at first, but it will open you to the hidden emotions and repressed thoughts in the unconscious. When you encounter these consciously for the first time, it can feel like a nightmare.

In the Four of Swords, we have someone who is experiencing the

Flow of Chesed in meditation. It's a Buddhist metta meditation of Loving-kindness, which begins with Loving the self and then radiating that Love out in ever-widening circles to include all; this is how the Buddhists express Chesed. But it's also a Night Vigil. The knight may be meditating on Loving-kindness, but he is also watchful for the demons that lie within.

Going within to tap into Chesed throws a light on the dark places where we don't feel Chesed and don't feel we are worthy of Chesed. These are some of the places we must heal in order to be in Relationship, to make a Connection that is spiritually Intimate. Because it is painful to experience these long cutoff emotions, we can see the figure in the Nine of Swords experiencing a dark night of the soul on this inner journey—a night that must be seen through with the open eyes of Chesed and without flinching, fear, or aversion in order to pass through it whole and healed.

The pleasure of deep Connection—spiritual, emotional, intellectual, and physical—is our birthright. That is the compassionate promise of Yesod of Chesed in Yetzirah, if we use our discriminating intelligence to keep our eyes open and our minds free of projection in the experience.

Day 6: Yesod of Chesed in Assiyah
The Nine and Four of Pentacles

_____ *within* _____

After the three previous difficult pairs today, this pairing comes as a relief! In the Nine of Pentacles, we see a woman who has channeled the energy of Yesod of Chesed in the world of action to create a garden of abundance. She is enjoying the fruits of a good life that has been earned through disciplined action. It's not merely a garden, it's also a vineyard, and in both Jewish and Christian symbolism, the vineyard is a symbol not only of fecundity but also of the spiritual life. In Judaism, the vine represents the people of Israel and the bounty of the Divine. Wine is part of every ritual meal and is sanctified by a blessing that speaks to the transformation from grapes to wine. So of course, this imagery continues through in early Christianity.

> I am the true vine, and my Father is the vinegrower. He removes every branch in me that bears no fruit. Every branch that bears fruit he prunes to make it bear more fruit. You have already been cleansed by the word that I have spoken to you. Abide in me, as I abide in you. Just as the branch cannot bear fruit by itself unless it abides in the vine, neither can you unless you abide in me.
>
> I am the vine, you are the branches. Those who abide in me and I in them bear much fruit; because apart from me you can do nothing.[7]

In this card, we see the Pentacles shining on the vine. This in fact is profoundly Jewish: all creation is holy.

But the woman in the Nine of Pentacles is alone in what appears to be a private garden. And Yesod is the Sephira of Connection, Bonding, and Relationship. Perhaps the connection here is to the Divine rather than to another human. It may be that the woman has chosen to give her life to work that helps realize the Divine in the world. In this way, the card can be seen as expressing the joy and rich inner life of spiritual pursuits that are further reflected in the world.

Then there's the image of the hooded falcon, a symbol of discipline and sexual self-control. So this card could be seen not only as a turning away from Relationship, but also as the sublimation of the sexual urge into one's work in the world as a spiritual path. However, not everyone who sublimates his or her sexuality into work does so as a spiritual path. This very sublimation may well be behind a major social development in the United States, where in 2015, for the first time, the number of unmarried adults outnumbered married adults. About thirty-one million of these unmarried adults live alone.[8] This doesn't mean all these people are unhappy or lonely. Many people find fulfillment in life without marriage. But the question is, Where does one put the energy of the natural desire for Connection?

In the Four of Pentacles, where the Flow is being stopped and held and where it is mediated by the Yesodic energy of the Nine of Pentacles, we have a day where outer Relationships can take a back seat to building financial success for solitary pleasure.

We could also see the figures in these cards representing stereotypical roles in a heterosexual Relationship—where the man concerns himself with money and may even be secretive about what he earns, while the woman retreats to her garden. Their Relationship suffers because of this division. So this could be a call to consider whether you take either of these roles in Relationship, regardless of gender.

Still, Yesod of Chesed is very much about Creating a fruitful Bond with another person that is built on Love. So this pair can help you examine your ability to share what you Create with this energy to build Connection.

Questions for reflection and contemplation: Day 6

1. (Wands) What fears or defenses does the prospect of Intimacy activate? What is the most Intimate thing you could say to God? Say it in a prayer.

2. (Cups) Examine any ways that you use your position in the world to block Intimacy; how can you release this block?

3. (Swords) Do your relationships have a strong enough Foundation to enable the expression of difficult emotions such as anger? What is your experience using substances or behaviors to avoid Intimacy or feeling loneliness?

4. (Pentacles) In what ways do you channel your desire for connection into your work? In what ways does your Relationship with money affect your ability to be Intimate with another?

Day 7: Malchut of Chesed

Accepting Love and Being True to Who You Fully Are in Relationship

Today is the seventh day of the Omer, which is one week of the Omer.

Today is the first day that completes a week; it's the first day we experience the Sephira of Malchut, which, with no energy of its own, receives and reflects all the energy from the nine Sephirot above it. Sounds heady. But the meaning is simple: everything in the world is Divine energy in a multiplicity of manifestations, and it is all here for us to experience, to see it clearly for what it is and celebrate its many blessings. It's all here for us. So today is the day when each of us should strive to see our place in the world clearly and experience all as a manifestation of the endless outpouring of Divine Chesed. This outpouring is for your sake.

One word used to define Malchut is Kingship, which can point to the danger of seeing everything as here for you. Because while there have been many Noble monarchs in history who have seen their position as one of service, overall they're in the minority. Kings can be arrogant. They feel entitled; indeed they have a title, and it's the highest there is. That's why Rabbi Bunem Simcha offered the teaching that we should all have two pockets with a note in each. In one, the note reads, "For my sake was the world created." But when we feel entitled, it's time to be reminded by the other note that without this Divine outpouring, we are "but dust and ashes."

As humans, it's hard to remember both truths at the same time. But together they are the truth: the world is a manifestation of Divine Love, here for us. Without it sustaining the world (and us) in every second, we are but dust and ashes.

Day 7: Malchut of Chesed in Atzilut

The Ten and Four of Wands

_____ *within* _____

In the Ten of Wands, we have someone who is experiencing Divine Love in all its manifestations as a burden. It's become too much to bear all this Love, all this creative energy. We all know someone who has a life filled with blessings, yet all they can do is complain. There is a culture of complaint that comes out of an old superstition that if you say how good things are going, you'll jinx them. You may know the old Yiddish phrase "*kineahora*," said in response to someone saying how good things are going in order to ward off the evil eye. Well, there's a strategy that goes one step further and doesn't even admit to how good things are going. So in answer to a question about one's health, instead of saying, "My health is terrific, kineahora," someone would say, "Oy, don't ask," and launch into a litany of complaints. It's about an attitude. I'm suggesting that it's possible that the man in the Ten of Wands is the recipient of great blessings but is responding from a culture of complaint.

Looking at this card in another way and thinking of the celebration in the Four of Wands, I can also see this card as a man bringing the gifts of Loving-kindness for everyone to share at the celebration. He is the one who has taken the Responsibility to gather the sparks of the shattered vessels. He has taken on the joyous burden of Tikkun Olam.

Not all of us are strong enough to do this, and while we are enjoined to take Responsibility in repairing the world, we aren't expected to do the whole job by ourselves. That would be overwhelming (and is in fact one of the dangers of Chesed out of balance). So this card can also be seen as a caution not to take Responsibility for everything. Sometimes the best way to give and receive Love is to share Responsibility.

Day 7: Malchut of Chesed in B'riah

The Ten and Four of Cups

_____ *within* _____

In Jewish myth, the rainbow is a sign of God's promise not to send another world-destroying flood. Chesed, though, can be connected to the image of a flood. It washes over and through everything. And as we've noted, this can be experienced as either liberating or terrifying (or both). In the aspect we see in the Ten of Cups, though, liberation and celebration are clearly the feelings we're meant to come away with.

So here in the Ten of Cups, we have a family of four dancing beneath a rainbow arcing across the sky, with ten cups arrayed within it. Leaving aside the heteronormativity of the scene (after all, the Waite-Smith Tarot was created by people who came of age during the Victorian era, even if they themselves lived unconventional lives), the image and its symbols suggest that this is a very happy family, where it's okay to feel and express the full spectrum of emotions. Children who grow up in such an environment develop not only good skills of expression but also a Grounded Self-Possession that is experienced by others around them as a kind of Dignity. This is the Sovereignty of Malchut. The children dancing in the card enjoy a sense of security that should be the birthright for all of us but is so often short-circuited by damaged family dynamics. These are children who will grow up to be able to Love fully and completely, whose Love will not impose selfish constraints on another nor result in a need to pretend to be anything other than who they truly are. So while the young man in the Four of Cups still appears to have some block to receiving the Chesed that is rightly his, the ultimate promise of Malchut of Chesed in B'riah is freedom from anything that takes away from fully giving and receiving Love.

Day 7: Malchut of Chesed in Yetzirah
The Ten and Four of Swords

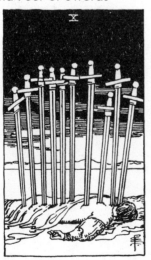 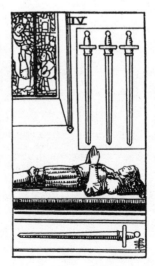

_____ *within* _____

The Ten of Swords is one of those dramatic cards: people see it in a reading and get upset or become afraid. Some tarot practitioners like to say that it's nothing to be afraid of, that the card is about the death of something we need to let go of—a defense, an outworn belief, or the thing that really doesn't want to die: the ego. Nothing to be afraid of here? Have you ever noticed a defense going without some furious resistance?

There's a reason this thing that needs to die has ten swords sticking out of its back! It's strong and hard to kill. Sort of like a psychological or spiritual Freddy Krueger, it's not gonna die. Like Rasputin, it will have to be shot again and again before it's really dead, if it ever really is. It hardly seems like we're in the week of Chesed, right?

Remember, this is in the world of Yetzirah, of the intellect, and in the suit of Swords, discriminating intelligence. And in the Chesed card, the Four of Swords, we have the knight-to-be in his Night Vigil, keeping watch for the inner demons that must be faced. This is not a battlefield where he will have to kill these demons. It's an internal landscape where the (not so) simple task is deep awareness without reacting with desire or aversion. Because in meditation, awareness without reaction is the practice that weakens and eventually kills these demons. These demons are the unskillful habit patterns of the mind that are pierced with the discriminating insight of the Ten of Swords, and when these habit patterns are seen and recognized for what they are, they die a little. Sometimes we have to learn to recognize them again and again before they totally die. Sometimes we only need to see them once. But once we have seen them, without aversion, with clarity and Love for ourselves, we are no longer enslaved to them. We are then truly the Sovereign of our soul; we are transformed, free.

Day 7: Malchut of Chesed in Assiyah

The Ten and Four of Pentacles

_____ *within* _____

The Ten of Pentacles is the last numeric card in the Minor Arcana, and it is the only card in the deck that explicitly depicts all ten Sephirot in the Tree of Life. But unlike the Four of Pentacles, where the figure is interacting with the pentacles, holding tight to three of them, these objects seem to be floating in the air, unseen by all the people pictured in the Ten of Pentacles. Everyone in the card seems to be a recipient of the material benefits of Divine Flow. But where's the Love? No one seems to be connecting to anyone else. It's as if everyone in the scene is like the figure in the Four of Pentacles: they have theirs, and they're not sharing it with anyone else.

The only reason we call this suit Pentacles is that Waite decided to add the star to the center of the disk in the suit known previously as Coins, and there are two things to consider when we think about this decision. First, that the Pentacles can still be seen as money, as coins. After all, we're in the world of Assiyah, and as Madonna expressed it so eloquently, "We are living in a material world, and I am a material girl." However, Einstein taught us that matter multiplied by the speed of light squared is energy, and the star inscribed inside each disk is a reminder that they're not just matter, they're not only money, they're also energy that's just moving very slowly.

The issue raised by Malchut of Chesed in Assiyah is whether we're going to see another person through Madonna's eyes or Einstein's. Are you only worth your net worth, or is your value beyond valuation? Is your relationship to others based on material gain, or do you approach everyone else as an individual with equal Dignity, regardless of what's in their bank account? Because the suit of Pentacles is about practicalities and pragmatism, there's a danger of relationships becoming transactional: what can you do for me? This sees the other person as a stepping-stone or a tool; in other words, an object, as opposed to an expression of Divine Love made manifest in the world.

This is the razor's edge of therapeutic relationships, whether with a healer or a guide of any kind. The role of the guide is to see the Dignity of the client, to see that the client is an expression of Divine Love. But the therapist is also dependent on the client for income. Your feelings about material blessings or, more directly, money, can either strengthen or undermine such a relationship. But approaching this dynamic from a nondual point of view, it's possible to see the financial arrangement as an expression of one's spiritual commitment to the relationship.

When I see the old man in the Ten of Pentacles, I am reminded of a story from the Babylonian Talmud in which Rabbi Joshua ben Levi meets the prophet Elijah and asks him when the Messiah will come. The prophet tells the rabbi to ask the Messiah himself, since he can be found sitting among the beggars outside the city gates of Rome. When the rabbi finds the Messiah and asks him when he will come, he is astounded at the answer: today. However, when the Messiah does not come that day, the rabbi goes to Elijah and says that the Messiah lied to him. But Elijah tells him that the Messiah meant he would come if people would follow his teachings today. It's highly doubtful that either Waite or Colman Smith knew this story, but I find a real resonance with the image in the card. The old man is the very picture of patience and wisdom. If everyone pictured in the card related to the others by seeing the Divine in them, the Messiah would have no need to come, because God's Kingdom (and Queendom, since Malchut is also associated with the Shekinah) will have been established here on Earth. And indeed, looking at the Four of Pentacles, we can note that the man in that card sees and interacts with the Pentacles: his feet are planted firmly on two of them, showing that he knows the ground he stands on is holy and he knows "the kingdom of God is within you."[9] When we all know this truth within ourselves and can see it in everyone else as well as in all creation, there'll be no need for the Messiah to come.

Questions for reflection and contemplation: Day 7

1. (Wands) Have you ever felt overwhelmed by the Flow blessings in your life, or have you known someone whose life is filled with blessings yet they seem burdened by them? What is your habitual response when someone remarks about the Flow of blessings in your life: are you a "kineahora" type of person, do you react with an "oy, don't ask" kind of response, or do you express gratitude for the Flow?

2. (Cups) Consider the full spectrum of your emotions: which emotions are the hardest for you to feel and express? Why do you think that is? What is your experience with the ability to feel the Flow of several emotions at once; for example, being angry and loving at the same time, or happy and sad? When in relationship, what is your experience with being able to be fully present to the full spectrum of your partner's emotions?

3. (Swords) What are the patterns of thought or beliefs that have blocked you from the Flow of Love in your life? What old thought patterns need to die?

4. (Pentacles) Consider your therapeutic relationships, whether as a guide or client: how do you surf the dynamic of being Present to the Divine in the other while honoring the financial arrangement? What are your thoughts and feelings about money and the Flow of resources in a therapeutic relationship? What are your feelings around this issue? How are financial relationships in your life expressions of a spiritual relationship?

WEEK 2

Gevurah

IT'S WEEK TWO. Metaphorically speaking, we're on the trek through the desert. Imagine that long line of ancient Israelites—men, women, children, and the "mixed multitude" of people who went with them. Plus animals, tents, and belongings. Without the discipline of Gevurah holding everyone together, people would have wandered off in all directions.

I am a gay man who is a child of the sixties, and Gevurah can feel like "the establishment" to me. Authority that defends the rules without soul. Law without compassion. And that is indeed part of the shadow side of Gevurah. But to look only at the shadow side suggests there is a lack of balance that must be addressed. Gevurah is the Sephira associated with the Torah because, after all, the Torah is the Law. That's not to say that the Torah is free from severe laws that show no compassion—consider the death penalty for a son who disobeys his parents.[1] However, Gevurah is an essential component of the Tree. Everything is out of balance without it. But the Severity of Gevurah on its own chokes the life out of everything.

Remember, it's Gevurah at work in restraining Chesed, which on its own is overwhelming. Some Kabbalists believe that creation began with Gevurah—with the Divine Limiting Itself through the constriction of the Tzimtzum so there would be space for our experience of reality.*

---

*Rabbi Isaac Luria's mythic account of Creation begins with the Tzimtzum. In the beginning, the Divine Presence filled the universe, so there was no room for Creation. Thus, the Divine contracted Its Self in order to create a space for Creation. This contraction is known as the Tzimtzum. This suggests that creation is separate from the Divine. However, despite this "contraction," the Divine Presence is understood as filling the universe. It is only our limited perception that makes it appear otherwise. For more on this topic, see "How the Ari Created a Myth and Changed Judaism" by Howard Schwartz on the Tikkun website.

There is a protective quality to Gevurah that can get lost in our (my) projections onto authority.

During the second week, we get to explore our relationship with this difficult energy, how it works in our life and relationships, and how it is expressed through the lens of the other Sephirot.

Day 8: Chesed of Gevurah

Creating Structure without Stricture

Today is the eighth day of the Omer, which is one week and one day of the Omer.

Just like the yin-yang symbol, Chesed and Gevurah are always in dynamic tension, and there is a little bit of the other in each of them. On the second day, we explored Gevurah in Chesed. Here, the focus of the pairing is reversed, and we get to consider how this shift in focus changes the meanings of the cards, how it shades the energies of the Sephirot, and the issues they raise for us.

Over the course of the next six weeks, there will be many other days when we encounter card pairs we've seen before, but in a different order. And today is the first time, though this is the structure of the practice, as you will see. Notice how this seemingly simple change can change everything.

Day 8: Chesed of Gevurah in Atzilut

The Four and Five of Wands

_____ *within* _____

You've seen these cards before: they're the same cards for the second day, the Gevurah that is in Chesed. But here the order is reversed. A change of order may not seem like much, but Counting the Omer is a practice not unlike mindfulness meditation. It calls for being aware of subtle shifts in energy.

So what is Chesed that is in Gevurah? How is Love expressed in Discipline? Consider the simple traffic light. It's an example of many of the characteristics of Gevurah: Law, Structure, and Form that express care for both pedestrians and drivers. The Flow of traffic is directed with safety, and in order to do that, people as a society must come together and agree on this Structure. Of course, this is a pretty Assiyatic example for the cards in Atzilut.

Both the world of Atzilut and the suit of Wands are connected to will. We can see this in the action of the man in the Five of Wands, holding his wand up in a position to command the attention and obedience of the other four people pictured in the card. This is Love expressed in the will to create Structure and Discipline out of the chaos he sees before him. This is the wand of Psalm 23, in which the psalm-ist sings, "Thy rod and thy staff, they comfort me." This is not a wand to be used as a cudgel to beat someone into Discipline—the way Zen monks whack your back if you're not sitting in perfect zazen style. This is the staff of the shepherd guiding his flock, an expression of Loving guidance and protection. Where is this energy of Gevurah expressed through Chesed at work in your life?

Day 8: Chesed of Gevurah in B'riah

The Four and Five of Cups

_____ *within* _____

The very shape of a cup is an example of Gevurah in the world. It creates a Structure that holds and, in the case of, say, a pitcher, directs the Flow of liquid. So let's consider again the potter throwing the Form of a cup on the wheel. One of the potter's hands is on the inside of the Form being shaped, the other is on the outside. The force on either side must be perfectly balanced. On the outside is Gevurah, Discipline, holding the Form and giving Structure to the clay body. On the inside is Chesed, Expanding out and lifting up the Form with a Loving touch that understands the imperfections and Limits of the clay body. When Love is expressed through Structure and Form, the results can be beautiful. So it is with Chesed of Gevurah. This is not Form for the sake of Form; it is Form infused with meaning.

A potter friend of mine once asked somewhat philosophically of the experience of throwing on the wheel, "Do I center the clay, or does the clay center me?" When you can express Chesed of Gevurah, you're coming from your center and connecting to the Center that is everywhere.

Looking at the Five of Cups, we see that overly strict Discipline can lead to loss or that being Judgmental focuses too much on loss. But a Disciplined approach that includes Love sees that all is never lost and that (in the Four of Cups) the Flow just keeps coming. With balanced Discipline, we can direct that Flow and share it.

Day 8: Chesed of Gevurah in Yetzirah

The Four and Five of Swords

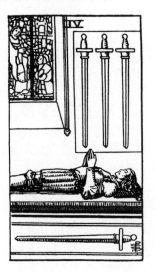 

——————————— *within* ———————————

The figure in the foreground of the Five of Swords has what looks like a spiteful smirk on his face—the nasty glee of an unpleasant winner. In the distance, two other figures wander off. They've dropped their swords on the ground. One seems to be grieving—walking away in shock and leaving himself undefended. This is an image of schadenfreude: the man in the foreground is taking pleasure in the misfortune of others as he picks up the discarded swords.

So what does this have to do with Gevurah? As Law, Gevurah is necessary to keep the universe from chaos. But the feeling here is less the Law of the Divine and more the Law of the jungle, which has no pity. Gevurah is also the pivot point where the Tree connects to what is referred to in Jewish mysticism as the Sitra Achra, or the other side: the world of the demonic, the world of evil, the Shadow Tree. The other side is always present and looking for opportunity. It can warp the Judgment that is Gevurah and appear in our lives as defeatist self-criticism or as someone outside who really is hypercritical, spiteful, contemptuous, and without empathy.

Part of the message of the Five of Swords is that even when you face a defeat or setback, you can't drop your defenses and walk away. And here is where the Four of Swords and Chesed come in. The knight-to-be is not holding a sword either. He is using the sword of intelligence to look within and gather strength so that he can act with that strength out of compassion rather than spite. The meditator is armed with the sword of discriminating intelligence against the attacks of the inner critic.

When you reflect and look inside, you may well find that you're not immune to feeling spiteful. It's nothing to be ashamed of, since all of us have these feelings at times, but it is dishonorable to act them out. And this is where the Four of Swords puts the break on the energy of the Five of Swords. It does the inner battle against the desire to humiliate another. It awakens us to the voice of the inner saboteur who is lying in wait to take our swords of clarity, leaving us to feel contempt for others or ourselves.

When we're dealing with Gevurah in the suit of Swords, criticism and Judgment become especially sharp, so it's an opportunity to look at your own style of criticism, because the energy that belongs to Chesed of Gevurah provides you with a chance to reflect on the way you criticize others (and yourself). It's a call to be mindful, using awareness to find the Love and express the Love within criticism instead of simply expressing a sharp Judgment.

Day 8: Chesed of Gevurah in Assiyah

The Four and Five of Pentacles

_____ *within* _____

One of the words associated with Gevurah is Severity, and there are few pairings that feel as Severe as the Four and Five of Pentacles. Who would not feel compassion for the two beggars, one shoeless in the snow, huddling against the weather as they walk outside a church? It's true that there are many so-called religious people who have no compassion for the homeless or the poor, and there are many houses of worship where they preach that poverty is God's Judgment. This is the unbalanced Severity of Gevurah at work in the world. But this unbalanced Severity can appear within each of us, leading to the question, Do I have a Judgment of myself that keeps me from feeling the Love of the Divine and that keeps me feeling outside, in spiritual exile?

The great Hasidic teacher, the Baal Shem Tov,* told a story of a king who built a palace with no doors and surrounded by high walls in

---

*Rabbi Israel ben Eliezer (1700-1760), the founder of Hasidism, was known as the Baal Shem Tov, which means "Master of the Good Name." This title is a reference to the fact that he was known as a miracle worker who used practical Kabbalah to effect cures. He also was a master storyteller whose message was one of mystic joy.

concentric circles. The king then offered great rewards to anyone who could get in to see him. Many tried. Those who managed to scale a wall were met by guards who gave them gold and jewels so that they grew satisfied and stopped trying to see the king. Only the king's son realized that the walls and the gold were all illusions. He passed through them all to see his father.

The beggars in the Five of Pentacles may well share the illusion that there is no way inside the church and that they're not welcome. They may suffer from the delusion that they aren't worthy of the Divine Presence. This is severe self-Judgment, though of course it may be introjected; that is, they may have internalized criticism that came from others. It could also be the case that because these people are suffering, either because of poverty or illness, they feel abandoned by the Source. Their pain and suffering clouds their ability to find Divine comfort.

When we consider how the Chesed of the Four of Pentacles mediates Gevurah, we see a man who knows that the ground below him is holy, the sky above him is holy, and the heart within him is holy. He doesn't let the Structure of an institution blind him to his Divine connection. His message to the beggars in the Five of Pentacles is that the star engraved on the disk is also within you.

We can also look at the Four of Pentacles and see the shadow side of Chesed. It shows someone who, like the people in the Baal Shem Tov's parable, let his love of gold become a spiritual obstacle. Either way, this pairing of cards should serve as a wake-up call from the delusion of self-imposed spiritual exile.

Questions for reflection and contemplation: Day 8

1. (Wands) What structures have you created in your life that are an expression of love? What are the structures in your life that you experience as an expression of love?

2. (Cups) How does your discipline help you express your love?

3. (Swords) How often do you examine your motivations before offering

criticism? Is your criticism sharp or contemptuous, or is it expressed with love? In which close relationships do you find yourself expressing Judgment sharply—and why?

4. (Pentacles) What Judgments do you hold about yourself that keep you in spiritual exile, that keep you from feeling Divine Love? Think about the different communities where you are a member: In which of them do you feel judged? Where do you feel welcomed? What about yourself or what actions have you taken in your life that make you feel unacceptable to the Divine? How might you heal this break?

Day 9: Gevurah of Gevurah

Learning Restraint in Judgment

> Today is the ninth day of the Omer, which is
> one week and two days of the Omer.

This is the second of seven days where the Sephira of the week and the Sephira of the day are the same. And of them all, Gevurah of Gevurah is perhaps the most challenging. Do the work of this day, but beware of falling into a well of self-criticism.

Day 9: Gevurah of Gevurah in the Four Worlds

The Five of Wands, Cups, Swords, and Pentacles

_____ *within* _____

This is a difficult day, when I often experience the strength of the shadow side and the negative possibilities of this Sephira. Severity of Severity. Discipline within Discipline. A very constricted place. Mitzrayim in fact—the narrow place of slavery we have escaped from. And here we are, nine days out, facing the slavery within. What might that slavery be?

Are you white-knuckling this practice? Are you being rigid in your approach to a spiritual Discipline? Is this an energy you recognize? I certainly do. I can get pretty rigid about things and be a real hard-ass sometimes. And Gevurah of Gevurah is the place of rigidity, of Structure devoid of love. I've been in institutions, organizations, and companies where I felt this, and I've felt it within myself. Part of the challenge of this day is to sit with this energy without being squashed by it, to feel this energy without identifying with it: feel the spacious-ness around it knowing that it is within you but that it is not you.

Where Chesed is boundless, Gevurah is all about Boundaries, building a wall. As you know, there are important, positive reasons for Boundaries, but there is also the possibility of using these Boundaries to prop up the ego. Gevurah is the pivot point on the Tree for the Sitra Achra, where the will of the ego takes precedence over Divine will. It either doesn't recog-nize Divine will or makes the mistake that the egoic will is an expression of the Divine will—the delusion that is the source of evil.

So I always have to remind myself that Gevurah is an essential energy and that because there are many characteristics and key words that can be used to describe the energy of Gevurah, to simply think of it as Discipline of Discipline or Severity of Severity is reductive and simplistic. Because Gevurah, in its role of boundary setting, also has the quality of Restraint. So another, more positive way to look at the energy of the day is as Restraint of Judgment. Looked at this way, Gevurah of Gevurah is having the Restraint to keep from Judging another or oneself.

There are times when it's important to show this Restraint. I've worked as a creative director in the world of advertising, and part of this job means I've had to review and Judge work developed by my team for creativity and strategy. When I look at work by seasoned professionals, I know I can speak directly about any issues I might see. But when a junior team presents work, I know that if I don't show Restraint in my critique of the work, the team won't be able to hear or learn. They are overwhelmed by Judgment and take it personally, as so many creative people do. I've made this mistake a few times with less experienced writers and art directors who weren't able to take in important criticism because my words were not Restrained, not balanced with Love. And believe me, you don't get good work from people when this happens. So for me, a very important exercise for this day is to consider how to Restrain my more Severe side and to know when it's appropriate to express it fully.

The Buddhist in me notes that Gevurah of Gevurah is also the Form of Form, which from a Zen perspective is actually emptiness of emptiness. Wonder of wonder, miracle of miracles!

When I lived in Japan, I found myself chafing under the Form in this highly formal society when I first began to study Sogetsu ikebana—one of the three main schools of Japanese ikebana flower arranging. Even though Sogetsu is the most modern of the schools, a beginner starts with a basic Form and does it again and again. When you look at the diagram of the Form, you can see it is very, well, formal.

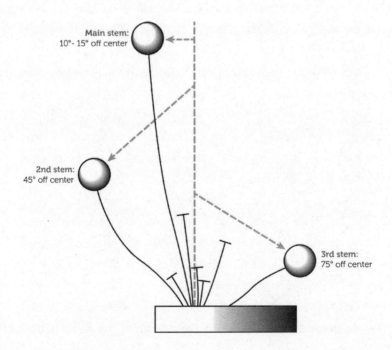

Main stem:
10°- 15° off center

2nd stem:
45° off center

3rd stem:
75° off center

The arrangement of the flowers is quite fixed. When I first started working in this most basic of Forms, if I varied an angle by so much as a degree, my teacher would move it. If I tried to improvise something because I felt it would be a little more interesting or creative, she would move it back to the proper Form. I resisted this for some time, and then I surrendered to it, and I learned the freedom of Form. For that matter, when I realized how truly different the arrangements looked from student to student, I was stunned. When I saw how varied this one Form could be from week to week, I was impressed. And when I considered that no matter what, the arrangement always looked natural, I became a disciple. Eventually, I received a license to teach in the Sogetsu school.

How do you create or respond to Structure in your life? Do you follow it and find the freedom in that structure? Do you resist? Is it something imposed from outside or something you joyously take on and make truly your own? This is a long preamble before actually getting directly to the cards of the day. Perhaps you have already made some of the connections between the images and these thoughts, but I want to specifically address the images in relation to Gevurah.

In the Five of Wands, we have a situation that seems chaotic, with someone trying to establish authority in a contentious group. This figure wants to impose Structure and Organization in a situation where they might naturally arise through competition. Of course, they might not. What you see helps you recognize your own projection onto the energy of this Sephira.

The Five of Cups can be seen as the result of the lack of Discipline and Organization: the figure in the card has lost the contents of three of the cups in the image. This image speaks to my own struggle with Organization. I once threw away a sapphire pendant that held great emotional value after a move. I had packed it in such a way that it would not be discovered if someone decided to go through my things in search of valuables, but I didn't write down where I packed it—and only after I threw out some of the packing materials did I remember where I had hidden it. The Discipline of keeping things Organized with a packing list (or perhaps being more trusting) would have prevented this loss.

In the Five of Swords, we see what happens in a society when

Structures and Discipline break down. The figure in the foreground feels no compunction in taking what isn't his to gain advantage. Here, the social Structure is essential to keep negative impulses in check. It protects us from others—and from ourselves.

The Five of Pentacles feels like a message from Charles Dickens's *A Christmas Carol*. It's the Ghost of Christmas Future showing how Judgment without compassion leads to suffering. This can be just as true of society's Judgment and the way you Judge another—or even yourself.

Questions for reflection and contemplation: Day 9

1. (Wands) How do you create Structure in your life? When do you feel the need to impose Structure? When are you comfortable waiting to see if Structure arises naturally?

2. (Cups) Has an inability to live by a schedule or in an organized way damaged your well-being or relationships? How are you experiencing the Discipline of this daily practice so far?

3. (Swords) If no one could see or know, would you do something society doesn't approve of? Have you ever given in to the voice of the little devil on your shoulder? How do you resist Structure in your life? What is your relationship to Discipline?

4. (Pentacles) When and why does your Judgment or criticism of others (or yourself) cloud your compassion? How do you express Restraint when giving criticism of another?

Day 10: Tiferet of Gevurah
Seeing the Beauty in Structure

Today is the tenth day of the Omer, which is one week and three days of the Omer.

Yesterday, I wrote about ikebana and Discipline in my discussion of Gevurah in Gevurah. Today is Tiferet in Gevurah, and one way of looking at this Sephirotic relationship is through the Beauty of Form, or how Discipline is expressed through Beauty. So once again, the example of ikebana seems appropriate, as does any art Form, with the accent on Form. After all, a sonnet is as highly formalized as a haiku. So today is a good day to meditate on the demands of a Discipline and how it channels our creativity and enables us to bring beauty into the light.

Alternatively, this day can also be considered as a time for expressing the Compassion within Discipline. I think of the advice given in the twelve-step world: easy does it. This is a recognition that someone in recovery needs to be easy on himself or herself. After all, there is much internalized shame and Judgment when one is in recovery, and there is no perfection in recovery (or anywhere in life). Simply recognizing that we are all human, that we all fall, is to experience Compassion for ourselves and for all those who fall once or again and again. This is not excuse making or abrogating responsibility; it is the simple recognition that there is no perfect Form, and to quote Taylor Mac, "Perfection is for assholes." In a twelve-step program, there is Compassion for a fall with the understanding that the Discipline must be undertaken again immediately. When you fall off the horse, you just get right back on it.

Day 10: Tiferet of Gevurah in Atzilut

The Six and Five of Wands

_____ *within* _____

Yesterday, when looking at the Five of Wands, I suggested there was the possibility that Order could arise out of the chaotic scene. And in fact, what we see in the Six of Wands is the establishment and expression of a kind of Order. We have moved from chaos to conquest. Because Tiferet is associated with the Heart, when I see how the conquering hero's horse is covered, I wonder if he is defending against his animal instinct. This poor horse is covered up by the trappings of either war or a tournament, making natural movement extremely difficult. Is this a message that in this card, the "hero" has had to cover or in some way tame his Heart in order to take Control?

As denoted by Waite, one of the themes of all the sixes is unequal relationships. By imposing a Structure that elevates him, does the rider lose contact with the others on the ground? Does he lose the empathy that is part of what gives Tiferet its Beauty? Is the "leader" in the Five of Wands who went on to mount the horse in the Six of Wands able to express Compassion from his position of leadership, or has he lost touch with it?

Day 10: Tiferet of Gevurah in B'riah

The Six and Five of Cups

_____ *within* _____

The Five of Cups is a picture of loss, but what is it that has been lost? When doing a divinatory reading for someone, the meaning often can be gleaned from the cards around a specific card and the general theme of the reading. Here, rather than reading, we are interpreting the image in this card in relationship to its corresponding Sephira—Gevurah—for the purpose of reflection, contemplation, and meditation. Since the job of a cup, like Gevurah, is to contain, I think of this card as illustrating what happens when an emotional container is broken. This is the breakdown of a psychological Structure in the world of B'riah—an emotional loss that has led to an unmooring and a loss of emotional perspective. The figure in the card is in mourning. This is the very picture of grief. And in today's pairing of Cups, this emotion is mediated by the feelings we find in the Six of Cups. Often the Six of Cups is interpreted as a feeling of nostalgia. Also, because this is Tiferet, the Sephira of Compassion, the feeling of being comforted in the face of loss is reinforced. Certainly, comforting oneself with nostalgia for the past in a time of loss seems reasonable. However, there is a danger lurking here— something that Jason Shulman, the founder of the Kabbalistic Healing school A Society of Souls, calls the B'riatic Defense. This is when someone escapes from or denies the uncomfortable feelings that arise in the face of a difficult reality by claiming to be on a higher spiritual plane. There's a kind of hazy fog around these people that mutes their emotions. Rather than clarity, people who exhibit the B'riatic Defense live on a pink cloud of denial. It's not an uncommon problem in some people who first discover a new spiritual Discipline. The B'riatic Defense shares the hazy quality we see in nostalgia, though it's more about a situation in the present. This defense paints a gauzy fantasy over inconvenient or uncomfortable feelings to create a false spiritual glow. Psychologically, this is known as spiritual bypassing.

Either way, one can see the issue of avoiding these difficult feelings by escaping into nostalgia for an imagined fantasy of an ideal past or by escaping into the fantasy of being on a higher spiritual plane where all is love and Compassion and messy, unwelcome feelings don't penetrate. The B'riatic Defense is a kind of false Compassion: it's pretend Tiferet.

This is entirely antithetical to the nature of Tiferet as an open Heart willing to bear all feelings, pleasure, and pain and to see the Beauty in all of them. There is a Japanese concept that captures this experience of feeling pleasure and pain simultaneously: *mono no aware*. It's sometimes translated as "the beautiful sadness of things," reflecting a wistful awareness of the impermanence of Beauty that heightens one's experience in the moment. This is the Beauty of Compassion for mortality—the very heart of Tiferet—and it's what underlies the Japanese appreciation for the Beauty of cherry blossoms.

The Japanese approach to loss, which is influenced of course by the Buddhist teaching of *anicca* (impermanence), is also reflected in this pairing. In the Five of Cups, we are faced with impermanence leading to a grief that is constricting the ability to see past it to what remains. With the Six of Cups, we can go in either of two directions with that loss—denial in the haze of nostalgia or acceptance of loss as part of life without denying the grief but by holding it with compassion—by giving the pain space and love.

When I look at this pairing through my Jewish lens, I see in the Five of Cups the myth of the breaking of the vessels—the Lurianic myth of the first creation when the Sephirot were not arranged in a balanced relationship, so they broke, scattering shards, called *klipot,* (and the light hidden within) throughout creation. Because the structure that held the Sephirot was too rigid—with too much Gevurah—it cracked. But the Divine Source started the process again, this time with the Sephirot arranged in the structure of the Tree of Life, so the energies balance each other. Today, in Tiferet of Gevurah, we see the raising up of these shards in the lifting of a cup by one figure in the Six of Cups as he is about to present it as a gift to the other figure. It is the recognition that we are all broken in some way and that the path of healing, that is re-storying to wholeness, is one of Compassionate (and thus flexible) Discipline.

Day 10: Tiferet of Gevurah in Yetzirah

The Six and Five of Swords

_____ *within* _____

What happens when there's a breakdown of the social Structure? When the function of the authorities to protect us from the unscrupulous isn't working? When moral limits are seemingly ignored for personal gain? When I look at the story in the Five and Six of Swords, the phrase that comes to mind is "seeking refuge from a breakdown in the social Structure." It's as though the boat being guided away in the Six of Swords was waiting at the water's edge in the Five of Swords to carry people away to safety.

As a youngster growing up in Brooklyn, I remember seeing adults in the neighborhood who had numbers on their arms—survivors of the Nazi death camps. My great-uncle Alfred was one of the few who managed to escape from Auschwitz. Somehow, he made his way from occupied Poland across Europe to England. But the United States wasn't taking any refugees, even though his brother (my grandfather) lived here and had become a citizen. When I see the Six of Swords, my family history comes to mind. The people in the boat look like a woman and child huddled together as they seek safety on another shore.

As I write this, the United Nations High Commissioner for Refugees reports that an unprecedented 65.3 million people around the world have been forced from home. Among them are nearly 21.3 million refugees, over half of whom are under the age of eighteen. Ten million of these people are stateless, which means they are denied a nationality and thus also denied freedom of movement, employment, health care, and other basic human rights. The number of people who have been displaced today surpasses the numbers at the end of World War II.[2] So let's not avert our eyes, but consider the man in the boat who is ferrying the people in the Six of Swords away. What is his story? Who is he? Is he a Good Samaritan helping these people escape? Is he a mercenary who has taken their money to guide them to safety? Because the Six of Swords corresponds to the Sephira of Tiferet, I prefer to think of him as acting out of Compassion.

Between xenophobia and compassion fatigue, in 2015, the United States accepted a grand total of seventy thousand refugees, with fewer than three thousand of them from Syria and a little more than twelve thousand from Iraq.[3] This is a human crisis that is a reflection of humanity's spiritual crisis. In the Torah, YHVH commands the people to "befriend the stranger, for you were strangers in the land of Egypt."[4] This does not change in the New Testament: "For I was hungry, and you gave me food: I was thirsty, and ye gave me something to drink, I was a stranger, and you welcomed me . . . just as you did it to one of the least of these who are members of my family, you did it to me."[5]

There is great pain crying out across our planet, and from the place of Tiferet of Gevurah, we are urged to open our Hearts to that pain and take Disciplined action that is also careful to make distinctions. Of course, the United States can't take in 63 million refugees. As it is, there has always been a very strong nativist current in our political system. Tiferet of Gevurah is both the compassion that is within discipline and the compassion that is within boundaries. The first of these says we must take Compassionate action in a way that is Disciplined and principled and gets results. The second says we need to know our Limits; Compassion fatigue is real, as any caregiver can tell you. It is possible (and essential) to practice healthy, ongoing self-care while successfully continuing to care for others.* Remember, this is a path of restoring Balance. In a world as out of Balance as ours, you should know the depth of your Heart and the measure of your ability to respond. But all three of the Abrahamic traditions—Judaism, Christianity, and Islam—demand that we respond, as individuals and as a society.

Day 10: Tiferet of Gevurah in Assiyah

The Six and Five of Pentacles

within

Here in the Six of Pentacles, we see someone who is literally measuring his ability to respond. We see a man who is clearly well off dispensing alms to two unfortunate people. He holds a Balance scale to underline this point. Waite considers one of the themes of the sixes to be "unequal relationships," and certainly, this card illustrates this point.

Looking at these two cards, you can see they share a certain symmetry. In both cards, there are two people in dire circumstances,

---

*If compassion fatigue is an issue in your life, there are resources, starting with the website of the Compassion Fatigue Awareness Project.

and both of these people are below and to either side of the representa-
tions of the suit, the Pentacles. In the Five of Pentacles, I noted that
there was no door into the church: these people were literally walled out.
In the Six of Pentacles, they receive some monetary relief from a man
who seems to be giving with an air of superiority that creates distance.
I see this playing out in the world around us as Structural inequality—
a system that is built specifically to keep some people down. I see this
pairing as asking us to consider how Structural inequality Limits our
ability to see oppression or privilege as well as how it determines the
measure of Compassion we bring to the situation.

Of course, we can look at the man giving alms in the Six of
Pentacles as doing what he can to restore Balance. Is it possible, since
this is Tiferet of Gevurah, that he knows the Limit of what these two
supplicants can receive? All of these are possible ways of looking at the
situation, and all raise questions about how we relate to the energy of
this Sephirotic pair.

Questions for reflection and contemplation: Day 10

1. (Wands) When you find yourself in a rigidly hierarchical Structure,
how do you express empathy to people both below and above you?

2. (Cups) Think about any relationships where you may have been
too rigid: How has that affected your ability to stay open? How has
loss affected your ability to be flexible? What roles would Balance and
Compassion play in healing these issues? What does Compassion in
Discipline mean to you personally? How is it expressed in your life?

3. (Swords) What would be a Disciplined and Balanced way to express
your Compassion for strangers or protect them in times of need?
What does the Beauty in Structure mean to you personally? How is it
expressed in your life?

4. (Pentacles) What are the ways that you benefit from Structural
inequality in the world? What are you doing to help repair this
inequality?

Day 11: Netzach of Gevurah

Perseverance Furthers

> **Today is the eleventh day of the Omer, which is one week and four days of the Omer.**

For Discipline to truly be successful, it must include the quality of Endurance, and this is Netzach of Gevurah. It's just the eleventh day in this practice of counting, which is indeed a Discipline, though hardly the most demanding one. It requires Endurance for just forty-nine days. Yet there have been years that I have missed days (and sometimes weeks) here and there.

Missing a day can be like taking a step off a path. Once the step is taken, it can feel easier to rationalize the next step off, until you're deep in the woods. This is where Endurance must be considered the ability not only to follow through but also to get back on the path if you've fallen off. This is the ongoing Victory of Netzach in Gevurah. Humans are imperfect. We're not meant to reach perfection; we can't. But we must try, gently and lovingly, with an Endurance in Discipline to be our best.

Day 11: Netzach of Gevurah in Atzilut

The Seven and Five of Wands

_____ *within* _____

In the Five of Wands, we can interpret what's happening in a number of ways: it's a group of young men in competitive play; it's a real fight (and there's someone who is either trying to stop it or take leadership in some way); or, as some have suggested, it's a barn raising. All of these interpretations can be looked at through the lens of Gevurah. But when the Five of Wands is paired with the Seven of Wands, the reality of struggle comes to the fore.

The constellation of meanings that orbit Netzach include "Endurance" and "Victory." Isabel Radow Kliegman pointed out that the man in the Seven of Wands is wearing one shoe and one boot, and she interpreted it as a statement of nonconformity. He is certainly outnumbered, but he is standing his ground and not backing down.

Society tells us in so many ways that speaking our truth—or speaking an inconvenient truth—isn't welcome. One of my favorite plays is Henrik Johan Ibsen's *An Enemy of the People.* In it, the main character is a doctor who discovers that the mineral baths crucial to his town's tourist income are contaminated. When he brings this information to the attention of the local newspaper, the editor thanks him and prints the story. But the mayor of the town (who is also the doctor's brother) demands that he retract his findings because it would damage the town's economy. In a town hall meeting, his findings are questioned and his expertise is dismissed. The newspaper withdraws its support. The people of the town turn against him. He loses his job, his family is attacked, and his home is vandalized. Written in 1882, this story could have been ripped from today's headlines. When concerned citizens in Flint, Michigan, had their water tested by an environmental engineer from Virginia Tech, the engineer's findings were disputed by the powers that be until this issue became a national scandal. Scientists who expose public health issues become pariahs and victims of internet trolls who threaten real-world attacks.

In the world of Atzilut, Netzach of Gevurah enjoins us to stand up for our ideals in the face of the tyranny of the majority. It also stands as a warning against introjection, which can cause you to attack your best self and defeat it. This takes the Endurance of Discipline.

Day 11: Netzach of Gevurah in B'riah

The Seven and Five of Cups

within

Previously, in the suit of Wands, one of the things the cards suggested was introjection—psychically taking in the values or judgments of others. Here in the suit of Cups, we're going in the other direction to projection.

Yesterday, when we were looking at the Six of Cups, one of the blocks to experiencing the Real fully was a flight to nostalgia—a fantasy of the past. Here the Seven of Cups suggests another block—in this case, fantasies of the future. When the Israelites were on their way out of Egypt, making their way through the desert, there was all kinds of complaining. There was nostalgia for Egypt: slavery wasn't so bad, was it? And there were negative fantasies of the future: we're going to die here in the desert. Both of these types of fantasies take us away from the present moment, which is Eternity. And Eternity, interestingly enough, is another facet of Netzach. In the Five of Cups, the figure is not living in the present but is focused solely on what is lost. He can't see the full cups remaining or the path ahead. In the Seven of Cups, the figure can't see the present because he is completely caught up in so many possible fantasies of the future.

This is the plight of anyone who takes up meditation: the mind doesn't want to stay still and in the present moment. The job of the meditator is to simply bring the mind back to the present again and again with compassion. It takes a lot of training for the mind to finally quiet down; the practice of meditation is a Discipline that calls for Endurance. I know that when I first started meditating, my mind would avoid the present moment by rushing to stories of the past when I felt I was a victim of some kind of injustice so I could feel righteous anger (an addiction from which many of us suffer). Or I would veer away to fantasies of what would happen in some upcoming situation—how would I spend the money I'd win in the lottery, how I'd be recognized as such a great meditator that I'd be appointed as a teacher or some other such nonsense. All these distractions and temptations arise when we begin a Discipline—a spiritual practice. Endurance in this Discipline gives us the clarity gained from living in the moment to see through the fantasies of the past and future so that we can be fully present and know the next right action to take, free of projection.

Day 11: Netzach of Gevurah in Yetzirah

The Seven and Five of Swords

_____ *within* _____

What an interesting pair we have here. In the Five of Swords, there's the smirking victor, and in the Seven of Swords, we have the sneaking trickster. The first thing I noticed about this pairing of cards is that in the Five of Swords, the man in the foreground is holding three swords and seems ready to collect the remaining two on the ground. In the Seven of Swords, the man who is sneaking away has five swords in his hands. It's almost as though this second figure is resetting the balance and returning the stolen swords to their rightful owners. One way of looking at this Sephirotic pairing of Netzach of Gevurah in Yetzirah is as the Endurance or Victory of Justice. There is a yin-yang quality of these two sneaky images together—a tit-for-tat way of settling things that keeps the situation in a kind of balanced dynamic of imbalance, with energy going back and forth but nothing really changing.

What's happening here is really the Endurance of injustice,* which is an unfortunate reality in our world. It calls for Perseverance on our part to work to establish Justice, even as we know it will never be perfect and it will not Endure forever. But because we know the principle of Justice innately, regardless of the fact that perfect Justice is unattainable, we are commanded to always seek it out.† In the world of Yetzirah, the intellectual understanding of Justice is pure. However, we don't live in the realm of ideas.

What happens when you think about the figures in these two cards as brothers? As if they were kids feuding over their toys or the last Hasmonean kings of ancient Judea, the brothers Hyrcanus II and Aristobulus II, whose feuding over the throne allowed the Romans to swoop in and take over the country. Each brother sought to undermine the other, so they missed the greater danger threatening both them and the kingdom. There was no respect for Boundaries and no trust. We can see this in both cards.

Because the figures in both cards are violating Boundaries, we can turn the question to this practice and ourselves. How well are you

---

*Remember, every Sephira includes its shadow opposite.
†"Justice, justice shall you pursue." Deuteronomy 16:20

Persevering in this Discipline of this practice? In what ways do you undermine yourself in this Discipline? Do you keep strong Boundaries around your practice in order to protect it from those who have no respect for spiritual pursuits or from those whose definition of spiritual pursuits doesn't include your practice?

Day 11: Netzach of Gevurah in Assiyah

The Seven and Five of Pentacles

_____ *within* _____

We've already considered the Five of Pentacles as suggesting a rigid religious institution that has forgotten its true purpose, one that exiles those whom we are commanded to open our doors and hearts to: the poor and broken in body and spirit. This is one of the shadow sides of Gevurah. But Netzach of Gevurah is about Victory and Perseverance of Discipline, and in the Seven of Pentacles, we see a man who, on his own, has Persevered in tending his garden and is about to reap the rewards.

What kind of garden is this? Because we are in the world of Assiyah, we're not speaking in metaphors—though the image suggests that money can grow on trees (or, in this case, a vine). In earlier versions of the tarot deck, this suit was known as Coins, and to this day people interpret this suit as related to money and wealth. But there is more going on in this suit as designed by Waite and Smith. Because there is a five-pointed star in the center of the disk, it signifies the spiritual energy that is within the material, and certainly the man with the hoe has put not only physical energy into the care of this garden but also spiritual Discipline.

On a spiritual level, this pairing could suggest that if you are faced with a rigid institution that doesn't accept your spirituality, it makes sense to tend your own garden and exercise spiritual self-care. Certainly, Counting the Omer is a traditional practice, but this way of practicing it is outside the walls of conventional religious institutions. Of course, if you've come this far, you already know that there are great rewards to Persevering on your own path. I don't mean to suggest giving up on religious institutions. Consider the long, hard work of many people in the Conservative movement of Judaism whose patient struggle was rewarded when the Committee on Jewish Law and Standards ruled that it was not a violation of *halakha* to ordain gay and lesbian rabbis.* Similarly, Soulforce sponsored Equality Riders—young Christians who saw discrimination as injustice—to visit fundamentalist Christian colleges and open a dialogue in a Christian context.

This kind of work takes Perseverance of Discipline; otherwise these sacred activists would have given up long ago. While there are rigid institutions that seek to exile some from their community, spiritual exile can only be self-imposed. In the meantime, it is important that we persevere in opening the doors and hearts of these institutions. Certainly, not all will change in my lifetime, but I recall the words of Rabbi Tarfon: "It is not your duty to complete the work, but neither are you free to desist from it."[6] And that calls for Netzach of Gevurah.

Questions for reflection and contemplation: Day 11

1. (Wands) Think of a time in your life when you were called to stand up for something you believed in: Were you able to stand your ground?

---

*The root of the word *halakha* means "the way," so that in a way, it's like the Buddhist word *dharma*. Except that in common usage it refers to the laws of Jewish life—the laws of the Torah as interpreted by generations of rabbis in the Talmud and other sacred documents.

If so, what gave you the strength? If not, how did you feel afterward?

2. (Cups) What do you do to stay Focused on the now instead of a fantasy of future rewards? Do you have trouble staying Focused on a goal? What distracts you and why? Where in your life has your Discipline been weakest? Why?

3. (Swords) What thoughts undermine your ability to do this work? Where do those thoughts come from?

4. (Pentacles) What do you do to guard your spiritual practices? Do you keep a Boundary around them in time or space? Where in your life has your Discipline been strongest? Why?

Day 12: Hod of Gevurah

Getting Yourself Out of the Way of Your Self

Today is the twelfth day of the Omer, which is one week and five days of the Omer.

Sephirot are like kanji—those Chinese ideograms used not only by the Chinese but also the Japanese. In Japanese, kanji have a minimum of two pronunciations and can have at least two different meanings. Add to this that in Japanese there are a great number of homonyms—words that sound the same (and are written with different kanji) but that mean very different things. This is why haiku and really all Japanese poetry doesn't translate well. A translation fixes the meaning to one thing, when in fact, as it is read and understood by the Japanese, the poem has multiple layers of meaning, each casting reflections on the other.

Sephirot are like kanji in this way: no one word captures each Sephira's characteristics. Thus, key words for Hod can include Surrender and Humility, to name a couple, just as Gevurah can be thought of as Discipline, Judgment, or Structure. In this way, the meditative quality suggested by the different combinations of today's key words could include Surrender to Discipline (and I am not talking about bondage and domination here, though there is a spiritual quality to that practice as well) or it could be about Humility in Judgment. Which works better for you? Or is there a different combination of key words that resonates more for you?

Yesterday, I wrote about the Soulforce Equality Riders. A few years ago, after they had visited a number of institutions on the East Coast, they arrived in New York City, so I had a chance to meet some of them. I felt that I was in the presence of both those interpretations of the energy of Hod of Gevurah. These young people had Surrendered themselves to the Discipline of nonviolent activism, Surrendered their egos, and faced down threats of violence as well as actual arrest. In this way, they were an inspiration. You could say that they also expressed Humility in Judgment because while they might have had a Judgment about Bob Jones University, they approached the school with Christian Humility (not sure how that's different from any other religion's Humility, but . . .). They were also the target of Judgment, and when that happens you learn to become careful of this energy yourself.

Day 12: Hod of Gevurah in Atzilut
The Eight and Five of Wands

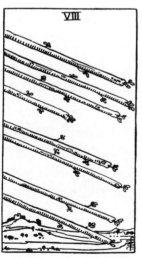 

_____ *within* _____

The Eight of Wands is devoid of human presence, with all the wands pointed (and headed) in the same direction. In the Five of Wands, the wands themselves, as extensions of the "quarreling" people, are all pointed in different directions. The expression of Gevurah in the Five of Wands captures one of the shadow sides of the Sephira in that there seems to be no consensus on what the action should be; there are no rules, and everyone is trying to establish himself as the one to set the rules. There's a lot of ego involved here. But Hod, the lens through which we experience Gevurah today, is about Humility and Surrender; ego is left at the door. One of the teachings when reflecting on this pairing is that when we let go of our ego in service of a greater purpose, our strength grows.

Hod is one of the two Sephirot related to prophecy, and there is important information in this pairing in Wands for those who meditate. For help with this, let's look at the experience of the prophet Elijah:

> Behold, YHVH was passing by—and a great and mighty wind tore the mountains and shattered the rocks before YHVH. But YHVH was not in the wind. After the wind there was an earthquake, but YHVH was not in the earthquake. After the earthquake there was a fire, but YHVH was not in the fire. And after the fire, there was a still small voice. As soon as Elijah heard it, he wrapped his face in his mantle . . .[7]

When we first sit down to meditate, there are often storms and all kinds of inner upheaval. This is Elijah's experience: he is trying to hear the voice of the Divine, but he is overcome by a blast of wind, then an earthquake, and finally, fire. These are all metaphors for the mental distractions we face, the inner turmoil that makes it hard to connect with the Source. But once all this turmoil settles down, one is able to hear the "still, small voice."

In the Five of Wands, we are dealing with a mind full of undisciplined and often contradictory drives. You can almost hear the crack of the wands striking each other like thunder or the earth quaking. The ego is fighting with everything it has to keep the mind from settling down. But once it does and the mind is quiet and one-pointed, the ego steps out of the way so there is space for the Divine energy to provide an epiphany. That's what we see in the Eight of Wands: hurtling down from the heavens all in one direction comes a great flash of insight. All the divided egoic energy of the Five of Wands that has worked to resist Surrender has dissipated, giving one the Humility to sit, receive, and channel the greater energy from above.

Day 12: Hod of Gevurah in B'riah

The Eight and Five of Cups

_____ *within* _____

In the Five of Cups, we are confronted by an image of human suffering. The card shows someone focused on the lost cups rather than those remaining, someone who struggles with attachments to feelings, emotions, and Judgments. Then, in the Eight of Cups, we see someone who is not suffering from any obvious loss or material want. Nevertheless, the figure in the Eight of Cups has turned his back on those eight cups to go off in search of something. What does this figure seek? Because Hod is the Sephira of Humility and Surrender, there is a quality of asceticism to this image, and since this is the week of Gevurah, this could be a Surrender of attachment to one's Judgments in search of equanimity. That's one interpretation from my Buddhist side.

Then of course there's my Jewish side. I mentioned on Day 10 how the Five of Cups brings to mind the Shattering of the Vessels. In Lurianic Kabbalah, the first time the Sephirot were emanated they were not in relationship, so that the power of the Divine light overpowered and broke these containers, and the shards were scattered throughout all Creation. The shattering occurred not merely because the Sephirot were not in relationship, but because the Structure (Gevurah) was arrayed in such a way that it was overly rigid (a shadow quality of Gevurah), leading to the splintering of the vessels and the light they contained. Rabbi Isaac Luria's mythic story also happened to provide a theological reason for the exile of the Jews from the Holy Land. Since the sparks were scattered throughout the Earth, the Jews needed to disperse to find and raise these sparks in Tikkun.

The figure in the Eight of Cups has restored what has been lost in the Five of Cups, but there are still shards of light to be found and returned to the Divine. He has Surrendered his ego to go off in service to the world. He recognizes he has a mission that calls for him to turn his back on what he has achieved in life to go and seek out the sparks that are his destiny to find.

The fifth Lubavitcher Rebbe, Rabbi Sholom DovBer, taught that a person is drawn by the Divine to places where the sparks that it is their Divine mission to raise up are to be found.[8] Setting out on this mission of raising the sparks is taking on a Discipline that must be done with Humility. Every day of this count—and really, every day of our conscious lives—we are on this mission.

From a twelve-step point of view, this work is the work of the eighth and ninth steps—listing all the relationships where one's addiction has harmed them (becoming conscious of the broken shards in one's life) and then making amends (doing the work of Tikkun). This not only repairs the outer relationship but heals the inner brokenness, a gathering up of the shards of our broken self so that we can hold the light of recovery.

Day 12: Hod of Gevurah in Yetzirah

The Eight and Five of Swords

_____ *within* _____

This doesn't look good, does it? In the Five of Swords, the Gevurah card, we see the breakdown of Discipline, Law, and Boundaries—the shadow side of Gevurah. The Eight of Swords seems to connect directly to the quality of Hod, which is Surrender, though it doesn't look so positive either. We know how Surrendering the ego to a Discipline can be a positive experience of growth, but there are some situations where Surrender isn't appropriate. When we're facing a situation where the social Structure is breaking down and Boundaries aren't being observed, Humility and Surrender are a trap. There is a way in which Humility in the face of the negative power of Gevurah is a willful blindness to danger—a false hope that things will turn out well. There is a trust in the power of the intellect: both the suit of Swords and the Sephira of Hod are connected with intellectual ability and discernment. However, a doubling of this power suggests a blindness to emotion and intuition.

Jewish culture has always been highly literate, and Talmudic study is extremely intellectual. My family came from Germany, a European culture known for its devotion to the intellect. My family trusted in that intellectual culture; they simply could not believe that their great civilization would descend into madness and irrational hatred. When I see the figures in the Five of Swords wandering off, having dropped their defenses, I see people who have lost their ability to discern and recognize the abuse of power so they no longer guard their posts, securing the Boundary. In the Eight of Swords, Surrender results in a self-imposed blindness to danger. So when I see these cards together, I see a Holocaust in the making. How blind can people be? Consider this quote from a *New York Times* article dated November 21, 1922:

> Several reliable, well-informed sources confirmed the idea that Hitler's anti-Semitism was not so genuine or violent as it sounded, and that he was merely using anti-Semitic propaganda as a bait to catch masses of followers and keep them aroused, enthusiastic, and in line for the time when his organization is perfected and sufficiently powerful to be employed effectively for political purposes.[9]

When you don't have an experience of that level of violence in your history, it's hard to imagine the reality of it. It's easy to bury your head in the sand or become complicit in your own victimization.

Surrender and Humility are important qualities. Discipline and Structure are essential. But they both have a shadow side, and when this shadow side of Humility in Discipline is activated (and people can be gaslighted into thinking this way), you must do everything you can to free yourself: this is another Mitzrayim. It is not for nothing that the Passover Haggadah, the ritual retelling of the Passover story, includes the words, "In every generation, they rise against us to annihilate us." Pay attention.

Day 12: Hod of Gevurah in Assiyah

The Eight and Five of Pentacles

_____ *within* _____

So far, we've been looking at the negative implications of the Five of Pentacles as expressed by religious institutions. But for a moment, let's simply look at the pentacles shining through the stained-glass window. This is one of the few cards where we see the diagram of the Tree of Life, though in this case only as far as Gevurah, the Sephira of that card. To me, there's a suggestion here that, while an institution might fall short of its ideals, the light of the Divine always shines through with the energy of all the Sephirot. The Divine countenance shines down on us, if we will only look up to see. But in this card, the woman is looking down, while the leper's face is turned away from the window. When we are lost in our suffering, it can be easy to turn away from the light. When we Judge ourselves harshly (often through introjection), we blind ourselves to the light that is always available to us. In fact, there is a kind of arrogance in this harsh self-Judgment (or harsh Judgment of others), as though one knows better than the Source. And that's a shadow side of Humility in Judgment.

From a twelve-step point of view, this Sephirotic relationship connects to the plight of the addict and the solution to his problem. In the language of the first three steps:

1. We admitted we were powerless over our addiction—that our lives had become unmanageable.
2. Came to believe that a Power greater than ourselves could restore us to sanity.
3. Made a decision to turn our will and our lives over to the care of God, as we understood God.[10]

The people suffering in the Five of Pentacles are certainly a picture of powerlessness, and we've considered how this card can indicate spiritual self-exile. Certainly, addiction can be seen in this way as well—as a kind of self-Judgment that one is not worthy of Divine love.

For anyone struggling with addiction of any kind—or even just for someone who is finding it hard to make a change for the better, step three is a Surrender of one's own will to the Will of the Source. It's turning one's face to the light in the window and finding that light in everything one does, even in the most Humble work, which is what we can see in the Eight of Pentacles.

Because we are in the world of Assiyah and the suit of Pentacles, part of my experience of this pairing relates to a change in status in my career. I was once a senior executive earning quite a good salary in advertising—an industry that values youth. Now that I am in my sixties, like the people in the Five of Pentacles, I find myself on the fringes of my industry, no longer welcome by corporations that previously valued my abilities. I could, like the people in the Five of Pentacles, feel abandoned and exiled. And it's true, one could make the case that I'm a victim of age discrimination. But holding on to victim status would not have changed the reality that I needed employment, so I started taking temp jobs; sometimes I found myself working next to people who once worked for me. If I held resentment, I would only be hurting myself: I would suffer, the work would suffer, and the people around me would feel it and suffer. I'd lose that job quickly. So my goal was to

Surrender to the Discipline of the work and find joy in work done well with Humility, one of the lessons of the Five and Eight of Pentacles. I looked to the words of Viktor E. Frankl to guide me, and he faced a much more dire situation than mine: "Everything can be taken from a man but one thing: the last of the human freedoms—to choose one's attitude in any given set of circumstances, to choose one's own way."[11]

There are lots of reasons one could face feelings of suffering upon entering a workplace. But Frankl's words, and today's pairing, show there is a way to be free from that suffering.

One last look today at the suffering in the image of the Five of Pentacles. I've written about this suffering being the result of spiritual self-exile, but I'd also like to consider how self-criticism feeds the endless desire for self-improvement. It may seem like an odd thing to say in a book about spiritual refinement, but "self-improvement" can be used to bludgeon the spirit. It doesn't matter how many self-improvement books you read or workshops you go to if you can't accept who you are and where you are right now. The people in the Five of Pentacles may thus repeat their victimization with harsh self-criticism. But the man in the Eight of Pentacles has given up; he has Surrendered the concept of self-improvement (and for that matter, maybe even the concept of self) and has found peace. To be able to love and accept yourself right now as you are—to give up the tyranny of self-improvement—is to experience freedom from a different kind of Mitzrayim. And once that freedom is experienced, you start to free up the energy necessary for change. An interesting paradox: if you want to change, start by loving where you are right now with no goal of changing.

Questions for reflection and contemplation: Day 12

1. (Wands) Think of a time when you were in (or led) a group or team that was at cross-purposes. Then think of a group where everyone really worked together. What made the difference?

2. (Cups) How have your experiences of loss in your life influenced your spiritual search? What lessons have you come away with from the losses in your life?

3. (Swords) Have you ever been complicit in your own victimization? If so, how? Do you blame yourself for this, or can you feel compassion for yourself? What is your relationship to your inner intellectual? How reliant are you on your intellect to solve your problems? Have your intellectual insights ever felt so threatening that you blinded yourself to them?

4. (Pentacles) What would it feel like to give up on yourself as a self-improvement project? What would your life look like?

Day 13: Yesod of Gevurah

Intimacy Can Blossom in a Strong Container

> Today is the thirteenth day of the Omer, which is one week and six days of the Omer.

One week and six days in, today's energetic field is about reinforcing Connection through Discipline. For many Jews, this can sound like an inner scold saying, "You should call your mother every day." And indeed, there's a degree to which that's true; Connection that lasts requires this kind of Discipline. You'll always be Connected to your mother, but most Relationships require regular investments of time and emotion. More than that, deep Relationships require us to bring a meditative focus to these Connections in our lives where we have made a commitment.

Day 13: Yesod of Gevurah in Atzilut

The Nine and Five of Wands

_____ *within* _____

What are the Rules of engagement? In the military, they're defined as the Laws or guidelines given to military forces and/or individuals that define the conditions, degree, and manner in which the use of force may be deployed. And certainly, the images in the Five and Nine of Wands suggest that the use of force is at question here. Then again, the word *engage* can simply mean to Connect, join together, contract, or employ. When a couple has agreed to wed, they're said to be engaged. So this simple verb covers a lot of emotional territory.

Because the Five of Wands is an expression of Gevurah, it carries the meaning of Rules, Structure, and Law. The Nine of Wands, as Yesod, is about Connection. What we see when we put the cards together is a story of someone who has engaged with the world in some way and has been wounded by that engagement. It's possible that one or more of the people in the Five of Wands were not playing by the Rules, and someone got hurt. But we all have to recognize that even in the best of circumstances, where everyone is following the Rules, there is still the possibility of injury, whether physical, emotional, spiritual, or psychological. Anyone who plays a sport can attest to this.

Counting the Omer is a practice of spiritual refinement, but as I'm sure you know, just because people claim to be "spiritual" doesn't mean they won't come to blows with each other. Consider the case of the Church of the Holy Sepulchre in Jerusalem. This complex of tombs and chapels is considered by all the world's Christian denominations as the site of the Crucifixion, burial, and Resurrection of Jesus Christ. Six Christian denominations in particular—Greek Orthodox, Armenian Apostolic, Roman Catholic, Coptic Orthodox, Ethiopian Orthodox, and Syriac Orthodox—share jurisdiction of this holy site, and they have been notoriously unable to keep the peace among themselves. Just a few years ago, there were brawls between monks from Greek Orthodox and Armenian Apostolic monasteries that were so violent the Israeli police had to be called to break them up. Regardless of who has jurisdiction, these worshippers clearly aren't following the Rules set down by the Church Fathers or by any of Christ's teachings of love and nonviolence. But you can look at every religious organization and find a violation of its most basic tenets in its history. I walked away from Judaism at age thirteen because I felt that certain teachings were an expression of spiritual violence. When I returned, in my forties, these teachings were still an issue, but because there were people who had remained actively engaged with the tradition and these issues, things had changed. Today the Conservative movement in Judaism ordains LGBTQ rabbis and marries same-gender couples.

You probably haven't found yourself throwing physical blows (or being attacked) in a house of worship. But have you ever been the perpetrator or victim of spiritual violence? How has it affected your Relationship with your spiritual community?

Before things changed, I found myself teaching at the center of the Conservative movement: the Jewish Theological Seminary. When I started, I felt defensive, but like the image in the Nine of Wands, I kept an opening in my defense. I was not going to wall myself off. I understood that to stay engaged and committed to a Relationship, whether to an individual or a community, it might mean that sometimes I would get hurt or that I might hurt someone else. This is one of the lessons that comes with the Sephirotic energies of this day: while there are Rules to engagement, Relationship is messy by nature, and there is always the chance that someone can get hurt. It comes with the territory. But with a commitment to keep an open heart and to stay Connected, deep Bonding is possible.

Day 13: Yesod of Gevurah in B'riah

The Nine and Five of Cups

_____ *within* _____

When we're having a healthy experience of Yesod, it balances the inner-directed and outer-directed energies of Netzach and Hod. It's sort of like what the psychologists Gay and Kathlyn Hendricks teach as the Loop of Awareness—a practice of learning to shift one's focus and attention from within to without and back again in ever-quickening oscillations so that you're able to place your attention on both inner and outer experiences at the same time, while being able to process both. It's being fully present to yourself and to another simultaneously. For Yesod of Gevurah in B'riah, though, as you can see from the Five of Cups, the attention is focused on a loss and is stuck there. Because we're in the suit of Cups and the world of B'riah, this could be an emotional loss, so that focus is inward and away from Relationship.

In the Nine of Cups, the focus is outward: it looks as though we've arrived at a banquet and the host is ready to greet us, albeit not with open arms but with his arms crossed over his heart. It's as though the host of the party wants the social Connection and has put on a good face, but inside he's hurting from a loss that he doesn't want people to see. So while he may be sharing his table with a lot of people, he isn't really being genuine.

This pairing suggests you look at your own Loop of Awareness to see how your inner experience and outer presentation reflect each other. The energy of Yesod, when balanced and held in a strong container, promotes an inner and outer intimacy. So it's a good day to consider ways you might be withholding your authentic self in Relationship— what your excuses might be, what defenses might be in place.

Day 13: Yesod of Gevurah in Yetzirah

The Nine and Five of Swords

_____ *within* _____

In Ronald Decker's groundbreaking examination of the connection between Joseph Gikatilla's *The Gates of Light* and the meanings of the Minor Arcana, one of the observations he makes is that the suits can be divided into two categories, corresponding to the words of Deuteronomy 11:26: "See, this day I set before you blessing and curse." He sets up these categories as spiritual blessings and curses, represented by the suits of Cups and Swords, respectively, and material blessings and curses, represented by the suits of Pentacles and Wands, respectively.

I find this division useful at times, and in this particular pairing of the Five and Nine of Swords, the images certainly feel like a curse. In the Nine of Swords, it's as though the figure is waking up from the nightmare of the Five of Swords. It could be that the figure in the Nine of Swords is tormented by the guilt of actions taken in the Five of Swords. Or the images might reflect on the loss experienced by the figure in the Nine of Swords.

For this pairing, where the Five of Swords suggests a betrayal, I found myself reflecting on an action I took years ago that betrayed my own values and hurt a dear old friend. I wanted to write an article that shared an event in his life. I would change the names, locations, and other details to guard the privacy of the people in this story, but my friend was concerned for the safety of his community, so he asked me not to write about it. It seemed too good a story to let go of, though, and I decided that no one would ever find out who these people were or even if I were making it all up. So I wrote the article, and it was published. Now, no one was hurt. Nothing was investigated or discovered. (The event described was not illegal, but it would have led to consequences for members of an organization.) But I had betrayed my own values and my old friend, and I found myself waking up in the middle of the night, in guilt and pain, not unlike the figure in the Nine of Swords.

Gevurah as Limitation is a container—a container for the trust that is the Foundation of Intimacy. I had violated that trust, and my Relationship suffered for it. My friend wouldn't have even known about this betrayal if I hadn't told him, and I knew telling him would lead to a break in the friendship, which it did for a number of years, adding grief onto my attack of conscience. But not owning up to my actions would make this a friendship of false Intimacy.

In the Jewish tradition, the commandment, "You shall not go up and down as a talebearer" is often interpreted as a commandment against gossip, but it's about more than just gossip.[12] The idea is not to say anything about another person, even it is true, even if it is not negative, even if it is not secret, and even if it doesn't seem as though there is the possibility that it could hurt anyone.

There is a story told about a man who once spread lies about the rabbi of his community. Eventually, he felt guilty and ashamed of what he'd done, and he went to confess and seek forgiveness from the rabbi. The rabbi gave the man instructions to perform a task of penitence: "Slice open a feather pillow and scatter the feathers to the four winds." The man was glad to have such a simple task and followed his instructions. When he returned, the rabbi gave him the second part of the task, saying, "Now, find and gather the feathers." That's when the man realized that although he was repentant, just as there was no way he could find and gather the scattered feathers, he could not call back the words he had spoken.

Today it's easier and more dangerous than ever to be a "bearer of tales." With just a simple click, you can send a "news" story filled with falsehoods around the world to be seen by millions. You might not be "Intimately Connected" to any of the people in the story, yet your actions create a Connection that can have devastating results in the lives of people you will never see or know. So the interpretation of the Five of Swords, which we looked at as also being an image of the breakdown in the social contract, is also appropriate here. Written more than three thousand years ago, the biblical commandments on the subject of speech couldn't be more immediate or relevant.

This pairing of cards, about the Connection that comes out of a strong Container, can help shine a light on all the ways one has fallen short of protecting that Container in Relationships.

Day 13: Yesod of Gevurah in Assiyah

The Nine and Five of Pentacles

_____ *within* _____

So far, we've been looking at the people in the Five of Pentacles as without material resources—poor. There is no arguing with that when you see people walking barefoot in the snow. And we've considered them as exiles from a spiritual institution. But one of the many meanings of Gevurah is Strength, and it certainly takes strength to withstand the conditions pictured in that card. So what if we considered this pairing as the Connection/Bonding that is in Strength?

In the Nine of Pentacles, the Connection we're looking at is an inner Connection rather than one that is between people. This woman has a strong Foundation of Connection within herself that has enabled her to manifest her aesthetic in the world in the creation of her garden. It is the externalized image of a rich inner Relationship. What if this is the Relationship between the two beggars in the Five of Pentacles? Certainly, we wouldn't be surprised if the poor woman abandoned the leper, since lepers are often forsaken by all. But there she is, by his side.

My synagogue runs an overnight shelter for homeless New Yorkers.

It's not a big shelter; there's room for just ten beds. Our guests come in the early evening, and they receive a dinner prepared by congregants. Before they leave in the morning, they receive a light breakfast. I haven't volunteered there many times, but when I have, I've been struck by the closeness of this downtrodden community. In particular, I remember a couple that had pooled their meager resources and were working together to sell T-shirts on the street during the day. They had met in the shelter system, formed a Bond, and worked together until, eventually, they had saved enough money to be able to leave the system and afford a small apartment together. When I spoke with them one evening over dinner in the shelter, I was struck by the fact that, in taking on the Discipline of working together, their Bond grew deeper and each of them grew stronger individually. So while on the outside they looked impoverished, on the inside, they shared a rich Relationship that gave each of them Strength.

Questions for reflection and contemplation: Day 13

1. (Wands) What techniques or practices do you have to help yourself stay open when you feel hurt or attacked in a community you value? How do you stay open to Relationship while being wary at the same time?

2. (Cups) Remember a time when you had to put on a happy face even though you were feeling very sad. By "faking it till you make it," did the experience help you Connect with a deeper happiness, or did you find yourself feeling alienated or split away from yourself and those around you? Why?

3. (Swords) Do you owe amends to anyone whose trust you have violated? Have you ever forwarded or posted something online that you knew wasn't true? If you have spread information that you thought was true and subsequently learned otherwise, what can you do to try to undo the damage? Commit to a social media and internet practice of scrupulous adherence to verifiable facts.

4. (Pentacles) What is your experience of finding Strength and support in shared suffering? If you've ever felt that you walled yourself off from another's suffering (or that someone did this to you), how did that affect your Connection?

Day 14: Malchut of Gevurah

Healthy Boundaries Make Healthy Relationships

> Today is the fourteenth day of the Omer, which is two weeks of the Omer.

Sovereignty within Structure. When you have a Strong Structure, you can have a Strong sense of who you are—assuming the Structure is built on your deepest values. Within that Structure, you're the queen. Or king. This is a day that reminds me of the phrase, "Good fences make good neighbors." With a healthy social Structure that defines Boundaries, people can relax and feel secure with each other. That's just as true for physical fences as it is for a psychological sense of inviolable Boundaries. When these Boundaries are healthy, Sovereignty comes with the understanding that there is a Sovereign above and within us all that binds us together. That we are all made "*b'tzelem Elohim*," in the image of God.[13]

A rabbinic parable points out that when the Roman emperor minted a coin with his face on it, the image was always the same. But the Divine created all humanity "b'tzelem Elohim," so that no two people are alike, yet each with their own Nobility. Malchut of Gevurah carries with it the Awe and respect for the Divine unity that is present within the diversity of creation. When you live with this awareness, you live with respect for the Nobility and Boundaries of all people.

Day 14: Malchut of Gevurah in Atzilut

The Ten and Five of Wands

_____ *within* _____

As you have probably realized, you can see the same image differently in different pairings and contexts. In this pairing, I see the group of young men in the Five of Wands participating in a "brainstorming" session. And the man to the far left with his wand raised high, as though to command attention, seems to me to have the winning idea that the others haven't come around to yet. Then again, he could well have a "bell the cat" idea that, while a brilliant solution, has little chance of being put into effect. Or he'll be delegated with the burden of carrying it out. One of the things I learned in the world of advertising is that the more good ideas you have, the higher you climb the corporate ladder. And then, rather than generating ideas, you oversee others tasked with that job. You become more of an administrator. You can well end up like the figure in the Ten of Wands, burdened down with Responsibility. You may get to be the boss, but I can tell you from my experience, it's a mixed blessing.

Here's where Malchut comes in. It's about Sovereignty. Not being Sovereign or king over others but being Self-possessed. Because if, like the man in the Five of Wands, you end up in command, you may find yourself carrying a heavy burden—whether it's the safety of others under your charge or the success of a project that many depend on. Organizational Structures, or social Structures, are generally set up to avoid putting so much on one person's shoulders, but sometimes the Structures are abusive and create situations where people are over-burdened. Often our own psychology colludes in this.

On this the fourteenth day, we're at Sovereignty that is in Discipline or Structure. When unhealthy, this takes us out of relationship because we believe that the Responsibility is all on our shoulders and that the Structure will collapse without us to keep it all in place. This leads to resentment and a sense of grandiosity that tells us that we're the only ones capable of doing things right. But when the Boundaries of Gevurah are working correctly, one's Sovereignty is part of a larger Structure in which we are supported as we support others. We take on healthy Responsibility that does not seek to take on more than is our due.

Moses himself was not free from this problem. During the journey of the Israelites on their way to Mt. Sinai through the wilderness, Moses's father-in-law, Jethro, came for a visit. Upon seeing Moses sit before all the Israelites, serving as a Judge in counsel for all their disputes, Jethro said to him:

> What you're doing is not good for you. You'll not only wear yourself out, you'll also wear out your people. This task is too heavy for you alone; you cannot do it just by yourself.[14]

Jethro told Moses to appoint magistrates from among the tribes and Judges over them so that Moses would not have to Judge every case. Was Moses a micromanager? Well, he didn't have the benefit of a management training course. He was just thrown in the deep end of the pool (or Red Sea, as the case may be) by Ehyeh Asher Ehyeh, so he took it all on. Only after instruction by Jethro was he able to let go. Trying to do it all wasn't good for him, and it wasn't good for his people. So what do you need to let go of? What responsibility should you be sharing?

Day 14: Malchut of Gevurah in B'riah

The Ten and Five of Cups

_____ *within* _____

The Baal Shem Tov taught that in the king's palace there are many gates and that there are many different keys for these gates, but there is one master key that opens all the gates to take one to the inner chambers of the Divine palace, and that master key is a broken heart.

You have to have some rain for there to be a rainbow, but if you get stuck looking down at the puddles, you'll miss it. The promise of this pairing is that your broken heart can serve as a master key to reach the Source.*

The trap of the Five of Cups is the Constricting and contracting of the heart in order to armor against the grief while at the same time holding on to it tightly. Only when you open fully to this deep grieving can you then feel the spaciousness that surrounds your broken heart. Only when you fully allow yourself to go to pieces can you discover the wholeness that you're never separate from. Of course, it's only human to contract against the pain. The practice of opening to one's pain is

---

*For those struggling with this issue, *The Gate of Tears: Sadness and the Spiritual Path* by Rabbi Jay Michaelson is an excellent spiritual guide.

gradual, and there is no calendar or schedule for you to follow. But when you are strong enough to go fully into the depths of your pain, you discover how high you can ascend to the heavens. Continuing to mix metaphors, the heart is a faucet. If you stop up or get stuck in the flow of sadness seen in the Five of Cups, you also stop up the flow of joy seen in the Ten of Cups.

In every great story or epic, the heroine or hero must descend into a kind of hell before she or he can return with the "healing elixir." In this pair, I see the injunction to make your own descent: you have to fully face and own the loss and grief of the Five of Cups in your life to heal and feel the joy of the Ten of Cups. In your own story, you must fully own the grief of loss or Limits in order to fully find a joyous connection to the Divine Presence and your Sovereign self that leads to the joy we see in the Ten of Cups.

Day 14: Malchut of Gevurah in Yetzirah
The Ten and Five of Swords

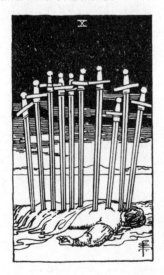 

_____ *within* _____

"If you must break the law, do it to seize power: in all other cases observe it." This quote has been attributed to Julius Caesar, whose story can be summed up in these two cards. As a successful general, he seized power, thus betraying and bringing an end to the Roman republic. As a dictator, he was assassinated by members of the Senate. So here is yet another way to look at the Sovereignty within Severity—as a perverse fortification of the ego that's ultimately a dead end. It results in total isolation and a psychic or physical death.

Is there a positive way to read this pairing? Perhaps if we consider it the end of a bad cycle. As I noted in the introduction to the Sephira of Gevurah, it gets a bad rap. We need Limits, we need Boundaries, or we end up in lawless societies where the strong seize power and might makes right. This pairing seems to suggest that when you violate your inner sense of ethics or break the social Structure, you will ultimately end up a victim of this destruction, not unlike Caesar.

Day 14: Malchut of Gevurah in Assiyah

The Ten and Five of Pentacles

_____ *within* _____

In our last pairing for the week of Gevurah, the Sovereignty within Severity reflects spiritual impoverishment amidst material plenty. The severe institutional response in the Five of Pentacles that keeps the poor outside the church is mirrored in the disconnection between all the people in the Ten of Pentacles. So even though the people in the Ten of Pentacles aren't suffering from material want, they lack a connection to the Divine Presence, the Immanence of the Shekinah that underlies the entire material world. The people in the Ten of Pentacles can't see the Tree of Life that sparkles in the air before them. But while Malchut in Assiyah (the Ten of Pentacles) is the place where the light of the Source, the Divine Structure of Creation, is most veiled, it's also the only card where the Tree is fully visible. Why might that be?

Certainly, this is the place we're all starting from, since we live in the world of Assiyah, so it serves as a sign to us that the Tree—access to all the Sephirot—is available to us right here, right now, whether we see it or not. As Moses said to the people:

It is not in heaven, that you should say, "Who will go up to heaven for us and bring it to us so that we can hear it and do it." Nor is it across the sea, so that you should say "Who will cross the sea and bring it back to us that we can hear and do it?" No, I tell you that the word is already with you—it's in your mouth and in your heart, so that you may do it.[15]

For those who are following the path of ascent, Malchut, while the tenth Sephira, is also the first gate. This is true in Gikatilla's *The Gates of Light,* and it is the first step in the path that initiates in the Order of the Golden Dawn followed. Indeed, in the image on the Ten of Pentacles, we see an old man seated at a city gate—not unlike the frontispiece of the Latin translation of *The Gates of Light* (see page 154).

Unlike the old man at the gate in the Ten of Pentacles, though, the man in the frontispiece image (alternately identified as either Gikatilla or Rabbi Isaac the Blind) reaches out to take hold of the Tree: he can see through material reality to the Divine Structure underlying all.*

---

*I have often wondered whether Pamela Colman Smith was familiar with this image and was influenced by it when she designed the Ten of Pentacles.

This is one of the hidden teachings behind the commandment that Jews put a mezuzah on their doorposts: in the mezuzah are the words of the Sh'ma—the statement of the radical unity of Creator and Creation, of the simultaneous immanence and transcendence of the Divine. So whenever you pass through a door or gate (just as the people in the Ten of Pentacles are at the city gate), you are reminded that as you move from one space to another, you are never out of the Divine Presence. Even the poor couple making their way through the snow in the Five of Pentacles have immediate access to the Divine love that keeps "faith with them that sleep in the dust."*

The gate is always before you, and it is always open.

Questions for reflection and contemplation: Day 14

1. (Wands) Where are you taking on unhealthy Responsibility in your life, or conversely, where are you avoiding your share of healthy Responsibility?

2. (Cups) What has caused you to Constrict your heart to avoid pain in your life? Take a moment to feel within your heart if there are any ways you are Constricted in this way now. What can you do to feel the spaciousness around that pain? How can you create a sense of safety so that you feel secure enough to try to open your heart to this pain?

3. (Swords) What beliefs or opinions do you hold with rigidity? How can you create a sense of spaciousness around those beliefs so that you can relax that rigidity?

4. (Pentacles) Look around you right now—with your eyes, with your heart, and with your soul. Try to feel the sparkle of Sephirotic energy that surrounds you and is within you. What was your experience?

---

*This is a line from the Amidah, the "standing" prayer recited three times a day, every day by observant Jews, which also includes these lines: "You sustain the living with lovingkindness . . . support the falling, heal the sick, loose the bound, and keep faith to them that sleep in the dust." One can interpret the final clause as referring to both those who are dead and buried and the poor who sleep on the ground outside. See page 54 of *The Standard Prayer Book,* translated by Simeon Singer.

WEEK 3

Tiferet

THE WEEK OF TIFERET COMES AS A BALM after the difficult week of Gevurah. One of the characteristics of Tiferet is Harmony; it's the balance of Chesed and Gevurah. While Tiferet is often known as "Beauty" or "Truth" in English, I have always felt that even these big concepts are too small a description. Tiferet is at the center of the Tree of Life. In the middle between left and right, top and bottom, located at the Heart, both metaphorically and physically. It is the place of the open Heart that holds the tension between the Love of Chesed and the Severity of Gevurah, and it fully feels that tension without running from it. So while Tiferet is a place of Harmony, it is a Harmony that is born out of a Dynamic Balance. And as such, one goal of this week is to be able to feel the Harmony in Dynamic Balance, to cultivate the ability to feel Chesed and Gevurah from a centered place, to feel it all with Compassion and without breaking.

Day 15: Chesed of Tiferet

Finding Joy in Harmony

Today is the fifteenth day of the Omer, which is two weeks and one day of the Omer.

Thesis. Antithesis. Synthesis. Tiferet is first Sephira that is born of the synthesis, the Harmonizing of the two previous Sephirot. And like a child that is born of two parents, this birth is an occasion of joy. With this Harmony, the overwhelming Flow of Chesed is right-sized by the

156

Restraint of Gevurah. And this brings a sense of joy and an appreciation of Beauty to daily life; we have left the realm of the seeming monotone for a more nuanced experience of reality that includes room for a multiplicity of shadings to our everyday encounters. It gives us the ability to recognize the interplay of Divine energies in all that surrounds us and to recognize this interplay as Beautiful. And as we grow in our ability to see this Beauty, our Love and joy grow too. Today is a good day to look for this celestial chemistry as it scintillates around (and through) you.

Day 15: Chesed of Tiferet in Atzilut

The Four and Six of Wands

_____ *within* _____

We start the week with Chesed of Tiferet, the place where there is complete Love for this place of Dynamic Balance, where unconditional Love for the difficult Balance of being fully human gives rise to joy.

We can see this Balancing act right away in the Six of Wands. If you want to experience Dynamic Balance in action, ride a horse. You must shift in response to every movement, and every movement of your own will create a response in the horse: it's not only a physical Balance, it's also a spiritual Balance between the higher will and animal instinct. The Six of Wands is the only Minor Arcana card (except the knights, of course) with the illustration of a horse and rider.

Riding a horse sets this man apart from those surrounding him; the fact that he can Balance Chesed and Gevurah, his Love and Severity, is why he is recognized and celebrated as a leader. I noted earlier that this is also the Balance of will and instinct, which connects with Keter above and Yesod below. The ability to hold this Balance, rather than an accident of birth, is what defines true nobility.

If you've ever ridden a horse, you know the experience of exuberance it can unleash (a strange paradox considering that the horse is leashed, but perhaps that's the Gevurah and Chesed again). And above that, there is a kind of communion of spirit with the horse, a relationship and recognition between beings that can open the Heart and flood it with Love and joy for all creation. It is an intimate intimation of the oneness of all being, where for just a moment—and only for a moment—the boundary between horse and rider falls away. Because while Tiferet Balances Chesed and Gevurah, in Chesed of Tiferet that balance is tipped toward Chesed and the dissolving of boundaries.

I remember one day I was walking along Sixth Avenue on my way back to my office; it was a beautiful spring day, and I was filled with joy. As I walked, I took in the Beauty of everyone on the street, many of them lost in thought. Some of the people kept their eyes down in the way people do to avoid contact on a crowded street in a city, even when we were so close we could touch each other. Some people looked straight ahead, but their eyes were focused on some inner goal or story instead of seeking some outer connection. It was the full panoply of humanity that is often on display on a New York City street, and it was Beautiful to me. And then my eyes were caught by the eyes of another man who was looking at me looking at everyone else. Now, this was Chelsea, and you might think that this was a cruising situation. And indeed, this man was very attractive. But that wasn't the energy I felt from him. The man was a young Lubavitcher Chasid, and as we made eye contact I felt a thrill of joy; I felt he could see that I was looking at the world with eyes of wonder. And I felt that he was looking at the world—and me—the same way. For a moment—just a moment—we were both awake to the joy and Dynamic Harmony of creation, and we connected in that instant wordlessly, with wide smiles. There was no need to speak. And I never saw him again. But I have never forgotten that moment. It was an awareness of the deeper spiritual Harmony that connects us all. You may well have had a similar experience in your history. If you have or haven't had this experience, this is a propitious day to keep your eyes open for just such a moment, when the Love that is Chesed tips the balance of Tiferet toward the Harmonious dissolving of boundaries.

Day 15: Chesed of Tiferet in B'riah
The Four and Six of Cups

_____ *within* _____

My first memory of smelling the fragrance of honeysuckle is when I was around five years old. There was a bush near the building where I lived, and the scent was so strong and wonderful that I asked my mother what it was. She held me up to the blossoms so I could take in a good sniff. It was heaven. Sometimes, when I look at the Six of Cups, I remember this moment. Yes, I know the flowers in the card are lilies, but this is the memory the image triggers in me. And it's always good to explore anything the images call forth.

As I've noted before, in the modern tradition of tarot reading, one of the meanings of the Six of Cups is nostalgia. And I find that nostalgia can be like gauze pulled over difficult emotional memories. But reading a card according to just one meaning is reductionist, and the memory of honeysuckle leads me to another interpretation. I am always amazed and somewhat envious of how easily children can be absorbed by something that interests them and how almost anything can interest them. How quickly they can find the fun in almost any situation. So on this day of Chesed in Tiferet, in the Six of Cups, I see the Beauty of a child's emotional reaction to the gift of a simple flower.

In this card, the flowers are held lovingly in the containers of the cups, and they are in full bloom. Just as a child is held in the emotional container of Tiferet provided by parents. In such a place of Balance, when presented with something as Beautiful as a blossom, Love and joy arise naturally from within.

Of course, the blossom is Beautiful. But more Beautiful is the impulse to give or share such Beauty with another: this is the true Beauty we see in the Six of Cups. Perhaps there is a time you can recall when you received just such a simple gift and found yourself filled with the spirit of Love and Harmony, even if only a moment before that you were feeling down. In this way, the act of receiving awakened the energy of Chesed of Tiferet within you. Or perhaps there was a time when you found yourself compelled to give such a gift to another, and the two of you found yourselves together in a Beautiful communion. This is another manifestation of Chesed of Tiferet in B'riah.

In my practice, there have been years when I came to this, the fifteenth day, Chesed of Tiferet, and like the man in the Four of Cups, I just wasn't feeling it. Even as it seemed as though blessings kept coming, my heart was closed to this Beauty. I've learned that while you can work on opening your Heart even when it's closed, you can't force it. And to beat yourself up for not feeling open is a trap; it's falling into the shadow side of the day. This is where the Acceptance Prayer found in the *Big Book* of Alcoholics Anonymous comes in handy. It's a good time to practice Love and Compassion for oneself—when in this "shut down" frame of mind, accepting it with Love and Compassion is exactly the Chesed of Tiferet response.

Rachamim is the Hebrew word for Compassion, and this is also one of the names for the Sephira of Tiferet. The root for this word, *rechem,* means womb in Hebrew, which points to the way Compassion holds those who need it. On days during this week when it is hard to enter the feeling of Tiferet, especially in your relationships, remember to have Compassion for yourself. And if that means spending time alone, in a space that gives you the sustenance of the womb on an emotional level, then that's just what you need.

Day 15: Chesed of Tiferet in Yetzirah
The Four and Six of Swords

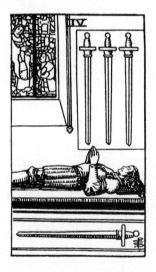 

_____ *within* _____

The history of Judaism is a history of broken lineage. From the destruction of the Temple and the enslavement of the people in exile in Babylon to the Holocaust, there hasn't been a century where the Jewish people and the wisdom of the Jewish tradition weren't in peril of extinction.

When I think back now on the rabbis who were my teachers when I was eleven years old, I can understand now that they were only twenty years past the experience of the Holocaust. And while my own family was affected by this genocide, I had no real understanding of my teachers' experiences. I could only see their failings as teachers. Now I realize that these men, many of them survivors, were severely traumatized by their experiences.

The greatest teacher of their generation, the Piasetzna Rebbe, Kalonymus Kalman Shapira, was devoted to educating the young with Love; he was also a teacher of Kabbalistic meditation. While he was held prisoner in the Warsaw Ghetto, he was given an opportunity to escape, but he chose to stay with his congregation. He was transferred with them to a concentration camp in Trawniki and was murdered with all the prisoners in that camp in 1943.

Before Shapira was transferred out of the ghetto, he buried some of his papers in a strongbox with a letter requesting that if it were found the papers be sent to his surviving family in Israel. Miraculously, they were found many years later, and this chain of transmission, which could have been lost, was restored, since among those papers was a short book, *Experiencing the Divine: A Practical Jewish Guide*. This book included the meditation instructions he gave to a group of his students. And we are fortunate that it has been translated and published in English as *Conscious Community: A Guide to Inner Work*. This is the kind of teaching that was only passed on from teacher to chosen students, face-to-face.

I have read some of the sermons he gave in the Warsaw Ghetto, and I have studied his meditation instructions. I was shocked to discover that these instructions could have been lifted right out of a Vipassana meditation retreat. But then, the instructions themselves are not tied to a tradition: they are steps anyone can take as they develop a sharp intellect and a spirit of Love in Compassion. In fact, if you read any of his surviving works, including the sermons he gave while imprisoned in the ghetto, you will recognize just such a spirit at work.

These thoughts and feelings crowd my mind when I consider

Chesed of Tiferet in Yetzirah. In the world of Yetzirah, we're encouraged to discover what the wisdom of the Jewish tradition offers on the subject of Love within Compassion. And with this pairing of cards, I read the Four of Swords as a call to consider the meditative teachings within the tradition that, like the people in the Six of Swords, have somehow managed to make their way to safety.

If Judaism is your tradition (or is a tradition you're interested in exploring more deeply), today is a good day to explore just these kinds of texts. If yours is another wisdom tradition, seek out those teachings that might have been lost, but somehow survived. If you're Christian, consider reading the Gnostic Gospel of Thomas. And if, like me, you can recall having teachers who failed you in some way, find the Love in Compassion for them today.

Day 15: Chesed of Tiferet in Assiyah

The Four and Six of Pentacles

_____ *within* _____

The Four and Six of Pentacles are an interesting pair for the Flow and Love in Compassion. Because we're in the world of Assiyah, which is the world of action, and some action must be taken to participate in the Flow. Traditionally, within Jewish practice, this action is called *tzedakah,** the religious obligation to give charity, which we can see being played out in some way in today's pairing.

In the twelfth century, Rabbi Moses ben Maimon, also known as Maimonides or the Rambam, wrote of eight principles for giving charity. Consider the images in the cards as you think about these different levels of giving tzedakah: Which level best describes what's happening in the image in the Four of Pentacles? Where does the man giving alms in the Six of Pentacles fall on this, ahem, scale? Which level best describes the way you approach giving charity?

Here are Maimonides's eight levels of charity:

1. The highest-level action you can take is to give an interest-free loan or an outright grant or to work with or find employment for the recipient so that they no longer need to rely on others and can contribute personally to the flow.
2. Give to someone anonymously—so that neither of you knows the other's identity—through a known and trustworthy public charity.
3. Your identity is not known to the recipient, but you know to whom you're contributing.
4. Give publicly through a trustworthy organization without knowing to whom you're giving. However, the recipient knows who you are and that you have given.
5. Give to a person directly—right into their hand—before being asked.
6. You only give to another after being asked.
7. Even when you don't give enough, but you give with an open heart and a smile, this is still worthy of being called tzedakah.

---

*In Hebrew, the root of the word *tzedakah,* most often translated as "charity," is the word *tzedek,* most often translated as "justice" or "righteousness." *Tzedek* is also related to the word *tzadik,* a righteous or saintly person. One of the beliefs of mystical Judaism is that there are always at least thirty-six hidden *tzadikim* (plural) on the planet, and the power of their righteousness is essential to the continuation of humanity.

8. The lowest level of charitable action is when you feel forced to give tzedakah out of obligation, so that you do give something, but not out of any willingness to do so. Some readings of this lowest level suggest that it's not about giving only out of obligation but also giving out of pity—not out of the love of sharing but out of some feeling of guilt.

I know I've given in every one of these ways. But every day is a new opportunity. And because the world of Assiyah is about taking action, this day in particular is a good time to give tzedakah at the highest level possible and to commit to it as part of one's regular spiritual practice.

Questions for reflection and contemplation: Day 15

1. (Wands) Whose presence in your life gives you joy? If you haven't expressed appreciation to that person lately, write a short letter of gratitude and send it today.

2. (Cups) Is your heart feeling open or closed today? Express gratitude in prayer or in writing to the Divine for the depth of your heart from the depth of your heart, regardless of whether you're feeling open or closed.

3. (Swords) Are there any teachers in your life who have been a source of Love and Compassion? Express your gratitude to them in prayer or by journaling about them. Are there any teachers in your life who have seemed blocked and unable to Love their students? See if you can feel Compassion for them and express that as well in a way that feels appropriate.

4. (Pentacles) When you give charity, which level of giving as defined by Maimonides do you prefer? Why? Give charity in a different way that pushes your comfort level today.

Day 16: Gevurah of Tiferet

The Role of Judgment in Compassion

Today is the sixteenth day of the Omer, which is
two weeks and two days of the Omer.

Judgment sounds so, well, Judgmental. But being able to discern the
Truth is an essential skill. Expressing Compassion without first ascer-
taining the Truth of a situation may assuage the feelings of the one who
wishes to be Compassionate. But if the response isn't Balanced appropriately, rather than helping the situation, it can be harmful.

A real-world example on the macroscale would be the emergency
response to a natural disaster. An organization flies in with supplies,
like powdered milk for the children. However, when the water supply is
unsafe, powdered milk is worse than useless. This is Compassion without Discernment.

A biblical example of Judgment or Discernment in Compassion
might well be the story of King Solomon deciding between two women
claiming to be the mother of a child.[1] Consider that story as you contemplate today's paired cards. In this story of Solomon, what initially
looks like a very Harsh and Severe decision is what ultimately reveals
the Truth, resulting in the right outcome.

Of course, the Sephirotic pairings create a kaleidoscope of dynamically shifting energies, so that depending on where you are today, you
might consider Gevurah of Tiferet as the Form of Beauty. Or the
Discipline of Truth. The Restraint of Compassion. The Organization
of Harmony. Play with the Sephirotic key words to see how your experience of the energy meets this day.

Day 16: Gevurah of Tiferet in Atzilut

The Five and Six of Wands

_____ *within* _____

Looking at the Five and Six of Wands, I see the underlying Structure (Gevurah) in the Dynamic Equilibrium of Harmony (Tiferet). One of the ways we can look at the men in the Five of Wands is as Morris dancers. In this traditional English folk dance, the dancers often carry sticks that they use in what looks like a chaotic fight but is really a highly-Structured event.* Conversely, watch some people practicing t'ai chi, a martial Discipline that has a Form and Structure so that it can look like dance. And if you've seen films as varied as *Robin Hood, Star Wars,* or *Crouching Tiger, Hidden Dragon,* you have seen fight scenes that were choreographed. I don't mean to downplay the competition we can see in the Five of Wands, other than to say that within the context of Gevurah of Tiferet in the world of Atzilut, we're looking at a kind of competition that's taking place on another level, giving rise to collaboration.

_____

*Oddly enough, the Morris dance traditionally takes place on Pentecost. You can see an example on YouTube under the title "Beltane Border Morris Dance Up the Sun (May Day 2016)."

Atzilut is the world of the psycho-spiritual, and we can think of the image in the Five of Wands as an expression of intrapsychic conflict that's a reflection of a Structure that's too rigid to hold the contradictions within. An example from my own experience was my struggle as a youngster to reconcile my emerging sexuality with my religious tradition.

Another way to look at it from a more emotional point of view (even though this is Atzilut) is the story in the Pixar film *Inside Out*. In this movie, five emotions are vying for control of a young girl's personality. And that's one way to think about the Five of Wands: all the people pictured in the card are aspects of your Self, competing for dominance.

In the Six of Wands, all these competing aspects have now been Harmonized and united toward a higher goal. Of course, at different times, different figures will be sitting on that horse, since Tiferet Harmonizes Chesed and Gevurah in Dynamic Equilibrium. But it is a Harmony that unites your inner spirit around a focused purpose. Tiferet finds a way for the self to live with its internal contradictions. And that way is through the Compassion that comes from the Balance between self-love (Chesed) and self-criticism (Gevurah).

The Compassion of Tiferet enables a person to accept self-criticism without going down the drain of negativity. And the Restraint within that Compassion also enables one to feel self-love without getting all fuzzy in a pink cloud. This is a Compassion that responds dynamically to changing conditions, feels the pain of all these inner conflicts, marks the Boundaries of that pain, and then surrounds it with tenderness. The ability to do this on both the personal and community levels is what makes a great leader—the leader we see in the Six of Wands.

Day 16: Gevurah of Tiferet in B'riah

The Five and Six of Cups

_____ *within* _____

One of the things Gevurah reminds us in the Five of Cups is that life is a Limited time offer: we have an expiration date. Unlike Chesed, which would keep expanding out eternally, Gevurah sets Limits on everything. Can you remember the first time in your life you experienced the Limitation of "no more?" It was most likely when you were an infant and you were hungry. And then in what seems like the blink of an eye, we rocket ahead to our eighties or nineties and find the Limits of our lives as we come to that bodily Limit, death.

In the Five of Cups, the figure in black has come up against loss and the Limiting nature of Gevurah. But we're in the week of Tiferet, and this is the Gevurah that is in Tiferet, so shouldn't that mediate things? Well, look at the Six of Cups. It's often interpreted by readers as looking back on the innocence of childhood with nostalgia, but the feeling I come away with here is a warning from a shadow side of Tiferet.

One of the names for Tiferet is Truth. And the Truth is, there is loss. There is Limitation. And this is something I can't deny or pretend away. To do so is to promote a false Harmony in my relationships with others and within myself.

In Tiferet we feel the full power of Gevurah's Severity in equal measure with the Benevolence of Chesed. Shut down to one and you shut down to both. I'm sure you've seen people who are shut down in this way.

In the Object Relations school of psychology, when an infant experiences Limits on its desires, it expresses rage and grief in its crying because it feels its very existence is threatened. It has internalized its relationship with the mother. And to hold the tension of not getting what it wants, the infant splits the mother internally into the good mother and bad mother. The child's ultimate psychological health depends on its eventually being able to heal that split and to hold both the mother's love and the mother's setting of Limits together. As we develop the ability to experience the complexity of this reality, we have our first experience of Tiferet's dynamic tension.

The feeling of powerlessness we all experienced as infants and as children still lives deep within us. Tiferet asks us to open to this deeply hidden pain instead of papering over it with the haze of nostalgia. It asks us to hold this pain with Compassion so that we can feel deeply and fully. It asks us to hold the pain of others and share our Strength and Compassion with them. But first we have to be able to do this for ourselves. And that's some of the important inner work of this Sephirotic pair.

Day 16: Gevurah of Tiferet in Yetzirah

The Five and Six of Swords

_____ *within* _____

The Judgment side of Gevurah, like the suit of Swords in the tarot deck, is about discriminating intelligence. The ability to separate things out and decide between them. This takes a sharp mind because the ability to separate things out is connected to an understanding of Law, Structure, and Discipline. So all these ideas are connected. But the Gevurah of Tiferet in Yetzirah is the ability to see differences and separate things out with an open Heart—fully feeling the pain that separation or Judgment can entail. This sounds abstract, but it has important implications for humanity and very personal ones as well.

Sometimes we have to separate ourselves from others whose values or behaviors can be dangerous to our own spiritual path. We may have a friend who abuses drugs or alcohol and who wants to take us down that path. Or perhaps we have been down the path of addiction and have come out of it. To remain sober, we must separate ourselves from those who would have us return to old ways. These may be deep relationships of long standing. And making the decision to part hurts. This is one aspect of Gevurah of Tiferet in Yetzirah—seeing who or what we must separate ourselves from, without disparaging Judgment but with the ability to feel and honor all the emotions around that.

In the Five of Swords, we can see a situation where there has been a Boundary violation, that there's someone who isn't entirely trustworthy. And in the Six of Swords, we can see that there are people who have made the decision to separate themselves from that person and situation. There's a sense of mourning in the Six of Swords, that it breaks the Heart to leave, but leave they must.

This is an important lesson of Gevurah in Tiferet, because when we come from the place of Tiferet, we are showing our wounds openly. We are revealing our imperfections and making ourselves vulnerable. Setting a Boundary around this, or knowing when and where showing vulnerability can be risked and when it is inappropriate, is one of the meditations of this day.

Internally, this pair can be about ways in which you might have colluded in the violation of your Boundaries. I know I've done this and felt the regret and sadness visible in the Six of Swords. This is when it's wise to remember that Tiferet includes having Compassion for yourself.

Day 16: Gevurah of Tiferet in Assiyah

The Five and Six of Pentacles

_____ *within* _____

You've seen this pair before, on Day 10, but with the cards in opposite positions. Because today we're looking at Gevurah within Tiferet in Assiyah, in this pairing I see the Discernment in Compassion. Certainly, the man dispensing alms in the Six of Pentacles is being Compassionate. And because he carries a scale, we know he understands Limits and Boundaries. It may well be that he has within him the experience and memory of a time when he needed Compassionate aid from someone else, and he is passing it forward.

One of the dangers this pairing warns against is operating out of a kind of poverty consciousness, living in fear of material want or seeing the world as a place where there isn't enough for everyone. This is a shadow side of Gevurah in this pairing. Many people avert their eyes from homeless people, and they shrink from a beggar asking for a few coins. Why is this? An encounter like this can activate poverty consciousness, which can be terrifying, so rather than face our inner fears of material want, we create a psychological Boundary and look away from those in need.

Gevurah of Tiferet in Assiyah gives us the opportunity to look at this inner fear with Compassion. It asks us to Discern what is true about the blessings of our material reality and to have Compassion, both for our fears and for others who are suffering from material want.

Questions for reflection and contemplation: Day 16

1. (Wands) Think about situations where you had to Balance your competitive and collaborative instincts: When have you been successful, when not, and why? How do you find Balance when you're faced with internal competing or contradictory desires?

2. (Cups) How has your experience with loss or Limitations affected your ability to express empathy or Compassion for others? Recall a time when you tried to paper over the pain of another so that you didn't have to reconnect with your own pain: what did that feel like and how did it affect your relationship?

3. (Swords) Where can you really be more open and vulnerable in your relationships? And where are you being open in a way that isn't healthy? What is your experience setting healthy Boundaries in a relationship that also calls for Compassion? What is your experience with people who take advantage of your Openheartedness? What is the best response to that? Have you had to cut off relationships because of Boundary violations of any kind, and if so, are there any feelings you have about this that need Compassion? Journal about this.

4. (Pentacles) What is your experience with your own fears when confronted with the poverty or material want of others? What can you do to keep your Boundaries and still express Compassion appropriately?

Day 17: Tiferet of Tiferet
The Heart of the Matter

> Today is the seventeenth day of the Omer,
> which is two weeks and three days of the Omer.

In some ways, Tiferet of Tiferet feels connected to a Japanese concept: 物の哀れ; that is, mono no aware, "the beautiful sadness of things." This Beautiful sadness includes joy, which is an example of the paradox of Nirvana and Samsara simultaneously coexisting. It is the beauty of the open Heart.

When you meet a person who is living from the place of an open Heart, you can't avoid seeing that person, regardless of who they are or what they look like, as Beautiful. And when you can see it in that person, it is because the Openheartedness that already lives within you, awake or not, has been activated by their presence. In the presence of a bodhisattva, the experience of nonduality is activated momentarily. This is Tiferet of Tiferet—the momentary gift of experiencing the Love, Beauty, and Harmony of the universe.

For this very Buddhist meditation on a Jewish mystical practice, I offer this quote from the second Dalai Lama (1475–1542):

All things in Samsara and Nirvana are but mental labels and projections.

Knowing this one knows reality; seeing this one knows what is true.

Day 17: Tiferet of Tiferet in the Four Worlds
The Six of Wands, Cups, Swords, and Pentacles

_____ within _____

The journey out of our spiritual Egypt is an inner journey, seeking the One in our own Heart. In *Radical Judaism,* Rabbi Arthur Green says that even within the Torah itself (Deuteronomy 30:11–13), we are told not to take the story of the journey to Sinai literally, but that we are to understand the story as a metaphor for an internal process.[2] This is a journey to our Heart of Hearts, and these four cards each give clues to how to make this journey successfully.

In the Six of Wands, we see the rider on his horse, the man who rose from the group in the Five of Wands to lead the way. And because one of the faces of Tiferet is Truth, one message here is that you should be led by your deepest Truth. But how do you know your deepest Truth? It calls for searching your Heart way below the waves of emotion on the surface level, past the defenses, past the joy, past the momentary infatuations, and descending within to the deep stillness at the center—the Balance point where all these swirling emotions are at rest and where you can hear the call of this inner leader. The first time I found my way to this place, I was stunned by the Beauty I saw all around me. I wish I could tell you I am able to reach this place anytime I want. I can't, but I know it's possible, and I know that I won't get there by trying, but by waiting and listening. In the meantime, my Heart works like an alarm bell, with pangs instead of clangs, when I make a choice that isn't following my deepest Truth.

In the Six of Cups, we are being told to drop our guard; in this card, you can see a guard with a weapon who is leaving the scene. Between the viewer and the scene, there is a row of cups, creating a boundary that is clear but less defended than having an armed guard. Innocence must be protected, but not necessarily with a halberd. For Tiferet of Tiferet, the Six of Cups shows us that having an open Heart is a risk, that boundaries must be clear but not impermeable.

In Tiferet of Tiferet in B'riah, we are being asked to remember what it's like to have the pure Openheartedness of a child. And we are being reminded that in our Heart of Hearts, purity is always there, as expressed in the prayer: *Elohai neshamah sh'natatah bee t'horah hee* (The soul which You gave me is pure).[3]

There's a body of water in the Six of Swords, suggestive of a river. Is it the Jordan or is it Lethe? The river you choose will lead you to a different interpretation. But what is clear is that mythologically speaking, crossing a river means passing through a difficult period to reach a new state of being. In the Buddhist parable of the raft, crossing the river means reaching enlightenment. If we're talking about the Jordan, it's reaching the "promised land," though, as I like to point out, the Torah ends before the people cross over, and then the cycle of reading the Torah in the synagogue begins again with Genesis: there is only the journey. For the Greeks, there were five rivers that set a boundary around the Underworld. Lethe made you forget your troubles. In fact, it made you forget everything. In each of these crossings, there is some kind of transformation.

In the Buddha's parable, the monk who crossed the river continued to carry his raft with him, thinking he might need it in the future even though it was weighing him down. In the Tanakh, when the people reach the other side of the river, we are out of the more mythic story of the Torah and have moved a little closer to history with the stories of tribal warfare in ancient Canaan. So when working with this card, I have asked myself what myths or practices have been part of my path that are in fact now hindrances to progress. What should I "forget" in order to experience the peace on the other side? Certainly, holding on to any kind of tribalism only serves to keep me separate from others, and even a spiritual practice can be tribal if I insist that this culturally contingent path is universal.

Looking at the passengers in the boat, there is an air of sorrow about them. And because the suit of Swords is the suit of intellect, the image brings to mind the words ascribed to King Solomon: "For with much wisdom comes much sorrow and whoever increases their knowledge, increases their heartache."[4] Because I'm the kind of person for whom thinking can lead to endless rumination, worry, and anxiety, I also come away with a suggestion that this kind of obsessive thinking only obscures the luminous awareness that is our birthright—our promised land. I can't let this kind of thinking sink my boat. It means letting go of the mental objects that arise and distract. Getting lost in obsessive thought is losing one's Balance—one of the themes of Tiferet. I'm not suggesting we lobotomize ourselves and repress our memories, forget our pasts. But simply letting thoughts go as quickly as they come is a way to inner Harmony. And a hidden message of this card for me.

One of the practices during the Omer count is to recite Psalm 67 every day, because it has 49 words. So for the seventeenth day, we look at the seventeenth word in the psalm: *yoducha,* meaning "they will thank you." The image in the Six of Pentacles is a situation that calls for gratitude, but is it the gratitude of the beggars to the merchant or to the One behind the merchant? Is it the gratitude of the merchant to the beggars for providing him with an opportunity to practice the mitzvah of tzedakah or to the One behind the beggars (and himself) for opening his eyes to that One? The answer to all these questions is YES! Here, because we are in the world of Assiyah, we are being shown a way to take action—how to be Compassionate in a way that transcends the duality of Chesed and Gevurah to experience the One heart that animates all hearts. Giving back (or paying it forward) to express gratitude is also a way to reestablish Balance in the flow of the material.

Questions for reflection and contemplation: Day 17

1. (Wands) Think about some situations that have thrown you off Balance, situations in which you found yourself reacting rather than considering and weighing all possibilities. How could you have brought the inner harmony of Tiferet in Tiferet to those situations. And what can you do in the future when faced with similar off-putting circumstances.

2. (Cups) What would letting down your guard and opening your Heart while maintaining a porous boundary look like in your life? Where in your life can you let down your guard a little more?

3. (Swords) What beliefs (religious or otherwise) do you need to let go of to experience greater inner Harmony? How do you Balance the more restrictive beliefs of your tradition with your desire to go beyond them?

4. (Pentacles) Think about times when you have been the recipient of generosity: how can you repay the generosity by paying it forward?

Day 18: Netzach of Tiferet

Finding the Victory in Truth

> Today is the eighteenth day of the Omer, which is two weeks and four days of the Omer.

The number 18 has special significance in Jewish tradition. Since the letters of the alphabet are also numbers, every word also has a numerical value. The letters for the number 18, *chet* and *yod,* spell out the word *chai,* which means "life." Next to the Magen David,* this word in Hebrew is the most popular symbol you'll see on necklaces and amulets worn by Jews. This gives an added level of meaning to the Sephirotic pairing of the day. I think of the story of the first Shabbat service held after the

---

*The Shield or Star of David, the six-pointed star made of two interpenetrating triangles, represents the essential oneness of the transcendent and immanent.

liberation of the Bergen-Belsen concentration camp. As the prayers of the recently freed Jews concluded, a British army chaplain shouted out, "Am Yisrael chai"—the people of Israel live. This phrase is a statement of the Endurance and ultimate Victory of the people and the call to Persevere in one's Compassion, even in the face of monumental cruelty.

How does can one continually keep one's Heart open, and at the same time, how can one Endure a completely open Heart? This is nothing less than the job of being fully human, fully alive. This is the work of Netzach of Tiferet, and the cards for this day will give us clues on how to embody this work.

Day 18: Netzach of Tiferet in Atzilut

The Seven and Six of Wands

_____ *within* _____

Like the man on the horse in the Six of Wands, the man on the top of the hill in the Seven of Wands must keep his Balance. The figures in both cards are solitary and surrounded at the same time. In the Six of Wands, the rider is surrounded by followers or supporters. We could even see the man in the Seven of Wands as the man on the horse in the previous card, but now his followers have turned on him.

The image in the Seven of Wands reminds me of the game I used to play when I was a child—King of the Hill. Behind my house, there was a small hill that been built up of earth taken from nearby construction. All the kids in the neighborhood played there, and King of the Hill was one of the most popular games. It's not a very nice game: it's all about aggression and staying on top. The game teaches that cooperation is situational, since an ally to topple the king may be the one who will try to topple you if you get to the top. And it teaches the one at the top that no one can be trusted. It's a paranoid's delight. And what is the "king" defending? An illusory title with no real power.

In Netzach of Tiferet, the defense should be of Compassion. One of the best ways to embody this Sephirotic pair is by giving ongoing defense or support to someone or some cause in need of Compassion. But the cards also suggest that a trap in this pairing is the defense of ego. The only person we see in the Seven of Wands is the man defending himself. Who, or what, is holding the other wands? Is this a real attack, or does the man only think he's being attacked? While I played King of the Hill when I was a child, I began to see a similar game played around me as I grew older, one called by therapist Robert de Ropp the Cock on Dunghill game, though it's only a game in the saddest sense. The players are people who are hungry to be famous and talked about, and they measure their happiness and success by how often their names appear in the media.[5] Today I think this would extend to how many followers one has on Twitter or Facebook. Just recently, it was revealed that some people pay for social media followers (that aren't real people but are actually bots) so that they appear to be more famous and influential than they really are.

This is the unhealthy side of Netzach of Tiferet: Perseverance in the service of the ego. And I am not immune to its pull. I know the ego prison of checking obsessively to see how many "likes" I get for a social media post. The pairing of the Six and Seven of Wands asks us to examine this dynamic in our lives and directs us to live out the positive side of this pairing, Endurance in Compassion, so that we are steadfast in our support for people and causes in need of help.

Day 18: Netzach of Tiferet in B'riah

The Seven and Six of Cups

_____ *within* _____

It takes Endurance to create a work of Beauty. It takes Focus. And today I find the cards leading me to reflect on my relationship to creative work. For today my take on the scene in the Six of Cups is that we're looking at a gardening project. Each of the cups is being used as a planter, and the row in the front of the scene creates a kind of permeable boundary around the garden. It reminds me of the planters that ring the deck of a summerhouse I've visited. The two figures in the card image may be deciding where to place the cup one of them is holding.

Maintaining a garden filled with flowering plants is no simple task. It requires daily attention, but the reward is Beautiful. This is Netzach of Tiferet in B'riah, Endurance in the creation of something Beautiful. Looking at the Six and Seven of Cups, it's clear to see that one of the dangers to watch out for is distraction.

So let me paint a little Martha Stewart–style scenario here: in the Seven of Cups, the figure is imagining lots of different ways to use these cups to make something Beautiful. Have you ever had an object or a group of objects that you wanted to use in one project and then thought, wait, I could use them here . . . or there? The figure in the Seven of Cups has a lot of great ideas on how to use the cups. The problem is that he can't decide which idea to pursue or gets distracted and doesn't Persevere in its execution. I can't tell you how many projects I've started that have ended up unfinished for this reason.

Creating something Beautiful takes Focus, Endurance, Perseverance. And I am not only talking about sticking to a decision or physical Endurance. We're in the world of Cups/B'riah. And so this kind of creative work also calls for emotional Endurance. All the more so because in Tiferet, we must have the Endurance to hold the Balance of all our emotions as we keep our Hearts open.

I know that when I am doing creative writing, all kinds of emotions come up. Sometimes I don't want to face these emotions; I can point to several works that I abandoned simply because I didn't have ability to Endure the powerful feelings that arose as I was writing. It was harder to distract myself back in the twentieth century when I worked on a typewriter. But with a computer, which can be a door leading anywhere in the world, it's extremely easy to distract myself from difficult emotions with a simple click. There was a time when I worked in front of my screen with a stopwatch; the rule I created for myself was that I stay focused on my writing for fifty minutes at a time. After that period, I had ten minutes to stretch, snack, or surf the internet. But when that ten minutes was up, no matter where I'd ended up online, it was time to get back to work. Working this way gave me the ability to Persevere through my distractions and difficult emotions to not only finish the work, but to also put more of my Heart into it. That's the work of this pairing.

Day 18: Netzach of Tiferet in Yetzirah

The Seven and Six of Swords

_____ *within* _____

I've mentioned before how the Six of Swords reminds me of the Buddhist metaphor for enlightenment as crossing to the other side of a river. The controversial teacher Osho taught that you have to be your own boat, boatman, and passenger and that once you reach the far shore, you should dedicate yourself to helping others make that crossing.*

But what happens if the boatman in the Six of Swords gets three-quarters of the way across the river ferrying his passengers and then decides it's too hard to keep rowing? I know from my experience sitting in meditation that it's easy for some thought to come into the mind that undermines my Endurance.

The Six of Swords is my path to Compassion—both my work on

---

*See his *Eighty Four Thousand Poems,* a "darshan diary" in verse that is unpublished but available online from several sources. Osho is perhaps better known as Rajneesh, and here's an example of someone who taught spiritual truths while using his position to abuse his followers and amass great wealth. I like what he wrote, but as with many who achieve spiritual "power," he fell prey to his own shadow.

myself and my work on behalf of others. The Seven of Swords is the antithesis of Endurance, however. The "occult" name of the card is the Lord of Unstable Effort. It's about giving up even as Victory (one of the qualities of Netzach) is within sight. Many times I have found that when I don't yield to the urge to give up, that is exactly when I reach a breakthrough. And many times I have given up—jumping right off the meditation cushion as though I didn't have another ounce of strength to sit.

You can hear people giving up in this way when they say, "I'd like to help, but what difference could I really make?" as an excuse not to make a Compassionate choice. They're defeated even before making the effort. This undermining energy saps them of belief in their own agency. I've been there.

This is the sneaky, trickster energy of the Seven of Swords, disarming us of our Determination. And here, on Day 18, the day of chai, we're being reminded to choose life. To choose to go forward in the face of any inner voices of resistance. To choose to Persevere and to overcome our false belief that our effort won't make a difference.

Day 18: Netzach of Tiferet in Assiyah

The Seven and Six of Pentacles

_____ *within* _____

I was chatting with a friend of mine earlier today about his work: he helps documentary makers get their films out in the world. Hardly any theaters show documentaries these days, and even if they make it to TV, there are so many entertainment choices out there that the important voices of these filmmakers can go unheard. My friend does work that is needed in the world, and it's the kind of work that should be very satisfying, but he can feel very frustrated by how few people his organization reaches. When I was on the board of a local LGBTQ film festival, I often felt the same way; we worked very hard to help underrepresented voices be heard by the community. And I never felt satisfied. That's when I try to remember the words of Martha Graham, who once said to Agnes DeMille, "It is your business to . . . keep the channel open. . . . No artist is pleased. There is no satisfaction whatever at any time. There is only a queer divine dissatisfaction."[6]

Why do I bring all this up today? Let's look at the cards. In the Six of Pentacles, we have what looks like a successful merchant giving alms to the poor. It would be easy to feel as though simply giving a few coins isn't going to really make a difference in these people's lives as a justification for not giving. And when we look at the Seven of Pentacles, we see someone who has done hard work—who has in fact Persevered in that work over the seasons to reach this time of harvest. Except he has this expression of dissatisfaction even though he has a crop of seven pentacles—and that's not nothing. So let's return to the circumstances of why Graham gave that advice to DeMille.

Agnes DeMille was a choreographer, and she felt that work she'd poured her heart and soul into had been ignored by the critics and the public. But then she was hired to choreograph the musical *Oklahoma!* which became wildly successful. Suddenly, her work was being praised, even though she felt that the dances she choreographed for the musical weren't her best work. For Graham, however, the feelings about the work are less important than the need to "keep the channel open."

For Endurance in Compassion in Assiyah, our own dissatisfaction with our work is the trap that can sap our Endurance. When I was dissatisfied that the crowds did not come to a particular movie I felt was important, it sapped my will to keep working on the film festival. Of course, I didn't know how that film affected the few people who did see it. For all I know, it could have changed someone's life. But I don't know, and I can't let my passion to share be undermined by attachment to what I think should be the results of that effort. Because I don't really know, and in most cases, I can't know. My job is simply to persevere in doing the work. That's true of my work in the world, and it's true about my inner work on this Omer journey, which isn't even halfway over. Keep your channel open. That's a message to Persevere in your work, which is your Compassionate gift to the world, regardless of how it is received.

Choose a cause. Make it yours. And add your voice to the chorus of Compassion. Lend your hands to do the work with the knowledge that you may feel it's never enough—or that you may never know the result—and Persevere. Remember the words of Rabbi Tarfon: "It is not your duty to complete the work, but neither are you free to desist from it."[7]

Questions for reflection and contemplation: Day 18

1. (Wands) When have you been Steadfast in your Compassion for others, even when it has been unpopular? What can you do to demonstrate your ongoing Commitment to stand up for the Truth?

2. (Cups) What do you use to distract yourself as a way of shutting down your Compassion or creativity? When difficult emotions come up to weaken your Resolve in a project, how do you deal with them while remaining Resolute in your Endurance?

3. (Swords) What undermines your Endurance? What ideas or stories do you tell yourself that sap your Resolve? Are those stories true? What practices can you use to defeat this undermining energy and strengthen your Resolve?

4. (Pentacles) Do you nurture your creativity and Persevere in practicing it regularly? Does your judgment of your creativity prevent you from continuing to practice or share it? What can you do to strengthen your practice?

Day 19: Hod of Tiferet

Witness and Withness—Humility in Compassion

Today is the nineteenth day of the Omer, which is two weeks and five days of the Omer.

The "com" in *compassion* points to the ability to be with someone's suffering. Certainly, you can have a desire to alleviate this suffering, but first you have to be with it, understand it with patience and Humility. Sometimes we run to fix something before we truly understand it out of a wish not to feel the depth of another's pain. There are times when simply the act of recognizing and sitting with another's pain is one of the best ways to be helpful.

This means your ego—the one that wants to avoid pain and puff itself up with pride for helping another—has to get out of the way. This may be one of the reasons that when the Temple stood in Jerusalem, the high priest was prohibited from wearing shoes when he led services. After all, when barefoot, the high priest could feel every stone and pebble, so while his title was "high," he was not above feeling pain and suffering, and he was reminded that as high priest, his job was to be a witness to the pain and suffering of the people.

Being a Compassionate witness means meeting people where they are and seeing them without judgment or pity (which is condescending).

"With-nessing" is Compassion that brings companionship, so that others don't feel alone in their suffering.

These qualities of witness and withness are the characteristics of Hod in Tiferet. They produce a Humility that enables the ego to step aside and allows for true Compassion. When we can do this, we can sense the other characteristics of Hod—Glory and Splendor in those we are with.

Day 19: Hod of Tiferet in Atzilut

The Eight and Six of Wands

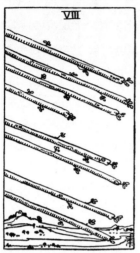 

_____ *within* _____

I still get chills when I read Shakespeare's *Henry V.* The night before the battle of Agincourt, the English were outnumbered by the French four to one, and they knew it. During the night, the king, in disguise, made his way through the camp, listening to the fears of his soldiers and sharing his courage. As the morning came, he delivered a rousing speech, urging his army to stand together as a "band of brothers."

In the plays that chronicle the rise of the seemingly careless and carefree Prince Hal to his ascension to the throne as Henry V, we are witness to a leader who learns how to use Humility to build an emotional bond of comradeship with the men he leads into battle. I think of Henry when I look at this combination of the Eight and Six of Wands.

In *Henry IV,* parts I and II, Prince Hal appears in the role of the prodigal son—spending his time with wastrels and drunkards. But we learn that this is just a role and that he's been using this time to learn a common touch, how to connect Compassionately with the people he will someday lead. So that when he is finally elevated to the crown, he ascends to the throne with somber Humility.

Because Henry puts his ego aside and is truly with his men, they give him their Hearts and fight with a unified spirit that wins the day against the highly hierarchical French. I see this in the Eight of Wands, the one card in the Minor Arcana where there is no human figure—and thus no ego either. The wands are headed all in the same direction, as inexorably as the arrows of Henry's longbow men rained down on the opposing army.

Anyone in a leadership position who has forged a team with one Heart knows how essential their own Humility is to the process. Humility in Compassion not only helps the one in need, but it also inspires others to emulate this quality. And it creates a force of love as direct as an arrow from heaven.

Returning to the qualities of witness and withness, Humility in Compassion is an essential characteristic of the best therapists. By holding back any egoic desire to rush in and advise a client how to fix things, their attentive presence enables the client to fully feel their feelings in a space that feels safe, loving, and healing. This is primarily what I learned to do when I worked as a peer counselor at Identity House, the oldest volunteer LGBTQ counseling center in the country.

This is also a skill I bring to my work as a tarot card reader. While I am not a therapist, my job is to hold a space for a client without judgment and without projecting my own ideas or solutions in answer to their question. My job is to (not so) simply interpret the information in the cards and to help a client uncover their own meaning in the cards. Obviously, my own experience, intuition, and knowledge will come into play, but when I am able to get my ego out of the way, the information feels as though it comes through me, like a bolt (or eight wands) from the blue. So you might not be surprised to know that the Sephira of Hod is connected to prophecy and divine inspiration.

Day 19: Hod of Tiferet in B'riah

The Eight and Six of Cups

_____ *within* _____

What did the religion you grew up with as a child teach you about God? Children often grow up with a Santa Claus–style God, as the famous song written by John Frederick Coots and Haven Gillespie goes: "He sees you when you're sleeping, he knows when you're awake, he knows if you've been bad or good . . ." And it's almost always a "he." And just as we learn there's no Santa Claus, many of us also rebel against this childish and limited conception of God. Many of us walk away from organized religion entirely.

Just as we were taught that there's this hairy thunderer in the sky with a parental or paternal system of reward and punishment, many of us were also brought up to believe that the God we were taught to worship was the only God. That other religions—or even denominations of the same kind of religion—worshipped false gods and were damned to hell. And most of us were taught to believe the Bible as literally true. But to quote the Christian version of that book, "When I was a child, I spoke like a child, I thought like a child, I reasoned like a child; when I became an adult, I put an end to childish ways."[8]

So what does all of this have to do with the Eight and Six of Cups? In the Six of Cups, I see an atavistic desire to return to this relationship to God as parent. Because it was something we learned at the youngest age, even when we put away this childish belief, something of it still clings to our psyche. So my understanding of "nostalgia" in the Six of Cups in this pairing is the unconscious pull of the child's emotional relationship to God. In the Eight of Cups, I see someone who is turning away from the idea of a parental God who acts in history with an egoic demand for validation.

Just as we learn that our own ego is illusory, we also come to understand that there is no deity with an ego. Learning to let go of one's own ego also entails letting go of our egoic projection that there is a God with a personality. After all, even if we are made in the image of God, that God is not a person.

One of the effects of this awareness is the freedom from religious chauvinism and the development of spiritual Humility. One result of this shift can be a move away from the structure of the organized religion you grew up with to explore the deeper journeys that your religion provides, since every tradition offers just such a less trodden path. Or it can mean exploring in other faith traditions to find the truth available there and experience its vision of Glory.

For Hod of Tiferet in B'riah, with the Eight and Six of Cups, the Humility of Compassion doesn't feel like the right combination of qualities for me—at least this year, since each year of this practice is different. But the permutation of key words also gives us Splendor of Truth or the Glory of the Heart, and both capture the work of this day for me: finding the deep roots of childish belief within me and uprooting them to discover the Glorious Truth of the Divine.

Day 19: Hod of Tiferet in Yetzirah

The Eight and Six of Swords

_____ *within* _____

I once saw a bumper sticker that read, "Meditation: It's not what you think." It took me a minute to get it, but then I had a very good laugh. As someone who often places too high a regard on the intellect, meditation taught me thinking can be a roadblock to progress on the path. And that is part of the double-edged image of the Eight of Swords. Swords is the suit of the intellect, and here we see a woman who is bound by her overreliance on the intellect. It has rendered her unable to see things as they really are. She is a prisoner of preconception and thinking that could be obsessive. Looking at the negative side of Hod, this could suggest a thought pattern that reflects feelings of powerlessness—a story that I tell myself about my own victimization and persecution and that keeps me trapped and sapped of my own agency.

At the same time, we could read this image as the opposite: rather than being a prisoner of thought (which surrounds her in the guise of swords), the woman in the image has chosen to ignore these swords/thoughts and go deep within. Which makes this card, like the Four of Swords, an image of meditation.

I remember the first time I went on a ten-day Vipassana meditation retreat. At first, while the schedule was intense, during each sitting, meditators were free to change position, stretch, or leave the hall for a few minutes. But on the fourth day, after spending three days learning the basic technique, we were taught the Vipassana technique, and during that sitting, we were asked to make a "strong determination" not to move for the duration of this instruction period. Not to open our eyes, move our arms, hands, or legs. It lasted almost two hours, and it was one of the most difficult disciplines I'd ever taken on. For the remainder of the retreat, every day there were three separate sittings, an hour each, that were called sittings of *addithana,* sittings of strong determination. This mirrored the Buddha's own vow of resolute determination not to move from his position of meditation, stable as a rock, until he reached enlightenment and demonstrated the Submission side of Hod, from a positive point of view.[9]

Now you may be thinking, wait a minute, isn't resolute determination more in the realm of Netzach? And you'd be right. Except that here, this exercise of resolute determination means putting aside all the thoughts, stories, or ego projections that come into your head, separating them from one's observation of simply what is, free from judgment. It is a Submissive practice of Humility. So when I see the Eight of Swords paired with the Six of Swords—a card that can be seen as a card of the seeker headed toward the far shore of enlightenment—I am reminded of my own Submission to the discipline of addithana as I experienced the waves of strong thoughts and feelings that urged me to get up and leave the meditation hall.

And for meditators, just as for the people in the boat in the Six of Swords, the waves will come. The water looks placid at first, but the waves always come. And we must use all our boatman's skill of keeping the boat of our mind Balanced and "stable in resolute determination," free of ego so that we may reach the other shore.

This is a message and a practice that I always need to remember as I work through this forty-nine-day path. Because my mind wavers, my determination flags, and I sometime let my ego stories get the better of me. That's when it's time to have Compassion for myself—and then start over.

Day 19: Hod of Tiferet in Assiyah

The Eight and Six of Pentacles

_____ *within* _____

As a gay man, I never expected to be a father. But in the early nineties, through an orthodox Jewish study group, I met a single mother who was in graduate school and working a part-time job. Now, your first question might be, What's a queer Jewish Buddhist doing in an orthodox Bible study group? It's a long story. What's important, though, is that I bonded with the mom's seven-year-old son immediately: he was a little red-headed kid with glasses who liked to read. And as a red-headed man with glasses who liked to read, I felt a real connection. I could see the mom needed help with childcare, and I needed a child in my life. I hadn't even known I needed a child; when I came out, I closed the door on the possibility of ever being a father, so I was stunned by how much emotion stepping into a fatherly role brought up.

And it was a fatherly role; I was at their apartment several nights a week to help him with homework. On weekends I took him to museums, movies, plays, and playgrounds. And because I understood that his mother's struggle wasn't only with time but also with money, I began to contribute to the household financially. This brought about a huge change in my life, as I understood for the first time from the inside the pressures that having a family can put on a working parent.

Up to that point, I had been floating through my career, happy to do what was expected without trying to move up the corporate ladder. I had less responsibility and more free time even if I had less money. But once I became part of a family unit, unorthodox as it was, I began to kick my career into high gear; I wanted to earn enough money to make life easier for them. I had to take care of business in order to take care of other people.

I was no longer living just for myself. This isn't news to you if you're a parent, straight or gay. But it was a new experience for me. And when I see the Eight and Six of Pentacles as Hod of Tiferet in Assiyah, this experience comes to mind.

Like the man in the Eight of Pentacles, I had to Surrender myself to my work and subsume my ego to climb the corporate ladder in the service of higher goals. And not unlike the merchant in the Six of Pentacles, I had to Balance my life and my income so I could share both in a way that made me part of something larger, rather than playing the role of benefactor that would only serve to create distance and keep me outside.

I've always had mixed feelings about my work in corporate America, but it has been very good to me. And I recognize that the material blessings I receive in reward for my work are blessings that must be shared. It's why before I became part of this family unit I contributed to a charity that supported children in other countries. And why I continue to give to nonprofits dedicated to helping others. This is one practice of Hod of Tiferet in Assiyah: working not only for myself but also for others. And on this day, I rededicate myself to this practice. How is the dynamic of Hod of Tiferet in Assiyah at work in your life?

Questions for reflection and contemplation: Day 19

1. (Wands) Have you ever given yourself to a leader or a cause with your whole Heart? How did it affect your experience of the pressures and issues in your own life? Have you ever had the experience of your pride or ego trying to force Harmony in a situation? What was that

experience like? If you recognize your pride or ego threatening Harmony in a group, what can you do to evoke your own Humility to counter it?

2. (Cups) What beliefs do you hold about your religion that reflect a childish understanding of the Divine? How does that affect your opinions of other religions and spiritual paths? If there is a religion or spiritual path you have judgments about, try to find some sacred teachings in that tradition that are universal and no different from teachings in your own tradition.

3. (Swords) Think about an idea or opinion you hold that is very fixed—one that you feel so strongly about that you can't hear the other side. Then try to let go of that opinion—really consider the humanity on the other side of this issue—and write a counterargument to what you believe that would help you see the other point of view, even if it doesn't change your mind. Ask for advice or guidance about an issue that feels stuck from someone you respect, even if he or she doesn't hold the same opinions you do.

4. (Pentacles) How does your work in the world support others or a cause larger than yourself? Does making this contribution or giving this support set up a barrier of feeling superior or does it open you to shared vulnerability and humanity? How does it help you experience the "withness" of greater presence?

Day 20: Yesod of Tiferet

Harnessing the Passion in Compassion

Today is the twentieth day of the Omer, which is two weeks and six days of the Omer.

Today is the first time during the count that we connect two Sephirot on the middle pillar: Tiferet, the synthesis and dynamic Harmony of Chesed and Gevurah, with Yesod, the synthesis and dynamic tension of Netzach and Hod. Both Yesod and Tiferet mediate the energies directly above them in a bond of mutuality. Tiferet radiates love throughout the body, and Yesod of Tiferet directs that love and Compassion outside, in the desire to Connect. This can be with another person, or it can be expressed as a lust for life.

Mapped onto the body, this is the connection of the genitals to the heart—the Heart's desire, experienced as a kind of longing, the passion in Compassion. Emily Dickinson wrote, "The heart wants what it wants." When the Heart's truth is expressed in the passion of sexual union, the Connection is so much more than just sexual: it generates a strong Bond of Intimacy.

Yesod can bring a kind of superglue quality of Bonding to Connection that can result in deep spiritual relationship or lead to an obsessive or addictive affect when it is out of Balance. Tiferet's true Heart can bring vulnerability in its openness to feeling not only love but also pain. So together they direct the energy of (com)passionate commitment toward Bonding deeply to another in a heart Connection. In a relationship, this is a powerful energy that helps provide a stable Foundation even as outer conditions change. An example that comes to mind are the vows "in sickness and in health, for richer or for poorer."

When these two Sephirot are connected, one can express spirituality in sexuality. I think about the advice Rabbi Zalman Schachter-Shalomi, z"l, would give to boys he tutored for their bar mitzvah. First, he would ask, "Do you masturbate?" And after the embarrassed silence and the admission, he would counsel them to take their time and to "let God in." Rather than divorce the sexual from the spiritual—and deny the body—he understood that damming (and damning) up this energy with shame would make it harder for one to bring a spiritual approach to sexual union with another.

Of course, when Yesod is out of balance in this pair, we're faced with the problem of promiscuous passion, possibly compulsive sexuality or substance addiction. And a person may make use of the feelings in Tiferet to create the illusion of Connection, but such a person is only interested in personal satisfaction. There can be a narcissistic neediness in Yesod of Tiferet to watch out for. And because of the addictive possibilities in Yesod, it's important to look at how committing to someone or to a cause out of Love or Compassion can be used to avoid something one needs to look at in oneself—making an outer Connection to avoid the inner Connection. Let's see how the cards address these issues.

Day 20: Yesod of Tiferet in Atzilut
The Nine and Six of Wands

_____ *within* _____

One of the ways we hide our hurts is by propping up the ego, and that's a dynamic I see in the pairing of the Nine and Six of Wands. In the Six of Wands, consider the man on the horse as defending his wounded Heart by achieving greatness to put himself above others—creating a superior exterior. Ah, but underneath we can see the vulnerability and hurt on display in the Nine of Wands. We've all known someone who pretends to be above it all, but who really is lonely and hungry for Connection. But you can't be in a truly Intimate relationship when you're on a high horse.

I am familiar with this dynamic in my own life. I have guarded my hurt Heart by masking it with an air of superiority. And I've hidden my longing to Connect behind a stockade of past hurts. But this is a self-defeating strategy. The Heart remains guarded, not only to others but also against itself, so that one doesn't even feel the loneliness and longing to connect. But the desire to Connect doesn't go away, so even though he is hurt, the man in the Nine of Wands still leaves a narrow breach in his wall of defenses. In fact, the man on the horse in the Six of Wands is surrounded by people who support him; he just manages to keep enough emotional distance by physically (and psychologically) holding himself over them.

The result can be a relationship that is marked by the inability to share true feelings. And I have a room full of past partners who can attest to my issues in this department. The difference today is that now I can see it, and I hope I'm conscious enough most of the time not to fall prey to this dynamic. But when I'm not, I hope I'll have a partner who is not afraid to point it out; I just have to be ready to hear and respond appropriately.

Day 20: Yesod of Tiferet in B'riah

The Nine and Six of Cups

_____ *within* _____

What happens to the generous Heart when it has been wounded? The answer may be in this pairing of the Six and Nine of Cups. In the Six of Cups, one child is offering a cup with a blooming flower to another. (Tarot people read the figure on the left sometimes as an adult, sometimes as another child, and as you can see, depending on the combination of cards and what I'm examining, I'm willing to accept either view.) In the Nine of Cups, a man sits in front of an array of empty cups on a table behind him, his arms crossed over his heart. Both the child with the lily and the seated man are wearing red hats and red hose. It's almost as if something has happened to squash the generous impulse of the child so that he has grown into a man who has become smug and self-satisfied: he is alone in this image and not sharing the cups, which are empty anyway.

I also see the Nine of Cups as a man who is greeting his guests at a banquet, and the cups have yet to be filled. However, his position suggests that his attitude toward his guests is one of superiority. Rather than an open Heart of generosity, his Heart is blocked, and his guests must provide him with something, perhaps praise or flattery, before he gets out of the way and orders his servants in to fill the cups so his guests can enjoy them. He uses his wealth to fill the empty cup of his Heart; he is emotionally insecure and thus demands a kind of emotional payoff from his guests.

In both cards, there is an array of cups that can be read as creating a boundary of some kind. There is the fence of cups in the Six of Cups that runs across the bottom border of the card so that the two children are on the other side of this fence. And in the Nine of Cups, the table on which the nine cups sit runs the width of the card behind the seated man, so that while you may be a guest in his house, he will only let you get so far in.

In earlier discussions of the Six of Cups, I've mentioned how the card can be read as a loss of innocence. So we can consider this pairing as the frustrated desire to Connect through a Heart whose generosity has been blocked by some past hurt or trauma. It's as though the compassionate generosity of spirit on view in the Six of Cups has morphed into something more self-serving or defensive in the Nine of Cups.

An old partner of mine once remarked on my habit of giving large parties. And indeed, there was a time in my life when I loved to create crowded get-togethers of the very different kinds of people I knew. But what he said was more about my unconscious motivation. He suggested that I was a "social loner," by which he meant that I used the crowds of people to Connect with the individuals only superficially. That these parties were a way of surrounding myself with people I liked, but also a way of preventing them from getting too close to me. As you may have noticed by now, I have a habit of finding psychologically astute partners who call me on my stuff. And this pairing of cards reminds me of his observation. Of course, there are many ways one can appear to be fostering Connection with others when in fact one is really distancing oneself. It's a tendency I have to be on guard for, and perhaps it's a characteristic you're familiar with in your life in some way, though I hope not.

Day 20: Yesod of Tiferet in Yetzirah

The Nine and Six of Swords

_____ *within* _____

Loneliness. Regret. Loss of a loved one in a breakup. Or by death. Guilt. I have experienced all these feelings, and I know they are at their most intense in the middle of the night. So when we come to Yesod in the world of Yetzirah as portrayed in the Nine of Swords, the Connection to another is broken, and our Hearts are broken as well.

One of the characteristics of waking in the night to fears is that our thinking becomes obsessive; it's hard to stop thinking negative thoughts in this situation, and our fears multiply. It's also my experience that when I allow myself to be controlled by the fears and negative projections, it poisons my Relationships. I judge myself with ferocity and can find no Compassion for myself. And my thoughts create the negative reality I'm afraid of in my Relationships with others. This is a place of deep pain, and whether based in reality or out of mental projection, the pain is real. What is the best way to approach this pain?

Because today is Yesod of Tiferet, the easy answer is with Compassion. But there are traps here as well, and the Six of Swords suggests one of these traps. And this is one of those times when which version of the Waite-Smith deck you have can lead you in very different directions. Because in several of my decks, the far shore in the Six of Swords is colored a kind of gray. The predominant feeling is moving from a more colorful, if difficult, place (the choppy blue waves on the near side of the boat) to a less colorful place (the almost blank expanse of the water on the far side of the boat and the gray land and trees on the far shore). I mentioned in the section for Day 17 how one could see the passage across this body of water as crossing the Lethe, the river of forgetfulness. And I find myself remembering the memorial service of my first boyfriend, who was one of the first people to receive a diagnosis of HIV. The service was at the home of his mother, who was a model of efficiency in greeting people and organizing the day. I was an emotional wreck and experienced for the first time the wracking sobs of grief that come when a piece of your heart has been ripped out through such a loss. His mother, seeing how distraught I was, approached me with some advice. "There's only one way I could get through this," she said to me. "Xanax."

Many doctors will prescribe sedatives of one sort or another for grief, but there are just as many doctors, as well as psychologists and spiritual counselors, who say that sedatives interfere with the grieving process. These medications flatten out the emotions and muffle the obsessive thoughts experienced in these crisis moments.

Because we're in the suit of swords, this intellectual approach to grieving, one that short-circuits the emotions, is Compassion that is afraid of passion. In our society today, one way we try to short-circuit the grieving process and all its emotions is with drugs, and I'm not talking only about the grief that comes with a loss through death. All kinds of emotional pain are sedated. Mind you, this is not a screed against sedatives or antidepressants; I am simply saying that as a society we are quick to medicate emotions rather than deal with them.

Let's look at the people in the cards again. In the Nine of Swords, the person in bed is alone, with their eyes covered. And in the Six of Swords, the passengers in the boat are huddled, hooded, with their eyes down instead of looking ahead. They seem to be within themselves rather than comforting each other. They are together, yet alone. So here we have another clue to the solution for this condition. As the old song by Friend & Lover (written by James Post) goes, "Reach out of the darkness, and you may find a friend."

A Heart Connection is the answer to a broken Heart. A Heart Connection can give one the strength to endure the pain of a broken Heart and to see the far shore of grief with hints of color instead of unending gray. The only way out is through.

We can also look at this card pairing from a twelve-step point of view—with swords as needles, perhaps. The Nine of Swords is very much a card of "hitting bottom." One way I look at the issue of addiction and compulsive behavior is as a disconnect between Yesod and Tiferet. When they mutually inform each other, the spiritual and the physical, sexual, or generative aspects of ourselves are aligned within and in Relationships with others. When they are disconnected, Yesod is always looking for someplace to pour its Generative energy, and when it's not informed by Tiferet, the choice can be, to use the Buddhist phrase, unskillful. Alcohol or drugs, sex or gambling—when you hit bottom, whatever form the addiction takes, it isn't pretty. But hitting bottom means you can now start on your way back up.

When you're new in a twelve-step program, sobriety feels like the world has been flattened. Without your drug of choice, the heightened apprehension of addictive thinking becomes covered in a kind of haze. Which brings me back to the Six of Swords: we can see the people in the boat as headed toward sobriety, which when glimpsed from afar and not long after hitting bottom looks like a gray world. But this is the result of the addictive thinking; thus, the swords still in the boat are in the way of the passengers' ability to see what's ahead. One way I like to think about the story in this card is that as they make their way across the water to the other side of addiction, the people in the boat throw over the swords one by one as they do the inner work to set themselves free. So that by the time they reach the other shore, they are free of addictive thinking and they can see the green on the trees instead of dull gray world. Once again, the only way out is through—and with Compassion for yourself.

Day 20: Yesod of Tiferet in Assiyah

The Nine and Six of Pentacles

_____ *within* _____

What if we looked at the merchant giving alms in the Six of Pentacles and the woman in the garden in the Nine of Pentacles as a married couple—the masculine and feminine energies of these two Sephirot interacting? With these cards, I think it makes sense to consider Yesod of Tiferet as the Foundation of Beauty. When we look at the people in the cards, one is out in the world and sharing his worldly blessings with others and the other is tending the garden at home and using the gift of material blessings to create a fertile space for creative energy to find expression. The hooded falcon suggests the harnessing and channeling of sexual energy to be unleashed when appropriate. The snail could be a clue that indeed the man in the Six of Pentacles and the Woman in the Nine of Pentacles are the same person, since snails are hermaphroditic. We can look at these cards as portraying the Divine Marriage within, expressed in the world as the Compassion that is born out of passion. When we have a Heart Connection and a sexual Connection with another person, the boundaries fall away and it's easier to feel Connected to all humanity.

The snail also Connects us to the cyclical nature of, uh, nature, so that we can see the merchant who goes out into the world and the marketplace and then the woman in the garden who takes time to go within, to retreat and find sustenance from the natural world as part of a cyclical movement of going out and going within. This is an external metaphor for the loop of awareness that creates Intimacy in relationship and Harmony within the soul. But whether they are a story about Intimacy between two people or about the Harmony of an internal relationship, these cards show the result when the desire to Connect and Create is Bonded securely to the Heart.

If there is any warning in this pairing of cards, it may be in the position of the mendicants receiving alms in the Six of Pentacles. They are kneeling on the ground, so their position makes the act of Compassionate giving not one of reaching across from one Heart to another person, a shared recognition of the humanity that Binds giver and receiver, but one of establishing a distance between the people. The solitary woman in the Nine of Pentacles can also be seen as an expression of emotional distance, with the hedges of the vineyard creating a fence that keeps the unruly garden outside her well-cultivated world at bay. It's easy to feel superior, to feel above others when one has both emotional and material resources at one's command. This is one of the many dangers of the popular "prosperity gospel," which comforts the comfortable with the belief that the blessings they enjoy are the result of their faith in God.

Because we are in the world of Assiyah, this pairing also suggests examining how you center yourself and perhaps giving voice to your spiritual and sexual urges in an inner dialog between them.

Questions for reflection and contemplation: Day 20

1. (Wands) In what ways do you create distance in Intimate relationships? Do you hold yourself above the other or put the other on a pedestal? How do you expect to get hurt, and do you prepare for it by walling yourself off in some way? How does this manifest in your sexual relationships? How might you heal the split?

2. (Cups) When do you appear to be open to Connection, but you're really not? Sit for a minute in the same position as the man in the Nine of Cups and imagine you're greeting guests in this position. How does it feel? Are there any familiar thoughts or feelings? What comes up?

3. (Swords) Have you ever used substances or compulsive behavior to avoid feelings (or been close with someone who did)? How has this affected your relationships? Has it ever led to a breakup? Is there anything you can do to heal this, either between you and another person or within yourself?

4. (Pentacles) Is your Compassion built on a strong Foundation? Do you Bond with others in the desire to Create? How does your Creative work express your Compassion? How do you bring Harmony to your sexual and spiritual desires?

Day 21: Malchut of Tiferet

The Dignity in Compassionate Action

> Today is the twenty-first day of the Omer,
> which is three weeks of the Omer.

Malchut, as the tenth of the Sephirot, is the culmination of them all and is often looked at as Sovereignty or Dignity. However, it is also the Sephira that is about manifestation on the earthly plane of this world, which is a world of imperfection. For this reason, I will take a bit of a different interpretation from the classic look at the energy of the day and suggest that this is where we look at the limits of our Compassion. I don't mean the kind of limits imposed by Gevurah. In the world we live in, our own Compassion is going to be imperfect. Because the Truth is that we are not realized beings. And we are not even Sovereign in our own lives. When we recognize this, really get it at our core, we can also have some Compassion for ourselves in our imperfection. And as we work to bring Compassion into the world, we understand that our Compassion is limited and imperfect.

In Christian Cabala, Tiferet is identified with the Sacred Heart of Jesus—an open wound that takes on the suffering of the world. In Malchut of Tiferet, we are deeply aware of that suffering; we feel it because we are not separate from the world. This means we must bear our own suffering with Dignity and that as we work to lessen the suffering of others, we do nothing to lessen their Dignity.

In the realm of Malchut, Compassion is manifested in the world. In other words, it is *Compassion in Action,* which just happens to be the title of a book by one of my Queer HinJu* Heroes, Baba Ram Dass (cowritten with Mirabai Bush). For Ram Dass, Compassionate action is the outer expression, and complementary to, inner exploration: acting compassionately is the work of peace and justice and is a recognition of our interconnectedness.[10]

Choose your path of Compassionate action. Start small but do it consistently. Just like this practice of Counting the Omer.

---

*HinJu = A Jewish person who also observes Hindu practices.

Day 21: Malchut of Tiferet in Atzilut

The Ten and Six of Wands

_____ *within* _____

The man on the horse in the Six of Wands knows Responsibility must be shared. He's only carrying one staff, and the people around him each have a staff of their own. He knows that for his followers to feel a Heart connection to the team, each of them must also feel their own Sovereignty, have a sense of personal agency, and feel recognized with Dignity and respect as an individual. When the horseman shares both this Compassion and respect, his team returns those feelings with recognition of his true leadership ability.

But there are leaders who neither feel a Heart connection with their team nor are willing to give them the agency and respect they deserve. There was a creative director I worked for who would stand over his art directors' screens as they worked on a layout; you could watch him try to keep himself from taking over. But the moment always came when he took the controls from a subordinate and finished the layout himself. He could not share the Responsibility, so he was always on edge and feeling overwhelmed, not unlike the man burdened by the bundle of staves in the Ten of Wands.

When I was promoted to be a group creative director, I knew there would be some administrative tasks. But my focus was on inspiring greater creativity and on creating a more cohesive and happier team. I didn't realize that I'd have a budget and would have to divide up raises and bonuses based on my judgment of each team member's contribution. I didn't think about how I would have to decide whom to cut if we lost business. And I didn't anticipate how wearing corporate politics would be on my Heart. There are some tasks that the leader can share. And there are other tasks that are his or hers alone. When we can approach the Responsibilities we are given with a sense of Balance and Harmony, and a sense of Self-Possession, these tasks will not be as great a burden as we see in the Ten of Wands.

Day 21: Malchut of Tiferet in B'riah

The Ten and Six of Cups

_____ *within* _____

For Compassion in Action to be most effective, it must be matched by inner exploration. The goal isn't for us to feel good about being Compassionate; it's about feeling our Connection to everyone and helping to restore the Dignity and recognize the Nobility of those we assist.

This is a Grounded Compassion that comes from the understanding of impermanence. The four children in the Six and Ten of Cups will grow up (well, not according to Keats, but that's another urn). The flowers in the cups will fade and die. The rainbow in the Ten of Cups is evanescent—a moment of Beauty that is gone in another moment. So what remains?

The spirit of generosity and Openheartedness in the Six of Cups remains. The willingness to look for what is both Beautiful and True in the rainbow, even as it disappears in the sky. There is nothing less Grounded than a rainbow. It would seem to be more a symbol that goes with Tiferet, representing the harmony of colors that come together in the one clear light. And in some ways, this is the message of the Ten of Cups here: the rainbow may be beautiful but remember to stay Grounded. True Harmony stays balanced, even as conditions change. Because change they will.

One of the phrases that comes to mind for the Ten of Cups is "and they lived happily ever after." Except there is no "happily ever after." When we reach a ten card, we have come to the end of a cycle, and a new cycle will begin. Reaching the end is worth celebrating, just as the family in the card seems to be celebrating. But to borrow a phrase from the Buddhists, after enlightenment, the laundry.

The Voting Rights Act was passed in 1965. It was important and worth celebrating. But it didn't end voter suppression. Marriage equality was established by the Supreme Court in 2015. The night of the decision, I was dancing in the street, celebrating with several thousand people in Greenwich Village. But it hasn't ended gay conversion therapy or the epidemic of homelessness among LGBTQ youth abandoned by their families or the attempts by the so-called religious right to roll back these advances. As I write this, students from Parkland, Florida, the site of yet another mass shooting in a school, are meeting with state officials who oppose common-sense gun laws, and they're getting a firsthand experience of the effect of dirty money in politics.

In the pair of the Six and Ten of Pentacles, I am reminded not to be blinded by a childish naïveté while being encouraged to cultivate a childlike optimism and Openheartedness that confers Dignity on everyone, even those who oppose my causes, as I work to change things for the better. Demonizing our opponents brings out our own demons. Acting for my cause should not include anything that diminishes the humanity of those who oppose these causes—even if their strategies include diminishing my humanity. I refuse that equation. It's a trap that continues the cycle.

Day 21: Malchut of Tiferet in Yetzirah

The Ten and Six of Swords

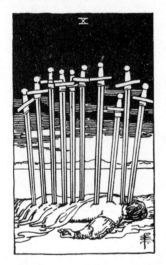 

_____ *within* _____

The call to Compassion in Action does not mean making a martyr of yourself. While we are called on to make sacrifices, the Balance of Tiferet asks that we do so mindfully, so that we aren't left feeling like victims.

In the Ten of Swords, we have come to the death of an idea, the end of the line for a negative way of thinking if we're lucky and if we've been doing the work. Otherwise, this negative thought process is likely to do us in. Of course, even if we've managed to escape this mind-set, it has likely had unfortunate results in our lives.

An extreme example for this pair of images might be the Japanese phenomenon of *karōshi,* or death by overwork. Consider the story of a twenty-two-year-old nurse who died from a heart attack after thirty-four hours of continuous duty five times a month. We all want to have a nurse who is devoted to our care. None of us wants a nurse who neglects her own health. But this young woman believed that this is what she had to do—and this is not just a Japanese issue. Our own training system for doctors in the United States requires young residents to work 80 to 100 hours a week, with some working as much as 135 hours a week. Our society has created a kind of hazing system for medical personnel, and for some reason we have bought into the idea that this is acceptable and a good way to train people in Compassionate care. This is crazy thinking that taken to an extreme will kill us, and most likely will hurt other people in the process.

The root of this dead-end thinking can be a virtue taken to extremes; as I said, everyone wants a nurse who is truly devoted to caring. We all want a doctor who, in the face of an emergency, can work through the crisis no matter how long it takes. And this is where the Balance of Tiferet in this pair comes in: we need to bring Balance back to this way of thinking. As we can see in the Six of Swords, sometimes even as we try to restore balance, the habit pattern of our mind makes it hard to see past these patterns, just as the swords in the boat make it hard for the passengers to see to the far shore.

Sometimes this belief system comes from an outside group, and we buy into it to become part of that group. Sometimes it's a set of ideas we grew up with and never challenged. But all of us carry some ideas that have a negative impact on our lives and relationships. And the challenge of the Six and Ten of Swords is to recognize what the dead-end thought process is in our own lives, then to not become a martyr to it but to reject it.

Day 21: Malchut of Tiferet in Assiyah

The Ten and Six of Pentacles

_____ *within* _____

The path between Malchut and Tiferet is a straight line passing through Yesod, with Tiferet representing the Messiah and Malchut as the Shekinah. So there's a way in which this pairing is also a symbol of the inner union of male and female—a reunification within the Divine and within ourselves. What can we do to help further this goal? Since we are in the world of Assiyah and working with the Sephira of Malchut, it's clear that in this case real action in the world outside is essential for healing the split within the world inside.

The world outside is clearly pictured in the Ten of Pentacles: we see men and women, children, adults and the elderly, the animal kingdom and the kingdom of humans. We even see hints of the world of nature and the world of the arts in the decorated cloak covering the old man seated at the city gate, with repeating patterns of bunches of grapes surrounding what appears to be a lyre (the instrument of King David). Superimposed over this crowded scene are ten pentacles suspended in midair, unseen by the people in the image, in the pattern of the Tree of Life. So we understand that the continued existence of our material world depends on the ever-flowing Divine Sephirotic energy, whether we're aware of it or not. Every now and then, we catch a glimpse of this energy at work in our lives.

In the Six of Pentacles, we're given to understand that we are recipients of a Divine Compassion that wisely and generously Balances what we need with what we are able to hold safely. One goal in the Omer practice is to strengthen our physical and spiritual container so that we are able to receive more of this energy.

Questions for reflection and contemplation: Day 21

1. (Wands) When expressing Compassion, how can you preserve and protect the Dignity of others? What can you do to recognize and encourage their Dignity?

2. (Cups) What are the practical actions you can take to express Compassion for another? When momentary setbacks pull you into pessimism, how do you bring yourself back? How can you have both a wounded Heart and an open Heart?

3. (Swords) What is your experience of martyring yourself to help someone else? Where have you forgotten your own Sovereignty in your desire to care for another? How do you feel about it? What part of this is your responsibility? Can you regain your Sovereignty without withdrawing your Compassionate response?

4. (Pentacles) What actions do you take to help make the world a more Compassionate place? What action will you take today?

Netzach

AUGUST 15, 1945, WAS THE FIRST TIME in history that the emperor of Japan spoke to the people of his country. The cities of Hiroshima and Nagasaki had been destroyed the week before by the first (and I hope the last) use of atomic weapons in war, and it was clear that Japan had lost. In the last years of the war, as the tide turned against Japan, the civilian population endured great privation and suffering. And up to this point, the militarism that had overtaken Japanese culture, denying even the possibility of surrender, had primed the people to commit suicide rather than surrender. But in his speech, Emperor Hirohito did not ask for this supreme sacrifice. In what was perhaps the understatement of the century, he said, "The war situation has developed not necessarily to Japan's advantage." He was announcing the surrender. So why am I writing about this for the week of Netzach, which is often defined as Victory? Because it is also defined as Endurance, and as the emperor told the people, "We have resolved to pave the way for grand peace for all the generations to come by enduring the unendurable."[1] This Endurance is passive Endurance.

A different kind of Endurance I learned in Japan was what they call *ganbare* spirit, a never-give-up attitude (the surrender notwithstanding), a call to Endure and overcome. It's a recognition that sometimes you must fight for what you believe. This is not passive Endurance; it's a highly energetic Drive to succeed. And that's another side of the Endurance of Netzach.

Of course, as with all the Sephirot, there are shadow sides to Netzach, from stubbornness and pigheadedness on one side to passivity and submissiveness on the other. And on the stubbornness side, we can look once again to Japan and soldiers like Hiroo Onoda, who hid in the jungles of the Philippines until 1974 because he refused to believe Japan had surrendered.

But when the energy of Netzach is balanced and healthy, it gives you the inner Drive to express your individuality as you face the headwinds of conformity. It gives you the strength to Endure in difficult situations. And it supplies the Determination to carry on—an especially important trait when taking on a discipline. Like this one.

Day 22: Chesed of Netzach

Love Endures All Things

> Today is the twenty-second day of the Omer, which is three weeks and one day of the Omer.

Okay, I have to admit it, saying Chesed of Netzach out loud can sound like you've sneezed. It's the opening day of the week of Netzach, the qualities of which include Endurance, Victory, inner Strength, and Ambition. And today is the day that such energy is mediated by Chesed, or Loving-kindness.

Simply put, Love Endures. And so I turn to a source on the subject that most Jews aren't likely to quote, Saul of Tarsus.

Love bears all things, believes all things, hopes all things, endures all things. Love never ends. But as for prophecies, they will come to an end; as for tongues, they will cease; as for knowledge, it will come to an end. For we know only in part and we prophesy only in part, but when the complete comes, the partial will come to an end. When I was a child, I spoke like a child, I thought like a child, I reasoned like a child; when I became an adult, I put an end to childish ways. For now we see in a mirror dimly, but then we will see face-to-face. Now I know only in part; then I shall know fully, even as I have been fully known. And now faith, hope, and love abide, these three; and the greatest of these is love.[2]

Directly under Chesed on the Tree of Life, Netzach shares its outgoing nature. So while Netzach has Drive and Ambition, today the motivating force of it all is Love. And really, every day this is true, because as Saul/Paul knew, Love abides.

On this, the first day of the week of Netzach, you can feel good knowing that despite all obstacles, nevertheless you've Persisted in this discipline of Counting the Omer as an expression of self-care and self-Love.

Day 22: Chesed of Netzach in Atzilut

The Four and Seven of Wands

_____ *within* _____

Imagine for a moment you are the man in the Seven of Wands. He stands alone before a group of attackers, his staff angled so that it can block the blow of any of the six staves arrayed against him. He's not holding the staff as a weapon of aggression so much as a statement of defense. If you were in his position, what would you be defending?

The Four of Wands may be his answer; consider the image of the chuppah-like structure as Abraham's tent, open on all four sides, as expressing the values and relationships worth defending and fighting for. You can only have such a structure in a place where safety and security are guaranteed. This is underlined by the fact that the action is taking place outside the walls of a town. City walls are not common in the twenty-first century, but there was a time when cities were surrounded by walls to protect the residents from attacks. Even New York City had a wall; in the seventeenth century, the Dutch colonists built a wall at the north end of what was then New Amsterdam to protect themselves from the native population. That strip of land has been known for centuries now as Wall Street. But the people in the Four of Wands feel safe enough to celebrate outside city walls. Everything about the image suggests openness and Love, abundance, connection, and celebration. Look at the figures in the lower left-hand corner of the card. It's not entirely clear what they are doing, but I imagine them to be holding hands in a line and dancing. If this is the home of the man in the Seven of Wands, his motivation to stand his ground is to defend this society's Love and openness. Because as we all know, a society's freedom is not guaranteed. And sometimes we are called on to stand up and fight for what we Love.

For me, that's what my activism in the LGBTQ movement is about—not merely standing up for Love, but at the beginning, fighting for our very right to Love. Ultimately, the slogan for marriage equality became "Love wins." And because today is Chesed of Netzach, in this imagined story of the man in the Seven of Wands, I believe that Love Endures and is Victorious.

Day 22: Chesed of Netzach in B'riah

The Four and Seven of Cups

_____ *within* _____

This is the week of Netzach—Endurance as well as Victory. And today, as Chesed of Netzach, we experience Love in Victory, the "boundary-less" Love in Endurance. Certainly, nothing Endures without Love. Endurance requires Love to go on. And Victory without Love is empty; it is being right at any price.

When we experience Chesed in Netzach, we have the Love that allows us to Endure the disappointments in our life, in our work, in the causes we work for. But what happens when we're wounded by Love in one way or another?

In the Four of Cups, the figure seated at the base of the tree seems to be ignoring the new Love that is being offered. Perhaps he has had other experiences (the three other cups) that have left him feeling defensive in some way; hence, his arms crossed over his heart. He may be projecting a host of fantasies and fears onto this cup, such as the figure in the Seven of Cups is doing. That figure's past experience is coloring what is before him, so he can't see clearly what it is. Under these conditions, not only will Love not Endure, it may never even take root. He could be projecting his fear that what's being offered will hurt him (the snake in the cup). Or possibly projecting positive qualities that aren't really there (the figure that's hidden under a shawl).

Almost all Love relationships start in projection—putting positive shadow qualities on the beloved. The work of relationship is owning those qualities and learning to Love the real person underneath one's projections. That's how true Love Endures. To do this, we must own the shadow we project, healing the inner split within an intimate relationship.

For the Jungians, a classic example of this is a heterosexual man projecting his sensitivity onto a woman because unconsciously he views it as a negative quality for a man and positive for a woman. So regardless of whether the woman is sensitive or not (though as the psychotherapist Fritz Perls noted, we never project onto a blank screen), he probably will see this in her.

Not an issue for gay men, right? Wrong. One of my partners pointed out to me that most of my previous boyfriends have been on the fey side; they exhibit feminine qualities that in our society are judged negatively in a man. In fact, this is even an issue in gay male society, where so many dating profiles include the misogynistic message: no femmes.

Feminine gay men carry a projection of fear for these "straight-acting" gay men—of being "obviously" gay and thus a target of straight society. It's both internalized homophobia and misogyny at work. My history, though, is different. I seek out "feminine" men. I'm a gay man who generally "passes" as straight if I don't announce myself. And like straight men seeking their shadow femininity in relationships with women, I do the same thing with the men I fall in love with, though I am conscious of the dynamic.

One man I was with for ten years was someone who could be described as flaming—stereotypically effeminate and not quiet about it. Like the man in the Seven of Wands, he was unapologetic and stood up for who he was. And like the man in the Seven of Cups, I projected my inner feminine aspect onto him.

Femininity is a quality I would be ashamed of if I expressed it myself, but it's what I love in other men. Conversely, I find men who are stereotypically manly unattractive. For years after I became an adult, I never referred to my male friends as men; they were always "the boys." Why? Because I identify "men" with insensitivity, casual cruelty, and aggressiveness. Of course, I know lots of straight men who are very sensitive and lots of gay men who are not. But I am not free of these stereotypes and projections. Owning these shadow projections, a negative expression of Chesed in Netzach, is part of the psycho-spiritual healing I work on. And for me, the pairing of the Four and Seven of Cups brings up this issue. What does it bring up for you?

Day 22: Chesed of Netzach in Yetzirah
The Four and Seven of Swords

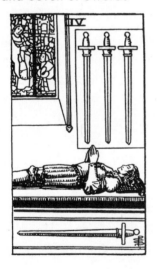 

_____ *within* _____

I'm an introvert; I'm okay one-on-one, but large social gatherings leave me depleted energetically, so much so that I tend to leave parties early. At conferences, if I have a hotel room, I often take time away to spend by myself recharging. I consider this self-care, an expression of Chesed as self-Love, a way of opening to refill the stores of Chesed inside. And in today's pairing of the Four and Seven of Swords, this is one way I see the four card.

This can include meditation, which is one way I've interpreted this card before. But sometimes meditation can be used as a defense. The esoteric name for the Four of Swords is the Lord of Rest from Strife. In other words, a kind of retreat. This would seem at cross-purposes to the energy of the week, which is Victory. But taking the time for self-care is a strategic retreat, especially if you've been taught to focus on other people first, and this can definitely be a Victory.

However, when we look at the Seven of Swords, it doesn't look like a retreat is the right approach today. It can be a way to undermine whatever successes have been gained, since this card, as a shadow side of Netzach, can be read as self-sabotage.

I know this dynamic: there have been occasions when I took time for myself that was less about recharging and more about running away from social interaction. Being in a group of people can activate all my old defenses and fears of rejection, and rather than facing these defenses and breaking through them, I can retreat to my comfort zone of solitude. However, this doesn't serve my growth, and it cheats me from meeting people I would really like.

One of the defenses that can be revealed through this pairing is the result of having one's Love betrayed by another. This doesn't have to be romantic Love, though it could certainly be that. But it could also be about the love for a sibling who you discover has been actively undermining your relationship with your parents or stealing directly from you. This kind of family wounding can result in deep defenses that play out as an attitude of mistrust that permeates all relationships: the other is guilty until proven innocent. The problem with this kind of basic mistrust is that one can never really feel secure: no one is ever really proven innocent. If this is a dynamic active in your life in any way, today is a day to examine its effects and consider how to free yourself from it.

Another dynamic we can see in this pairing is the case of someone who, when facing a competitive situation, retreats from active confrontation to a more passive-aggressive undermining of the other for a sneaky, underhanded Victory. This can manifest as putting forth a caring, spiritual persona (the Four of Swords) while delivering a sneak attack (the Seven of Swords) through words that seem well-meaning but, in reality, are cutting. Do you know anyone who fits this description?

Another dynamic we can see in these cards is that of someone who builds a persona of Loving spirituality while engaging in sexual profligacy. I've been guilty of both these dynamics in the past, and these are character defects I always need to be on guard against.

There is of course a positive way to look at how Chesed of Netzach is expressed in this pairing of cards. Both Chesed and Netzach share the quality of outward movement; neither of them has any respect for boundaries. And while this is mostly a negative trait, in the world of Yetzirah, though, this can lead to innovative ideas. Creativity is rarely the invention of something totally new. Most often it is a combination of existing ideas that have never been put together before. Chesed of Netzach is the opposite of rigid thinking; it can be a free-roaming mind, unafraid to break down categorical thinking to open new vistas of possibility. This can call for trickster mind; the trickster is a boundary crosser. The figure in the Seven of Swords can certainly be a trickster who is defanged of any real malevolence by the mediation of Chesed. (I can even see him as Bugs Bunny, sneaking out of a garden with a bunch of carrots.) This is the role of the sacred trickster in the myths of many societies where they understand the paradox that while boundaries need to be respected, a dynamic society also needs to have its boundaries tested and disturbed regularly.[3]

Of course, that doesn't mean other people like having the boundaries of their thinking disturbed. In 1883, at a dinner in honor of the graduates of Hebrew Union College, nonkosher food, such as shellfish, was served. This was crossing a boundary even in the Reform Judaism of the nineteenth century, so that more traditional Jews were scandalized. This event led to the founding of the more traditional Conservative movement in American Judaism.

When Picasso unveiled his masterpiece *Les Demoiselles d'Avignon*, it was considered scandalous, even by his closest associates and friends. Its emphasis of geometric shapes instead of presenting natural human figures was one of the opening shots in the cubist revolution in art. Its appropriation of African masks broke the boundaries between

European art and so-called primitive African art. And it influenced artistic expression throughout the world.

Some of the most successful innovations in religion, art, law, commerce, and science are the result of crossing boundaries between disciplines. These examples of breaking boundaries are rooted in Love—the desire to create something new and better to share with the world. And at its best, this is what today's energy of Chesed of Netzach celebrates.

Day 22: Chesed of Netzach in Assiyah

The Four and Seven of Pentacles

_____ *within* _____

We've seen this pairing before, though with the cards in opposite positions, on Day 4. On that day, I considered the pairing relative to external conditions—working for a boss or a company that doesn't value its people. With the positions reversed, though, I am moved to consider the inner motivations we bring to work.

Back in the eighties, there was a book titled *Do What You Love, The Money Will Follow.* It seemed as if everyone I knew was reading it; the book became a best seller, and it certainly changed people's lives. I read it too, because at the time I had no love for the kind of work I was doing. By many people's judgment, I was successful, and I was making good money. But it felt hollow to me. At the time, I was writing TV commercials for video cameras, and while I didn't feel that the work I was doing was bad for society, I also didn't feel fulfilled by it. (The role of advertising in the decline of our political culture is another thing entirely.) I was grateful I wasn't working on a factory assembly line—having seen what they were like when I visited manufacturing clients—but there was a disconnect between my passions and my livelihood.

There's a reason that book was a best seller. I would guess that the vast majority of working people in the world aren't working at a job they Love. The way I've dealt with this in my life has been to take side jobs that allow me to express my passions. I've worked as a teacher of traditional storytelling in a religious school. I've also worked as a teacher of creative writing. And over time, I've learned how to bring my Love of humanity to work—building relationships with coworkers that enable all of us to better share our gifts. These are some of the ways I've worked to deal with this issue in my life. All this is prologue to one of the issues presented in the pairing of today's cards.

In the Seven of Pentacles, we see a farmer whose tilling of the soil has yielded a fine crop. But he seems downcast. It's a good image for anyone who feels unfulfilled upon the successful completion of a project in which they have no emotional investment. It's just a job to be Endured. And we know there is no emotional investment in this work because of what we see in the Four of Pentacles.

The cards that correspond to Chesed can be about an outpouring of Love into the world. But in the suit of Pentacles, the card shows a shadow meaning of Chesed. The flow is stopped up. It seems the man in this card is more interested in money. So that one motivation for the figure in the Seven of Pentacles could be simply economic; he's doing this work only for the money. Lots of us have to do this. But it's work we must Endure, and there is little to no Love or satisfaction in it.

Another way to look at this pairing is putting the energy of Netzach into a kind of Driven workaholism as a defense. In the Four of Pentacles, money and possessions are being used as an emotional shield, just as the pentacle is held in front of the man's heart. So that despite the success that comes in the Seven of Pentacles, it's a hollow Victory because there is no Love fueling it. Nevertheless, this is someone who Persists in working this way. Like one of the Hungry Ghosts from one of the Buddhist hells, no success will ever be enough because the rewards are being used to fill emotional or spiritual needs that can't be satisfied.

In the first example, we have someone who is unfulfilled but understands the root cause and seeks to address it by finding a way to express Love in Endurance. In the second, we have someone who is unfulfilled and unconscious; he does not even realize his dissatisfaction because it's channeled back into the Drive for more.

Questions for reflection and contemplation: Day 22

1. (Wands) What causes have you Committed to working for, no matter what? When you are defending yourself or others, how do you stay connected to Love? If you find yourself more Driven by anger, what can you do to reconnect to Love?

2. (Cups) How do you recognize and own your own projections in relationships? When facing the emotional challenge of reconciling the real person versus your projections, what do you do to make sure your Love Endures?

3. (Swords) What defenses do you habitually use to avoid inner or outer connection? Why do you think these defenses Endure? What can you do to weaken them? Do you recognize any of the dynamics in this card pairing as active in your life? Or does this pairing reveal another personal dynamic that is calling out to be recognized and reconciled? How can you do that?

4. (Pentacles) If you are working at a job that you don't Love, how else can you channel your Chesed in the workplace? If you're using work and the need for money to defend yourself from feeling the Flow, why are you doing this? And what can you do to restore Flow and Love in this situation?

Day 23: Gevurah of Netzach

Endurance Requires Discipline

> Today is the twenty-third day of the Omer,
> which is three weeks and two days of the Omer.

What's the difference between a spiritual discipline and a spiritual practice? I think of it this way: When I am at a morning service reciting prayers, I am working on one of my spiritual practices. When I get out of bed every morning at 6:00 a.m. for months on end to be at the prayer service, that's a spiritual discipline. And clearly, it is a Discipline of Endurance.

When all the voices in my head are saying, "Stay in bed," especially when there is freezing rain or snow outside, the Gevurah in me, my Discipline, is what gives me the strength to Endure the cold. Some days I want to run out of the service halfway through. Discipline keeps me in my seat.

During a ten-day Vipassana meditation retreat, meditators are asked to follow a code of Discipline, part of which is the daily schedule of meditation from 4:00 a.m. to 10:00 p.m. Eventually, we learn Endurance by sitting for certain periods of time without any movement whatsoever, by simply sitting and watching the mind's reaction to the body's sensations with equanimity. It sounds painful, and it can truly be painful. But it can also lead to a transcendence of pain and an understanding that sees through suffering in a way that is freeing. In this situation, it is the Discipline that gives Endurance its strength.

There is a short Hasidic tale that illustrates this:

A Hasid decided to undertake a fast from one Sabbath to the next. Only a few hours before the fast was to end, he thought he was going to die if he didn't at least take a drink of water. It so happened that he was on his way to his rabbi's home when he saw a well, so even though he had taken a vow of fasting, he went to the well to take a drink. Just as he was about to bring the water to his lips, he realized he had less than an hour left to endure his suffering. He had endured so long already, so he decided he couldn't give up now and break his vow. He centered himself in his Netzach and started to walk away from the well without drinking.

All of a sudden, he was filled with a delicious tingling: he was feeling pride that he had kept his vow. Except now he was tempted by feelings of superiority and pride. He could not let himself be seduced by pride. For a moment, he stood stock still, not knowing what to do. Then he chose to take the drink of water, deciding this would be better than falling prey to feelings of moral superiority. So he turned back to the well, but just as he brought the ladle of water to his mouth, his thirst completely disappeared.

So may we all learn to free ourselves from both desire and pride through Discipline in Endurance, clear sight, and compassion.

Day 23: Gevurah of Netzach in Atzilut

The Five and Seven of Wands

_____ *within* _____

Does the Five of Wands represent choreography or chaos? Does it show the beginning of an Organized building project or the middle of a fight?

Are the people in the card engaging in a Structured competition, such as a sport? If that's the case, what looks chaotic is really Organized by specific rules that keep things from becoming dangerous. How you respond to this card colors your experience of Gevurah of Netzach in Atzilut.

If we look at the people in the Five of Wands as being Organized, then the result should be Enduring. But if we see them as a group that's divided among themselves, with each wanting to have his or her own way, the outcome undermines the possibility of anything that Endures.

Creating a story from the two images, we could imagine that the man on the far left in the Five of Wands has raised his staff as though he wants to lead or control the others. But once he gets their attention, they turn on him so that he becomes the man facing off against a line of staves arrayed against him in the Seven of Wands. It's as though by trying to Organize and take Control of the group he unites them, but not in the way he intended, since they unite in opposition to him. In this case, the controlling, shadow side of Gevurah turns the energy of Netzach against it.

How could this play out within our own character as an inner dynamic? It's as though the rigidity of the inner control freak wants to stamp out the frequently messy process of innovative thinking. Of course, this can play out between people too.

The Five of Wands could also be a commentary on the quality and motivation for one's Endurance. It could be a Determined inner response to the experience of "dis-Organization" and lack of Structure—inside or out. I have a friend who grew up in a particularly chaotic environment; his mother lived in Haight-Ashbury in the sixties, and he had many half-siblings from different fathers. It was a highly disorganized "hippie" lifestyle. This affected his character so that when he turned eighteen, he chose to live in one of the most highly organized and structured environments, one designed to test and strengthen a person's Endurance: he joined the armed forces. And it was an excellent choice for him, since it grounded him in a Discipline that was in contrast to his life growing up.

As you play with the key words for this pairing, you may find other combinations more relevant for you. Discernment in Endurance suggests recognizing when to keep going and when to let go. Limits in Ambition could indicate an issue with understanding how one's determined pursuit of a goal can affect relationships. Ambition also suggests a desire to lead, possibly as the sole leader, while the image in the Five of Wands contrasts this desire with a more consensus-based style of leadership, where vigorous discussion is part of the process. The sheer gusto of Netzach can be off-putting to others. Someone with a lot of Netzach often has a big personality that Dominates the room, just as we expect the man facing off his opponents in the Seven of Wands will Dominate them. A strong Netzach personality can be both enlivened and contained by the Structured competition of the Five of Wands. Is this your personality? Do you know someone like this? How does your understanding of these energies guide you in this relationship?

Day 23: Gevurah of Netzach in B'riah

The Five and Seven of Cups

_____ *within* _____

With the Five of Cups, Limits are always in the picture. If we think of the Seven of Cups as Ambition, then the cards can be a commentary on what happens when you have a lot of unfocused goals. Certainly, there will be some success. But as some of the goals are met, a Focus on achieving more can lead to losing what's been gained. There's a recognition here that there's a Limit on what you can achieve, that you can't have everything you want even if you are Focused on your goals. A healthy acceptance of Limitation can help Focus you on goals that are not only achievable, but that will also be Enduring.

Because I've worked as a creative director in the advertising industry and the suit of Cups includes creativity in its constellation of meanings, I could interpret the message in the Seven of Cups as being that imagination and creativity are Limitless. But when your Focus is on the past, on what's been lost or on ideas that don't work, you lose the flow of creativity. I can hear my introjected therapist telling me to make "I" statements. So I will.

I can recall many times when I've found it hard to let go of an idea that was rejected by a supervisor or a client. And when that happened, I tended to get rigid in my thinking, and that affected my ability to come up with new ideas. Nothing strangles the creative process like rigid thinking.

The effect of rigid Gevurah thinking in Netzach is that it can transform the positive quality of Perseverance into its shadow quality, stubbornness. In the Five of Cups, there is a lack of Discernment; the figure cloaked in black can't see the big picture. And this lack of Discernment affects the figure in the Seven of Cups, for without Discernment, he is unable to choose a goal and Persevere in reaching it. Everything is pie in the sky.

Of course, you can read the Five of Cups as the Discernment that comes after having made a mistake and regretting it. It can be about acknowledging the negative results of having made bad choices. And because the Seven of Cups can be read as one of the negative sides of Netzach, we can see the image as relating to temptations that have led to dissipation (no Perseverance) and/or addictive patterns (Tenacity applied to problematic behaviors or substances).

The issue here, though, is that while there is regret and sadness over making bad choices, there is no movement away from those choices.

This is the negativity of an inner Judge without the Determination to change. If you've ever heard someone say something like, "I wish I could stop doing _____, but I'm just a screwup and can't get anything right," then you're in the presence of one of the shadow manifestations of Gevurah of Netzach. This is a particularly difficult dynamic to come out of because of the deep-seated self-Judgment. But the first step is awareness. If you see this dynamic at work in your life, the day to start working on breaking it is today. It won't be over in a day. But making a strong Determination to break free of it on the twenty-third day gives you the extra energy from the positive expressions of these Sephirot to do the work that needs to be done.

Day 23: Gevurah of Netzach in Yetzirah

The Five and Seven of Swords

_____ *within* _____

In this pairing, we come face-to-face with some of the uglier tendencies of the human heart. The negative side of Gevurah expressed in the Five of Swords is the extreme opposite of the loving "Boundary-lessness" of Chesed. Here the Boundary stops at the outer level of one's skin, because for the person in the Five of Swords, that is the only Boundary that matters. This is someone for whom the only motivation for anything is self-interest, regardless of rules or Laws. And any actions that serve this self-interest are right.

In the Seven of Swords, we see negative Netzach at work, with someone who is running away from obligations and responsibilities. When faced with a test of Endurance, this is someone who takes the first opportunity to leave. And he's not only leaving others behind, but he's also making off with their swords—leaving them relatively defenseless. And he does this without guilt, because his highest value is the self-interest of negative Gevurah.

Taken together, this is the card pairing of the traitor. A mole in the CIA. An elected official whose only motivation is graft and greed. A sexual predator who is only interested in their own satisfaction and has no care whatsoever for the other except as an object of satisfaction. In a marriage, this could be someone who is a serial cheater or someone who is willing to force himself sexually on his partner.

A person who lives this way is a sociopath. But because this is the suit of Swords and the world of Yetzirah, it doesn't have to be about someone who acts this way in the world. This combination asks us to look within and consider whether we have ever had thoughts like this. We may never have acted them out, but we may have entertained revenge fantasies that include this kind of nasty action.

So is there any way of looking at these cards and this combination in a positive way? I think they can offer guidance when one is caught in the influence of the negative expressions of these Sephirot. Rather than looking within, it can be time to look around: Are you in a situation where your Boundaries are not respected? Where you are being asked to take on too much responsibility, or where someone else's shirking of responsibility means more work falls on your shoulders? Have you helped this along by being agreeable and not drawing a line in the sand marking your Limits? These cards can be a warning of a dynamic that victimizes you. And if it's a dynamic that feels familiar in your life—a pattern that has repeated a couple of times—then it's also time to ask whether something in you is attracted to this situation.

Think of the story of the ancient Israelites. They did not become slaves to the Egyptians overnight. Their bondage happened slowly and by degrees, so that each degradation could be excused or played down until one day an entire people lost their agency. We've seen this happen to individuals, and we've seen it happen to other groups in our world. It can happen in a society, in an organization, or even in a family. And if it's happening to you, these cards are a message: get out now. The process of Counting the Omer is learning to set yourself free of all kinds of enslavements and learning to take on spiritual responsibility. If these cards depict your Egypt, it's time for your Exodus.

Day 23: Gevurah of Netzach in Assiyah
The Five and Seven of Pentacles

_____ *within* _____

My father was a child of the Great Depression. In those days, with landlords struggling to find tenants, apartments were sometimes offered with two months' rent free. His family would move in, and then just before the two free months were up, they would move out in the middle of the night. More than just once. This meant his early education was often interrupted. He left high school to fight in World War II and never went back to get his degree. So he was a high school dropout, and opportunity to succeed in the world felt closed off to him. When I was a child, I didn't understand that my family was struggling financially. But it weighed heavily on my father, and it wore down his self-esteem.

Sometimes when I look at the Five of Pentacles, I think about my father's experience, how he would stand over my bed when I was a child and repeat like a mantra, "You're going to go to college." When I did go to college, it felt like the distance between us grew; I had entered a world that was barred to him, just as the two people in the snow outside the church are excluded from the warmth and comfort inside.

But like the man in the Seven of Pentacles, he was a hard worker and he Persevered. His businesses never succeeded in the way that he'd hoped. In fact, many times he was on the edge of failure. But through it all, he saved what little he could. And he invested this money, never touching it, so that when he retired, he was surprised to discover that he could live comfortably and without the economic worry that had been his constant companion.

He was a man of Limited means and education. Despite his shame about this, he became Disciplined and Determined to provide his family with a better life and greater opportunities. And ultimately, he succeeded.

Some people use the Limits life has placed on them as an excuse to stay on the outside. Some use these Limits as the fuel that fires their Determination to change their situation.

There's a kind of "I'll show you" attitude at work here. If you're told you'll never amount to much, you might accept that story and make it come true. Or you could challenge it and come out on top.

Of course, sometimes when you get to the top it doesn't really satisfy. That's when Five of Pentacles–type thinking claws its way back into one's consciousness with a story that no matter how well you succeed, you're not really deserving, or that your success could be taken away at any time. Or perhaps you have worked to escape the story of Limitation only to find that while you've succeeded financially, it feels hollow because you've neglected your soul in some way.

Today is a day to look at where you've put your Focus and

Determination, to consider your motivations and take stock. Determine whether you're on the right course, and either renew your energy or change direction. Consider how invested you are in your decisions and choices and determine whether you're unwilling to review them. Because Determination can be either a virtue or a hindrance.

Questions for reflection and contemplation: Day 23

1. (Wands) Does your Endurance come from a grounding in Organization and Discipline, or is it a reaction to disorganization and chaos? How does this color the character of your Endurance?

2. (Cups) Do you have a bad habit that you've tried to break in the past but failed? If so, examine its origin, create a Structured plan to set yourself free of it, and then make a strong Determination to follow this plan.

3. (Swords) Have you ever betrayed someone out of self-interest? If so, reflect on this and write about whether you have changed or how you would act differently in this situation today. If you are currently or ever have been in a situation where you've been taken advantage of in this way, reflect on how you might have colluded in this and what you can do to escape this dynamic now.

4. (Pentacles) Consider your financial goals: What motivates them? How good are you in Persevering to reach these goals? When you reach a milestone, are you satisfied or do you feel that something might be missing? What is your relationship to financial Limitations and the Limits of financial success to solve your problems?

Day 24: Tiferet of Netzach

Finding Compassion in Victory

> Today is the twenty-fourth day of the Omer,
> which is three weeks and three days of the Omer.

How does one keep an open Heart in a state of Determination? Being Resolute suggests closing down in a way, white-knuckling your way through something unpleasant. Gritting your teeth and bearing it. Yet today is about doing quite the opposite, feeling Compassion for one's own suffering as one Endures and using that Compassion as fuel for your Fortitude. It's also a day for learning to be patient with those one is often impatient with. When you open to the feelings underneath impatience in a kind of reflective meditation, you can come to an understanding of its origin and then soothe it with Compassion.

Another aspect of the day's energy is Compassion in Victory. One reason I grew up feeling proud of being an American was the Marshall Plan—how after World War II, rather than pillage and impoverish our defeated enemies, we helped rebuild their societies. I only wish I could feel that pride today. That is a society-wide example, though. How does this play out personally? We all compete in many ways. In the business world, in the highly competitive business of advertising, I have been very competitive. And part of my practice is holding my competitors in my heart. Not always easy. This is close to the Buddhist practice of metta meditation. Or for that matter, the message of a rabbi from two thousand years ago who seems to have been taken up as the teacher for a whole other family of religions.

And because you have been doing this work of Counting the Omer, which has meant opening to some of your darker impulses, today is a good day for an Openhearted experience of your Endurance in keeping up this practice. Here is where your love and Compassion for your deepest, Truest self has enabled you to Persevere day by day. (And don't beat yourself up if you miss a day here and there, because you're at this day right now.) That's something to celebrate.

Day 24: Tiferet of Netzach in Atzilut

The Six and Seven of Wands

_____ *within* _____

Here we come across the same cards as on the eighteenth day, though as we progress through the Sephirotic relationships, their order is reversed. How does Tiferet support the man defending himself in the Seven of Wands? Fighting for one's Truth, one of the names for Tiferet, can fuel his Endurance. Of course, we all know that having Truth on your side is no guarantee of Victory, but intrapsychically, knowing the Truth is a Victory.

One of the reasons the man in the Seven of Wands has the Fortitude to stand up for himself is that already, deep within his Heart, he knows he will be the Victor in this situation. He knows his own Truth, and he knows how to Balance his Chesed and Gevurah in Harmony so that he has the tools to achieve his goals and Persevere.

Just as the leader in the Six of Wands keeps his Balance atop his horse, Tiferet gives you just the Balance you need to keep on keeping on and to stand up for yourself in all kinds of situations. If there are any negatives to watch out for here, they are in the possibility of a lack of balance. If the rider in the Six of Wands thinks too highly of himself, so that he considers himself above the others, he's eventually in for a fall, which is what we may be seeing in the Seven of Wands.

Compassion and Balance are what keep the rider on his horse. His Compassion for those he leads and for himself. His Balancing of Chesed and Gevurah in his leadership. However, if he loses this Balance, it can lead to overreach. If you recognize times when your Ambition has gotten the better of you, eclipsing your Compassion for others (and even yourself), this pairing should help you execute a course correction.

I know this situation quite well. When I was first promoted to be a creative director, leading teams of people, I was a well-liked supervisor. I inspired the teams to greater creativity and worked hard to ensure that we all enjoyed a work/life Balance—no mean feat in the ad biz. Over time, though, I lost my Balance, and because of that I lost the confidence of my teams. I'm not proud of that. But I learned from it.

Day 24: Tiferet of Netzach in B'riah
The Six and Seven of Cups

_____ *within* _____

What gives you the strength to Persevere? Consider the image in the Six of Cups, where the cups form a permeable boundary—each of them filled with a blooming flower. The Balance of Tiferet has created a safe space in the Heart that enables love and Compassion to bloom. The Heart has become a sanctuary of Beauty. And this sanctuary can give you strength to Endure and Persevere in the face of trials.

This kind of sanctuary in the Heart is often the result of an upbringing where the parents understood the balance of Chesed and Gevurah needed by the child. It builds a sense of boundaries that provides love with the security it needs to flourish. And when Netzach draws on this kind of Tiferet, it has the Focus to move mountains and the Drive to see any project through to completion.

And with such a base of Tiferet, the figure in the Seven of Cups knows exactly which of the cups floating in the air before her is the right choice. There is a feeling of security in that choice and a Determination to do what needs to be done to fully realize the goal of what is, in the card, something only in the imaginal stage.

I did not have an upbringing where my parents understood how to apply a Balance of love and discipline. And this directly affected my ability to Focus my energy and apply it with Determination. To be blunt, I was a lazy kid. Smart, but lazy. So when I had a school project that called for sustained work, I often let it go. And I knew I could; my mother, rather than setting a strong boundary and making certain I met my deadlines, would often finish the work for me, with me sitting beside her as she talked me through what she was doing. My father set chores for me to complete before I would receive an allowance, chores that were age appropriate. Did I do them? Most of the time, no. Did I still get an allowance? Yes. Too much Chesed, not enough Gevurah, destabilizing my Netzach until I dealt with the consequences of this as a young adult.

Like many people, I learned self-parenting skills later to make up for the times in my childhood when my parents didn't have the Balancing skills of Tiferet. I had to: I went to work in an industry where deadlines are not very flexible and you have to deliver.

Day 24: Tiferet of Netzach in Yetzirah

The Six and Seven of Swords

_____ *within* _____

I like to think of the effect of this Sephirotic pairing in the suit of Swords as the "Robin Hood impulse." In the classic 1938 film *The Adventures of Robin Hood* with Errol Flynn and Olivia de Havilland, there's a scene in Sherwood Forest just after Robin's men have stolen treasure guarded by Sir Guy of Gisbourne. Robin led Marian to see the peasants that had been downtrodden by the predations of the Norman nobles and to show her how he gave them food, medical attention, and sanctuary. While Marian was moved, she was still suspicious, so she asked what he planned to do with the gold that had been stolen. Robin jumped onto a table and called out to all his men, asking, "Shall we keep all this treasure for ourselves?" And they responded to a man, "It's for Richard, to save the king!"

    The spirit of Compassion we see at work in the Six of Swords, with a ferryman giving aid to what appears to be a downtrodden mother and child, is the motivation for the trickster in the Seven of Swords when we're considering Tiferet of Netzach in Yetzirah. While the ferryman keeps the boat in Balance, the trickster has the Ambition to restore Balance by stealing from the powerful.

The movie and the legend of Robin Hood are inspiring. But whenever I read a story of a so-called modern-day Robin Hood, the reality never quite lives up to the legend. Like the image of the man in the Seven of Swords, there's always something a little off-putting about these stories.

While the Hollywood version looks good, with a real sense of Compassion as the source of the action, in real life, it often seems that the motivation is more revenge than a sustained desire to restore Balance. I must admit, I am no stranger to these kinds of revenge fantasies. But two injustices don't restore a just society. I've always believed that Compassion is the motivation at the Heart of progressive tax rates. They're not about punishing the wealthy so much as they are about sharing the responsibility of paying for social services, with those who are most able to bear that burden contributing more.

A more benign way of thinking about the dynamic of these cards is breaking the law to bring attention to an injustice and to right it. Like sitting at a segregated lunch counter and courting arrest to protest racial discrimination. Or climbing the Statue of Liberty to protest immigration policies. Of course, while that's breaking the law, it's nonviolent. But in a less positive example from the 1960s, we have the Weather Underground, whose members went from being just another anti-war protest group to become a domestic terrorist organization. They robbed banks and killed police officers. They rationalized this violence as justified in response to state violence, though ultimately they were just bank robbers and bombers without Compassion. They thought they weren't any different from Robin Hood, and since I didn't live in thirteenth-century England I can't know that they weren't; maybe they were right—except without the Hollywood veneer of romance.

This impulse to respond to injustice by breaking the law goes back a lot further than the thirteenth century: Moses killed an Egyptian overseer who was beating Hebrew slaves. He then fled Egyptian justice and his life of comfort as an adopted member of Pharaoh's family and escaped to Midian.[4] Justice through retaliation when there is no justice by law is also one of the themes of *The Oresteia,* the trilogy by Greek playwright Aeschylus about the revenge-murder of Clytemnestra by her son Orestes. Societies and individuals have wrestled with this since the dawn of human civilization. And as we can see, there are degrees of retaliation ranging from nonviolent protest all the way to murder.

How do these impulses live within you?

Day 24: Tiferet of Netzach in Assiyah
The Six and Seven of Pentacles

_____ within _____

Sometimes when I look at the cards, I think about the Peshat meaning before looking at other levels of meaning. Peshat is one of the four levels of traditional Jewish interpretation of a sacred text; it's the literal, surface meaning without metaphor or digging for secret teachings. And interestingly enough, when you line up the four levels of interpretation with the four worlds in Kabbalah, Peshat corresponds with Assiyah. So starting with a Peshat interpretation of the Six and Seven of Pentacles makes sense.

In the Six of Pentacles, we have someone often described as a merchant, giving alms to two beggars. He holds scales in one hand—taking the Balance of Tiferet and literally showing it. The relationship between him and the beggars appears to be unequal. We do not know what is in the merchant's Heart, but we know he feels enough Compassion to give them alms. Perhaps the merchant sees and feels their shared humanity, and his taking action that recognizes this restores some Balance to the relationship.

In the Seven of Pentacles, there is a young man who is working the land, and the fact that his crop is producing fruits (okay, Pentacles are not literally fruits!) tells us that he has been very carefully tending this crop. Farmers often work up to sixteen hours a day in their fields in all kinds of weather since food crops require constant care and attention. His Perseverance in this work results in a bounty that can be shared. The farmer has no guarantees, since a hailstorm, early frost, drought, or a flash flood could ruin the harvest. But he Endures.

So what is the relationship between these two figures—the city-living merchant and the rural farmer? The very day I was thinking about this, I received an email from my synagogue reminding me that it's time to sign up for our community-supported agriculture program.

When you sign up for your share in this program, you pay in advance for a whole season of fruits and vegetables. This means you are sharing the risk with local organic farmers. If the weather is bad, the pickings are slim. If the weather is good, you have an abundant box of super-fresh produce.

Most of us today don't have a connection to the lived experience of farmers; we get our produce from supermarkets that get their produce from industrial providers and factory farms. It's just a transaction. Participation in a community-supported agriculture program isn't charity; it creates community of shared risk and reward and guarantees a living for people whose livelihood depends on the vagaries of the weather. And it creates real relationships—not the unequal relationship of the merchant and the beggars, but a community of equals among the members and between the members and the farmers.

Members feel real anguish for the farmers when the weather destroys all their hard work. Farmers work with real love in their hearts, not only for the land they're working but also for the people they're helping to feed because they know them.

Farmers aren't the only people who are motivated by Compassion and Balance to work in fields that call for great physical and emotional

Endurance. Think of the doctors and nurses who work in ICUs to save people's lives and the firefighters who rush into burning buildings to rescue people. Their work is not always successful. Without Balance they would burn out quickly.

Perhaps there is a way in which you are motivated by Tiferet so that you have the Netzach to continue working at some task. Or perhaps you recognize how you benefit from someone who does such work and how this binds you in a relationship. Today is a good day to consider and celebrate these relationships.

Questions for reflection and contemplation: Day 24

1. (Wands) Ambition, Determination, and Persistence are all qualities of Netzach, and in and of themselves, they are not an issue. See if you can recall any times in your life when these qualities may have blocked your ability to feel Compassion for others, whether friends, colleagues, family members, or competitors. See if you can recall any times when someone else's expression of Netzach felt insensitive to you. What are your feelings about these experiences? Looking back, can you see any ways you could have brought Balance to the situation?

2. (Cups) How has your upbringing or your childhood experience of learning to internalize the Balance of Tiferet affected your ability to Persevere in a task?

3. (Swords) What is your experience of the "Robin Hood impulse" in your life? Have you ever felt the desire to right injustice by breaking the rules or the law—retaliating in some way—to restore Balance as you understand it? Does your response to others who break rules or laws to restore Balance change depending on who they are and what they see as injustice? Can you feel Compassion for both the perceived victim and perpetrator in these situations? Why?

4. (Pentacles) In my example of membership in a community-supported agriculture program, I describe what I think of as the "web of mutual Compassion" that fuels Endurance. What are examples of this dynamic at work in your life, and what can you do to honor them?

Day 25: Netzach of Netzach

Passive Endurance vs. Active Endurance

Today is the twenty-fifth day of the Omer,
which is three weeks and four days of the Omer.

When we look at the key words for Netzach, it becomes clear that there are at least two kinds of Endurance. There is the Endurance that is passive, which is often about the capacity to live with suffering without complaint. And there is the Endurance that is active, the Determination to achieve something. Some of us are better at one of these than the other. Often someone who is better at active Endurance, for example, studying for the bar exam or working eighty to one hundred hours a week as a medical resident, will find it much harder to passively Endure pain that is unconnected to a goal. Conversely, some people who have learned to live with difficulties through passive Endurance become worn down and find it hard to marshal the energy and Endurance to work toward a goal. That said, Enduring pain and suffering with grace is an inner Victory.

There are also those who, having learned to Endure in a situation where they seem to have no agency, are able to take the energy of Endurance and harness it to meaningful, sustained action. Such people are an inspiration to all of us. And there is a movement in the United States that exemplifies this attitude, with an anthem of hope in Endurance (based on the lyrics of "I'll Overcome Someday," by Rev. Charles A. Tindley):

> *We shall overcome,*
> *We shall overcome,*
> *We shall overcome someday.*
> *Oh, deep in my heart,*
> *I do believe,*
> *We shall overcome someday.*

Day 25: Netzach of Netzach in Four Worlds

The Seven of Wands, Cups, Swords, and Pentacles

_____ *within* _____

So far, my reading of the Seven of Cups has been about the shadow side of Netzach—the lack of Focus that saps Endurance. But there is another way to look at the image on this card. The advertising executive Leo Burnett once said, "When you reach for the stars you may not quite get one, but you won't come up with a handful of mud either." Sure, the figure in this card most likely isn't going to win all the prizes floating in the air. She may not reach any of them. But it's a good bet she's going to come away with something.

In the introduction to this day of Endurance squared, I wrote about the great anthem of the civil rights movement, "We Shall Overcome." The image on this card calls to mind another civil rights song: "Keep Your Eyes on the Prize."

I know that I never thought I would see marriage equality become the law of the land in my lifetime. It seemed like a fantasy, like one of the castles in the air in the Seven of Cups. While I believed it would happen someday, I had no faith that I would live to see it. But both "We Shall Overcome" and "Keep Your Eyes on the Prize" are not just about Endurance, they're also about the Endurance of faith.

The man in the Seven of Wands, who is standing up against the majority of people who oppose him, shows not only Endurance in his ability to withstand all this opposition but also the Endurance of his faith in his ultimate Victory.

The person in the Seven of Cups has an Enduring faith that the better world they imagine is possible and that if they reach for it, they may not win it all, but they won't come away with a handful of mud.

I believe this commitment to faith is also at work in the Seven of Pentacles. The image in this card brings to mind the words of Jesus: "No one who puts a hand to the plow and looks back is fit for the kingdom of God."[5]

For those of us who've never worked the land, this sounds rather mystifying and harsh. But when Jesus lived, most people lived close to the land and agriculture. They understood that to successfully move forward, one's attention needs to be focused on what is ahead without being distracted by what has been left behind. You can't plow a straight line ahead if you're not looking ahead.

Oddly enough, the gospel song "Keep Your Eyes on the Prize" seems to have been based on an earlier song called "Keep Your Hands on the Plow," which is a direct reference to this Bible verse. And in the Seven of Pentacles, it suggests that if your faith is Enduring and your commitment is strong, you will see the fruits of your labor.

That leaves us with the Seven of Swords and someone who doesn't have the power of endurance; rather, this is someone with poor impulse control. I had a friend who, for some reason, when faced with certain temptations, just could not control himself. If he had an impulse to do something, he did it without thinking through the consequences. And there are consequences. I don't often mention this detail on the card, but you may notice in the lower left, just below the tips of the swords, there is a group of people, one carrying a lance, who have noticed the man sneaking off. Perhaps they are part of this encampment and, having seen what's happening, they're on their way to right the situation. Which does not bode well for this trickster.

I know that whenever I make a strong Commitment to anything, there's an undermining energy within me that seeks to undo my efforts. In the twelve-step world, I've often heard it said that while you're working the steps in a meeting, your addiction is outside doing push-ups. It's important to always bring to awareness the unconscious countercommitments and impulses that can undercut your efforts at Perseverance.

Questions for reflection and contemplation: Day 25

1. (Wands) What is your capacity for Enduring the criticism or opposition of others; are you able to consistently have faith in and stand up for yourself, or does doubt creep in and sap your ability to Persevere? What is your experience with this?

2. (Cups) How much have you been willing to Endure and how hard have you Persevered in your life to make your dreams become a reality?

3. (Swords) When you make a Commitment, are you awake to any inner voices seeking to undercut your goals? How persistent have they been throughout your life? What do you do to make sure you "stay the course"?

4. (Pentacles) How do you stay Focused on the task at hand and the goal ahead? What do you do if you get lost because you are looking back on past failures? How does your experience with this change depend on the kind of goal you're working toward? When your Persistence bears fruit, are you able to take satisfaction in your work, or do you feel stuck in some way?

Day 26: Hod of Netzach

The Victory That Comes from Surrender

Today is the twenty-sixth day of the Omer, which is three weeks and five days of the Omer.

In the twelve-step world, "white-knuckling" is holding on tight to sobriety with a kind of nervous willpower and fear of slipping. As a strategy, it might work at first, but it wears away at the soul rather than strengthens it in the ability to Persevere in sobriety. It is antithetical to the positive kind of Endurance found in Netzach.

The spiritual genius of the twelve steps is the recognition that to Endure in sobriety, to be the Victor over one's addiction, first one must Surrender to it. That doesn't mean you let your addiction take over. It means you know that all your efforts on your own to beat this addiction have failed. This is the first step: admitting your own willpower is not enough. And the next Surrender is of your own will to a Higher Will. This is the essence of the second step, that people working the steps: "Came to believe that a Power greater than ourselves could restore us to sanity."[6]

The quality of Hod, which includes Surrender and Humility, is what enables one to Endure and ultimately Triumph in situations where we have little or no power. This means accepting reality as it is. After all, in an argument with the Universe, there is no question who is going to lose.

I know from my own experience that by humbly accepting the truth of my powerlessness, the willpower I was holding on to tightly could relax into a Will greater than my own. It's a process of aligning one's spirit to the Will of one's Higher Power, to use the phrasing that sidesteps the God issue in the twelve-step world. And when you can really do that, the experience of Surrender in Victory becomes an experience you'll always be grateful for. I know I am.

Day 26: Hod of Netzach in Atzilut

The Eight and Seven of Wands

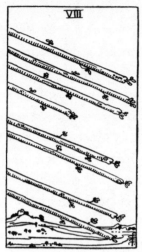 

_____ *within* _____

The man who is steadfastly standing his ground in the Seven of Wands is about to get some serious assistance. The cavalry is coming in the Eight of Wands, but it's not the kind of support that comes riding in on a horse or with any people. That's because the man in the Seven of Wands has just discovered a new source of inner strength that takes his Endurance to the next level.

This inner strength appears because the man in the Seven of Wands, even though he is standing up to defend himself, is free of ego. And when his ego gets out of the way, he reaches into a deeper well of Endurance that is a direct channel to the Divine. His Humility is what gives him greater strength. From a spiritual standpoint, this is something many people understand, but in the practical world, sometimes it doesn't seem so clear. So let's look at this in the realm of the personal.

I don't know how you'd feel if you were the man in the Seven of Wands, but with six people taking arms against me, I'd take it very personally. Now we're in the suit of Wands and the world of Atzilut, so while we can consider this as a physical attack on a person, we can also interpret this as an attack on a person's ideas and ideals. And who isn't personally attached to their ideas? I know that when one of my ideas is disparaged, I have a habit of taking it personally. But there is great freedom when you can put your ego aside. It's kind of a psycho-spiritual jujitsu that doesn't let your opponent land a blow and then turns all that energy against your opponent.

I know that when I don't take things personally, I'm not busy reliving past hurts or thinking about the personalities of the people I'm in opposition to. And by not concentrating on a bruised ego or on the personal issues being projected onto me by others, I free up a great deal of energy to concentrate on what really needs to be defended.

I know I didn't feel this way when I was a child. You probably heard the same saying from your parents: Sticks and stones may break my bones, but names will never harm me. I didn't believe it when I was a kid: names *did* hurt me. But that's because I cared about what other people thought about me. When you surrender to the realization that you can never control what other people think of you, you're free to take all the energy you were expending on trying to control this experience and turn it to more productive and satisfying things.

Day 26: Hod of Netzach in B'riah

The Eight and Seven of Cups

_____ *within* _____

"If there be a prophet among you, I, YHVH will reveal myself to him in a vision, and will speak with him in a dream. "[7]

Because Netzach and Hod are associated with prophecy and because the suit of Cups can be related to connecting with your own and the collective unconscious, let's look at the Seven and Eight of Cups in relation to visions and prophecy. If you're someone who feels a connection to a source of information that feels like it's coming from outside yourself, or even if you're someone who never feels any such connection, this pairing can have important information for you.

Think of the man in the Seven of Cups as someone who often receives such information through visions. Maimonides looked at the text quoted above and made the distinction between the information received in visions and in dreams. In fact, Judaism makes distinctions between twelve levels of prophecy. And for Maimonides, visions were not always clear; they were allegories, and as such were subject to interpretation. Just because you have a vision doesn't mean you're going to get the meaning of it right. Even those who had dreams, which according to the text is one example of where you can hear the voice of the Divine, don't always understand what's being said to them. But we have a long lineage within the Jewish tradition of dream interpretation, starting with Joseph, who interpreted the dreams of other prisoners when he was held captive, eventually leading to his being brought before Pharaoh to interpret his dreams.

And what did Pharaoh see in his dreams? In the first, it was seven fat cows eaten by seven gaunt cows. Then seven full stalks of grain devoured by seven scorched stalks of grain. And how many cups are in the Netzach card? Seven!

The problem, though, is that when you have a vision and your Netzach is out of balance, you're not going to be able to understand the vision clearly. Your own ego can't get out of the way, so that while there might be some understanding, it will not be free from projection. For that matter, one might have a problem discerning which vision is truly from the Divine and which vision is entirely projection.

But when Netzach is balanced with Hod, when the ego can step aside, the ability to interpret these visions increases. In the Eight of Cups, we see a figure walking away from an arrangement of cups. The esoteric name of the card in the Golden Dawn tradition is the Lord of Abandoned Success. And because I often think about these images with biblical stories in mind, I see this as an image of Moses leaving Egypt after he has killed the Egyptian slave overseer. He has turned away from the wealth and comfort of his position as a prince in the court of Pharaoh and is headed to the wilderness and the mountain, where he will encounter the burning bush.

Moses is the one prophet in the Jewish tradition who spoke with YHVH "mouth to mouth."[8] And why is this? In the same chapter of Numbers, it explains that "the man Moshe was exceedingly humble, above all the men that were on the face of the earth."[9]

Certainly, it takes a certain kind of Determination, a Netzach quality of putting oneself forward, to share one's vision of the Divine. And as many prophets have learned, by stepping forward, they've had to Endure criticism and disparagement from others. But when that is balanced by Humility in Hod, the Glory and Splendor of this vision is not only made clearer, but other people also are more likely to hear its meaning.

When writing about this using the examples of Joseph and Moses, it all seems out of the realm of our daily lived experience. But I can think of times in my own life where this Netzach/Hod dynamic has affected my ability to share my experience of the Divine. I remember the first time I came back from a Vipassana retreat, and I was so filled with the joy of the experience, I felt I had to share it with everyone. This is a human trait I've noticed not only in myself but also in many other people; you have a spiritual experience and the impulse is to share it with as many other people as possible. However, I found that what brought people to ask me about that experience was not my announcing it to everyone but instead how they saw a change in the way I lived my life. Humbly living the experience and the ways that it changed me led people to want to learn more about it. But trying to tell them as though I had come down from the mountain with the tablets turned people off.

One message of the Seven of Cups can be that you're getting a message and that the best way to more clearly understand that message is to get your ego out of the way. A "Cups" experience of Divine connection is a feeling connection. This is described in Hebrew as the Ruach HaKodesh, when one is overcome by a feeling of the presence of the Holy Spirit, which is the meaning in English of Ruach HaKodesh. Christian Pentecostalists place a great emphasis on this experience, and they see evidence of connection to the Holy Spirit in the speaking of tongues. In the Christian Bible's story of Pentecost, when the apostles spoke in tongues, it meant that they were able to go out into the streets and preach the gospel to others whose language they previously could not speak. Today, when one is overcome with the Holy Spirit, it doesn't mean that suddenly you can speak French, Indonesian, Hebrew, or any other known language. Which is why I remain wary of anyone who claims to interpret what information is being communicated in this experience. So many preachers seem to be filled with ego that their ability to clearly understand any messages they may receive feels extremely compromised to me.

Which brings me right back to the cards. All of them. Because I don't only use tarot cards for reflection and contemplation. Like many people, I sometimes also use them for divination or prediction (divination, of course, meaning reading the Divine Will in cards or coffee grounds or what have you). And like many people, I have also gone to have my cards read by others who do divination. Some readers claim to be purely intuitive, and they use the cards as a prop for clients as they somehow connect to information. Others actively search the cards for meaning and interpret them, with or without intuitive flashes of insight: this is more my experience.

As a reader, I have to work to separate whatever projections I might bring to a reading with a client, because often that's my own ego getting in the way. But it's not always easy to determine what's a projection and what's an intuitive flash. What I do know is that if I feel any ego attachment to the interpretation, then indeed my ego is getting in the way of delivering clear information.

If, as a client, you have ever had an experience with a reader who takes the position that they have access to information that you need to protect yourself—for example, a reader who tells a client that they are suffering under a curse that only the reader can lift, for a substantial fee—you're in the presence of a scam artist. And in most places, that reader is breaking the law.

However you choose to seek Divine guidance, the pairing of the Seven and Eight of Cups has information for you on how best to receive and share that information. And if you're a tarot card reader, there is much you can learn about your inner dynamic when reading for other people by studying all the Netzach and Hod card pairings, the Cups in particular.

Day 26: Hod of Netzach in Yetzirah

The Eight and Seven of Swords

_____ *within* _____

In the suit of Swords, we see the negative expression of Hod of Netzach, and with both out of balance, the possibilities for trouble are manifold. When in balance, Hod and Netzach are in a reciprocal relationship. Netzach is there to make sure that Hod's Humility doesn't turn you into a human doormat. Hod is there to make sure that Netzach's Drive doesn't run roughshod over everyone else.

When all is in balance, Hod's Humility includes the recognition that anyone can transgress; thus, forgiveness is important. And Netzach's Drive comes with the understanding that having transgressed, one needs to apply that Drive to making restitution and seeking forgiveness.

In Jewish law, when one transgresses against the Divine, one atones on Yom Kippur. But if you transgress against another person, Divine atonement is not forthcoming until you have asked forgiveness and made restitution to the person you wronged.

In the Seven and Eight of Swords, whether you look at this pair as illustrating an intrapsychic dynamic or a situation between two people, you can see that the cards' corresponding Sephirotic relationship is not healthy. And if you recognize the images as representing issues in your own life, they also give clues on how to repair things.

In the Eight of Swords, we have someone who has taken the Humility of Hod to extremes, so that she's allowed herself to be taken advantage of. So much so that it has restricted her ability to act in her own interest. And what's more, she has closed her eyes to the situation; she may not want to admit that someone else has done this to her or that she has colluded in her own victimization. Meanwhile, the perpetrator, in the Seven of Swords, is making off with the goods.

This works intrapsychically when one's Humility, one's Hod, is so damaged that one is unable to recognize the Divine Splendor in all creation, which particularly makes someone unable to see that other people are also made in the image of the Divine, b'tzelem Elohim. When you don't see others as expressions of the Divine made manifest, it's easy to treat them without respect. And that's a recipe for seeking your own Victory with no concern for the dignity or humanity of others.

When the Talmudic sage Rabbi Nechunya Ben HaKana was asked by his students to what virtues he ascribed his longevity, he answered that he never sought respect at the expense of another.[10] His own Humility was a check to balance against his Drive.

Day 26: Hod of Netzach in Assiyah

The Eight and Seven of Pentacles

_____ *within* _____

In these two cards, we have images of people who are working, doing something practical, which is only appropriate given that we are in the world of Assiyah. But there is a subtle difference between them, and you can see it simply by following the gaze of the figure in each card.

The man in the Seven of Pentacles is staring off into the distance rather than looking at the fruit of his labor. What is he thinking about? Since this is the Netzach card, perhaps he is already looking ahead to the rewards of his hard work. Instead of seeing the Divine Splendor in the work of his hands and recognizing that his success is not his alone, he may be like the figure in the Seven of Cups, imagining all the things he can get when he sells the harvest. Of course, there is still much work to be done. Harvesting the fruit of the vine is not any easier than planting or caring for the crops over the course of the season.

The man in the Eight of Pentacles is focused solely on his work. While he has hung some of his work on a post as a display, there is no sense that he's done this out of vanity. His Humility keeps his ego out of the way so that he can keep doing what needs to be done without getting lost in a fantasy of what he will do when his work is done. This means he is in the moment and more likely to do good work because of it.

Here in the world of work, Hod helps keep Netzach focused and grounded on the task at hand so that Netzach will eventually reach the goal of Mastery.

For a moment, let's think about the Pentacles not as products but as people—as colleagues the figures in the card are working with. The man in the Seven of Pentacles isn't thinking about them at all. He's busy imagining his rewards, and there's no indication he's willing to share them. But the man in the Eight of Pentacles is happy to share the credit, showing the others off to their advantage even as he keeps working himself. As always in the Tree of Life, it's in the balance between these two places where we find real satisfaction, where we are recognized for our achievements, and where we share the recognition and rewards with others.

Questions for reflection and contemplation: Day 26

1. (Wands) What is your experience when you're defending your ideas? Are you able to detach your ego? If so, have you ever felt greater strength result from your ability to let go? Conversely, have you ever felt stuck in such a situation, and if so, what is the connection between being stuck and holding on?

2. (Cups) How do you seek Divine guidance? If you use the cards to do this for yourself and others, how do you distinguish between your projections and the information you're receiving? Look at the images in the cups in the Seven of Cups: what do the contents of each of the cups mean to you today? How would you have interpreted them differently in the past or for another person?

3. (Swords) While setting your ego aside can strengthen your Endurance, too much Humility can sap your ability to Persevere. What is your experience with this dynamic—either in your own life or as you have seen it play out with family or friends?

4. (Pentacles) When you work with others, what is your experience with the ability to share credit for success? Think about when you've worked on a long-term project: what was your relationship to the end of the project while you were in the middle of it, and how did thinking about the rewards of the ending distract you or help focus you?

Day 27: Yesod of Netzach
The Connection That Fuels Commitment

Today is the twenty-seventh day of the Omer, which is three weeks and six days of the Omer.

The Bonding in Endurance—sometimes one's ability to Persevere is greater because of a Bond with another person. In the Day 19 section, I wrote about how I finally engaged my Drive in my career only when I found myself Connected in a family unit and wanting to help provide financial support. It was this Bond that fueled my Perseverance. I made a Commitment to my career because of my Connection in this relationship.

In a crisis, the Bond of love can set adrenaline on fire so that you're able to do things you wouldn't be able to do in everyday life. We've all heard stories about the mother who lifts a car off her child pinned under it. And I believe these stories because once something similar happened to me. When a boyfriend became violently ill, I carried him down three flights of stairs and into a cab and from there into the doctor's office. I could never have done that had it not been for our Bond of love: I was able to access deep reserves of Netzach Drive energy through the power of Yesod.

I've also written about the dark side of Yesod, and that side can manifest in this pairing too. The Connecting energy of Yesod is indiscriminate: it will go in any direction if it isn't being directed consciously. So Yesod can be the seat and seed of all addictions. And because like all the other Sephirot, Yesod is a Divine energy, its power, dark or light, is great. When Yesod is frustrated in the search for Connection, the result is a psychic energy that the Buddhists call a Hungry Ghost. Thus, the twenty-seventh day can be very unhealthy if you're unconscious of this energy, because if shadow Yesod is fueling your Endurance, you can find yourself stubbornly Committed to actions that are not in your best interest.

Day 27: Yesod of Netzach in Atzilut

The Nine and Seven of Wands

_____ *within* _____

Feeling defensive, are we?

Yesod can bring a Grounding energy to Netzach, and that grounding is through Relationship, Connection with others. Relationship can fuel the Drive and Determination of Netzach while keeping it Connected to human values. But when we look at the Seven and Nine of Wands, it's clear that the man in the Nine of Wands has been wounded in Relationship and is wary of Connection. He has walled himself off defensively, though there is a gap in his defenses, perhaps showing that he still wants to Connect, even if he is suspicious.

The Seven of Wands also contains an image where a defensive stance is taken. Together, these images make me think about my own prickly defensiveness. Because I have my own Yesodic wounding, I am quick to take offense and ready to fight when I feel attacked. Like the man in the Nine of Wands, I can be suspicious of anyone approaching me; I want to trust, but my experiences have made me wary, and I have been known to project bad intentions onto those who hold no such feelings. This is one of my character defects, and it's something I keep working on. In fact, looking at the man in the Seven of Wands, I recognize what my stance in the world must have looked like to others when I was in my twenties. I'm not as bad today, but it's still an issue that calls for greater consciousness on my part.

Because Atzilut is the world of ideas, rather than look at how this has affected my heart relationships, I think about how this issue has affected my relationships in the world of business, where I work with others in ways that are both collaborative and competitive. In a creative department in the advertising world, the better your ideas, the more successful you are. Though often, as in the world of film and theater, while an idea might originate with one person, the process is ultimately highly collaborative. But I can be very defensive about my ideas in ways that have sabotaged the collaborative process, thus preventing these ideas from being realized and preventing me from being promoted. Add issues of prejudice into this situation, and it's a recipe for career disaster.

When I began my career in advertising in the late seventies, it was a very WASPy industry. The shift to more diversity in the business has been chronicled in many memoirs by industry greats who often founded their own agencies because they couldn't get hired by the old-line Madison Avenue shops. And one of my first agencies was just such a famous old-line shop. The creative director who hired me was Jewish. And after I was there for a few weeks, I noticed something odd. Everyone in his group was Jewish, and everyone else in the other creative groups and in the other departments throughout the agency was not. I even heard us referred to as "the Jewish group." Management came to us when they wanted more "out-of-the-box" thinking. But we were in a kind of ghetto, and while there were people in the agency I became close with, I had a defensive chip on my shoulder since I could also sense the disdain for my group.

When there were internal agency competitions to win business, I was always hyperdefensive of my work because I believed that it wasn't my work that was being judged, but my heritage. Sometimes it was true, and sometimes it wasn't. But my defenses had been activated, and that made it impossible for me to see clearly what was really going on. And of course, my quickness to defend my work was interpreted by those people who were prejudiced as just another example of a "pushy Jew." My defenses played into the stereotype.

The thing is, though, I know if I had felt less defensive, had I been more open, I would have seen more openings available to me. And I would have trusted them more.

These defenses run deep in me. Even though I've done a lot of work to make them conscious in order to weaken them, I can often be caught off guard by my guardedness. This isn't made any easier when there are politicians today who use anti-Semitic dog whistles to speak to their supporters. But living on guard like this holds people at arm's distance. And that's not how I want to live my life.

There's one more way I want to look at this pair. As a gay man, I have often read the Nine of Wands as a card of a queer person who is in the closet, someone who comes from a family or cultural situation where they have grown up knowing who they are but had to hide it and hide the wounding of their identity. For me, this has fueled my activism, so that this pairing speaks to me in a particular way. But for those who remain closeted or whose wounds run deep so that their desire for Connection is frustrated by fear, the result can be a Netzach that is wounded (and wounding) as well. Consider the gay man who uses a cutting wit to hold other people at a distance.

Day 27: Yesod of Netzach in B'riah

The Nine and Seven of Cups

_____ *within* _____

In the introduction for today, I noted that Yesod helps us stay Connected to human Relationships as we pursue our goals. These Relationships can even be the fuel for our Determination. But when Yesod is wounded or defensive, this fuel is depleted or it directs our Perseverance in unhealthy ways. This is clear in the pairing of the images of the Nine and Seven of Cups.

In the Nine of Cups, the body language of the man seated on the bench makes it clear that the Connection on offer is shallow. The man leaves no room on the bench for anyone else—he's manspreading—even though the bench is wide enough for another to join him. He may be the master of a banquet, but he doesn't look very welcoming with his arms crossed in front of his heart. Because his legs are spread apart, the path to his genitals, however, is open, so that even though this is the suit of Cups, the Connection offered here isn't emotional. You can think of him as a wealthy man who knows his money can buy him physical Connection and that's enough for him. And the cups behind him can very well be trophies of past conquests.

We can see how this expression of Yesodic energy affects Netzach in the Seven of Cups: the man can't focus on any one Relationship, and he sees them all as possible trophies to add to his collection.

I've been on both sides of this equation at times. I can think of times when I was single and looking to meet a partner. Sometimes I'd be speaking with someone in a social setting, and while the person seemed to be interested, I could also see his eyes wandering the room to check out the other possibilities. He wasn't focused on me but was only looking for another conquest. And I've been just as guilty of this kind of behavior.

I've also been at family affairs where I have felt this dynamic in action. Have you ever been to a celebration of some kind hosted by family members whose only goal in inviting others was to show off how successful they are? They're not really inviting you to celebrate and share in their *simcha**; it's not about Connecting in celebration but about lording things over you.

In this kind of negative expression of Yesod of Netzach, a person sees others only as potential opportunities to increase their success in some way. People under the sway of this dynamic choose their Relationships on this basis. Here Yesod is not about Connecting deeply to others; it only sees them as either obstacles or support to be used in the pursuit of one person's goals.

This is perverting emotional Connection in the service of material success. If you know someone like this, you've probably felt used by that person at times. You may have done something like this yourself. I don't like to admit it, but I have. This pairing of cards shines a light on all those times, forcing me to consider where I might still be doing this in any of my relationships today.

One other way to consider this pairing is through the lens of addiction. The man in the Nine of Cups can be a high-functioning alcoholic; he looks successful to the world, and he presents himself as such, but he uses alcohol (or some other substance) as a substitute for

---

*Hebrew for "gladness or joy," this word often refers to a joyful celebration of blessings. It is also used as a given name.

or a defense against Connection. As a result, he can't see any of his relationships clearly; they are all seen through the haze of his addiction in the Seven of Cups. If this was a problem in your past, today is a day to consider the ways in which this issue still affects you and your Relationships.

Day 27: Yesod of Netzach in Yetzirah

The Nine and Seven of Swords

_____ *within* _____

We have come to the moment of the crisis in faith—when our wounded self-esteem undermines the feeling of worthiness and agency and when we have lost our belief that we are always in Relationship with the Divine Presence.

There are two stories in the Torah that come to mind when I see the Nine and Seven of Swords. First is the story of Jacob in Genesis, chapter 28, when he had run away from home and the anger of his brother Esau, whose blessing he had stolen. While sleeping in the wilderness with his head on a rock for a pillow, he had a vision of a ladder reaching up from where he slept into the heavens, with angels going up and down. When he awoke, he said, "Surely the LORD is in this place, and I did not know it."[11] He named the placed Beth El, the House of God (seemingly unaware that the Divine is accessible in any place at any time).

When we look at the Nine of Swords, the swords hanging in the dark are unseen by the person who is weeping. It might feel to the person in the card that the weight of Divine Judgment is above and against them, with the blades cutting them off from Divine Connection. But you can also see the blades as the rungs of Jacob's ladder, with the positive interpretation that God is in this place and that while the person crying in bed may feel cut off from Divine Connection, that Connection is there to be had. Even when you feel lost in the wilderness like Jacob. Or like the Israelites in their wanderings.

When the Israelites were wandering in the desert, Moses sent twelve scouts ahead into the Promised Land to report back to the camp on what they saw. Two of the scouts, Joshua and Caleb, gave a good report of a land flowing with milk and honey. But the other ten saw something else entirely:

"And there we saw giants, the Nephilim, so that to ourselves we looked like grasshoppers in comparison, and that's how they saw us too!" Hearing this all the people of Israel cried out in fear and wept all night long.[12]

The ten did not see with the eyes of faith the land the YHVH promised them. They still saw with the eyes of slaves, so that they saw themselves as grasshoppers. Even though these were people who had witnessed the Divine hold back the Sea of Reeds so they might escape Pharaoh's army, their faith was not strong. Like the figure in the Nine of Swords, they did not feel the power of the Divine Presence with them. And as former slaves, their Netzach was weak, further undermining their faith. This affected the whole community, who let the fears of the ten scouts keep them up all night, crying in fear.

We humans seem to be wired to forget. At least I am. I have had moments when I have felt a strong Connection to the Source of All

Life that has filled me with a deep inner peace. But a week later, something happens that disturbs my newfound equanimity, and my old fears return and blind me to the Divine channel that is always open.

This is an illusion, the self-deception that's at work in the Seven of Swords. But I have fallen prey to believing it. And that makes it just as real as if it were true, because it has kept me from seeing the opportunity to connect that's ever present. Today is a day to examine just what triggers this wavering of faith, what activates this self-deception. Because the more one falls into the trap, the longer the time spent wandering in the wilderness.

Day 27: Yesod of Netzach in Assiyah
The Nine and Seven of Pentacles

_____ *within* _____

It's time to get earthy:

> *"Where has your beloved gone,*
> *you most beautiful of women?*
> *Which way did your beloved turn,*
> *so that we may seek him with you?"*

"My beloved has gone down to his garden,
to the beds of spices,
to pasture his flock in the gardens
and to gather lilies."[13]

Let's go down to the garden together. Because in the Nine and Seven of Pentacles, that's exactly where we are. And with the two figures, male and female, the images it brings to mind are from the Song of Songs, the biblical celebration of sexual love that is unashamedly sensual and erotic.

We're in the world of Assiyah, the world of the physical, and there's nothing more physical than the earth itself and our bodies. And Judaism recognizes that the earth and earthly love are also spiritual. When the sages were deciding which books should be included in the canon of the Tanakh,* many were opposed to the inclusion of the Song of Songs for its highly sexual nature. But Rabbi Akiva† argued forcefully for its inclusion, interpreting it as an allegory for the Relationship between YHVH and Israel.

While earlier interpretations of these cards in other pairs sometimes have pointed to more negative expressions of their respective Sephirot, this pairing is nothing but joyful. It's an opportunity to look at your Relationship with your body and your experiences loving other bodies (not divorced from their souls) as spiritual experiences. Remember the star in the pentacle? It's singing to you in the words of Joni Mitchell's "Woodstock": "We are stardust, we are golden, and we've got to get ourselves back to the garden."

Here in the Nine of Pentacles, we can see the woman in the card is deeply Connected to the earth and the garden. With her one hand resting on the ripe grapes and a hooded falcon resting on her other, she is connected to the earth and the sky. Sexuality is controlled and

---

*The word *Tanakh* is an acronym, made from the words Torah, Nevi'im (Prophets), and Ketuvim (Writings), and it is used in Judaism to refer to the books of the Hebrew Bible.
†One of the greatest rabbinic sages of the first century CE. The Sefer Yetzirah is ascribed to him, though this is unlikely to be true.

channeled, resulting in fecundity. She waits for her beloved in this lush garden.

In the Seven of Pentacles, we find her lover. He is her partner in planting and caring for the garden. As he works, he looks off longingly in the distance, imagining them spending time together in this bower. Her Yearning for Connection feeds his Perseverance, his Netzach, in working to create this garden.

Yesod, in the Nine of Pentacles, shows us the deep Yearning of the soul for Relationship. There is a paradox here, because the woman in this card seems self-sufficient, and to a degree this is true, because she knows, even as she Yearns for Connection with the Divine, that she is never separate from It. But the experience of seeing the Divine in another and having another recognize the Divine in you is a different Connection. This is the love that the great Sufi poet Rumi writes about. And this is why she waits in the garden for her beloved.

This pairing shows the ideal of what Relationship can be. It promises that if we channel our energies wisely, we can experience Divine love in human love and see it reflected in nature all around us. Today is a day to examine just how we channel those energies and a reminder to see the star in the pentacle. We are indeed stardust.

But we're not just stardust. To quote another high priestess of pop, Olivia Newton-John, these cards tell us, "Let's get physical!" Yes, we are moving toward the marriage on the fiftieth day, and it can sometimes be hard to remember that this process is a courtship of your inner male and inner female leading up to that marriage. What would manifesting this inner courtship physically look like?

Today is a reminder and a celebration. The work of preparing the garden calls for the commitment of Netzach. You have demonstrated this commitment by doing the work to reach this point in the count. *Mazel tov!**

---

*This is a celebratory expression of congratulations. The word *mazel* in ancient Hebrew meant "constellation," so that using this expression was like saying you were born under a good sign of the zodiac.

Questions for reflection and contemplation: Day 27

1. (Wands) What are the fears that fuel your defenses in Relationship? How have they affected your ability to Commit to Relationship?

2. (Cups) Think of the times in your life when you appeared welcoming to someone but you were really closed off. Why was that? Think of any occasions when someone wanted to Connect with you and you deflected by showing off something about yourself. Why was that? Have you ever been on the other side of this experience? What was that like? What do you think was going on for the other person?

3. (Swords) Remember a time when your fear overwhelmed your faith. Looking back, see if you can feel where in that experience your Connection to the Divine was still present and available. Think back to a time when you feel that you betrayed your faith. What happened to your feeling of Divine Connection? Looking back, see if you can feel where in that experience your Connection to the Divine was still present and available.

4. (Pentacles) What are you doing to build, grow, and prepare your garden? Who is allowed in?

Day 28: Malchut of Netzach

Nobility in Endurance

> Today is the twenty-eighth day of the Omer,
> which is four weeks of the Omer.

I was only five years old at the time, but I remember the image in the newspaper, and it's a photograph you probably know: it's a picture of Elizabeth Eckford, fifteen years old, entering Little Rock High School on September 25, 1957, escorted by members of the 101st Airborne Division of the U.S. Army through a crowd of white people screaming vitriol and hate. In the photo, the young black woman holds her body erect, her head held high and her gaze looking only forward as she makes her way through the menacing crowd. She had made that same journey three weeks earlier, but she and eight other black students—the Little Rock Nine—had been barred at the door to the school by the Arkansas National Guard. And after that first day getting in to school, she continued to attend classes. Enduring ongoing harassment, she and the other black students were pelted with vegetables, spat on, and insulted on a daily basis for a year.

For me, this image illustrates the energy we must find within us on this day: Nobility in Endurance. We may never find ourselves in such an extreme situation as Elizabeth Eckford's. We may never be tested as the Little Rock Nine were. But should such a time come, may our love, our discipline, our hearts, our intention, our humility, and our connectedness all unite to give us the Nobility to Endure the inevitable setbacks until the day that we prevail.

Day 28: Malchut of Netzach in Atzilut
The Ten and Seven of Wands

_____ *within* _____

And Moses asked YHVH, "Why do you treat Your servant so badly? Why haven't I found favor in your eyes, since you put the burden of all the people on me? Did I give birth to

them, so that you command me: 'Carry them in your arms,
like a nurse carrying a baby' to the land You promised to
their ancestors?"

NUMBERS 11:11–12

It wasn't only the Israelites who complained in the desert. From the start, Moses didn't even want to take on the burden of leading the people, asking YHVH to "send someone else."[14] Like Jonah, he wanted to run away. He actually got YHVH to agree to send Aaron to speak with Pharaoh instead of him. And in their wanderings, when the people complained to him, he would complain to YHVH. Yet when it comes to Nobility and Leadership qualities, Moses is at the top of every Hebrew school list. Why is that?

In this card pairing, we can see some of these events in the story of Moses and apply them to our own experience with this Sephirotic pairing in our lives. In the Ten of Wands, there is a man burdened by ten staves, carrying them toward a destination, just as Moses felt burdened by leading the people toward the Promised Land. And as we know, Moses got the people to the border but was not allowed to cross into the land himself.

In the Seven of Wands, we have a man facing off against would-be attackers. In this pairing, I think of this image as Moses telling Aaron to throw down his staff in the competition with Pharaoh's priests. All their staves turn into snakes, but it is the snake born of Moses's staff that eats all the others. In this Victory, Moses does not claim it for himself, for it belongs to YHVH. And he Perseveres, even as Pharaoh hardens his heart and changes his mind time and again.

The responsibility of Leadership was a burden to Moses, but he was able to carry it because he embodied the virtues of all the previous Sephirot, and this strengthened his Determination to guide his people toward their goal, even though he faced constant complaints and open revolt. Despite feeling discouraged and weighed down, he kept moving forward.

Of course, he was able to do this because he had a face-to-face relationship with YHVH. And because we're in Malchut, the Sephira of the Shekinah, we are reminded that his spiritual source of strength was unified, both masculine and feminine (and beyond both). His experience of the Divine was both immanent and transcendent. And the tradition makes clear that there was only one Moses. No one else had that relationship with the Divine.

So what does this mean for us when we find ourselves in a position of Leadership or when we are inspired to take on a great work that promises much but also offers many burdens? The realization—the bringing into reality—of a vision requires marshaling the strengths of all the Sephirot within us. Because as we move ahead, there are always obstacles challenging us to face our very core. There is no room in this for complaint.

This is a tough one for me, because I was once a chronic complainer. Earlier, I wrote about the Ten of Wands and what I see as the culture of complaint. I still carry the voices of complaint in my head. I often refer to them as my inner Israelites. And this is when I need to call on my inner Moses. Moses complained too. The difference is that he shared his strength with the people, and he brought his complaints to YHVH. And the Divine hears all without complaint.

Day 28: Malchut of Netzach in B'riah

The Ten and Seven of Cups

_____ *within* _____

There's an advertisement for the "personal wealth management" division of a major bank that's running as I write this. The image in the ad is of a kid in a candy store. You can see all the colorful jars of candy on display from the child's point of view. The headline reads, "When was the last time you believed possibilities were really endless?"

I don't believe the premise of this ad. They're trying to convince their target audience that possibilities are indeed endless—especially if you have enough money to be a client. I oughta know. I used to write advertising for this bank. But the headline taps into several popular beliefs. First, the materialist's belief that if you have money, anything is possible. Next, the "New Age"* belief that with the right amount of intention and spiritual concentration, you can "manifest" anything. Last, the belief that many American parents teach their children: you can grow up to do or be anything you want.

Why do I bring this up? Just look at the cards. Usually, the Ten of Cups is interpreted in a very positive light. It's a lovely card, suggesting domestic joy. But when paired with the Seven of Cups, those cups in the rainbow might suggest a more illusory joy. It's as though the joy of the family is not because they have enough—and enough is as good as a feast—but because they believe the future is filled with unlimited potential. The Seven of Cups suggests that belief is unrealistic.

In Genesis, the rainbow was the Divine promise not to bring destruction on humanity after the devastation of the biblical Flood. So the celebration in the Ten of Cups can simply be relief after a calamity has passed, with the parents telling their kids, "You can grow up to be anything."

What happens when you give kids awards for everything? They grow up with the belief that they should be rewarded for everything. That is destructive to a child's Netzach, undermining the ability to pursue goals with Consistency and Commitment.

I don't want to be a Negative Nathan here, but there is a warning in

---

*I recognize this is a highly problematic term that spans a wide range of beliefs and practices for which there is no fully definable category. I'm generalizing. Something I generally don't like to do. Ahem.

this pairing. Yes, take joy in what you have. Yes, live with wonder and amazement at the Divine Presence throughout Creation. But don't let complacency and satisfaction rob you of your Drive or confuse you into believing in endless possibility.

The Ten of Cups can also be seen as an illustration of the Jewish value of *shalom bayit,* literally meaning "peace of the home" but referring more specifically to peace in the relationship between spouses.* However, while this is a beautiful value to uphold, the Talmud suggests it's okay to tell a lie in order to keep the peace in the family.[15] Once again, we are faced with joy that has the possibility of being based in falsehood. Certainly, if you come from a family where there was the appearance of harmony and you learn that was based on untruth, that can rob you of your Netzach and make it harder for you to distinguish between illusion and reality.

At the same time, it is part of the daily liturgy to thank the Divine three times a day for the "miracles which are daily with us."[16] To live with the gratitude and amazement that we can see in the Ten of Cups. And here is the distinction: miracles are indeed everyday occurrences. The hummingbird at the feeder. A shooting star. Photosynthesis. Reality is indeed miraculous. Fantasies, unfortunately, are not reality. Find joy in the real world of Malchut, and the miracles are there. Look for fantasies, and your Netzach will desert you.

---

*And on a completely tangential note, if the plural of mouse is mice, why isn't the plural of spouse, spice?

Day 28: Malchut of Netzach in Yetzirah

The Ten and Seven of Swords

_____ *within* _____

Yesterday, in Yesod of Netzach in Yetzirah, I wrote about the crisis of faith the Israelites experienced after hearing the false report of giants in the Promised Land delivered by ten of the twelve spies. Even after all the miracles they had witnessed performed on their behalf, they still suffered from a slave mentality. In the story, YHVH decides that such people would not be fit to enter the land as a new people and that this slave generation had to die off before the Israelites could cross the Jordan. So YHVH decrees:

> But as I live and as My glory fills the entire earth, none of the men who saw My glory and the signs I did in Egypt and in the wilderness, and yet who tested me these ten times and haven't listened to My voice, surely not one of them will see the land I promised to their ancestors. None of them who treated me contemptuously will live to see it.[17]

Each and every one of those times is right there to be seen in the Ten of Swords. With each act of spiritual rebellion, the people were cutting themselves off from the future. The only people from that gen-eration who entered the land were the two spies who gave a true report: Joshua and Caleb, who became the next generation of leaders after Moses.

We are more than halfway through the forty-nine-day period of the count. My experience with this discipline is that I Commit to it, I mess up a few days, I recommit, I miss a day, I recommit, I actively resist, then I get depressed, then I recommit again. It's a process. And this process includes a dynamic I mentioned back on the fifth day: the Upper Limits Problem. As I've worked this discipline over the years, I've found that when I'm doing really well and I begin to feel a Sephirotic flow of energy throughout my body, I'll do something to bring myself down. And often that something involves rationalizing a behavior that cuts me off from this flow. It's that undermining of effort we see in the Seven of Swords. Except the deeper I get in this work, the more extreme are the thoughts and behaviors I can fall prey to that take me out of it.

The Ten of Swords is both a warning and a reminder. Because the story of the Israelites being punished by not being able to reach the promised land is not a story of being cut off by the Divine. It's the story of a habit pattern of the mind that eventually cuts itself off from the Divine, that falls for the illusion that there is no possibility of *t'shuvah,* which means "return" or "repentance." This is hitting bottom. But it's not the truth, because there is always the possibility of return. That's why the dawn is breaking in the distance in the Ten of Swords.*

Rabbi Nachman of Breslov taught that no matter how far one may fall, never fall into despair, because a return to God is always possible—always.

Yes, we can all return. But Malchut of Netzach in Yetzirah tells us that Endurance is essential if we want to change. And that transfor-mation is hard. We always think ahead to the beauty of the butterfly. But the caterpillar dies. Something has to die. And one of the dangers in this pair is the stubborn refusal to accept the end of something. Difficult energies indeed for this pairing on the twenty-eighth day.

---

*People disagree: Is the sun setting or rising in this card? I choose to see it as sunrise, obviously, since ten is the end of a cycle and the start of a new cycle. A new day.

Day 28: Malchut of Netzach in Assiyah

The Ten and Seven of Pentacles

_____ *within* _____

> *And there came a man of God to Eli, and said to him,*
> *"Thus spoke YHVH: Did I not reveal myself to the house*
> *of your fathers when they were in bondage in Egypt to the*
> *house of Pharaoh?"*
>
> I SAMUEL 2:27

This is one of the biblical verses associated with Malchut in Assiyah in *The Gates of Light* by Joseph Gikatilla (as noted by Ronald Decker in *The Esoteric Tarot*), which connects it to the Ten of Pentacles in the pair above.[18] Eli was the high priest at Shiloh in the days of the Judges, and the "man of God" had come to reprimand Eli and let him know that his sons would be punished for stealing from the sacrifice. When the Hebrew Scripture uses the phrase "man of God," it can indeed refer to a person, but it can also refer to an angel, as was the case when Samson's mother received the prophecy of Samson's birth. All this is to note that when a "man of God" appears, whether a prophet or an angel, it is often to alert people to a level of reality of which they are usually unaware.

In the Ten of Pentacles, I think we are also receiving a visit from a "man of God." The figures in the card are uninterested in the old man seated just outside the city gate. He is ignored by all except the dogs, and he sits patiently waiting to reveal himself when the time is right.

When will the time be right? The clue is in the pentacles suspended in the air in the form of the Tree of Life—and unseen by all. The ability to see these shining disks, representing all the Sephirot, announces the immanence of the Divine Shekinah. When you can see them, you have reached the goal of Kabbalistic work—the experience of Messianic Consciousness. However, that time is not yet for the figures in the card. They have yet to reach this level of awareness. But it is always within their reach.

Messianic Consciousness can be theirs if they work for it. If they make the Commitment shown in the Seven of Pentacles and they work their inner garden. The man in the card is seeing the first fruits of his work. He is not there yet, but he can see that he has made progress and that his Determination is being rewarded.

The pairing can also reveal possible imbalances in your experience of Malchut of Netzach in Assiyah. It points to the trap of becoming so involved in the work that the focus is only within and not on other people or one's relationships. And without this dual inner/outer approach, ultimately, the fruits will wither on the vine.

Still, this pairing promises great rewards, and together these cards remind me of the promises of the ninth step in *Alcoholics Anonymous: The Big Book:*

> If we are painstaking about this phase of our development, we will
> be amazed before we are halfway through. We are going to know a
> new freedom and a new happiness. We will not regret the past nor
> wish to shut the door on it. We will comprehend the word serenity
> and we will know peace.[19]

At the end of Day 28, we are at the end of the fourth week and a little more than halfway through Counting the Omer. If you have been painstaking as you worked this path, you may already have had some moments of amazement. But whether quickly or slowly, the rewards will materialize if you work for them.

Questions for reflection and contemplation: Day 28

1. (Wands) Who are your inner Israelite complainers? Do they have a style or familiar subject of complaint that comes up regularly? How can you deal with them strictly but lovingly? What is your relationship to your inner Moses?

2. (Cups) There is a tradition in Judaism to say one hundred blessings a day. Spend today with an awareness of the everyday miracles that surround you. With each miracle, say this blessing to yourself:

   Blessed is the One, Divine Source of all blessings, whose miracles
   I have witnessed in this place.

Count these blessings as you say them, and use your Netzach to set the goal of reaching one hundred blessings on this day.

3. (Swords) What has to die within you for you to be reborn spiritually? What are you refusing to let go of?

4. (Pentacles) As you do this inner work, review how your relationships have gone over the past twenty-eight days—or during any time you put toward a spiritual discipline. Is there any way in which your concentration on inner work has been detrimental to your relationships? If so, start taking action today to repair these breaks and consider what you can do moving forward to make those relationships an integral part of this work.

WEEK 5

Hod

HOD IS OFTEN TRANSLATED as "glory" or "splendor." And one of my favorite lines in the liturgy is the angelic chant: "Holy, holy, holy, YHVH Tzevaot, the whole world is filled with His Glory."[1] This appeals to the panentheist in me, and I know that when I have been at my most balanced, I have been able to see glimpses of that Glory. Rabbi Min Kantrowitz offers an interpretation of Hod that suggests that seeing the Splendor of all Creation comes from an awareness that the Diversity of all Creation is holy.[2] I like this a lot; it feels right that Nature's Diversity is one of Hod's essential qualities. One clue of how to reach the state of seeing the Splendor in all Creation is in another quality ascribed to Hod, Surrender. A healthy ego is essential to live in the world. But a healthy ego knows when to get out of the way, and Hod helps activate that.

The word Hod has its root in the Hebrew *hoda'ah,* which means "gratitude." Developing an attitude of Gratitude increases one's Humility with the awareness that one is indebted to others. This is a powerful antidote to the dominating ego of Netzach. For just as Chesed and Gevurah are opposite ends of a spectrum that find balance, so too Netzach and Hod find balance together.

I've also mentioned that Hod is connected to prophecy. And certainly, to receive information from beyond one's limited ego and to communicate it clearly means Surrendering to the Divine. This week, we'll explore all these qualities and more.

Day 29: Chesed of Hod

Overflowing with Gratitude

> Today is the twenty-ninth day of the Omer,
> which is four weeks and one day of the Omer.

The psalmist wrote, "My cup runneth over."[3] Chesed is an overflowing of Loving-kindness. And Hod is Gratitude for the Flow of blessings we receive daily, along with an appreciation of the Splendor and Glory of Creation of which we are a small part.

Expressing one's Gratitude to another is the practice of Chesed of Hod, since the nature of letting another know how much you appreciate that person communicates your Love and demonstrates your Humility. So today would be a good day to write a Gratitude list, noting all the people, events, and blessings that you are grateful for and expressing that Gratitude personally where you can.

Even as we experience economic challenges, health issues, legal troubles, exile from communities of origin, and so much else, despite all these things, Divine love fills us in every moment whether we're aware of it or not. And making that awareness conscious starts with Gratitude. For indeed, our cup is overflowing.

Day 29: Chesed of Hod in Atzilut

The Four and Eight of Wands

 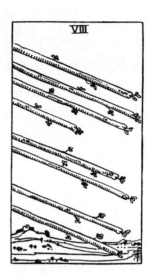

_____ *within* _____

In the Four of Wands, the structure is open, welcoming. It's a statement of faith in, and a celebration of, Divine Abundance. The two cards paired together have a message for us: as you prepare for the Divine Marriage within, stay open so that Divine Glory and greater blessings will rain down on you.

What about marriage between two people? Is there a message here for relationship? Yes! Not that you wouldn't already know that Love, openness, and Humility are essential for a marriage to be successful. With the Eight of Wands, this pairing suggests that marriage can be all the more passionate when these qualities are shared by both spouses.

Too often, when people think of someone who demonstrates Humility, the image is of someone who is quiet and withdrawn. But these cards show us that in Chesed of Hod, Humility can be an exuberant celebration of blessings. People who can feel Chesed of Hod in Atzilut find joy in the blessings that rain on others, and they're as Grateful for those blessings as they are for those that come to themselves. They feel Love arising naturally for the Splendor and Diversity of all Creation. Their sympathetic joy also activates the Gratitude and Humility of others.

Another way of looking at these cards? Because Hod is also associated with systematic thinking and the intellect, this could be seen as the Love in learning or the joy that arises from a "eureka" moment of discovery. (That's not Eureka O'Hara, the drag queen, though her performances have given me many moments of joy.)

Is there any possible negative reading of this pair? If you're someone whose Hod leads you to negate yourself or if you're someone who can get caught up in the ideas or actions of a strong-willed person, this could be a suggestion that you need to apply some of the boundaries of Gevurah to your expression of Hod. And we'll deal with that tomorrow.

For today may our hearts "overFlow" with acceptance and Gratitude for what is in this very moment and in every moment.

Day 29: Chesed of Hod in B'riah

The Four and Eight of Cups

_____ *within* _____

Just yesterday in Cups, I mentioned a phrase that's also the title of a Renaissance play: *Enough Is as Good as a Feast*. It comes to mind again today as I'm looking at both the Four and Eight of Cups.

In the Four of Cups, we could consider that the seated man has enough with three cups and that the fourth being offered to him is just too much. I've seen this with many people I know in the business world; they work to reach a certain level of success, and once they reach it, they're satisfied. But the world of business doesn't want you to stay satisfied; you have to keep moving up. And that comes with more responsibility that you might not want. It also comes with more rewards, which you may not find are meaningful anymore.

In a recent issue of the journal *Nature Human Behavior,* researchers reported on a survey of more than 1.7 million people. They determined that most people experience optimal well-being and are at their happiest when they earn about $75,000 a year. Of course, that number would change depending on where you live. But the really interesting thing is that they found that it's possible to make too much money, that after a certain point, emotional well-being and life satisfaction declined. They believe the reason for this decline is that after a certain point, material pursuits become unfulfilling.[4] This doesn't stop people from pursuing wealth way beyond what they can possibly use or even spend. And you don't have to be wealthy to be a compulsive shopper, which can also be a symptom of an imbalance in the Sephira of Yesod.

People stay in unfulfilling jobs, earning more than they need to be happy, because they are convinced they must keep on this path. This is the real rat race. And as the comedian Lily Tomlin noted, "Even if you win the rat race—you're still a rat."[5] We could see the young man in the Four of Cups and the man turning away in the Eight of Cups as the same person at different stages in the realization of this dynamic.

The younger man in the four card is at the choice point: he has enough, yet something is being held out before him as a mysterious reward at the next level. Will he reach for it and join the rat race, or will he ignore it and remain content with what is before him? The answer, if we say the man in the Eight of Cups is the same man, now older, is that he reached out and took the cup, setting him on a course that led him to having twice as many cups as before, yet left him still unsatisfied, so that he has come to another choice point. This time, he recognizes the mistake he made when he turned his back on a simpler yet deeper happiness. And he knows it is never too late to return, to do t'shuvah. So he turns his back on the material pursuits to find his way back to the One.

Now, don't get me wrong: in Judaism, the material is holy. Everything is suffused with the Divine. But Kabbalah and the Tree of Life are all about finding the right balance of all these energies that are flowing freely within you. If the Flow is constricted, as with the man in the Four of Pentacles, whom we'll come to again in a few pages, things are out of balance. If the Flow is overwhelming, as it may be for the man in the Four of Cups, things are out of balance. This is the imbalance that the man in the Eight of Cups is walking away from.

One of the imbalances in Hod is an extreme expression of Humility, leading to feelings of worthlessness. If this is the case, being the recipient of an unrelenting Divine Flow is very disturbing. If you feel you don't deserve these gifts from the universe, at some point you're going to flee. And that is also a possible dynamic at work in these two cards.

To get a little more materialistic, absolutely earthy in fact, you can also see the Four of Cups as a young man being tempted into a life of emotional dissolution of some sort and then see him escaping from it sometime later in the other card.

But any way you look at it, Chesed of Hod in B'riah suggests reevaluating your understanding of whether you deserve to receive the Divine Flow (hint: you do) and how much you really need to be happy.

Day 29: Chesed of Hod in Yetzirah

The Four and Eight of Swords

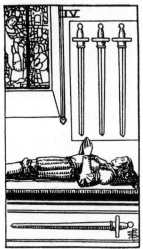

_____ *within* _____

The Sephira of Hod is connected to reason and the faculties of the intellect. And the suit of Swords has in its constellation of meanings "discriminating intelligence." Some tarot interpreters read the Eight of Swords as the imbalance that comes from overreliance on reason, turning away from intuition. In this pairing, though, I see it the other way entirely because both the knight on the bier and the woman bound and blindfolded can't see.

The knight has closed his eyes. And he has retreated from the world. The woman can't see the swords or anything around her. Why is she blindfolded? I see both figures not as being overreliant on reason, but as having turned away from the intellect and reason. If the woman were using her reason, she would know that the fabric that's binding her is loose enough for her to free herself and walk away. But having abandoned deduction, she is held prisoner by an illusion. We don't know what the bound woman is seeing in her mind's eye, but she must believe she is surrounded by danger to stand there motionless without trying to escape.

Similarly, we don't know what the knight is seeing (assuming he is meditating), but meditation brings up shadows from the dark recesses of consciousness. The whole situation reminds me of an etching by Francisco Goya, *The Sleep of Reason Produces Monsters.*

Goya believed that for society to advance, ignorance must be eradicated. While his understanding of the psyche preceded Sigmund Freud's by a century, he realized that in a mind without reason fantasies run wild—what was referred to in the great science fiction film *Forbidden Planet* as "monsters from the id." While he believed that reason needed to be relaxed to let the imagination loose, he also believed that reason is necessary to tame the imagination and give it the direction to make great art.

Why this image for Chesed of Hod? Think about someone you know who has sharp analytical faculties. Or perhaps this describes you. What happens when those critical insights are shared with others? They're often not welcomed, especially if they're coming from a woman in a situation where the men control things. This can lead to a retreat from engagement and hiding of these skills. It might look like

The Sleep of Reason Produces Monsters *by Francisco Goya*

Humility to hold back from sharing these insights, but the reality in a situation where these insights aren't welcome is that keeping them to yourself can be seen as self-care or self-preservation. One can be aware of one's insights and simply withhold them, which can leave a person feeling isolated. This is a retreat that leaves one alone. Or one can deny one's own gifts of intellect to oneself, thus transporting one's own intellectual faculties into the shadows—where the sleep of reason produces monsters. Both are traps to be avoided.

As always, there are other ways to see this pair. And there's one other I want to look at. Let's consider that both these cards illustrate different experiences of meditation metaphorically. And that in meditating, one uses the faculty of discriminating intelligence to see through to the heart of things—to the Glory of all creation. The Baal Shem Tov taught that the Divine Glory is present from the lowest levels to the highest in all worlds.[6] This means that in meditation, when you restrain the ego and watch all the mental phenomena that arise with both Humility and sharp analysis, the Divine Glory embraces all worlds and reveals Itself to you in all things. All things, good and evil. But what do you do when the *yetzer hara*, "the inclination to do evil," arises during meditation (or at any time)? The Baal Shem Tov taught that when such thoughts come, they are the residue of the Shevirat he-Keilim, the broken shards left over from the shattering of the first emanation of the Sephirot. Within these shards, within these urges, is the original spark of the Divine that must be liberated by our Tikkun. These shards veil the Glory within.* One must search within such urges to find their origin in the Divine Glory, the spark of holiness at the root of these urges. This is where the discerning intelligence of Hod is essential. One must see through to the Glory and raise the energy of that thought in the service of the Divine in a kind of conscious sublimation. This isn't easy, but it's one of the teachings of Chesed of Hod, and the Four and Eight of Swords illustrate the challenges of this practice.

---

*In the myth of creation in Lurianic Kabbalah, the first time the Sephirot were emanated they were not in proper relationship. Unable to hold the Divine energy, they shattered, and the resulting shards are spread across all creation.

Day 29: Chesed of Hod in Assiyah

The Four and Eight of Pentacles

_____ *within* _____

In his classic book *Flow: The Psychology of Optimal Experience,* Mihaly Csikszentmihalyi said that learning to control your inner experience enables you to determine the quality of your life.[7] When we look at the pairing of the Four and Eight of Pentacles, what is the inner experience being revealed in these images?

With the Four of Pentacles, Chesed, which is Flow and Love, we have someone who seems to be withholding and stopping up the Flow. If this is the inner experience of the man at work in the Eight of Pentacles, it could be because he is feeling resentment as he works. Rather than letting his creative energies pour into his work, he is holding back for some reason. Rather than feeling Humility in the working of his craft, he feels demeaned by the repetitious manual labor, so that he feels resentful on the job. This is the opposite of Surrender, and the result is far from happy.

We live in a society where most manual labor and service jobs have low social status. It used to be that working with one's hands was a respectable way to make a living, and while physically demanding, it could be fulfilling psychologically, emotionally, and spiritually. Even the physical demands could be satisfying when approached with the right attitude. However, the discipline that craftsmanship requires seems unnecessary in a world where 3-D printers can spit out in minutes objects that it once took workers hours or days to create. This has only accelerated the trend of disrespect for manual labor. In fact, as technological advances replace many of the jobs done by manual labor, the people who do these jobs feel greater insecurity and lower self-esteem.

As someone who has worked at jobs that called for repetitious activity, I get it. When I was in college, I took part-time jobs that I knew were just way stations for me. While the other people on these jobs would be there until they left the workforce, I was just passing through on my way to a "white-collar" job. I resented having to work at such jobs, and I looked down on my coworkers. I'm not proud to say that, but I was young and full of myself.

If I had approached these jobs with Gratitude for the opportunity to work and earn money and if I'd come to the work with a sense of play, my work relationships and experience would have been completely different. But like the man in the Four of Pentacles, I was stuck and was holding on to resentment that I was better than the jobs and the people I worked with. Rather than Humility, I was in the grip of grandiosity. (Note that the man in the Four of Pentacles is wearing a crown.)

This attitude affected my work, of course, so that it really wasn't very good. It's a miracle that I wasn't fired from any of these jobs. I had yet to learn how to control my inner experience, so I wasn't happy. And even though I learned this lesson, it's not as though I completely got it and worked with this understanding for the rest of my career.

Just a few years ago, I had to take a job that paid less than I had been earning before, and I had to do the kinds of tasks lower down on the business totem pole that people call "grunt work." I could have fallen back into an old unhealthy pattern, with feelings of low self-esteem and resentment. However, the words of a Jewish prayer for peace came into my mind: "We have come into being to praise, to labor, and to love."

Three deceptively simple tasks. Two of them, love and praise, are at the heart of Chesed of Hod. For to praise another is to show Humility about oneself as well as Love and Generosity of spirit, all of which the man in the Four of Pentacles is unable to express. But when you can do this, you open to Divine Flow, so that your labor, your work, becomes an expression of your praise and Love. When I've approached my work from this mind-set, with Humility, Generosity, and Love, it has unleashed great energy that transformed both my work and my experience of my workplace.

True and healthy Humility allows one to be more Loving and open, considerate and Kind. Unhealthy Humility is an expression of low self-esteem and is constraining, leading to resentment. Today is a day to consider how these dynamics play out in your experience of the world of work.

Questions for reflection and contemplation: Day 29

1. (Wands) What is your experience of Humility? Can you feel the Love that is within it? When have you experienced it as self-negating and constraining? When have you experienced it as a feeling of expansion that takes you beyond yourself? What was the difference between these two situations?

2. (Cups) Review the blessings in your life. Do you feel deserving of them? Do you express Gratitude for the Flow of Divine blessing in prayer? Today is a good day to do a mental inventory of your possessions: What are the things you don't need that you've been holding on to? Find a local charity, and give those things away.

3. (Swords) When do you hide your intellect from others? Why? How does that make you feel? When an "evil urge" arises in your meditation (or just in the course of the day), use your discernment to peel away the specific temptation itself to uncover the hidden good at the root. Journal about this experience.

4. (Pentacles) How have your jobs affected your self-esteem throughout your life? How have they affected your ability to express Love? How has your judgment about different kinds of jobs colored your experience of people who do those jobs? As you go through your day, try to see everyone engaged in any kind of work as being in service to the Divine—including yourself.

Day 30: Gevurah of Hod

Living in Awe of the Splendor of Creation

Today is the thirtieth day of the Omer, which is four weeks and two days of the Omer.

I have been blessed to spend many summer days on Fire Island, a long, thin barrier of land off the southern coast of Long Island. And when I was there, I made it my practice, as best as I was able, to wake up in time to see the sun rise over the Atlantic Ocean and, later in the day, to watch the sun set over the Long Island Sound. I've managed to arrange vacations so that I could witness the Perseid meteor showers in August. I've seen them over Fire Island, where we're far enough from the lights of Manhattan so that the Milky Way is dimly visible. And I've seen them while staying in a clearing near a stand of redwoods in Philo, California.

Looking up to the surprise of a murmuration of birds. Seeing dolphins at play. Experiencing the grandeur of elephants in a herd. These are all examples of the Splendor of Creation. Splendor is one of the many faces of Hod, and it is manifested in the infinite variety of nature. And in the face of such Splendor, who does not feel Awe, a face of Gevurah, and Humility, another face of Hod?

In fact, the ability to feel Awe is in a direct relationship to one's ability to feel Humility. When one has an encounter with the truly Awesome, Humility and Surrender are natural responses. So is terror, so I would be remiss if I didn't remind you that another face of Gevurah is Fear. And that "Awe full" and "awful" are not so far apart.

I haven't forgotten that Gevurah is also Judgment. But when we are in a place of true Humility, we do not Judge. Though we may be able to use our Discernment to better understand the things we stand in Awe of. Just before he died, the great scientist Carl Sagan reflected on this when he wrote about science as a source of spirituality in his book, *The Demon-Haunted World: Science as a Candle in the Dark,* suggesting that awe and reverence are the natural responses of a scientist studying Nature and that both humility and elation arise in the heart of the scientist studying the immensity and intricacy of the universe.[8]

In the Jewish liturgical calendar, the days from Rosh Hashanah to

Yom Kippur are known as the Days of Awe. But when I think about the experience available to us any day, I believe that if we are awake to it, all our days are days of Awe. And today in particular is a good day to go out into Nature and explore with a sense of reverence, Awe, and Humility.

Day 30: Gevurah of Hod in Atzilut
The Five and Eight of Wands

 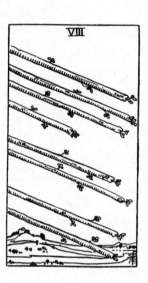

_____ *within* _____

Humility has its limits. Being Humble does not mean being a door-mat. The Gevurah that is within Hod is there to make sure you don't let other people take advantage of you. Just because one of the faces of Hod is Surrender doesn't mean you should Surrender to people who attack you. No one in the Five of Wands has dropped his staff on the ground so that he can be beaten by the others. They are all defending themselves vigorously.

The Surrender that we speak of in Hod is to the higher will of the Divine. Or as we saw on Day 12, which was Hod of Gevurah, Surrender to Discipline. But in Gevurah of Hod, we are being asked to use our Discernment even as we Surrender to Discipline or before we give our Devotion to a spiritual path. This is in direct opposition to the words of the early Christian theologian Tertullian, who wrote, "It is to be believed because it is absurd."⁹ But it is in complete harmony with the teaching of the Buddha.

In the Kalama Sutta, the story is told of how the Buddha was approached by the people of a town and questioned about what to believe.¹⁰ Between all the gurus and ascetics, the traditions and religions they were exposed to, they found it difficult to decide where to place their faith. His answer to them might be shocking to anyone who grew up in a tradition that demanded blind faith. He told the townspeople not to believe something because their teacher said it, or because it has been passed down for generations, or because it's in Scripture, or because they like the idea, or because it matches their bias, or because they trust the speaker, or because it's "common sense," or because it seems logical. He taught them that you should only believe things that you can test against your own experience of what produces good results.

When hardly a day goes by without some spiritual teacher or religious institution being exposed for abusing the trust of their followers, this continues to be sound advice. Use your Discernment before giving your Devotion. And the Devotion should be to the teaching, since after all, teachers are only human and almost certain to disappoint in one way or another.

Day 30: Gevurah of Hod in B'riah

The Five and Eight of Cups

———————————— *within* ————————————

Looking at the Five and Eight of Cups, I see a spiritual crisis that is the origin for a spiritual search. Just what do I mean by "spiritual crisis"? It has been defined as deep grieving or loss that leads to questioning the meaning of life or feeling that life is meaningless and that results in a dramatic change in how life is seen.[11] Such a crisis is often set off by a sudden and serious illness or the loss of a close relationship, often through death. You can see this loss symbolized in the overturned cups in the Five of Cups. And the response after the figure in black has grieved is for the figure to then turn away in the Eight of Cups to climb the mountain in the distance.

Experiencing the Limitation and Severity of Gevurah can be profoundly disturbing. Faced with the Limits of mortality, who wouldn't, at the very least, feel Humbled? This is the origin story of the Buddha, who, as legend has it, was brought up a prince and cloistered by his father so that he would not see any suffering in the world. But in just one day, the young prince came upon a corpse, a man who was very sick, and another who was elderly. He realized that all these things he was protected from seeing could not be kept from happening to him. And it led him to leave the palace in search for a way out of suffering. It's a good story, though whether it really happened, who can say? But then, as the storyteller in me likes to say, even if it didn't happen, that doesn't mean it isn't true.

The truth is that each of us has some sort of encounter that shocks us out of our dream state and sends us out to search for deeper truth. I have had several such shocks. I've lived through the worst of the HIV crisis, losing almost every boyfriend and many good friends that I met before 1980. I had my heart ripped out of my chest and sliced into pieces when a man I loved dearly fell into the darkness of mental illness and killed himself.

It was the loss of people I loved to the HIV crisis that sent me down a path that led me to discover Vipassana meditation. But like the vast majority of humanity, I tend to fall back into the waking dream state. So no doubt I will have a few more shocks ahead in my life. Rumi recognized this tendency when he enjoined people not to fall back into sleep.[12]

I hope that your wake-up calls will be gentle. And that you don't go back to sleep.

Day 30: Gevurah of Hod in Yetzirah

The Five and Eight of Swords

_____ *within* _____

In the Five and Eight of Wands, we saw that the quality of Humility does not require you to be a doormat. In the Five and Eight of Swords, we see the dangers of being a doormat.

In the Five of Swords, we see someone who exhibits many of the traits of negative Gevurah: a person who is willing to violate Boundaries, one for whom Law or Justice is meaningless and who does not feel Constrained by human decency. And the result for anyone who allows this kind of behavior to continue without protest or response is on view in the Eight of Swords; by closing their eyes and remaining silent in the face of Injustice and Boundary violations out of a negative expression of Humility, people put themselves in real danger. If you really believe that we are all one, then injustice against one is injustice against all.

How can you recognize this negative expression of Humility? You'll hear someone utter the seemingly reasonable phrase, "What can I do? I'm just one person." You may even find yourself falling prey to this mind-set. For all my activism, I sometimes do. It's easy to feel this way, to deny one's own power, because to take action takes us out of our comfort zone. And in fact, it can put us in danger. But the danger of not acting is greater.

The anonymous protester who stood in front of a convoy of tanks during the Tiananmen Square protests in Beijing, China, in 1989 did not ultimately stop the slaughter of hundreds and perhaps thousands of protesters. But he did stop that line of tanks, and we don't know how many lives were saved because of that action. We also don't know what went through the mind of the soldier driving that tank who decided to stop; how did it affect the rest of his life?

Oskar Schindler was a German industrialist during World War II who started out a devoted member of the Nazi Party. But he ended up spending his entire fortune bribing Nazi officials to save the lives of more than a thousand Jews. His efforts could have been uncovered at any time, and he would have been summarily executed. He was not a doormat.

These are extreme examples, for sure. But these extreme situations developed only because thousands of people closed their eyes and said, "But I'm only one person" in earlier situations that led up to them.

This dynamic can also be internal. We all have our inner Boundary violator. And worse, we can suffer the psychic damage of negative Hod. Like the negative thought that tells us that our actions won't make a difference for good, here negative Hod manifests as the thought that it doesn't really matter if we do something bad. We've all known someone who is a victim of that mind-set (and who thus makes other people victims of their actions). I've fallen prey to this mind-set myself. This is why I have found the twelve-step practice of making amends an essential discipline. And the sensitivity of those who developed this process was such that they recognized that one's behavior might have been so egregious that trying to make amends directly would only make things worse. And of course, there are those we've wronged who are no longer alive. So for those situations, the Divinely inspired recovering addicts who developed the twelve steps created indirect ways to make amends. I am forever grateful to them.

Day 30: Gevurah of Hod in Assiyah

The Five and Eight of Pentacles

_____ *within* _____

What happens in Hod when the Power of Gevurah is turned against you? When you have internalized rejection and negative Judgment? Some people put their heads down, deny who they are, and put all their energy into their work, hoping that doing excellent work will ameliorate this Judgment. They become overachievers who nevertheless have low self-esteem. This is the story told in the book written by Andrew Tobias, under the pseudonym John Reid, titled *The Best Little Boy in the World*.

This novelized memoir of growing up gay revealed a dynamic many gay men recognize and many other people, whether in a disparaged minority group or not, can also identify with. It's even come to be called Best Little Boy in the World syndrome. It's when a person will try to deflect attention from something they are ashamed of, but is an important part of who that person is, by excelling in socially accepted measures of success. For closeted gay men, this can mean becoming the school valedictorian, winning an Olympic medal, working for the most elite companies: it can manifest in all these ways and more. By overcompensating in these areas, people who suffer from this dynamic conceal their low self-esteem by erecting a facade of self-worth that only creates a deeper sense of alienation from others and the self. You can recognize this psychological principle at work in the pairing of these two cards.

Of course, one doesn't have to excel to fall prey to this mind-set. Because excelling means standing out, and that too can be dangerous. So you can see negative Hod manifesting in people who don't want to be seen—the people who keep their heads down at work, plugging away in life, trying not to make any waves so that no one realizes that fundamentally there is something about them that is unacceptable (or at least so they believe). So many people live quiet lives of suffering in just this way, and it breaks my heart.

Questions for reflection and contemplation: Day 30

1. (Wands) Have you ever felt failed or betrayed by the actions of a spiritual teacher? How did this affect your relationship with the teachings? Are the teachings still valid for you? How much do you investigate a teacher before you decide to follow their path?

2. (Cups) What have been the spiritual crises in your life that sent you on the path of a spiritual search? How have the practices or teachings that you found supported you in times of crisis?

3. (Swords) Thinking back to situations in your life when you could have stood up for what is right but did not speak out or take action: how do you feel about it now? What could you have done differently? Is there anything you can do now? Think back to any times you may have rationalized boundary-violating behavior on your own part. What did you tell yourself? What amends are due to others and yourself? How and when will you make those amends?

4. (Pentacles) Reflect on whether there are any ways that you use something you excel at to deflect attention from something about yourself that you're ashamed of. What can you do to more fully accept yourself? Do you know anyone who seems to employ such a similar deflection strategy? What can you do to show that person that they're fully accepted without triggering a shame reaction?

Day 31: Tiferet of Hod

An Open Heart Is Always Full, but Never Full of Itself

> Today is the thirty-first day of the Omer, which is four weeks and three days of the Omer.

We have come to Compassion in Humility. An open Heart knows how to put Compassion into action in a way that is empty of self. (And not devoid of self at the same time, since this is a non-dual path.)

The Sefat Emet taught that the goal of Counting the Omer was to purify oneself of all desires so that in freeing ourselves from desire, our spiritual Egypt, we become truly free—Surrendering our will to the Divine Will.*

In this understanding, "empty of self" means simply (or not so simply) that the ego has stepped out of the way, allowing us to be fully free for our actions to be in alignment with Divine Will. As we purify ourselves through this practice of Counting the Omer, if we are doing it well, this can be what will happen as the heavens open on Erev Shavuot: we receive our Divine revelation and awaken to the Divine in every moment.

Of course, like any flower, that awareness will open and close and open and close. We will wake and go back to sleep (regardless of Rumi's entreaties otherwise). And that is simply the natural order of things. Unless you're the Buddha. Or the Sefat Emet.

Speaking of the natural order of things, you can also read Tiferet of Hod as Harmony within Splendor—the Dynamic Balance that exists throughout all Creation and the web of life. It's the dance of the interdependence of Nature at every level of existence. And this is a delicate Balance that humanity has been busy overturning at our own peril. We are witnessing the "Sixth Great Extinction," which

---

*Rabbi Yehudah Aryeh Leib Alter came to be called the Sefat Emet, after the name of his most famous work, which in English can be translated as the Language of Truth, or more colloquially, Straight Talk.

is destroying the food chain in our oceans, our forests, and our atmosphere.[13]

Back when I looked askance at Scripture, I read the following passage from Leviticus as transactional when YHVH says:

> If you faithfully observe my commandments and follow them, and
> I will send rain in their season so that your crops thrive and your
> trees grow heavy with fruit. Your harvest of grain and grapes will be
> of such abundance, it will last beyond the next time for sowing. You
> will have enough food to be full satisfied, and you will be safe and
> secure in the land.[14]

This is followed by a long warning of what will happen if we disobey these commands, and it reads, among other things, like a catalog of ecological disaster. So today I have come to see passages like this as a warning to respect all of Creation and live in Harmony with the Splendor of Creation, which is really one of the main teachings of Scripture. May we heed these warnings before it is too late.

Day 31: Tiferet of Hod in Atzilut

The Six and Eight of Wands

 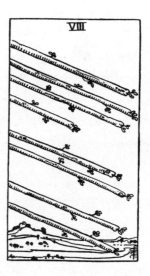

_____ *within* _____

In the American mythos of the Old West or even in the Grimms' folktales, if there's a man on a white horse, you know he's a hero. And here in the Six of Wands, we have a hero on a white horse—a leader, crowned with laurel. As I've noted in many of the other appearances of this card during the count, it takes Balance to ride a horse. It also takes Balance to be a successful leader. Today the Balance we'll be looking at is of Hod—Humility, to start.

When someone in a position of leadership has a healthy relationship with Humility, he or she is more approachable. It enables others to be more fully who they are, and it allows for others to share their opinions without fear of judgment. In fact, healthy Humility is welcoming; it actively expresses appreciation to others for sharing their opinions and ideas. It provides the ground for empathy. But when that Humility is expressed as a kind of withdrawn shyness, it can communicate disrespect for others. The leader is seen as cold and distant. And this can make a leader seem arrogant at the worst and defensive at the least. This is true whether one is in a leadership position or not, since all of us take the lead in certain situations in our lives.

Someone who went on to become one of my closest friends was shy in just this way when we first began to get to know each other. His reserve came across to me as a snooty arrogance, and I wrote off any thought that this relationship would develop in any direction. It took the sharper observation of another friend to suggest otherwise. And my friend was correct in his observation. I had misread the first man's demeanor and might have lost the pleasure of his company for the last thirty years had I not adjusted my understanding and responded in a way that enabled him to come forward.

At the other end of the spectrum is someone who is overly Humble. This can seem disingenuous, making the person seem like a "Uriah Heep" character whose expression of Humility feels both cloying and insincere. In a leader, it creates insecurity among the followers, since it suggests that the leader is either naïve or unqualified for the position. And if it is not disingenuous, this is the Humility of someone who has been beaten down.

This pairing, though, suggests a positive relationship with Balanced Humility and Gratitude. The Eight of Wands shows that a well-Balanced Humility can be the source of great strength of character. May we all enjoy such Balance in our relationships, and may our leaders exemplify the best of this Balance.

Day 31: Tiferet of Hod in B'riah

The Six and Eight of Cups

_____ *within* _____

One of the faces of Hod is Gratitude, and in today's pairing in the suit of Cups, it seems that this *middot,* this virtue, is more on display in the Six of Cups, where the illustration can be read as a child receiving a gift. But the Eight of Cups is the card that corresponds to Hod. However, in that card, someone who seems to be the recipient of many gifts is turning away from them. So what's going on here? Since I'm Jewish, let me do the traditional thing and answer this question with another question: Have you ever watched a very young child at play? There's no need for video games or screens, or even objects that are labeled as "toys." Children can find the wonderful and miraculous almost everywhere. And they can make anything into something to play with. At least until they (we) grow up.

We go from easily amused to easily bored. We need ever more things to distract us. And we lose our sense of Gratitude and wonder. That's the story I see in the pairing of these cards. The seeker in the Eight of Cups is leaving those gifts behind in search of a lost sense of the appreciation of Glory or, as the daily liturgy puts it, the "miracles which are with us daily."

In modern Hebrew, the word for "miracle" is *nes,* which in biblical Hebrew, meant "a banner or flag that points the way." Most of the time when the word *miracle* is used, it refers to something big and powerful that stops us, gets our attention: it's something that seems to defy the laws of nature, like a burning bush, for example. But the prayer in the liturgy is about (re-) awakening us to everyday miracles. And this is one of the messages of today's pairing in the suit of Cups—to reawaken our sense of Gratitude for these everyday miracles. Because they are the garments of the Divine, they are signs pointing to the transcendence that is always available in the immanent. Rabbi Nat Ezray suggests that we make the awareness of nes a regular spiritual practice. And that "at a time when we might be so consumed with the daily news that we lose perspective," we can restore balance to our lives by paying attention and by living in Gratitude for the daily nes.[15]

You don't necessarily have to go off on a retreat and leave the daily world behind like the figure in the Eight of Cups to regain an appreciation for the daily miraculous. Simply sit quietly and bring your attention to the beauty that surrounds you. It can be anything—even something that is not conventionally beautiful. Wait quietly: the very nature of the Divine is to reveal itself in all its Divine ecstasy.

Day 31: Tiferet of Hod in Yetzirah

The Six and Eight of Swords

_____ *within* _____

These two cards together make for a somber scene. The Six of Swords is one of the seven cards examined in this book where the faces of the figures in the cards are not visible. (There are several other cards with some faces visible and others turned away.) And in the Eight of Swords, while we can see some of the face of the bound woman, her eyes are covered so that she can't see others. In the version of the deck I'm using, the background landscape in both cards is also grey. A hushed silence seems to pervade both scenes.

If any two cards show the psychological scars of oppression, these two would be at the top of my list. Yes, the Six of Swords has the "Compassionate ferryman" taking the two figures away from danger. But they carry their psychic wounds with them, weighing down the boat. And I don't think of this vehicle so much as a boat, but rather that it represents the many escape routes of peoples throughout history. The Underground Railroad. The Kindertransport.

I lived for a short time in North Carolina in the mid seventies. Before moving there for graduate school, I had dated several African-American men in New York City. Though I knew that they faced challenges I did not, I was young and naïve: I did not notice them holding back anything of who they were when we were together. I would sometimes witness the daily indignities they dealt with; for instance, whenever we wanted to take a taxi, I would stand in the street to hail it, and my friend would stand back, his body language indicating we were not in any way connected. Only after the cab had stopped and I had opened the door would he step forward and move to join me. If he had been the one to try to hail a cab, not a one would have stopped. I knew how real estate agents and developers conspired to keep African-Americans in certain neighborhoods that bankers redlined for mortgages. But in North Carolina, it was another world entirely. There was no one in the gay group on campus who wasn't white. (Not to mention that it was also almost 100 percent Christian.) The local gay bar was segregated: not that African-Americans weren't allowed in, it's just that there was no mingling or socializing between the groups. The only black people I met and spoke with were the people I worked with.

When I first arrived on campus, to help pay for my expenses, since my student loans didn't cover everything, I got a job at the college cafeteria. Almost all the employees were black. The management was completely white. And for the first time, I saw the dynamic of cultural and linguistic "code-shifting" between the races.

When management was around in the kitchen or when the employees had to interact with students as they moved along the food line, I realized the language of these employees of color was subservient in a way that went beyond providing service. They kept their eyes down and did not meet the gaze of those they were serving. They kept their voices down and spoke softly, with deference. This was also how they treated me for the most part. Except because I worked with them in the kitchen, I also saw how they interacted with each other when management wasn't on top of us. That was when I began to get a sense of who each one of these people was as a real individual. They code-shifted out of the language of the oppressed to the language of equals in a shared culture. It was a revelation. And I knew that this was a world and a culture

I had never seen. These people were not at the march on Washington in 1963. These were oppressed people trying to live their everyday lives without bringing down further violence into their community.

Someone with no social awareness might mistake their deferential attitude as Humility. In a way you could say it was: it's the enforced Humility that's on display in the Eight of Swords. It's the inauthentic Humility of people robbed of their dignity.

I experienced this once again when I visited India. While there, I met a man who was eager to befriend me. He was also extremely deferential, and at one point, he expressly and directly said that he believed India would be a better place if the British still ran it. The British had been gone for more than forty years, but the psychic scars of colonialism still affected people in many more ways than this. I bring up this particular example because it's relevant to the pattern I see in these two cards.

Today this enforced, false Humility is under attack like never before. While it was extreme enough for me to see in North Carolina, that doesn't mean it didn't exist in New York back then—or now. Except that today more and more people of color are owning their dignity and demanding equal respect. And to many white people, that feels like a threat.

One of the meanings of the Eight of Swords is being blinded by one's preconceptions and biases, so that today this card manages to be relevant on both sides of the issue at hand: enforced, false Humility and blindness to internalized racism. Not merely blindness, because the result imprisons and impoverishes us all.

May we all be free of our biases, conscious and unconscious. May we all live in dignity and with a Balanced Humility that allows room for others to live in dignity as well.

Day 31: Tiferet of Hod in Assiyah

The Six and Eight of Pentacles

_____ *within* _____

Compassion in Humility calls for an outward movement of the soul. So while Humility is a pulling in to allow space for others, Compassion in Humility expresses itself in an outward flow of feeling of empathy for others. There is no room for judgment here. There is no room for pride.

Now, you might say, wait a minute, the merchant in the Six of Pentacles is clearly making a judgment; after all, he does hold a set of scales. But this is not negative judgment; he is making a determination of what is the appropriate response. This is the Balance of Compassion that is Tiferet.

In the Eight of Pentacles, we have our workman, who knows that he is working not only for himself and not only for his family but also for others whom he will share with. He knows there is a spiritual component to the physical work that he does. Just as much as his craft gives him the satisfaction of work well done, the Compassionate sharing of the rewards of his craft also opens his Heart to Beauty and Truth. His Humility means there is space in his Heart for Compassion. And by expressing his Compassionate Open Heart, he engenders greater Humility.

Truly, the virtues on display in these two cards give each other strength. And as you continue this practice of Counting the Omer, you have a chance every day to practice and enhance these virtues. Today you have the opportunity to examine whether your Humility causes you to pull in so much that you seem or actually become antisocial. Don't make the mistake of using Humility to be self-contained. For while Humility does require you to pull in to make space, it's not about withdrawing. Compassion helps Balance this motion. And the focus of the figures in the two cards shows this. Not only is Tiferet itself about Balance, but in relationship with Hod, they both form a Balance of inward and outward movement. So by practicing Compassion, you will activate your Humility. And by practicing Humility, you will activate your Compassion. And that's part of the Beauty of the Tree: touch one of the Sephirot and you touch them all.

Questions for reflection and contemplation: Day 31

1. (Wands) Think of someone you know in a leadership position who exemplifies Balance in Humility: it can be a world leader or a teacher you had when you were growing up. What is it about that person that demonstrates this quality in action? How might you bring more of that quality into your life?

2. (Cups) As you go through your day today, try to be aware of all the little miracles and say an inner prayer of Gratitude and Appreciation for each one. Such a prayer doesn't need to be any more complicated than "thank You for this blessing." At the end of the day, review your experience during the day: Is there anything you missed expressing Appreciation for? If so, express that Appreciation in a prayer just before bed. Notice any times when you felt resistance to this practice or when you felt there was something that did not warrant Gratitude or Appreciation. See if you can peel away the outer shell to find something within that calls forth your Appreciation.

3. (Swords) See if you can think of examples in your life when you have been witness to the Humility of the oppressed. You might not have

recognized it as such at the time, but looking back with new awareness, you might discover times when you saw people express a mask of deference to others that was more an expression of a power imbalance than true Humility. When have you worn this mask yourself? How did it make you feel?

4. (Pentacles) Find an action you can take that will express the Compassion in Humility, something that will work to activate both Sephirot within you, and take that action within the week.

Day 32: Netzach of Hod

Finding Endurance in Humility
Is Finding Victory in Humility

> Today is the thirty-second day of the Omer,
> which is four weeks and four days of the Omer.

When I think of Endurance in Humility, I think of the steel within the nonviolent resistance of Mahatma Gandhi, who equated the ability to stand up in civil disobedience with the capacity to hold unlimited suffering.[16] It was Gandhi's teachings that inspired Rev. Martin Luther King Jr. to train people in the practice of nonviolent protest and civil disobedience during the struggle for civil rights in the United States in the 1960s. And those of us who lived through that period witnessed this suffering as the Endurance in Humility of these brave protesters was tested throughout the South. You can see the horror of these images on YouTube today—police using attack dogs and fire hoses to disperse protesting schoolchildren, police on horseback trampling adult protesters, cracking skulls with nightsticks.

Then there was the bombing of a church during Sunday school classes. Four young girls were killed, and twenty-three others were wounded. Can you imagine how the protesters felt? How many wanted to stop turning the other cheek? How many wanted to fight back? Do you remember Dylann Roof, the young mass murderer who continued this reign of terror forty years later by entering a church in Charleston, South Carolina, and killed nine people in 2015? Do you remember the response by members of the church? It wasn't a violent response. It was a response of forgiveness and sadness. I can't rise to that response: the murder of eleven worshippers at a synagogue in Pittsburgh, Pennsylvania, in 2018 had me considering learning to shoot. I am not a pacifist.

Perhaps you're thinking that I've spent a lot of time writing about racism and the civil rights movement in our country in a book on tarot and Kabbalah. But this is one of the great moral issues that every one of us in this country must face, both as a society and as individuals. Part of my path is the ongoing struggle to wake up from my own unconscious racism, to see how systemic racism works in the world around me and then work to help end it. For me this is a spiritual issue, the spiritual practice of seeing all people as b'tzelem Elohim. And the heart of the Omer practice challenges us to be involved as best we can. That's why Rabbi Abraham Joshua Heschel was in Selma, Alabama, marching with Rev. King. And it's why Hillel's words from two thousand years ago still challenge us today: "If I am not for myself, who will be for me? And if I am only for myself, what am I? And if not now, when?"[17]

Today, as we are tested by renewed attacks on the fundamental spiritual truth that we are all made in the Divine image, we are called to live that truth without self-righteousness but with Humility. Gandhi taught us that civil disobedience required discipline, care, and attention and that standing up to evil was as essential as working to do good. For Gandhi, one can only practice nonviolent action when the heart and mind are in synch; together, they lead the way of truth and love, which always win. Tyrants may seem invincible, but they always fall in the end.[18]

Gandhi lived with great Humility, yet not without dignity, strength, and courage. Humility isn't a doormat. And Gandhi was clear that his practice of nonviolent civil disobedience requires discipline in order to Endure in the face of suffering. Gandhi found the Endurance in Humility. And that led to his Victory in Humility.

Day 32: Netzach of Hod in Atzilut

The Seven and Eight of Wands

 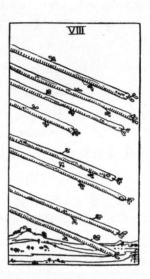

_____ *within* _____

Here we are in the middle of the week of Humility, and we have the interesting pair of the Seven and Eight of Wands. I've said quite often that Humility doesn't mean being a doormat. And here the cards bear that out: Humility has great strength within it. Humility does not mean refraining from action. On the contrary, it is meant to be a strength. Claiming humility as an excuse for inaction is an evasion of responsibility.[19]

As you can see, there is no inaction going on in the Seven of Wands; rather, there is vigorous action in play. Because we're in the suit of Wands and the world of Atzilut, we can consider this an action in the service of ideas and creativity. And looking over the key words that connect to these Sephirot, a good way of looking at this pairing is as the Determination in Inspiration. As soon as I think of these cards this way, the words of the great American inventor Thomas Edison come to mind: "Genius is one percent inspiration and ninety-nine percent perspiration." But there's more to these words than is usually quoted; he introduced this sentence by saying, "None of my inventions came by accident. I see a worthwhile need to be met and I make trial after trial until it comes."[20]

Just how many trials did Edison make before finding the right filament for the electric light bulb to work? By his own report, he tried more than six thousand different materials before succeeding. Now, that's Determination, Persistence, and Perseverance. He knew the strength of the original idea, and he didn't let ongoing failure stop him. Even more importantly, after this success, he kept going on to invent more things. Because Humility means there's always room for more Inspiration. Many people think creativity is a well that can run dry. But the Source of all Creation is active in every moment, and by doing this spiritual work, we can tap into this endless font of Inspiration. Indeed, authentic Humility can be a conduit to great accomplishment.

Day 32: Netzach of Hod in B'riah

The Seven and Eight of Cups

_____ *within* _____

Today, in the suit of Wands, I wrote about the Determination in Inspiration for Netzach of Hod. And here in the suit of Cups, we can see the very same Sephirotic pair in a negative dynamic. Instead of Determination or Persistence, in the Seven of Cups, we have a lack of focus. So in the Eight of Cups, instead of waiting for Inspiration, we see someone who has given up too easily and abandoned the work.

This could reflect someone whose Determination and Drive are based on a fantasy, so that when faced with reality that person is willing to walk away in search of a new fantasy to chase. I've seen this dynamic too often in the world of relationship. There are people who have a fantasy ideal of a partner, with an impossibly long shopping list of qualities to be checked off, and when someone doesn't meet up with this fantasy, the person is off in search of the next possible partner. Rather than approaching relationship from a place of Humility and a commitment to deeply listen to the other, these people are only thinking about what they think they want, so that they miss the totality of the person in front of them. This dynamic has only become more widespread with the advent of mobile dating apps.

I've also seen this dynamic at work in people who say they want to be famous singer-songwriters, authors, or actors. They imagine the rewards without actually sitting down to do the daily work (which is not always creative work—for example, applying for grants, networking, etc.) that leads to success. And in the end, their dreams remain empty and unfulfilled; then they blame the "system" for their failure rather than the fact that they haven't done the work. And they walk away from their dreams embittered by their experience.

These cards can also point to someone who is suffering from grandiosity in their fantasies of success, so that even if they do reach some level of success, it isn't good enough to satisfy them. They're unwilling to adjust the grandiosity of their dreams to the reality of their experience, so that regardless of succeeding in some respects, they see themselves as having failed. I've also known people who fit this description. And I hate to admit it, but in my younger and less mature days, I could fall prey to this kind of thinking.

For commentary on this Sephirotic pairing, again I turn to the Wizard of Menlo Park, Thomas Edison, who is attributed as saying: "Opportunity is missed by most people because it is dressed in overalls and looks like work." Of course, you've been doing the very hard work of this practice for thirty-two days now. Which means there's just a little bit more than two weeks to go. If you're feeling tired, discouraged, or drained at this point along this inner quest, take inspiration from Edison: he never gave up.

Take heart. Everyone gets discouraged. But you've got the power of Netzach in you, and it's within every Sephira, since of course the whole Tree is in each individual Sephira. It's always there to call on when you're feeling down.

Day 32: Netzach of Hod in Yetzirah

The Seven and Eight of Swords

_____ *within* _____

In *The Esoteric Tarot,* Ronald Decker divides the four suits into those that show blessings and those that show curses. And there's no question that today's pairing in the suit of Swords feels like a curse. The esoteric name that the Golden Dawn gave the Seven of Swords is the Lord of Unstable Effort. This is of course the shadow aspect of Netzach, and if the virtue is Perseverance, it's opposite can be seen as irresolution, vacillation, and cowardice.

When we look at the man in the Seven of Swords, he is someone who can be described as cowardly. Yes, we can see him as someone who has snuck into the camp to steal something, which takes a trickster's kind of courage. But in this case, I see him as someone who was part of the camp and who has decided to decamp with the goods, someone who was part of this army but who has decided it's safer to sneak away—and to take some valuables with him. He is both cowardly and untrustworthy. His cowardice is born of his inability to Endure; he can only envision a future of victimization, so he runs away and in so doing victimizes himself. He believes that to save himself from an imagined fate, it's acceptable to break his vows to stand with the others he is deserting and to steal from them as well.

In the Eight of Swords, we have someone who is afraid to move forward. This is a different kind of cowardice; it's the shadow side of Hod, where Humility has turned against oneself so that self-esteem is so lacking that the figure in the card feels completely helpless, even though we can see that the bonds holding her are loose and the swords do not surround her. She can free herself and walk away at any time. But she is blinded by her perception of being a helpless victim.

Together, these cards create the dynamic of competitive victimhood. At the international level, we can see this at work in how the Israelis and Palestinians both work to portray themselves as victims of the conflict. And of course, Israelis hold what they believe is the trump card of victimhood for the twentieth century, the Holocaust. But everyone from African-Americans to Armenians can fall prey to this kind of thinking. What is competitive victimhood? It's a mental framework where one believes that one's group has suffered more when compared with another group that's considered an outsider group that also has experienced suffering. For example, there is a sizable contingent of Americans who believe Christians are subject to religious discrimination in the United States that is greater than the discrimination LGBTQ people face.[21]

On the individual level, people who suffer from what is known as "victim identity" have come to define their identity around the crises, traumas, or other difficulties that have occurred in their lives, so that they believe that they have no agency (see the figure in the Eight of Swords) or that there is a "they" who will always kick them down, trick them, or betray them and that this can be used by the "victim" to avoid taking responsibility for his or her actions (see the figure in the Seven of Swords) and for the failures in his or her life.

Often such "victims" appeal to others to help save them from some situation, but then find a way to refuse help or sabotage the effort because it would change the narrative they live by. Even worse, on the personal level, some who suffer from this dynamic attract people who are bullies. You've probably seen people in relationships that fit this description.[22]

This is a particularly difficult psychological dynamic to free oneself from. As a queer Jew, unfortunately, I've had many opportunities to meet people in marginalized groups (and some from groups that aren't marginalized at all) who suffer from this misperception of reality, with the resulting lack of agency or acceptance of responsibility.

Together, these two cards represent the worst of these tendencies. And it's a true curse. So for a moment of comic relief, let me direct you to find a YouTube video of Monty Python's skit "The Four Yorkshiremen." In this wildly weird comedy bit, four successful men each try to outdo each other with their stories of being brought up impoverished and abused. It's a race to the bottom of victimization, and in this case it's very funny. When we see it among people we know, however, it is anything but.

Day 32: Netzach of Hod in Assiyah

The Seven and Eight of Pentacles

_____ *within* _____

Agriculture and manufacturing—two activities of our species that together distinguish us from all the other inhabitants of our planet—are pictured in these two cards. The figures in these cards are the recipients of the blessings of their work. In the Seven of Pentacles, the farmer sees the fruit of his labor, traditionally seen as a grapevine, which has connotations of transformation and holiness. The wine we create from the fruit of the vine is a blessing that we receive. When we drink this wine, we say a blessing that recognizes its Divine origin. That Source can be seen in the stars inside each Pentacle on the vine.

In the Eight of Pentacles, we see the craftsman creating something at his bench. What is he creating? It doesn't matter, because within the matter, the material, is the spiritual Source, and he is aware of this. He is working with the understanding that as he opens to his creativity, he is actually partnering with the Divine creativity that expresses itself uniquely through him, and he is fulfilling his purpose by actively contributing to the ongoing work of Creation.[23]

In readings, the Seven of Pentacles often is interpreted as feeling dissatisfaction with results (even when they appear to other eyes as successes). However, in this pairing with the Eight of Pentacles, I want to look at the way Netzach and Hod balance each other. Just as Chesed and Gevurah balance each other's energy, Netzach and Hod are energies that seem opposed in the names Victory and Surrender. But in *The Gates of Light,* Joseph Gikatilla says that the level of Netzach and Hod is the access point for one of the seven heavens: Shamayim. And this is the place from which we receive great strength and where we are gifted with the vision that is associated with prophecy. So for today, I'd like to read the farmer as someone who does in fact have the vision to see the Divine origin of the fruit he is harvesting.

Both the farmer and the craftsman see the Source that underlies all reality and have reverence for the Splendor of all Creation. So I see this pairing as the Triumph of Splendor. And because of the Divine's urge to know Itself through manifestation in multiplicity, I also see this pairing as the Endurance of Glory—the Eternal movement throughout the universe to the Diversity of Creation. This pairing can serve as a wake-up call to look at whatever you are doing, whatever you are making in the moment and see it as an expression of the Divine. Because as we work toward making our creative dreams a reality, we move closer to alignment with our Divine Source.

Questions for reflection and contemplation: Day 32

1. (Wands) When your Humility has been tested, how well has it Endured? Think of specific times when it Endured and when it did not: What made the difference?

2. (Cups) A dream without a plan of action to realize it is a fantasy. A dream with a plan of action brings the possibility of a goal achieved. Are you firm in taking action toward your goals, or do you vacillate? Do you worry that taking action to reach your goals is seen as self-aggrandizing by others?

3. (Swords) Do you see yourself as a victim anywhere in your life? Have you ever used victim status to excuse something you did or said? Who would you be without a story of victimization?

4. (Pentacles) What are you working on, building, or creating in your life? Visualize yourself doing this work as one piece in a mosaic that extends beyond what you can see. Know that you hold an essential piece of this mosaic and spend the rest of the day seeing everyone you work with or encounter as also holding an essential piece.

Day 33: Hod of Hod

Glory, Glory Hallelujah

> Today is the thirty-third day of the Omer,
> which is four weeks and five days of the Omer.

The thirty-third day of the Counting of the Omer is known as Lag B'Omer, which makes sense because it simply means "thirty-three days of the Omer." There are all sorts of special customs around this particular day that are of obscure origin. For that reason, many of these customs have fallen out of practice. But one custom is still popular today, and in Israel, it's a very big deal in the town of Meron, near Safed in the Galilee. That's the site of the tomb of Rabbi Shimon Bar Yohai, the author of the Zohar (as ascribed by Rabbi Moses de León, who was in fact the real author of the Zohar). Even without the Zohar as his legacy, Rabbi Bar Yohai is the fourth most-quoted sage in the Mishnah, and there are many mystical legends about him, including that on the day of his death, he passed down many Kabbalistic secrets to his followers. Whether or not this is true, the anniversary of his death is considered a *hillula,* a celebration, since the death of a tzaddik is considered the reuniting of his soul with its Divine Source in a Divine Wedding. So today, on Lag B'Omer, Jewish mystics gather at his gravesite to light bonfires and dance through the night.

This custom goes back centuries to the time of the eminent Kabbalist Rabbi Isaac Luria. There is a story told that on the Hillula de Shimon Bar Yohai, he went with his followers to light a bonfire and dance through the night. While they were dancing, an old man with a white beard appeared and joined Rabbi Luria in the dance. The face of the old man glowed, and as they danced, the face of Rabbi Luria began to glow as well. As the sun rose, the old man disappeared, and Rabbi Luria's companions realized they had been visited by the soul of Shimon Bar Yohai himself. True or not, the tale as told makes Rabbi Luria the spiritual heir of the man they believed wrote the Zohar (which can be translated as "radiance").

Stories with someone who has a glowing face also connect that person to Moses, who is described as having had a radiant face when he descended from Mount Sinai—that the Glory of YHVH was upon him.[24] And remember, Moses is described in the Torah as the most Humble man on Earth.[25]

I have seen people of many traditions with such a glow. It was when I saw my friend Anne with her face glowing in this way that I asked her what had happened to her, and that was my introduction to Vipassana meditation. This glow is the natural response of quiet joy when one's ego steps aside and recognizes with Humility that there is indeed a

Higher Power guiding us. However you find this radiance within, I say to you, "Glory, glory, hallelujah."

And if you have a teacher you revere, someone who opened vistas for you previously unimagined, today would be a good day to say a prayer of gratitude in your teacher's honor.

Day 33: Hod of Hod in the Four Worlds
The Eight of Wands, Cups, Swords, and Pentacles

_____*within* _____

The Humility within Splendor. The Splendor within Gratitude. The kaleidoscopic combinations on "doubling" days are in fact examples of the Splendor and the Glory. But on this day, I'd like to look at pure Humility since it is a quality that is much overlooked in this world of "selfies" and online narcissism.

People with a healthy sense of Humility aren't posting online photos of everything they eat and what their pet did today hoping for "likes." They are secure in themselves. Humility isn't self-abasement; it's not about holding yourself in low regard. It's about holding others in high regard—knowing that everyone you meet is just as much an entire universe as you are and giving space to that, being open enough to take the other person in with all their complications (because after all, you have complications too). In this way, Humility isn't about making yourself small; it's about knowing your full expanse within and opening to that expanse, that Splendor, that Glory in others.

The Hasidim teach the practice of *bittul,* which is sometimes translated as "self-abnegation," but I think that's too negative sounding when the reality is that it's more about selflessness in service to the Divine. This is a service that puts self-concern aside. And here is the key: what others think of you is completely unimportant. And indeed, what you think of you is unimportant. These are only thoughts. And the practice of Humility is a kind of meditation where you put any thoughts of yourself aside. Just as when you're meditating and you think about how good a meditator you are so that you've stopped meditating and fallen into a mind trap, so too when moving through the world with Humility, if you think about how good you are at being Humble, you've fallen into Humility's exact opposite: pride. This is a practice where all thoughts about the self are put aside, all judgments (positive or negative) are put aside as just thoughts. And as the mind becomes quieter, something amazing happens.

Rabbi Jonathan Sacks taught that Humility is actually a form of perception. When you can silence the "I" enough to hear the "Thou," Humility will open your heart to all Creation.[26]

Let's look at how the cards reflect this teaching. And as always, we'll start with the suit of Wands. The "I" is silent in the Eight of Wands; there is no one there at all. And you can hear the "still, small voice" in the wands racing down from the Heavens, always audible for those who have ears to hear.

In the Eight of Cups, the turning away from the pursuit of pleasures of the senses to go off on an inner quest is a Surrender of the self, and this is one way to move in that direction. However, I want to reemphasize that Judaism is not a path of renunciation of sensual pleasures. Pleasures are to be enjoyed, but with an awareness of the holiness within them. And of course, in moderation.

The Eight of Swords has gotten a bad rap throughout this book and in tarot books in general. But on this day, I'm staying with the meditation theme and Humility as a meditative practice. For those of us who tend to intellectualize everything, there is an important teaching in this card. If we consider the swords as representing discriminating thought—and the goal of this practice is to put these thoughts aside—then the woman in this card has literally and figuratively closed her eyes to these thoughts. Like any meditator, she holds her body still, the better to open to the inner stillness and open the inner senses to the Divine whisper. Part of the practice of Humility is the awareness of the limits of one's knowledge and thinking. This is one of those places where I run into trouble since I'm a know-it-all. Except, of course, I don't know it all. But I like it if people think I do.

There is a well-known Zen story of a professor who had studied Zen academically and who went to visit a Zen master to learn from him. While the master was making tea, the professor nattered on about his knowledge of Zen. As the master poured tea into the professor's cup, the professor kept talking until he noticed that the master had poured so much tea that the cup started to overflow. The professor blurted out, "Stop, the cup is full!" To which the master responded, "Like this cup, you are full of your own learning, opinions, and speculations. How can I show you Zen unless you first empty your cup?"

This is a very elegant way to tell someone that he's full of himself. And in the Eight of Swords, the figure understands this conundrum. She is someone who has great powers of intellect, but she also knows this intellect can be an obstacle in the practice of Humility. This doesn't mean one should reject the intellect; it simply means that we need to know its limits. The woman in the Eight of Swords knows the limits of intellect and is willing to put herself in a situation where it can't be her guide; even though it feels constricting and unnatural to her, she knows doing this can take her somewhere she couldn't go otherwise.

Finally, we come to our Humble craftsman in the Eight of Pentacles. Working hard at manual labor is often looked down on by those of us who work in glass towers in front of glass screens. He doesn't take that judgment into account. He doesn't feel any vanity either, even though he is turning out beautiful work. He has stepped aside inside himself so that the creativity flows through him. He sees the Divine working through him, and he feels joy and satisfaction in his work and Gratitude that he has been so gifted.

Together these four cards provide a road map for the deep practice of Humility. May we all walk this path together.

Questions for reflection and contemplation: Day 33

1. (Wands) How good a listener are you? Look up the principles of active listening and try to consciously practice these principles all day, with everyone you speak with. Notice the ways your experience differs from the usual. As you practice active listening, add one more instruction to the practice: listen for the Divine Whisper when you find time to be alone.

2. (Cups) Go on a social media fast for twenty-four hours. Notice any time you have the urge to post anything. Consider how you might be using social media to construct a story line or image of yourself to seek attention or approval. After twenty-four hours, before you go back, consider ways to bring the practice of Humility to your use of social media.

3. (Swords) What is the color of the wind? When you can do nothing, what can you do?

4. (Pentacles) Find something in your home that is handmade and that you don't look at or think about very often. Sit with it for up to thirty minutes, if you can. Listen to it with your heart and wait to see if the light within it reveals itself to you. Regardless of what you experience, when you are done, say a prayer of Gratitude for the person who made the object and a prayer of Gratitude to the Divine for bringing this object into your life.

Day 34: Yesod of Hod

The Connection of I-Thou Begins in Humility

Today is the thirty-fourth day of the Omer,
which is four weeks and six days of the Omer.

Martin Buber, whose study of Hasidism is the source of many of the Hasidic stories we know today, is best known for his book *I and Thou,* which examines the nature of Relationships between individuals and between an individual and the Divine. He contrasts the I-Thou Relationship with the I-It Relationship, which unfortunately is the basis of many Relationships. What's interesting, though, is that Relationships between people can move back and forth between I-Thou and I-It.

In an I-Thou Relationship, one person is fully open and present to the full humanity of the other person. This means that the active listening I wrote about in yesterday's section is fully focused on the other person with empathy and respect. And because this presence is based in Humility, it means that as practitioners, we are vulnerable. It means we are in a judgment-free zone with no preconceptions that distort the fullness of the other person. This urge to Connect in Humility invites the other person in, holds a place where that person can feel seen and safe to be completely who they are.

The very phrase "I-It" tells you that the Relationship with the other lacks respect. It does not see the other as fully human. At its worst, in this dynamic, the other person becomes an object to be used. But most of the time, it's less that we see the other as an object and more that we're protecting our vulnerabilities or judging the other in some way in which we are not fully present: we are holding something of ourselves back, which defeats authentic Relationship. This is at the root of our modern alienation, not only from each other but also from our selves. Strangely enough, trying to establish an I-Thou Relationship is destined to fail because the very process of trying objectifies the goal and the other person. Thus, the I-Thou Relationship is a Connection that arises in Humility.

For Buber, the Divine is the Eternal Thou because we can't bring any preconceptions or preconditions to the Relationship. We can only be present and open, and perhaps God will reveal God's Self. And this was Buber's observation of the story of the Hebrew slaves' redemption from Egypt and their experience at Sinai. Their new freedom and the witnessing of the miracle at the Sea of Reeds enabled them to be fully open and present, without any expectation (because expectations attempt to limit the Relationship partner, thus creating an I-It moment). So the entire people experienced an I-Thou moment at the foot of the mountain.[27]

As you know by now, I don't believe this is something that happened. But that doesn't mean I don't believe it's true. The Connection at Sinai is a template for what we must do to experience the I-Thou Relationship with the Divine in community. And Buber believes that by studying the Torah, the prophets, and the rabbinic teachings, we can similarly open ourselves, preparing the ground for such an I-Thou encounter.

I hope that as you read the holy texts from all traditions that are discussed in this book and as you do the work, you prepare the ground for your own I-Thou encounter with the Divine, and the Divine in all other people.

Day 34: Yesod of Hod in Atzilut

The Nine and Eight of Wands

 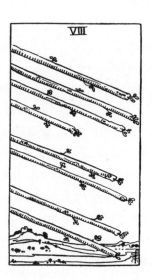

_____ *within* _____

The emotional wound symbolized by the bandaged head of the man in the Nine of Wands, along with the stockade of staves, tells us that while he has the urge to Connect, he is defensive and wary. This distorts his Humility so that it can be expressed—or experienced by others—as timidity.

The nature of this wounding and defensiveness is such that someone experiencing this dynamic can only bring negative preconceptions to any new encounter, which makes an I-Thou Relationship almost impossible.

But there is an opening in the stockade of staves in the Nine of Wands, and all you need is a moment of opening along with true Humility for an I-Thou moment to arise. And the Eight of Wands suggests that despite the wounding, healthy Humility is still possible.

The warning here, though, is that someone who exhibits true Humility can be perceived by others as weak, and for the bullies in the world, this is an invitation to take advantage of someone. Sometimes this Humility actually activates the bully complex in another person. This is not to blame the Humble person at all; it's an awareness that sometimes the behavior of a bully in fact arises out of the bully's fear of their own inner sense of powerlessness, a neurotic recapitulation of victimization in the past. Thus, it's very possible that the Humility on display in this pair might very well have led to the wounding we see in the Nine of Wands, though once again, this is not to place any blame on the person who is wounded.

Day 34: Yesod of Hod in B'riah

The Nine and Eight of Cups

_____ *within* _____

In the Nine of Cups, the I-It dynamic is fully on display with the man who appears to be hosting guests, but whose motivation seems to be to create an image of himself as successful. We've previously considered the cups in this card as representing emotional conquests, trophies if you will, so that each cup is really the objectification of a relationship.

The tension in this pairing with the Eight of Cups is that it seems that for all intents and purposes, we have someone who is at some level dissatisfied with a way of being and wants to leave it behind. However, the "geography cure" doesn't work; you can't run away from yourself. And if it really is an inner quest we're seeing in the Eight of Cups, as opposed to walking away from it all to go somewhere else, well, at the start of any spiritual quest, the old habits and ways of relating to others have not changed yet. There is just the desire and the will to change.

You can see this tension between the desire to change and the bondage to old ways of acting in the way some people Relate to (and project issues on) spiritual teachers—not as other human beings but as tools to reach a goal, even if it's defined as a "spiritual" goal. Or it could point to the desire to be seen as spiritual by others in the furtherance of building one's ego. This is one of the dangers of spiritual materialism as described by the Buddhist teacher Chögyam Trungpa Rinpoche.

I know I've used spiritual teachers in just this way. And I could even make the argument that I could use the writing of this book as a kind of trophy and as a way of staying separate from others even as I disclose my vulnerabilities. This is one of the traps of doing this work, and I hope my awareness of it keeps me from falling into this trap—or at least helps me see when I've fallen and gives me the Grace to admit it, pick myself up, and do my best to Connect authentically and with Humility.

Day 34: Yesod of Hod in Yetzirah
The Nine and Eight of Swords

_____ *within* _____

Imagine for a moment that the two figures we see in the Nine and Eight of Swords are in a Relationship. Obviously, it's not a very happy Relationship, but it's a dynamic I am familiar with. In this reading of the Eight of Swords, we have someone who is a prisoner of their preconceptions and judgments—and this not only makes that person blind to the fullness of other people but also blind to one's own prejudices. So even in a Relationship, there is always something of that person held back, unspoken. You can't fully show who you are because you can't fully see who you are. Someone in a Relationship with a person like this is likely to feel like the figure in the Nine of Swords—unseen, alienated, lonely, and full of grief. I've seen marriages where the man is in some way emotionally blocked and unable or unwilling to see this, held prisoner by punishing introjected societal restrictions on expressing himself, and where the woman ends up feeling isolated in the Relationship that should offer her the deepest and most Intimate Connection. Of course, this is a stereotypical view of the psychological divide between the genders, and this dynamic can go the other way entirely. Either way, though, this is a heartbreaking pairing, and one I am sadly familiar with from my own decidedly nonheterosexual experience.

As gay men go, I generally pass as straight, and unless I tell someone, other people assume I express the "default" heterosexual norm.* Most of the men I am attracted to, however, don't pass; they are often perceived as feminine in expression. I find this attractive. And some of the reasons for this include that my own masculinity is a shadow trait that I don't like, so I don't find traditionally masculine men attractive. Interestingly enough, my own femininity is also a shadow trait, so I seek it out in others rather than own it and integrate and express it myself. This has manifested in some of my relationships with other men, with me playing the role of the figure in the Eight of Swords and my partners dealing with the grief and isolation on view in the Nine of Swords. However, one old partner of mine had a different Nine of Swords experience. When I told him I thought our Relationship wasn't working and was beyond repair, he burst into tears. I thought he was crying because he was hurt and didn't want to break up. But he quickly disabused me of that idea. He explained that he was crying for me! He felt that I was so cut off from myself and so judgmental that I would end up alone. His words haunted

---

*Today academia has given us the unfortunate descriptor *cisgender* to describe this. I do not accept this labeling since for some people my gender role presentation would appear to be the default heteronormative male, but for others I would be quite queer. *Cisgender* is reductionist, and as such I reject this label.

me because while our Relationship truly was beyond repair, he was not wrong about my own issues and how they kept me isolated.

Over the years, I've worked very hard to remove the emotional blindfold and straitjacket that have kept me a prisoner. It's an ongoing process, and I'm a very different person now than I was those many years ago. But this is still a dynamic I deal with internally, and I can be a tough nut to crack sometimes.

Day 34: Yesod of Hod in Assiyah

The Nine and Eight of Pentacles

_____ *within* _____

This pairing suggests that working with Humility (in the Eight of Pentacles) is preparing the garden within for Relationship. It's almost as if the craftsman in that card is open to his inner Divine Feminine, which has arisen for him in the Nine of Pentacles.

Indeed, true Humility creates a space, a garden like the one in the Nine of Pentacles, which is a place of Foundation, a place of security where the Splendor hidden within Hod can express itself and where the Splendor can be Appreciated in the world of nature and in the fullness of another person.

By doing this work, by Connecting with the Divine Feminine through Humility, the workman in the Eight of Pentacles is not only whole within himself, he also can be fully present and whole before another person in Relationship and fully present in all the things he does. He sees the beauty and fullness in the work he creates, so that anyone who is similarly sensitive will see the garden within his work as well.

I believe this is why we respond on a both a visceral and a spiritual level (as though the viscera and spirit were separate) to certain handmade objects. When I lived in Japan, I began to collect traditional pottery. I was drawn to the spirit of the potter that I felt in the fired and glazed clay form. Because while I like having a lot of teapots, what drew me to the form was the "star" that I saw in the "pentacle." I sought out the potters whose work moved me most deeply, and I became friends with many of them because they saw that I saw that I could see them in their work. And not surprisingly, these were Humble men and women—true masters of their craft, yet without pretense or arrogance.

One of the marks of Humility in the arts is what the poet John Keats called negative capability—the ability of artists to tolerate pain, confusion, and intellectual uncertainty, enabling them to go beyond preconceptions to create something that captures an essential aliveness in their work. This is what I saw in the work of these potters. And Humility is essential to hold the tension of negative capability.

You could even say that negative capability is the ground of Relationship because it allows for the essential aliveness of the other to reveal itself, which is why I connect it to Humility.

Questions for reflection and contemplation: Day 34

1. (Wands) When has your Humility been perceived by others as weakness? Why do you think that happened? Have you ever mistaken Humility in another as weakness? When has the reverse ever been true: Have you ever been timid in a situation and been seen as being Humble? If so, for any of these situations, why do you think this was the case?

2. (Cups) Think about a time when you wanted to make a change in your life, a time when you felt strongly that you needed to do something differently, but you still didn't know what the next step would be and

you still felt caught by older ways of thinking and acting. How did you deal with the tension? What did you do that enabled you to take the next step? What can you take away from this to use in your daily experience?

3. (Swords) What is it that you see about yourself or your Relationship(s) that you pretend not to see? What blindfold are you wearing willingly? What blindfold have you been unconscious to but have had pointed out to you? How has it left you isolated or kept you from Connecting fully with another? It doesn't matter if you feel this is truer about your partner or about another person you know. Look at yourself.

4. (Pentacles) What can you do to prepare your inner garden? How can you nurture your Humility in ways that create a space for others and for Relationship to flourish?

Day 35: Malchut of Hod

When You're Secure in Your Dignity, Humility Comes Naturally

Today is the thirty-fifth day of the Omer, which is five weeks of the Omer.

When you're secure in who you are, you are comfortable with others and who they are. And you have the Humility to Appreciate not only your own Dignity but that of others as well. As an example, consider the heterosexual man who is so secure in his own sexuality that he is completely comfortable with queer men and isn't in the least bit nervous about expressing his feelings for them. There is no sexual charge or tension within him in the presence of men who love men, so that there is psychic space for everyone to fully be who they are. I am lucky enough to have some heterosexual male friends with this kind of Grounding in security.

Self-respect in Humility confers a Nobility of Presence that is immediately felt by others who meet someone who exemplifies these qualities. However, without Humility, self-respect can fall into a kind of pride that does not leave room for others.

Malchut is the Sephira that has no quality of its own; it is the vessel that receives the energy of all the Sephirot above. Of course, the ability to receive is a quality, but that's how Malchut has been described in the texts over the centuries. In combination with Hod, Malchut enables one to see and receive the true goodness in another—seeing their innate Majesty in a way that reveals the Nobility of both people.

In a way, Malchut of Hod is the apotheosis of the practice of Humility. It's almost like living with the consciousness of the healer in the Healing of Immanence—one of the first healings taught in Jason Shulman's A Society of Souls. In this practice, the "healer" simply regards and receives the Divine that is always present within the client.[28] I have found this deceptively simple healing practice to be profound because the practice heals the healer as well. And the results are, uh, simply Divine.

Day 35: Malchut of Hod in Atzilut

The Ten and Eight of Wands

 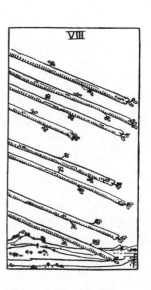

_____ *within* _____

The man in the Ten of Wands doesn't look as if he's feeling particularly Sovereign. He is weighed down by the bundle of staves, is bent over, and can hardly see what's in front of him as he walks back to town. The world of Atzilut and the suit of Wands are the highest and the closest (there I go, being directional and hierarchical, so please remember this is a metaphor) to pure spirit. So we could see the man in the Ten of Wands as weighed down by spiritual gifts or by the spiritual Responsibilities he has taken on.

The Eight of Wands often represents the gifts of the spirit, the gifts received by those whose Humility has created an inner space to receive them. So together I see these cards as the plight of Leadership in a spiritual community. These leaders are people of great spiritual gifts who have both the Sovereignty and Humility to lead a community, but who often end up overwhelmed and burned out by the Responsibilities and demands of the community.

You don't have to be a cleric to be in this position. Teachers, therapists, and leaders of many kinds are people who offer their gifts in service to a wider community, whether it's a school, a congregation, a clinic, or even a business. If you are a practitioner of reading tarot for others as an offering of guidance, this includes you.

One of the lessons of this pairing is to remember self-care. Share your gifts but remember to give them to yourself as well. Remember the instructions of the flight attendant: if the overhead oxygen bag drops, put it on yourself before putting it on the child next to you. You don't want to black out because you've put someone else's needs first. That doesn't help either of you. You're not being asked to sacrifice yourself, though there is an element of that in the image of the Ten of Wands. You can certainly see Christ carrying the cross in this card. But put the cross down: there aren't any Romans scourging you along the Via Dolorosa. If you've taken on more Responsibility than you can healthily handle, say so. Ask for the help you so readily extend to others. Create your own place of retreat.

Going from spirit to sex, one can also read this pairing as someone who has a great deal of sexual energy and is holding it back—possibly to channel it, to sublimate it in the kind of service I've been talking about in the paragraphs above. But it could also be that holding back this sexual energy feels oppressive. After all, in Judaism sexuality is a gift of the spirit to be shared. Rabbis are not celibate. But there are some traditions where sexuality is demonized. Yes, sexual expression needs boundaries and it needs to be channeled appropriately. True Sovereignty knows how to express this energy appropriately, whether physically, emotionally, or spiritually.

Last, we can see this as the situation of the gifted artist whose creativity is being held back in some way so that it becomes a burden. I have an artist friend who had been hospitalized for his alcoholism a few times. At first, I thought he drank because he believed it opened him to his creativity. But one day as I sat by his bedside in the hospital, he explained to me that he drank because it closed down the channel. He was overwhelmed by his creative urges, by the multiplicity of Inspirations that came to him every day. He couldn't hold the energy, so to disperse it or numb himself to it, he drank. So while it's true that many people may have a drink or two to let down their inhibitions, my friend was drinking heavily to do the exact opposite. Feeling oppressed by creativity is tragic to me, but I know that creative people are often the most sensitive people on the planet and that the level of stimuli we face in today's world can certainly be overwhelming. My artist friend eventually moved from the city to a small island, where he lives in a rural setting better suited to his nature and where he isn't over-stimulated so that he finally lives a more balanced life.

Day 35: Malchut of Hod in B'riah

The Ten and Eight of Cups

_____ *within* _____

Malchut is the Sephira of the Shekinah, the Indwelling Presence the Divine, or the Divine Feminine. While Keter, the Sephira at the top of the Tree of Life, is all about transcendence, Malchut and the Shekinah are all about Immanence—the recognition that the Divine is present throughout all Creation—and about allowing oneself to be held by, and Grounded in, this Divine Presence. Malchut of Hod points us in the direction of feeling Gratitude for the Indwelling Presence within the Splendor of Creation.

I usually see the Ten of Cups as a beautiful card, with the happy family aware of the Divine blessings that surround and suffuse them. The human relationships are loving, and the family members' relationships to the world around them are healthy because they're all based in this awareness.

This awareness also lives in the figure in the Eight of Cups, who is turning away from her past success in the world to seek something deeper. Sometimes one doesn't need to turn away from the world because of course the Shekinah isn't separate from the world. But there are definitely times when the clamor of the world and its pleasures can overwhelm the ability to sense the Divine within. And that's when it's time to turn away to seek reconnection within.

It's as though the person in the Eight of Cups is trying to get back to the innocence we see in the Ten of Cups. Note that the eight cups in the image create a kind of a fence, a boundary between the viewer and the figure who is turned away. The cups have a feeling of heaviness, a solidity that contrasts with the lightness of the rainbow cups in the other card. What's that about?

I collect typewriters. I have more than a dozen (not as many as Tom Hanks, of course, but then I don't have his money or the space for more; I don't even have the space for all the typewriters I do own). There are a couple of Corona 3 models from about 1915. An Oliver from about 1910. A Remington "Noiseless" from about 1938. A Franklin 7 from 1897. A Hammond from about 1915. And a couple of Olivetti Lettera 22 models from the sixties. Talk about heaviness and solidity. When I bought my first antique typewriter, I didn't think I was going to start a collection. As a writer and as someone who grew up with old Underwood cathedral typewriters as a child, the Olivetti (held in the collection of the Museum of Modern Art for its modernist aesthetic) when I was a teen, and the IBM Selectric at my first job, these old machines were the tools of my craft. I love the smell of the ink and machine oil that wafts from the type bed. But collecting became a mania. I lost sight of the love for what the objects represent and lusted after the objects themselves. This dynamic isn't unfamiliar to me, since I'd already been through this before when I first started collecting Japanese pottery.

This is the story I project onto the Eight of Cups: perhaps the man in the Eight of Cups is turning away from something that was once a source of connection to the Divine but that has become a barrier in some way. (And yes, I switched genders, but how do you know the gender of the figure in this card? It's one of the many cards where the gender is ambiguous, making it easy to project yourself, whatever gender you identify with, into the card.) So he walks away, seeking to find the original relationship he had with the world—one of Humility that allowed space for the Majesty of the world to reveal itself. We can see this relationship in the Ten of Cups. Perhaps once he has renewed that inner connection, he can return to these eight cups in a new way.

While my example was in relationship to objects, one can also start to take other people for granted. When you no longer respond to others with the Humility that opens space for them to grow and change in relationship, you are treating them like objects, and you've moved from an I-Thou to an I-It relationship.

This pairing speaks to the essence of the prayer sung at the end of the Torah service, when the scroll is returned to the ark. When I sing these words, my heart both aches and overflows with love. The prayer in English, with words taken from the Book of Proverbs and the Book of Lamentations, is:

> *It is a tree of life for those who grasp it,*
> *And all who uphold it are blessed.*
> *Its ways are pleasantness and all its paths are peace.*
> *Help us turn to You, and we shall return.*
> *Renew our lives as in days of old.**

---

*Proverbs 3:18, Lamentations 5:21. You've probably noticed that the Torah is referred to as a Tree of Life. Indeed, the Kabbalists believed all the secrets of Creation are hidden in the Torah and that it holds the energy of all the Sephirot. This is why for a Jewish Kabbalist, Torah study is essential. And it's why I find the occult Qabalah, which gives short shrift to the classic Judaic texts, somewhat ungrounded at the least and an anti-Semitic appropriation at the worst.

This is a renewal that reopens our hearts with Humility so that our eyes can see the Splendor and Glory that surround us.

Day 35: Malchut of Hod in Yetzirah

The Ten and Eight of Swords

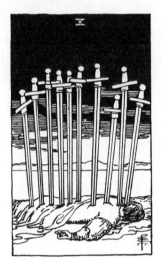 

_____ *within* _____

The Shekinah is not all sweetness and light. She is also the defender of the People Israel, and as such she has been described as having spears and meteors for hair.[29] And in the Ten of Swords, we see her in her most terrifying aspect.

While the suit of Swords is the world of the intellect, Malchut is the physical world, where death is a reality. So here we have followed blind intellect, or wrong thinking, to its inevitable end. This is hitting bottom for the addict. And if one doesn't do t'shuvah and turn like the figure in the Eight of Cups, the result is not going to be happy.

Paired with the Eight of Swords, where we are blinded by thinking that limits us, this illustration of the negative energy of these Sephirot stands as a warning to those who would persist in their delusions despite all evidence to the contrary. Unfortunately, when I see this pairing, I feel like I'm looking at those who deny the reality of climate change in the world and who are taking us all down this road to the destruction of the ecosystem that supports life on the planet. This blindness to the Splendor of the Creation that we are not separate from calls forth the Kali-like aspect of the Shekinah, which could destroy humankind and our world.

There is no stronger warning that while the Divine urge to know Itself is irrepressible and Creation is ongoing, the Divine will do what is necessary to maintain the balance of Creation. And those who destroy that balance will be destroyed in return. Then Creation will go on happily without us. Or with a new, hopefully improved version.

On the more personal level, this is a warning that whatever an individual does that takes that person down a path of blindness and the illusion of separateness, whether it's an addiction to a substance or an addiction to power or money, the ultimate result is death. Oh, it might not be a physical death immediately. But I am sure you've seen people who are dead behind their eyes. These are the true zombies, and when you encounter one, run. Oh, and please don't vote for one.

Day 35: Malchut of Hod in Assiyah

The Ten and Eight of Pentacles

_____ *within* _____

Remember that within each Sephira is a whole Tree of Life, extending fractally into infinity, reflecting the nature of the Infinite One. So that here, in Malchut of Hod in Assiyah, we come to the completion of a whole Tree of Life within Hod, where all of the Sephirotic energies are balanced through Humility. We are but two weeks away from the revelation of Sinai, and the Devotion we see at work in the Eight of Pentacles should at this point be activated in our lives so that we are now seeing glimpses of the Shekinah, of the Splendor in the material world, everywhere in our daily lives, as evidenced by the full Tree of Life visible in the Ten of Pentacles.

Seeing the Ten of Pentacles from within Humility, we can focus on how the people in the image are connected rather than disconnected. Our Humility allows us to see the fullness of these people. How the woman with a garland of flowers is smiling at the man with a spear. How the child holds on to her while reaching out, unafraid to pet the dog. And how the elderly man seated at the gate is also reaching out to a dog, completing a circuit of connection between them all, inside and outside the gate.

The whole Tree of Life sparkles in the air before us, in front of the gate, giving us the message that the entire world, everywhere at every moment, provides a gateway for us to reach out and touch the Divine.

In the last hours of the Yom Kippur service, the liturgy tells us the gates are closing. The metaphor of this day as the one Day of Atonement gives those last hours an urgency for those of us who live the metaphor.* It helps us further break open our hearts to seek our "at-one-ment" with the Divine. But for all the reality of our feelings of urgency, we know it's a metaphor, so that even as the *shofar* is sounded at the last moment of the service to signal the closing of the gate, we say that the gates don't finally close for another twelve days, at the last day of the Sukkot holiday, Shemini Atzeret. But as the Ten of Pentacles shows us, as long as we're alive, the gates are always open.

---

*One of my favorite books, which presents this holiday as both metaphorical and urgently true, is *This Is Real and You Are Completely Unprepared: The Days of Awe as a Journey of Transformation* by Rabbi Alan Lew, z"l.

Questions for reflection and contemplation: Day 35

1. (Wands) If you have a position of Leadership or Responsibility in a spiritual community, what do you do to take care of yourself? How do you hold that Responsibility so that your Humility remains healthy and open to others without violating your Sovereignty? If you are a creative person, how do you hold your creative Inspiration without discharging it fruitlessly or acting out in some way?

2. (Cups) Are there objects in your home that have given you a joy that has now receded because you see these objects every day? What can you do to revive that earlier feeling? Or is it time to let these objects go to someone else who will Appreciate them the way you once did? Is there a relationship in your life that once felt more alive? What can you do to renew your Appreciation of that relationship?

3. (Swords) Do something to honor the planet today. Examine the way you live to see what you can do in your daily life to lessen any stresses on the ecosystem. And do something to support an environmental organization. Ask someone you know intimately and trust to be gentle to tell you about your blind spots, and when you receive this information, take it in with Gratitude and without excuses. This is an exercise in listening and in learning information that might very well save your life. Pray for Divine assistance in getting past these blind spots.

4. (Pentacles) How does your Humility help you open your eyes to the gates of the Divine that surround you at your place of work? At home? On the street? These gates are everywhere. (Hint: your Humility is one of them.) Spend the day attuning yourself to their presence. Say an inner prayer of Gratitude each time you catch a glimpse of one of these gates.

WEEK 6

Yesod

ALL THE ENERGIES OF THE SEPHIROT come together and are held by Yesod before they all gush forth into Malchut. Much as Gevurah regulated and directed the energy of Chesed so that it would not overwhelm, so Yesod has the same function for balancing not only Netzach and Hod but also all of the upper Sephirot. This is the reason it is called Foundation. And because it brings together all the energies from above and weaves them together, it is also Bonding: it Bonds all the energies of the Sephirot, and it Bonds individuals to the Divine and to each other.

As the Foundation, the amount of energy it holds and directs is unfathomable. Yet we feel it, because it urges us to Connect, to Bond with the Divine and with other people. And this urge is, uh, urgent. It fills us with yearning. Thus, the energy of Yesod is often the most difficult to work with. In the previous weeks, it is almost as though we've been working out in a spiritual gym, making ourselves strong enough to hold all this energy and to face all the issues that the week of Yesod will bring up.

The week of Yesod is where our deepest, most stubborn issues of dependency and abandonment will arise to challenge us. Where our weaknesses and strengths in regulating our sexual energy and our speech will show themselves. Our desire to put all this energy into some Connection, almost any Connection, is so strong that without having done the work of the previous weeks, Yesod could bring us to unhealthy Connections and into the darkness of addiction.

One of the names for Yesod is El Chai, God of Life, and Yesod in many ways is the Life Force itself, looking for a place or a way to manifest. The shoot of a plant may look deceptively weak, but I'm sure you've seen shoots of grass that have cracked through the concrete of a sidewalk; there is immense power in this Life Force, and the previous weeks have been preparation for you to be able to direct this force with all the Love, Restraint, Truth, Balance, Endurance, and Humility you have. When you can bring all these qualities together in harmony, Yesod is the Foundation for spiritual Intimacy.

Day 36: Chesed of Yesod

The Secret Love Binding the World Together

> Today is the thirty-sixth day of the Omer,
> which is five weeks and one day of the Omer.

On Day 18, I noted that Hebrew letters are also numbers and that the letters that denote the number 18 spell the word that means "life." Well, today is eighteen times two—thirty-six—and in mystical Judaism, there is a tradition that there are thirty-six righteous people alive in every generation and that the very existence of the world depends on them. In Hebrew, they are called the Tzadikim Nistarim, the Hidden Saints, because tradition has it that no one knows who they are and that they themselves, because of their great humility, are unaware of their status.

The letters that makes up the number 36 are *lamed* and *vav.* So these Hidden Saints are more popularly known as the Lamed-Vavniks, and there are many folktales about them. Of course, the story that a small number of righteous people can save the world can be found in the first book of the Torah, in Genesis, when Abraham bargains with God to save the cities of Sodom and Gomorrah if there are ten good men there.

I like to think about some of these folktales on the thirty-sixth day because they show how the Love that these people have for the Divine and Creation help sustain it, Binding all of us together in its web, even if we are unaware of it. It's unlikely you'll discover a Lamed-Vavnik in your travels today, but it's a good day to see if you can feel the web of Love they weave that Binds us all together.

Day 36: Chesed of Yesod in Atzilut

The Four and Nine of Wands

_____ *within* _____

Both Chesed and Yesod share their movement of outward Flow. But where in the Four of Wands, that Flow is consecrated under a chuppah, in the Nine of Wands, that Flow is being held back by a stockade.

This Flow is a psychic/psychological energy, so that a physical stockade, such as the one in the Nine of Wands, isn't going to be much help. Even if we decide that the staves standing upright in a line are psychological defenses, they hardly create an impermeable wall. The break in the wall is only just a little wider than the other spaces between the staves.

The reason is simple: the wounded man in the Nine of Wands may be wary of Intimacy and Connection, but he wants them desperately. His yearning is fueled by the energy of Chesed in the Four of Wands and by the energy of Yesod in the Nine of Wands.

Between the inner Yearning for Connection and the outer, almost gravitational pull of Love, the man can't help but look over his shoulder past the line of staves. Is he looking because he expects attack or because he desires Connection? Yes. And yes. Unfortunately, if he finds Connection, he will be quick to take offense at slights that are, uh, slight.

This does not have to be a Connection to another person; remember, the Four of Wands is a card that looks forward to the Divine Marriage between the Deity and the People Israel.* So the bandage on the man's head could suggest he has been wounded by his tradition. He would not be comfortable standing under a chuppah because he wouldn't trust any spiritual authorities. So while he might have a great Yearning for the Divine, he also doesn't trust its earthly, organizational manifestations. He might be invited to this wedding, but he doesn't feel like a welcome guest or a willing groom.

As a gay man, I relate to this figuratively and literally. For many years, I felt wounded by the spiritual tradition of my ancestors, so even as that tradition started to evolve into acceptance and I began to look for welcoming congregations, I was still wary and defended. And after years of going to weddings of heterosexual friends, I began to be resentful of ceremonies that I was excluded from enjoying myself.

Someone who has escaped from a cult or any abusive spirituality group might very well suffer from a similar wounding, so that one could easily imagine such a person being suspicious of any organized religion or even a spontaneous spiritual experience. There are many other reasons one could feel excluded from one's tradition or organized religion; the very fact that you're reading this book means you may have traveled somewhat afar from the tradition of your birth, perhaps because you were wounded in your own explorations. Yet here you are, because just as flowers are heliotropic—they seek and turn toward the sun—so humans turn to God, seeking the Divine Light.

In the Jewish mystical tradition, our turning to the Divine is in response to some apprehension of the Light, and by turning I mean not only seeking but also "turning," as in t'shuvah. This turning of the

---

*Here I want to make a distinction between the People Israel—that is, the historical tribal group that is the origin of the modern Jewish traditions—and people who may not be Jewish at all. Inasmuch as the name Israel was given to Jacob after he wrestled with the angel and it means One Who Wrestles with the Divine, I consider anyone who does this kind of work just such a God-wrestler. So while such a person may not be a member of the Jewish people, he or she is of the People Israel. That's my universalist take on our particularist tribal origin story.

heart away from unskillful action toward apprehension of the Light and then aligning one's will with the greater Will is known as the arousal from below—Itaruta Diletata. It goes both ways, since when one aligns with the Divine, when one performs *mitzvot,* this creates an arousal that originates from above, known as the Itaruta Dile'eyla, which brings down blessings. I like that the word *arousal,* which in English has sexual connotations, is used for this spiritual attraction and Connection between humans and the Divine in this week of Yesod.

In Chesed of Yesod, we see that the Flow goes both ways. And if we can open our defenses, even just a little, like the man in the Nine of Wands, that Flow can heal our relationship to Intimacy with others and with the Divine Itself.

Day 36: Chesed of Yesod in B'riah

The Four and Nine of Cups

_____ *within* _____

Two figures are seated, both with arms crossed. One looks uncertain as the Flow continues to offer him its blessings. The other looks smug and satisfied since he has received many blessings from this Flow, though his position suggests he is blocking it from continuing. In the

Four of Cups, though, the young man's legs are also crossed, while in the Nine of Cups, the older man's legs are spread wide—not a surprise in a card associated with Yesod and sexual Connection.

One can view these two figures as the same person at different points in life, each with a different Relationship to the Flow of Love and the Flow of Intimate Connection. Perhaps the younger man does not feel worthy of this Flow of blessings. Or instead, the Infinite One keeps offering him the Flow of blessings, but he's reacting like a petulant child because either they're not exactly what he wants or not good enough for what he believes he deserves. Nevertheless, the cups keep coming so that by the time he is older he has amassed a table full of them that seem to extend even beyond what we can see, since the table and the row of cups are cut off at both ends. And indeed, each of the figures in the cards are also cut off—emotionally.

Rather than recognizing the impersonal nature of Divine Flow, the man in the Nine of Cups claims these blessings as his and his alone. He sits in the center as though he is the center of the universe and this is how he wants to present himself to the world. But is he really that smug and self-satisfied?

It could be that if he was the younger man who felt unworthy, now as an older man he feels like an impostor and hides this from others; thus, the tunic that covers him from his neck to his ankles and the tablecloth that hides what's under the table.

There's a famous story that originated with the great spiritual teacher and storyteller Rabbi Nachman of Breslov that this image brings to mind, "The Rooster Prince."

There was once a prince who went insane: he believed he was a rooster, and so he took off all his clothes and stayed under a table pecking at scraps. The king and queen called in doctors and healers of all kinds, but none of them could cure the prince of his delusion until one day a wise man came to the palace and claimed he could restore the prince. The king and queen, desperate for help, agreed. So the wise man took off all his clothes and joined the prince under the table!

After some time the prince asked, "Who are you, and what are you doing here?"

The wise man, like many Jews, answered the question with a question, "And who are you, and what are you doing here?"

"I am a rooster," said the prince.

"Me too," said the wise man.

After a while, the wise man put on a shirt, and the prince asked him, "What are you doing?"

"What makes you think that a rooster can't wear a shirt?" said the wise man. "You can wear a shirt and still be a rooster." So the prince also put on a shirt.

Each day, the wise man put on a new article of clothing, and the prince questioned him in the same way. And then each day, the prince followed suit, until they were both fully, uh, suited up.

Next the wise man signaled the king's servants to bring food on a plate from the table. And when he began to eat, he asked the prince, "What makes you think that you will stop being a rooster if you eat food from a plate? You can eat whatever you want and still be a rooster!" So the prince began to eat food from a plate.

The day came when the wise man asked the prince, "What makes you think a rooster must sit under the table? Even a rooster can sit at the table." And when the wise man got up from under the table and rejoined the king and queen, the prince joined him, completely cured.

Well, at least the story says he was completely cured. But it doesn't say that he no longer believed he was a rooster, just that it was okay for him, as a rooster, to dress, eat, and behave like a human. Now, Rabbi Nachman's stories were all allegories, and every time there was a king in the story, it was clear he was speaking about God. So the rooster prince was understood as the Jews, who, having endured centuries of persecution and exile, had forgotten who they were. And the only one who could remind them of their former state was a wise rabbi, in this case Rabbi Nachman himself, who by telling the story was reminding his audience of Hasidim that they were royalty.

Why am I telling this story now? As a storyteller, when I look at the cards I am sometimes reminded of specific tales. And looking at these two cards, I think of the young man in the Four of Cups as someone who feels unworthy of the blessing of Divine Flow; he thinks of himself as somehow an impostor. So as he gets older, he decides to act out his feelings of unworthiness by believing he is a rooster and hiding under the table.

And in the Nine of Cups we see him after he has been "cured" by the wise man, so that once again, he is seated before a table. Except his red hat with a plume suggests that somewhere deep inside he still believes he's a rooster, that he really isn't worthy of all these blessings. And he keeps the tablecloth covering the table all the way down to the ground so that if he's feeling a little, uh, peckish later on, he can go behind the tablecoth and peck at scraps underneath the table with no one seeing him. His "addiction" to acting like a rooster is somewhat under control inasmuch as he isn't living under the table full-time. But because the root cause of his delusion, his feelings of unworthiness, hasn't been addressed, he still keeps his arms crossed over his heart because he doesn't feel worthy of Divine Love and Connection. There is a degree to which he still sees himself as an impostor, and this keeps him from showing his heart to another.

This is a tragic scenario, but it is not an uncommon dynamic. So what would help effect a real cure that goes to the root of the problem?

The issue goes right back to the Flow that is central to both Chesed and Yesod. One must participate in the Flow; by sharing the blessings instead of crossing his arms over his heart, the man in these cards could thus become Connected to others in a web of Relationship. He must learn that these blessings are not his alone, that they are meant to be shared. And by acting in a way that puts his self-interest to the side, he will become authentically interested in others. He will no longer feel like an impostor—or terminally unique—because he will see himself as part of a community.

You may not have had such an extreme experience as this, but if there is any way in which you are stopping the Flow because you feel unworthy, remember, you are royalty. And the gifts you receive are to be shared.

Day 36: Chesed of Yesod in Yetzirah

The Four and Nine of Swords

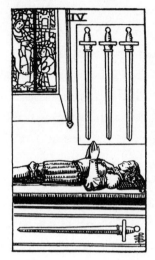

_____ *within* _____

When you lay the Four and Nine of Swords side by side as you see in today's illustration, the plane of the sarcophagus and the bed are such that the "pillow" on which the knight rests his head looks as though it could continue into the pillow of the figure in the bed. And as I looked at these two figures facing away from each other atop their respective "beds," another image came to mind: the cherubim atop the Ark of the Covenant.

There were very highly detailed instructions on how to build this sacred reliquary in Exodus, and atop the box were two cherubim. These angelic beings were not the cute little sanitized babies with wings you see on Valentine's Day cards: they resembled the Egyptian sphinxes or the Babylonian *shedu*. They were hybrid beings, most likely with the body of a lion or a bull, the wings of an eagle, and the head of a human. If you're of a certain age, your image of them is probably of the Ark as it was pictured in the Steven Spielberg movie *Raiders of the Lost Ark*. And this was inspired by the James Jacques Joseph Tissot painting of Moses and Joshua praying before the Ark, which gives the cherubim, portrayed as fully human-looking except for their wings, an art nouveau feel. In the painting, the cherubim face each other, and it is from the space between them that the voice of YHVH emanates. But in the tradition, the cherubim don't always face each other. According to the Talmud, their faces would miraculously change direction depending on whether the people looking at them were living in harmony with the Torah. If the cherubim were facing each other, the people were living in harmony with the will of God. But if the cherubim were facing away from each other, that meant the people had fallen away from God.[1]

We are two weeks away from the *hieros gamos* of YHVH and the Shekinah, but when we look at the images of the Four and Nine of Swords, it seems we're in need of some Divine Marriage counseling. There are still issues we need to face about the Relationship of our inner masculine and inner feminine, and there is little time left. And there may well be issues we need to address in our communication with a partner. So there is great urgency in the work of this week. And in particular, the work of this day.

Whether it's an inner dialogue or a discussion with a partner about how the Relationship is structured and how that affects what gets spoken and what does not, the relentless forward energy of Chesed of Yesod pushes us to come, uh, face-to-face with anything that gets in the way of Love and spiritual or interpersonal (as though there's a difference) Intimacy.

The figures in the cards depict the stereotypical male/female emotional split. In the Four of Swords, the man is in a place of silence. It is as though he has retreated from engagement and maintains an air of being above it all; he shows no emotion. Meanwhile, the figure in the Nine of Swords, which we'll denote as female in this reading, is expressing great emotion. It's a classic situation where the man holds his feelings in, which only makes the woman more emotional and unhappy. It's a crazy-making dynamic for a woman since it denies her inner experience and it denies her the experience of Intimacy with a partner.

Whether an inner experience, an interpersonal experience, or both, this split must be healed for one to be whole. We must fully face each other if we want to see the Divine as Moses did, face-to-face.

Day 36: Chesed of Yesod in Assiyah

The Four and Nine of Pentacles

_____ *within* _____

The male biblical figure associated with Yesod is Joseph, for his ability to withstand the seductive advances of Potiphar's wife. I don't see Joseph in this pairing, but I do see Potiphar and his wife. While Potiphar's wife is not named in the Torah, she is given a name and a story in an Islamic telling of the story that I love very much, titled "Yusuf and Zulaikha."

There are many versions of this story, and as in the biblical story, Joseph was sold into slavery by his brothers and bought by Potiphar, who is often identified as the captain of the guard in Pharaoh's palace. In these versions of the story, Joseph is described as so beautiful that no woman could look on him without falling in love with him, so that for Zulaikha to fall for him was not especially unusual. In fact, in the version of the story written by the Persian Sufi poet Jami, Joseph is described so erotically, and homoerotically, that even Potiphar finds himself attracted to the young man's almost supernatural beauty. And as evidence of this breathtaking beauty, the story tells of Zulaikha's inviting the neighboring wives to come for lunch because they had all been gossiping about her obsession with the young man. They were cutting oranges as he entered the room to serve them drinks, and in their amazement at his attractiveness, they all sliced their fingers without realizing it until he left the room.

What makes this Sufi version of the story so different from the biblical telling is that Zulaikha gave up everything for her love. She lost her husband, her home, and her social position. She sold what little was left of what she owned just to catch glimpses of him. Her own beauty faded, and she became blind. Yet her love did not die, and in fact, at the end of the story, her sight and her beauty are restored. The fire of her passion purified her love, and she was rewarded by God: Joseph found and married her. In this version by Jami, the story is an allegory of the soul's yearning for the Divine. There is also much other Islamic poetry that is homoerotic and uses this desire as a metaphor for the soul's desire for the Divine.

Of course, with Yesod, there is always the danger that this desire can stay on the earthly plane. In twelve-step programs for sexual compulsion, members are advised that when they see someone they find attractive, they should allow themselves to gaze on this beauty for three seconds and then look away while saying a prayer of gratitude to God for creating such beauty. This is not unlike the Baal Shem Tov's instruction to find the root of good that is hidden in desire.

In this pairing, I look at the man in the Four of Pentacles as Potiphar; concerned only with his position and possessions, he is unaware of the star, the Divine, hidden within these material concerns, so that he is not participating with the Divine Flow. The woman in the garden in the Nine of Pentacles is Zulaikha, languishing alone because her husband's attentions are elsewhere; the Flow of both Chesed and Yesod within her are damned up and awaiting the release that will come after she suffers for her love. For after all her suffering, an angel appeared with a message to Joseph from God telling him to marry her.

> *Mine eyes have seen her in humble mood;*
> *I heard her prayer when to thee she sued.*
> *At the sight of her labors, her prayers, and sighs,*

The waves of the sea of My pity rise.
Her soul from the sword of despair I free,
And here from My throne I betroth her to thee.[2]

So may your soul be free from the sword of despair, and may you find in earthly Love and Intimacy the path to the Divine.

A quick sidenote on one other way to look at this pairing. Consider these images with the lyrics of the song "A Bird in a Gilded Cage." There's no question that the desire within Yesod can turn toward choosing a partner for material wealth. And this is just one of the many other ways you can go with this pairing. My focus on the story of Zulaikha is a reflection of my own experience of this pair in the count; remember you can go in lots of other directions as long as they capture a facet of the Sephirotic pairing of the day. I hope that my examples speak to you in some way, but if not, I hope my examples show you how to find your own way.

Questions for reflection and contemplation: Day 36

1. (Wands) What is your Relationship to your spiritual community? Is this a different community from the one you were born into? If so, what is your Relationship to that spiritual community too? Do you have more than one spiritual community? If so, do you notice playing them off against each other as a way to keep from going into deeper Relationship with one of them? Are there prayers or rituals that bring up your defenses? If so, why? How might you heal this dynamic?

2. (Cups) Are there any ways you feel unworthy of the blessings in your life? If so, why? Consider sharing your blessings in a new and different way, possibly with new people, as a way of finding and feeling your rightful place of Connection in the Divine Flow.

3. (Swords) If you are in a committed Relationship, initiate a conversation that invites your partner to share with you questions or concerns in your Relationship that have not been voiced—in ways that are not blaming but are simple statements of feeling. Search within yourself for similar thoughts and feelings. Share these with each other while seated

face-to-face and while reminding each other of the love and respect you have for each other. Then commit to working out any problems and recommit to each other. If you are not in a committed Relationship (and if you are you can also do this), have an inner dialogue between your inner masculine and inner feminine; ask both of them to share with the other the ways they feel welcomed by the other and then say what about them feels unwelcomed. Have both voice their fears or defenses around those traits and say why they might appear to the other to be unwelcomed. Then have each inner voice welcome the other fully, so that together they may enable you to feel and express the full range of emotions. Thank them—and yourself—for the courage to do this.

4. (Pentacles) Has there been someone in your life whom you loved obsessively, whom you desired in ways that tested your sense of reason? Regardless of what happened in this situation, write a letter (that you are not to send) thanking this person for showing you the depth of your heart and your yearning for the Divine. Explain that what drove you to such extremes of feeling or behavior was the depth of this Yearning— not as an excuse, but as a way of telling yourself that this person opened a gate in your heart to the Divine. If this is true, write that now you know how to Connect with the Divine on your own and that you sincerely wish that Connection for this person as well. When you're done, burn the letter. If this is not something in your experience, in what ways do you see the Relationship between the couple in this card pairing as reflecting your own Relationships?

Day 37: Gevurah of Yesod
Setting Boundaries in Intimacy

> Today is the thirty-seventh day of the Omer,
> which is five weeks and two days of the Omer.

Yes, Yesod is about sexual Connection. But what is it about "no" and the setting of Boundaries that so many men do not seem to understand?

I have a memory from an old comedy skit that I can't place: in it, a man is forcing his attentions on a woman, and she protests, saying "Don't." Then she says "Stop!" He continues to press forward as she says "Don't," followed again soon after by "Stop!" But then the words run together so that what first was a protest has turned into an expression of desire as she says "Don't stop! Don't stop!" It was meant to be funny. Of course, today it seems anything but.

This was a message to men: women may say "no," but they mean "yes." Uh, no. However, it seems as though many men have internalized this message, whether they've seen this skit or not. And it's not just an issue between men and women.

I was raped when I was nineteen years old. Yes, me too. Though I feel that it's not entirely appropriate for a man to use this anthemic phrase that speaks to what feels like structural misogynistic violence in our society. And as someone who was also molested as a child, I have struggled a great deal with setting or observing sexual boundaries. But my story isn't uncommon. According to the National Sexual Violence Resource Center, in the United States, one in three women and one in six men experience some form of contact sexual violence in their lifetime.[3] And more than half of those who reported being raped, whether male or female, were violated by someone they knew—either an intimate partner or an acquaintance.

Stories like this are hardly new. The Tanakh tells the story of how King David's eldest son, Amnon, plotted to rape his sister Tamar. Once he had committed the crime, "Then Amnon hated her with intense hatred."[4] Sound familiar? It's always the victim's fault. And I'm sure his hatred was a projection of his own self-loathing and disgust. Often men act out their self-loathing in sexual violence, which is then reinforced by this action, setting in motion a cycle of assault.

For today, we'll look at the effects of broken Boundaries in sexual Connection. We'll also consider how the Boundary-setting Restraint of Gevurah can provide safety from sexual violence and how the Discipline of Gevurah can be part of a healthy relationship of Intimacy.

Day 37: Gevurah of Yesod in Atzilut

The Five and Nine of Wands

_____ *within* _____

We've looked at the figure in the Nine of Wands before as someone whose ability to accept or even tolerate Intimacy has been wounded. In this pairing with the Five of Wands, we can see the origin of this wounding in a Boundary violation. While the suit of Wands as Atzilut is not generally interpreted physically, we can't ignore the phallic nature of the suit, especially in the week of Yesod. So when I look at the Five of Wands in this context, several places where sexual abuse seems to thrive come to mind, whether orthodox yeshivas, high school football teams, Olympic ice skating teams, Hollywood studios, Congress, the Catholic Church, churches in general, or frat houses; people in all these settings can share a mind-set that has come to be known as rape culture.

If this phrase is new to you, rape culture has been defined as a setting where rape is pervasive and the perpetrators, who are often people in power or from privileged groups, are not only not held accountable, but their actions also are minimized because their communities don't want to ruin their futures (in the cases of student athletes) or their careers (in the cases of teachers, coaches, doctors, clerics, or legislators), thus revictimizing the person who was assaulted. Brock Turner, a Stanford University student on the school's swim team who was convicted of sexual assault, received what many at the time considered a light sentence, some say because the judge in the case had also attended Stanford, where he was captain of the lacrosse team. Turner's father protested against the prosecutor, who was seeking a harsher sentence, writing that the sentence would be "a steep price to pay for 20 minutes of action out of his 20 plus years of life."[5] Of course, there may be no clearer example of rape culture than the now infamous phrase, "Grab them by the pussy."

While the figure in the Nine of Wands is male, the dynamic being illustrated is not about the gender of the person being violated. Because rape culture is about establishing dominance and power, regardless of the gender of the victim.

These cards ask us to consider how we participate in rape culture. The phrase "Grab them by the pussy" was excused as "locker-room talk." But in Judaism, words have power, and words like this deny the dignity and agency of another. Of course, I've been guilty of such talk. Before I came out, I would participate in talk like this with other young men as a way of hiding who I was, so that I was doing violence to myself as well as to others. And as a gay man, I've objectified and sexualized other gay men in what is called "sport fucking," which is the seeking out of casual sex as both hunt and conquest—often going out with friends and competing to see who catches someone first. There are those who would say that's just boys being boys. No, that's boys socialized into a system by society.

Based on my own history and experience, that's what seeing this pairing brings up for me. It means I have healing to do, and I have to make amends to some people, and it means I must be more conscious moving forward. I can't speak the way I did when I was younger. I can't remain silent when other people say sexist, misogynistic things. And I have work to do in emotional and sexual Intimacy. My history is such that my stance in the world is not so different from the man in the Nine of Wands in that I am not very trusting and I enter almost every relationship expecting to be betrayed. Of course, this very stance helps create the thing I fear.

Your response to this pairing may be very different if you haven't had any experiences of abuse—and I hope that's true. It means your work around this energy also will be very different. But if you have had such experiences, as you do the work of this day, remember to be gentle with yourself. There's a way in which you can see the figure in the Nine of Wands as taking a "time out" to heal while leaving room for the possibility of Connection. If you're taking just such a break, it can be a very good thing. Just be sure it doesn't harden into your stance in the world.

Day 37: Gevurah of Yesod in B'riah

The Five and Nine of Cups

within

In the previous pair, the man in the Nine of Wands showed his wounds to the world, even if he deflected Connection. Here, in the pairing of the Five and Nine of Cups, we have a similar situation, with a traumatic wounding, but here the pain we see in the Five of Cups is hidden in the Nine of Cups. In the Gevurah card, we confront brokenness. And because the figure in black is looking down on the broken cups in a way that hides her face, the natural response is to interpret this as mourning, and while this can be the case, we can also interpret the situation as the figure feeling shame.

The figure in the Five of Cups could be mourning lost Relationships, lost innocence, or broken promises or vows. And this figure could be ashamed of actions they have taken that have led to this break. We can also think of this figure as experiencing their own inner brokenness as the result of abuse, either as victim or perpetrator.

Then we come to the Nine of Cups. I've mentioned before that this card can suggest high-functioning alcoholism, and any addiction can be a response to abuse or a way to numb feelings of loss or shame. Similarly, I've written about this card as showing someone with something to hide. He could be hiding how damaged and ashamed he really feels inside as a victim, or he could be hiding how ashamed and guilty he feels as a perpetrator. Or both, since so many perpetrators of abuse have a history of being abused themselves.

In this dynamic, the Intimate Connection of Yesod is blocked by past trauma that is unresolved and unacknowledged. This trauma does not have to be sexual, but it is probably the result of a Boundary violation or break of some sort. Until this is dealt with, the Connection on offer in the Nine of Cups will only be a surface, shallow Connection. And all the pleasures and emotions represented by the nine cups on the table will continue to be overshadowed by the three overturned cups in the Five of Cups.

Personally, I experience this pairing as about the loss of friends and lovers to HIV. As I write these words, I am sitting in a house in the Pines, on Fire Island, one of the most popular queer beach resorts in the country. Just the other night, while I was out with friends watching the sun set at the harbor, I heard a man in his early twenties ask an older man why he was single. I held my breath for a second, tensing against what I was afraid would be the reply.

"All the men I ever loved are dead; the man who was my soul mate died more than ten years ago," the older man replied.

If you had seen this older man dancing at a pool party earlier in the afternoon, you would not have suspected this sadness, for not unlike the man in the Nine of Cups, he puts on a good face. And he does enjoy his life, and he has many blessings. But he is still traumatized by the losses in the eighties and nineties of his friends and lovers. He has been unable to let anyone in to a new Intimate relationship out of Fear (another face of Gevurah) of reexperiencing this trauma and loss. But aside from that momentary reveal of his pain, his time out here looks to all who don't know his story to be filled with pleasure. And it is. However, it is pleasure shadowed by loss and grief. Sometimes he drinks too much; sometimes he uses other drugs as well to numb himself to the memories. How do I know all this? I know this man well, though he is not a housemate. His pain is a pain I have also known, and there are many like him in my generation. I pray for the healing of his heart and the hearts of all those so affected.

Day 37: Gevurah of Yesod in Yetzirah

The Five and Nine of Swords

_____ *within* _____

So far, I haven't spoken very much about the face of Gevurah known as Pachad—Fear. But in this pairing, I see Fear of Intimacy. It's the expectation that letting someone in for Intimate Connection will only lead to betrayal, Boundary violations, and pain. It's an expectation that could be the result of something one has experienced in the past or because one has seen the suffering in one's family after an infidelity by a parent.

The grief we see in the Nine of Swords can be because one has been betrayed or because one is ashamed of having betrayed another. We can look at the figures in these two cards either as a couple or as two aspects of one person.

Because Yesod includes sexual Connection as one of its facets, this seems like the obvious place to go. But remember, in Judaism sexuality is not separate from spirituality, so that a sexual betrayal can be a metaphor for a spiritual betrayal. And in fact, this exact metaphor runs through the Tanakh, though nowhere perhaps as directly in the book of the prophet Hosea.

The story opens with YHVH telling Hosea to find a prostitute and marry her. Why? So he will understand the sense of betrayal felt by the Divine. Yes, there are lots of stories of men who break their marriage vows—not least among them King David. But when YHVH is unhappy with the People Israel for breaking the covenant by worshipping other gods, the language used is one of sexual infidelity and prostitution, with YHVH as the "man." The people "whore" after foreign gods. So that YHVH tells Hosea:

> *I will punish her for the days of the Baalim,**
> *When she made offerings to them,*
> *And when she decked herself with earrings and jewels,*
> *And went after her lovers,*
> *Forgetting Me—declares YHVH.*[6]

While the offender in the Five of Swords is male and the grieving figure in the Nine of Swords appears to be female, the metaphor works for all gender combinations. If you break the covenant, you are breaking your Connection to the Divine, and there are consequences. So that not only does YHVH grieve, but so will you.

---

*Baal was a god worshipped by other ancient Near Eastern peoples; Baalim is the plural form. Baal also means "master" and "husband" in Hebrew, depending on the context.

I know this broken Connection because I have felt my Connection break. While I do not believe in the letter of all the commandments, I do know there are actions that, at least for me, are not acceptable behavior. These actions might bring other people closer to a sense of the Divine, but for me the result is the exact opposite. And knowing this, I have nevertheless persisted at times in such actions so that one evening I can remember feeling something break inside me—as though an energy channel in my spine was cut or went out of alignment.

Afterward, there were many nights when I felt like the figure in the Nine of Swords—out of alignment with my integrity and cut off from Divine Connection. But what is important to know is that there is always a way back.

The first two words of my bar mitzvah *haftorah,* which I chanted at age thirteen, before I walked away from Judaism for many years, were also from Hosea: "*Shuvah Y'Israel,*" (Return Israel). And YHVH promises, "Generously will I take them back in love."[7]

The path of return is not fast or easy. But the gates are always open to those whose hearts open to t'shuvah.

Day 37: Gevurah of Yesod in Assiyah

The Five and Nine of Pentacles

_____ *within* _____

The stone that the builders rejected has become the chief cornerstone.

PSALMS 118:22

How do we get from the Five of Pentacles, with its feelings of negative Judgment and rejection, to the Nine of Pentacles, the cornerstone that is the Foundation? Let's start with the card of Gevurah and look at the Relationship of the two poor people left outside the church in the snow. Their Strength in adversity is not the only thing that helps them to survive; they also apply that Strength to their Bonding with each other. So the difficulties they face together are what help them stay together, closely Connected spiritually, even if they appear to be in spiritual exile from the Church.

Despite the fact that they are outside in the cold, their Relationship of spiritual Intimacy is the garden in their lives that we see in the Nine of Pentacles. Having "found" each other, their Relationship also becomes the Foundation of their Strength.

Looking at their Relationship from the other side, from the Shadow Tree, the two figures in the Five of Pentacles could have Bonded over their shared resentment of being rejected and Judged negatively. They could take a "Fox and the Grapes"–type approach to their rejection and cast aspersions on the institution that has kept them outside. Like Groucho Marx, who is reported to have said, "I don't care to belong to any club that will have me as a member," they may wear their rejection as a badge of honor, knowing in their hearts that their Relationship exemplifies the spiritual values that the institution that has excluded and scorned them purports to maintain.

This is part of my own spiritual journey as a queer Jew. At age thirteen, the day after my bar mitzvah, I walked away from Judaism in self-exile because I knew I was gay and I knew that as soon as I came out I would be a "stone that was rejected." I went through stages that were angry and resentful. I went through a period of militant atheism. I found groups that offered spiritual gifts within the LGBTQ community, and I began my search for a path to the Divine that felt welcoming of all of me. I discovered queer spirituality. I found spiritual practices and traditions that helped heal my resentment, and eventually I found my way home to Judaism in the years of ferment before the Conservative movement shifted their view on lesbian and gay Relationships to acceptance. And I brought my experience in social activism to the denominational hierarchy in Conservativism.

The first time I went to Congregation B'nai Jeshurun for Erev Shabbat services, there just happened to be an LGBTQ social potluck dinner after services. After we said the blessings on the wine and the bread, Rabbi Marshall T. Meyer, z"l, said something I had waited many years to hear.

"We don't hold these events to show people how 'tolerant' we are. We do this because as a community, we are not whole without you," he said.

That was when I knew I had finally found a Jewish home. Though I have to admit, when I heard these words, they sounded so good I wasn't sure I trusted what I was hearing. But I kept going back, and soon I discovered that this rabbi walked his talk. And that this community was willing to struggle with the hard issues with respect, integrity, and love. Within a very short time, I found myself Strongly Connected to the community, to its leaders, and to their mission. I found myself Connected to the tradition I was born into in ways that opened me to a deeper Connection to the Divine.

Because you're reading this book, there is every possibility that you too have walked away from a tradition that made you feel rejected for one reason or another. Perhaps you've found a way to return, or maybe you've found a new home. Not everyone gets to return to their tradition in the way I have. But Strong Bonds can be forged in Intimate spiritual relationships that show there are gates to Divine Connection everywhere, and they are always open.

Questions for reflection and contemplation: Day 37

1. (Wands) What is your experience with Intimacy Boundaries? Have yours been respected or violated? Do you respect those of others? How has your experience affected your ability to trust others? If your Intimacy Boundaries are weak, what can you do to strengthen those Boundaries? If they are too defended, how can you open up safely?

2. (Cups) Have you ever had traumatic experiences of loss that make it difficult for you to open to new Intimacy? If you feel broken in some way, how does that prevent you from opening to deep Intimacy? Consider sharing your feelings of brokenness with someone you have a Foundation of Intimacy with. In Intimate Relationships, do you focus more on what could go wrong as a way of holding yourself back from going deeper? If so, what can you do to change that?

3. (Swords) What is your experience of betrayal in Intimate relationship? Do you choose trustworthy people to Bond with? If you have ever betrayed your own values, how did that affect your Connection with the Divine? What temptations do you face that leave you feeling disconnected or distant from the Divine? What actions can you take to reconnect?

4. (Pentacles) Have you ever Bonded deeply with someone in shared adversity? If so, did your Connection feel spiritually Intimate or did it feel desperate? Can it be both? If you ever felt cut off from your faith community, what did you do to maintain your Connection with the Divine?

Day 38: Tiferet of Yesod

Truth Is the Foundation of Intimacy

Today is the thirty-eighth day of the Omer, which is five weeks and three days of the Omer.

When I was ten years old, I was a compulsive liar. Looking back, I can't believe how easily I made the most outrageous claims about what I could do, even as these claims were easily proven untrue. It's probably one of the reasons my school recommended that my parents (who could not afford this at all) send me to a child psychologist for a couple of years. Dutifully, they did so, though it had absolutely no effect on my behavior at all. In fact, because seeing a child psychologist was considered shameful in 1960s Brooklyn, I lied to my friends about where I went every Tuesday after school, and my parents, who felt the same shame, colluded in this lie.

As I got older, much of this behavior receded, but it didn't go away entirely. My lying was not necessarily about anything important, and sometimes it felt automatic. I had a habit of saying that I had read books I'd never read, for example. It was in the service of building up my know-it-all status. Of course, lying meant I was always in danger of being found out to be a fraud and a liar. It wasn't until after my first Vipassana meditation retreat in my early thirties that I physically felt the effect of lying on my soul (despite the fact that Buddhists don't believe in a soul). But even with that, there's a degree to which this behavior still affected my closest relationships.

What ultimately led to a change was working with Gay and Kathlyn Hendricks in the workshops based on material in their book *Conscious Loving: The Journey to Co-Commitment*. They taught that there were three fundamental requirements for a conscious Relationship: feeling your feelings, telling the truth, and keeping your commitments. Pretty basic, huh? Well, I grew up in a family where my father was a serial adulterer, so that truth seemed kind of fungible to me.

This work taught me why I felt lonely even in my Intimate relationships. When you lie to your lover, you immediately create a distance, a wall that blocks off the truth of who you are. And then of course you feel as though the real you isn't being loved because in fact you're not showing the real you. This insincerity ultimately creates feelings of insecurity about the relationship.

This is one of the things that makes Intimate Relationship a spiritual practice; it demands a radical commitment to the Truth, which means there's no posturing or trying to manage one's image.* An Intimate Relationship is where all of you—both shadow and light—will be on view to your partner. And monogamy in such a relationship is the alembic that forces you to face that shadow with clarity and love. Monogamy is the container for Intimacy.†

---

*I grieve for the Facebook generation, which struggles with the distance between the image management of their online personas and the reality of who they are. Social media has made this split deep and epidemic.

†But what about open relationships? you may ask. What about polyamory? This is a big subject, enough for another book that I'm not the one to write. I know people in open relationships that are spiritually Intimate. I'm just not sure that I can live this way, so it's not my way.

I come from a family where cheating was a multigenerational behavior: both my father and his father were adulterers. Then, coming out into the gay world of the early seventies, where monogamy was, like marriage, considered a regressive tool of oppression, I was socialized into a rather promiscuous way of life. It took me a long time to settle down, because in Truth, the commitment to Truth and Intimacy can make for some very unsettling experiences. Such a commitment requires creating a strong container that can hold the dynamically changing nature of personalities in relationship.

Ultimately, though, this Foundation for Intimacy is the one place, apart from your relationship with the Divine, where your brokenness can be held with Compassion.

Tiferet of Yesod, as Truth in Intimacy, brings up all these issues. Then again, as we turn the kaleidoscope of Sephirotic meanings, we also come up against Compassion in Intimacy, Dynamic Equilibrium in Foundation, and Heart in Creativity, to name a few. The pair to explore is the one that is the hottest for you. Let's see what the cards reveal about these pairings.

Day 38: Tiferet of Yesod in Atzilut

The Six and Nine of Wands

_____ *within* _____

Looking at these two cards, they seem to pose a question: Can a love between two people of unequal status be truly Intimate, or is it doomed to end with resentment over unequal reciprocity? This is not an academic question: I have a friend who is married to a highly successful executive who pulls down millions of dollars a year in salary and bonuses. My friend's income sometimes doesn't go above five figures. This is further complicated by roles assigned by gender in our society. My friend is male and married to a woman. They have struggled with their perception of who the "breadwinner" is supposed to be and how to divide up child-rearing responsibilities. Their relationship did not start out with them in these positions; that's just how it developed over time. And that's one of the lessons of Tiferet: roles are not set in stone but are dynamic, and for Intimacy to survive these shifting roles, there must be a radical commitment to Truth and transparency.

I know this from my own experience because at the turn of the century I began an intimate relationship with a man who was twenty-five years younger than I was. And it wasn't an easy relationship, but what made it work was our commitment to transparency and Truth. This meant sharing our insecurities and fears about the Relationship. It meant being sensitive and awake to how we were judged by others when we were out in public. He knew that some people saw him as a gold digger. I knew some people saw me as a lecherous old man. We tried not to let these stereotypical projections become introjections, but when we did, we had to talk about it. I'd never met anyone his age who had the psychological depth and commitment to self-reflection he demonstrated. This enabled us to be emotionally naked with each other in a way that made us equals, because unlike the figures in the Six and Nine of Wands, we were constantly shifting positions and changing roles. Maybe not to the eyes of the outside world, since our age difference wasn't going to change. But so much else did. And within the container of that relationship, the constantly shifting (im)balance gave our connection its juice. And surfing that change is the Dynamic Equilibrium of Intimacy. That relationship ended after several years only because he was no longer able to live the commitment to sharing the Truth.

Of course, I say the figures in the cards don't change roles because like the figures on Keats's famous Grecian urn, they are static images. That's the warning to those of us who are in relationships that are unequal in one way or another. When people harden in a role or believe that roles won't shift and change, they're setting themselves up for falling off the horse or feeling the defensive resentment we see in the Nine of Wands. Or worse, the partners collude in staying exactly where they are with no change or growth because that might seem threatening in some way.

And here's the kicker: while the two relationships I've used here as examples are obvious in their inequality, every relationship has its imbalances. Giving and receiving are constantly shifting sands. If you're in a relationship and you don't think it's unequal in some way, you're probably sitting on a white horse and your partner is eyeing you warily. This pairing is an invitation to explore these imbalances with Compassionate Commitment to emotional Truth. Because there is no perfect reciprocity in love, but there can be honesty between lovers about how they are giving and receiving. And that is the Foundation for all love.

Day 38: Tiferet of Yesod in B'riah

The Six and Nine of Cups

_____ *within* _____

Joshua ben Perachya said: Get yourself a teacher. Find a companion to study with and challenge you. Don't prejudge anyone, but weigh all in the scales of justice leading with their virtues.

PIRKEI AVOT 1:6

For almost two thousand years, traditionally, the most intimate spiritual relationship a Jewish man had was with another man—his study partner. This custom goes back to the earliest days of rabbinic Judaism, and this is the *chaver*, the "companion," referred to in the quote from the Pirkei Avot above. Hevruta-style learning pairs two students to analyze sacred texts, most often from the Talmud or the Torah. This pairing teaches each member to think logically and make a reasoned argument to his partner. He also must listen carefully to his partner's argument. Each member will challenge the other's questions, as Joshua ben Perachya suggested, thus sharpening the thinking of the other. Together, they often reach new insights. As the custom has been practiced in traditional yeshivas, partners are often carefully paired and remain together throughout their schooling, so that these pairs can develop into deep, spiritually Intimate friendships.

So why am I writing about this custom? Because the relationship in the Six of Cups is sometimes interpreted as a joining of opposites in loving Harmony, and one meaning of the Nine of Cups is deep satisfaction. While I didn't grow up with a traditional Jewish education, I have participated in hevruta-style study, and I've found that it requires an awareness of the Sephirotic virtues represented by Tiferet, Yesod, and their respective precursor pairs on the tree: kindness, discernment, Truth, Balance, perseverance, humility, Creativity, Intimacy, and Bonding.

You don't have to be working from sacred texts to study in this way. When I would meet with my twelve-step sponsor weekly, we would read the Big Book together, and we worked with the text in exactly this way—going sentence by sentence, relating it to our own experience, and interpreting each sentence in ways that were most meaningful to each of us. And we challenged our interpretations to make certain we didn't fall into any kind of excuses for old behavior.

I have been in tarot workshops where I have been paired with another student, and I've used this style of study to find deeper meanings in the cards and deeper Connections to our lives.

It is a rich and rewarding way to study, with each student offering the gift of their full Presence to the other and each receiving great satisfaction in being deeply seen and heard. As each challenges the other with Compassion, the Bond of spiritual Intimacy grows.

Are there negatives to this pairing and this style of study? Well, as I've said before, I'm kind of a know-it-all. So I can be smug and superior, as the man in the Nine of Cups is sometimes interpreted to be. And I can see my partner as having only a child's understanding, so that I can dominate the debate and miss the gift I'm being offered by my partner. Like the man in the Nine of Cups, I can pretend to welcome my partner's opinion, creating a false Harmony.

The interesting thing about this custom, though, is that even if you have someone who starts out only pretending to participate authentically, the nature of the work is such that each partner will surprise the other with moments of emotional and intellectual Intimacy that disarm the defensive judgment and withholding that can be brought to the work. I know because I've been disarmed in just this way. And as the Pirkei Avot teaches, when "two sit together and interchange words of Torah, the Divine Presence abides between them."[8]

So may the Divine Presence rest between you and your sacred text study partner.

Day 38: Tiferet of Yesod in Yetzirah

The Six and Nine of Swords

_____ *within* _____

What happens when you withhold Truth in an Intimate relationship? What happens when you keep secrets or remain silent in the hopes that such silence will protect Harmony in the relationship? My experience is that it creates an inner alienation, a distancing. And that's just what we can see in the Six of Swords, which has in its set of interpretations keeping secrets or remaining silent instead of telling the Truth. The psychological distance created by this withholding is reified in the image of the people in the boat literally distancing themselves from a Relationship that we know nothing about. Except that the Nine of Swords can give us a clue. Because withholding never goes undetected. Oh, maybe the conscious mind doesn't know, but the unconscious does. I would even venture to say the conscious mind knows and pushes that information away because it's too threatening. And I can say this because I've watched my own mind do this.

I've been in Relationships where I have felt my partner withholding some information, and rather than press the issue, I kept silent myself so that both of us were promoting a false Harmony, putting on a façade of Intimacy. The more you do this, the more you end up feeling isolated and alone and filled with despair, believing that True Intimacy isn't possible. This kind of suffering is tragic and unnecessary. All it takes to avoid all that is two people committed to the Truth. Of course, there's a reason there's a story about Diogenes wandering around Athens in broad daylight with a lantern looking for an honest man.

It takes courage to press the issue and ask what's being withheld— or to be open and not withhold—because the Truth can be painful. Then again, the more distance one has from the Truth, the greater the pain of inner isolation. What looks like a move to protect Harmony in fact destroys it.

This brings me to the Japanese concept of harmony, known as *wa* (和), which is all about preserving the unity of the group through conformity. My experience of this custom is that it suppresses the truth of people's feelings so much that to express one's personal desires can be shameful. In what might seem like a harmless example, I remember after I first arrived in Tokyo, my colleagues and I would have lunch together regularly. I was always asked what I wanted for lunch first, and at first I just assumed this was because I was new and a guest in a way. But I soon realized that I was setting the table for everyone else. Because if I ordered chicken katsu, everyone would order chicken katsu.

A little more comical (and tragic) is that if I came home to find that my boyfriend had made a dinner for me, regardless of whether or not it was food I liked, I was supposed to eat it happily because he had made it for me. And I was supposed to say I loved it. Which meant he believed I loved it, and then he would make it for me more often. This example of dinner is something I experienced and is, by itself, not the most serious issue in the world. But this dynamic can occur within much more serious situations and can create a dance of distancing so that people never express their true feelings or desires. There's a reason that when the Japanese get angry, it's an explosion that seems way out of proportion to the situation: they're sitting on a veritable volcano of repressed emotion. And it's why, as much as I loved Japan, I knew I would have to return to the United States. The distance between the harmony of wa and the Harmony of Tiferet is that Tiferet doesn't hide the Truth of the tension in Dynamic Equilibrium and has Compassion for it—which is Beautiful. Wa submerges the truth in grey conformity. This might work for some people: clearly, it works for most of Japanese society. But it doesn't work for me.

Day 38: Tiferet of Yesod in Assiyah
The Six and Nine of Pentacles

_____ *within* _____

Is the man in the Six of Pentacles giving with an open Heart or is he controlling the situation? Let's consider that what he is giving isn't really money, but that he is sharing love. We all long to be loved fully and unconditionally. And we long to love another in just this way. However, our experience of being hurt and disappointed in love has left us habitually holding back, giving out only the small change of our selves. Having been hurt, we feel fear and anxiety when we give of ourselves—that we'll be left feeling empty and used. So even though we long to give of ourselves, to pour our love into another just as the Divine pours forth Its love into Creation at every moment, we measure out our love, sometimes keeping an inner secret accounting of tit-for-tat reciprocity, making love transactional.

This is one of the dangers associated with the Six of Pentacles. Yes, Tiferet is about Balance, but not the Balance of measuring back-and-forth reciprocity; it's the understanding that as we give, so we receive. That when we take care of someone else, we are also taking care of ourselves. And that because no role is permanent, while we may be giving now, we will be receiving later.

One way of thinking about the measured response of the man in the Six of Pentacles is that he doesn't want to overwhelm the receiver. What happens when you get more than you know what to do with? A Massachusetts Institute of Technology study showed that lottery winners are more likely to declare bankruptcy within three to five years than the average American.[9] And as for love, rather than money, well, giving people more love than they're comfortable with can activate defenses and old traumas. Showing restraint in giving that matches what the receiver can healthily take in is the True, Compassionate Balance of the Six of Pentacles.

Meanwhile, in the Nine of Pentacles, we have a different kind of restraint; this is the reining in of animal impulses in an exercise of self-control represented by the hooded hawk. Because we're in the Sephira of Yesod, this could well be sexual self-restraint.

Together, I see these cards as a teaching about Balancing the needs of the soul and the appetite of the body. They're about learning the difference between Yearning and Desire, which are two aspects of Yesod.

Yearning is fundamental to our experience as humans. It isn't focused on an object; rather, it is the soul feeling its separation from the Divine and longing to "re-Connect." When we allow ourselves to fully feel the depth of our yearning, we face our vulnerability. Desire is almost a defensive response to yearning. Because it is focused on an object that it wants to possess in some way, it provides the mind with the illusion of control: there is an object that can be possessed that will satisfy this feeling. Until, of course, desire rears its head again, since desire can never be fully satisfied. Desire is the shadow side of yearning.

You might look at the lovely garden in the Nine of Pentacles and desire to own it. But that garden was built not because the woman pictured in the card desired it; the garden is the result of cultivating self-restraint, so that the energy of desire went into creating a place where yearning can be experienced as something Beautiful.

Once again, though, I want to emphasize that Judaism sees sexual expression as offering the possibility of self-knowledge and transformation. But this is only possible when we peel back the skin of desire to reveal the yearning underneath. So that when lovers are fully present, joining together in the reciprocity of pleasure, the Divine Presence graces this union, giving the physical act a spiritual meaning. With right intention, physical Intimacy reveals spiritual Truth.

Questions for reflection and contemplation: Day 38

1. (Wands) What are the kinds of inequality you have experienced in your Relationships? How have you dealt with them? What were the conversations about them like? What does it mean to tell the Truth about your feelings without blaming someone for them? How can you listen to your partner talk about feelings without your feeling blamed? How have your roles shifted over the course of your Relationship?

2. (Cups) What is your experience of spiritual companionship in study? Consider reading a sacred text with someone you respect but don't necessarily agree with about some things, then analyze the text together, including what it means to each of you personally.

3. (Swords) What is your experience in Relationships in which there has been withholding? What happened when what was withheld was revealed? Do you believe there are things that can't be shared in an Intimate relationship? If you feel this way, what is it that can't be shared and why?

4. (Pentacles) What is your experience with tit-for-tat accounting in reciprocal Relationships? What does too much love—either giving or getting—mean to you? What does it feel like? What is your relationship with desire? Think of someone or something you desire, and try to feel underneath the desire to the yearning within it. What does it feel like? What does it tell you?

Day 39: Netzach of Yesod

The Ongoing Commitment to Intimacy

Today is the thirty-ninth day of the Omer,
which is five weeks and four days of the Omer.

There are two ways for a relationship to Endure over time. One requires the partners to remain unconscious, colluding with each other to avoid anything that would upset the stasis or challenge them to change or grow. The other requires making a renewed and daily conscious Commitment to remain grounded in integrity, radically honest, and fearlessly Intimate. It means staying open and vulnerable. This isn't an easy path. And it's not something that is "once and done." It is action that is taken over and over again over time. It is, in fact, a spiritual practice.

Making a daily Commitment to Intimacy will bring up your shadow Commitments. The voices in your head that tell you why what you're doing is wrong. The physical sensations in your body that feel uncomfortable so that you get scared that what you're doing is dangerous. You can try this yourself. This is the way to work with affirmations because an affirmation is not a mantra you repeat in the hopes that by repeating something over and over again it will become true. When you speak an affirmation aloud, the first step is to listen for your inner voice telling you why what you said can't happen. The next step is to scan through your body to see where you're holding tension in response to what you said and then explore what's hidden in that tension. I've done just this kind of work, using relationship Commitments and affirmations developed by Gay and Kathlyn Hendricks in a two-year training. It put me face-to-face with the fears and unconscious defenses holding me back from a successful Intimate Relationship.

We can see one of the greatest examples of how a shadow Commitment can sabotage a relationship right in the story of the Israelites at Mt. Sinai, the story that is at the culmination of Counting the Omer and that stands as a forewarning about your inner Israelites on the fiftieth day. The people had promised to remain faithful to YHVH, but while Moses was on the mountain receiving the tablets of the law, the people returned to idolatry and created a golden calf to worship. Even though they made the Commitment that "everything that YHVH has spoken, we will do and obey,"[10] the people's unconscious Commitment to remaining enslaved asserted itself.

May we all wake from the trance and renew our conscious Commitment to a faithful and enduring Intimacy, directly with the Divine and with the Divine as expressed in another person. *Keyn yehi ratzon.*

Day 39: Netzach of Yesod in Atzilut

The Seven and Nine of Wands

_____ *within* _____

Here's an unfortunate but familiar Relationship dynamic. Two sensitive people: one always quick to feel attacked and ready to defend himself, the other wounded and withdrawn. One wants Connection but sees it as confrontational and isn't afraid to be confrontational himself. The other is wary of Connection and mistrustful of both his own desire for Connection and of others who approach him. Somehow, people like this manage to find each other and get entangled in a Relationship that doesn't truly satisfy either, but neither believes anything else is possible.

The Tenacity of the man in the Seven of Wands is not seen as a positive trait by the man in the Nine of Wands. He experiences it as arrogant, controlling, and Dominating. Perhaps underneath this aggressive stance is an experience of being hurt in the past that the man in the Nine of Wands doesn't see or understand. Meanwhile, the man in the Seven of Wands sees the other as inflexible, dug in to a position, and unwilling to engage—as hiding out. He does not understand that this behavior is the result of past trauma. Neither of them is ready to cooperate, listen, and really hear the other, so that no matter how much the man in the Seven of Wands Persists in trying to reach the other, Intimacy remains out of reach.

It's easy to see that the man in the Nine of Wands is behind a barrier. But if you consider the possibility that the staves arrayed against the man in the Seven of Wands are only memories of the past, he is also behind a barrier of perceived persecution. People in this Relationship dynamic have provided retirement savings for many psychologists.

We can also view the Relationship between these two figures as one that is challenged by outside stressors. Minority groups face negative projections, stereotypes, and prejudices that are often introjected; for gay men this is the dynamic of internalized homophobia, and this mental health challenge creates many psychological obstacles for couples in Relationship. These are obstacles I'm familiar with from my own experience. But any kind of couple that faces outside stressors, from economic disadvantages and insecurity to racial or religious discrimination, brings that stress into the Relationship, with the possible results including divorce, abandonment, or domestic abuse.

So often a couple that comes together to find sanctuary from the world then brings the problems of the world into their Relationship. A conscious Commitment to confronting this dynamic can save the Relationship and make it not only a sanctuary but also a new Garden of Eden.

Day 39: Netzach of Yesod in B'riah

The Seven and Nine of Cups

_____ *within* _____

The longest and most successful Intimate Relationship I've had with another man was with my therapist: I saw him individually for more than twenty years. Talk about an Enduring Relationship. And after I finished working with him individually, I continued in a group with him for several more years until my work schedule made continuing impossible. When I looked at these two cards together, one of the many things I saw in the pairing was the Relationship between client and therapist. I could have written "one of the many things I *projected* onto this pairing . . ." Because that's some of what these two cards reveal about Relationship: how we project onto others and what the results of projection can be.

A good therapist knows how to recognize and hold a client's projections, eventually enabling the client to see that they have been unconsciously attributing (both positive and negative) thoughts, motivations, desires, and feelings that they can't accept as their own onto others. This projection occurs in both the therapeutic relationship and with other people in the client's life. So in the Seven of Cups, I see a client arriving with a whole slew of projections that keeps him or her from seeing others clearly and Relating to them with authenticity. And in the Nine of Cups, I see a therapist who is Committed to holding the client's projections without becoming entangled in them. Not a very traditional interpretation of these cards, I know. But in the context of Commitment in Intimacy, it is certainly one way to look at the cards.

A less positive way to see this pairing, and one that can be observed any day, is in the dynamic of romantic illusion. Shakespeare said it best: "Love looks not with the eyes, but with the mind."[11] Long before Freud or Jung, the phenomenon of projection was understood. That's not to say romantic projection can't be positive. Most romantic Relationships begin with mutual positive projection. The work begins when the reality of who the other person really is starts to peek through the projection.

Someone who is unable to deal with the reality of the other when the shine of projection wears off will go off in search of another screen to project onto. Such a person is a serial romantic, and no one can live up to the fantasy, so that person is never able to make an Enduring Commitment. Or that person will make a Commitment based on the fantasy, and when reality bursts the bubble, such an individual sees no problem breaking agreements because the object of the fantasy isn't agreeing to live the fantasy.

There is yet a darker version of this dynamic. Think of the person in the Seven of Cups as a student—perhaps a college or graduate student. And the person in the Nine of Cups as a professor. How many students see their teachers with stars in their eyes and develop a crush on them? How many teachers take advantage of this situation and sleep with their students? Of course, this power dynamic plays out in lots of places besides universities. Look at these two cards, and you can see a young person filled with romantic fantasies and someone with more power enjoying the trophies of so many Relationships.

We could also see the figures in both cards as the same person— someone who has projected fantasies onto many others, someone who has been in and left many relationships and is now alone and filled with self-justification, because after all, when you're busy projecting, it's always the other person's fault.

Now, I don't want to be a total Negative Nathan here. There are projections that also offer the possibility of positive transformation. The faults we most complain about in others, particularly our partners, often are issues that lie within ourselves. That's what Jesus was talking about when he said, "How can you say to your neighbor, 'Let me take the speck out of your eye,' while the log is in your own eye?"[12] And when you find yourself noticing the same speck in lots of other people, it's a clue there's a log in your eye.

When you make the Commitment to see and own your projections, they begin to lose power over you. But the mind is tricky, and it's not easy to do. It takes Determination and Perseverance, along with courage. But the result is greater Intimacy with yourself and others.

Without romantic projection, many couples would not have gotten together. But when the romantic projection wears off and the negative projections start to assert themselves, this is when the work of the Relationship really begins. Those relationships that experience Endurance in Intimacy are those where the couple has worked through these projections with fearless honesty, so that their Relationship is more alive every day. And they grow as individuals and in Relationship. Pretty good, right? Are you in?

Day 39: Netzach of Yesod in Yetzirah

The Seven and Nine of Swords

_____ *within* _____

Once, when these two cards came up together in a reading I was doing for a woman I knew, she immediately exclaimed, "I knew it, he's cheating on me!" You don't have a to be a tarot reader well versed in the many meanings of the cards to see that as a possible interpretation of this pair. And here, in the week of Yesod and Intimacy, infidelity, deceit, and betrayal are all issues we have to look at. Nothing poisons Intimacy like deceit. Nothing is more destructive to the Endurance of a Relationship than betrayal—sexual or otherwise.

So what do we do when we're working with these two cards on this day? Just like every other day, we search within. I have been in Relationships that were monogamous and Relationships that were open. Oddly enough, some of these monogamous Relationships were filled with cheating, while the supposedly open Relationships never involved anyone on the outside. But when this Sephirotic pairing comes up every year and I face this pair of cards, I have to look at any desires to cheat on my partner and what those desires are really about. Just like projection, putting my sexual Drive elsewhere is really about letting off steam about something I don't want to look at or talk about honestly. And when that pent-up Drive finds an unskillful means of expression, it endangers Intimacy.

It's important to note that there are three levels of Intimacy this deceit threatens. Obviously, it threatens the Endurance of Relationship with a partner. But it also endangers my own inner Intimacy, because in order to act out in this way, I have to lie to myself. And this endangers my spiritual Intimacy as well. So I am both the man in the Seven of Swords, deceiving another and undermining myself, and I am the figure in the Nine of Swords, feeling all the pain of having betrayed another, my heart, and my values.

This doesn't mean I don't notice attractive people and that I deny I find them attractive. I just don't dwell on it, and I don't act on it. Sometimes, sitting on the couch, my partner and I will see someone on TV that we both find attractive—and we say so. It doesn't make either of us jealous. It enlivens us and reminds us of our attraction to each other. But it's not like this hasn't been an issue in my life in the past. And I can't be certain it won't be an issue in my life again. It's something I have to remain watchful for.

I've also been in Relationships where my partner has cheated on me, and I've felt like the figure in the Nine of Swords. One of the dangers of such a situation is the desire to get even and declare that all vows are null and void (not out loud, of course, but by returning the betrayal tit for tat).

I'm Focusing on sexual betrayal because sexual Intimacy is one of the facets of Yesod. But there are many ways to betray Intimacy. The important thing, though, on this day is to keep the Focus within. If you've been in a Relationship where someone has cheated on you, the goal today is not to get lost in blaming the other. I'm not saying give the cheater a pass. But it takes two to tango, so you have to explore how your own inner dynamic may have contributed to the situation. And looking back to the previous pair in the suit of Cups, you have to consider what role projection plays in this issue.

Day 39: Netzach of Yesod in Assiyah

The Seven and Nine of Pentacles

_____ *within* _____

Night after night on my bed
I sought for the one beloved of my soul.
I sought, but I found him not.
I will rise up now and roam the city,
through the streets and the broad avenues,
I will seek the one my soul loves.
I sought, but I found him not.

SONG OF SONGS 3:1–2

The Yearning for love is Enduring; it Drives us even as we lie in bed at night to go out into the streets looking for love, and often in all the wrong places. The wisdom in the Song of Songs recognizes this Drive, and how, when it's followed without spiritual awareness, it leaves us feeling the dissatisfaction we can see in the Seven of Pentacles. The man in the card is filled with Yearning, and though he is tending his vineyard, for some reason he does not seem to hear the call: "O you who linger in the garden / A lover is listening; Let me hear your voice."[13]

The Song of Songs is attributed to King Solomon, or Shlomo in Hebrew. The woman in the poem is Shulamit, the feminine form of Shlomo. And both are related to the word *shalom,* or *shlemut,* which is often translated as "peace" but is perhaps more accurately translated as "wholeness." And this is the clue that the poem is not simply a celebration of erotic love; it is also a celebration of the erotic path to Divine unification. It is an understanding that we can find healing and wholeness in Intimate Connection.

So while we may be looking for love in all the wrong places, it's important to remind ourselves that what we really seek is wholeness. If you're in a Relationship and you're not tilling the garden together, that wholeness will elude you. And you may feel tempted to seek outside the relationship for it. But looking outside is walking away from Perseverance in Intimacy.

For a Relationship to Endure through all the seasons, you must pay close attention to how it is growing because a relationship that isn't growing, to take a phrase from Bob Dylan, is busy dying. And one can interpret the expression on the man's face in the Seven of Pentacles as considering how best to help the vine thrive. Does it need pruning? In the first couple of years of a vine's growth, it should not be allowed to produce fruit. It needs to strengthen its root system, its Foundation, before it can support the extra weight of fruit.

In other words, Intimate Relationships require the Perseverance of careful attention and hard work if they are to thrive and Endure. Then the rewards can be more than just physical, for in the physical, one may touch the Eternal for a moment.

Questions for reflection and contemplation: Day 39

1. (Wands) How do outside stressors affect your close Relationships? Which of the two defenses shown in the cards feels familiar in your Relationship experience—on your side, as well as on your partner's side. What can you do to break the pattern in a way that increases aliveness and Intimacy?

2. (Cups) In your close Relationships, whether with a partner, relative, or friend, what do you feel self-righteous about? What is a regular complaint that you gather evidence for? What do you Focus on that can't be changed or is out of your control? Your answers can give you clues about what you might be projecting in these Relationships. Choose one or more, and explore in writing why you are telling yourself this story and what its origin is within you.

3. (Swords) In what ways have you betrayed (or are you now betraying) your closest Relationships? Even if these violations seem small, write them down. In what ways do you betray your own values? If you have been (or now feel) betrayed, in what ways have you participated in this betrayal, and what rewards do you get from this dynamic?

4. (Pentacles) What techniques do you practice to make sure your Intimate Relationships Endure? When you feel lonely, what do you do to feel Intimate Connection? Where do you search for it? What "unskillful" actions do you take to cover up your yearning for Connection, and how do you break free from this dynamic?

Day 40: Hod of Yesod

Humility Creates the Space for Intimacy

Today is the fortieth day of the Omer, which is five weeks and five days of the Omer.

Forty is another significant number in the Jewish tradition. It's the number of days and nights that Noah and his family (and the family of Creation sans unicorns, basilisks, and dinosaurs) spent on the ark. It is the number of days and nights Moses spent on top of Mount Sinai receiving the law from YHVH. And after, when he descended to find the Israelites worshipping the golden calf, it became the number of years they had to wander in the wilderness before entering the Promised Land.

Traditionally, one also had to be forty years old before being allowed to study Kabbalah. It's as though it's the number that denotes a kind of spiritual ripening, a readiness to begin the work of transformation. I've wondered about this restriction, along with all the others—starting with the restrictions of maleness and marriage. Yes, I started out angry in reaction to what I perceived as discrimination, pure and simple. But over time, I've come to see these restrictions as an imperfect response to a serious issue. The people who put these restrictions in place came from a very different time, place, and experience. Today these specific restrictions are unnecessary. But I have come to understand some of the thinking behind them.

I've mentioned before that I'm a bit of a know-it-all. And when I was younger, I knew even more of it all! Which meant there was no room for anyone else's knowledge or experience. And really, that translates into there being no room for anyone else, period. But reality has a way of knocking sense into folks like me. Though the longer it takes to learn this lesson, the harder reality knocks. I needed the Humility to know that I didn't know. The rabbis who set up the restrictions around Kabbalah study must have had people like me in mind; I was more grounded and open, with greater Humility, by the time I reached my forties. It's true, there are people who go the other way, who become more closed down as they get older. But most likely those folks are not the ones who are looking to study on this path. As the book of Proverbs teaches, "Do not rebuke a scoffer, for he will hate you; Reprove a wise man, and he will love you. Instruct a wise man, and he will grow wiser."[14]

With the Humility to recognize there is wisdom to be learned from others, there is room in the heart and mind for Intimacy. Let's see how the cards reveal this dynamic in Relationship.

Day 40: Hod of Yesod in Atzilut

The Eight and Nine of Wands

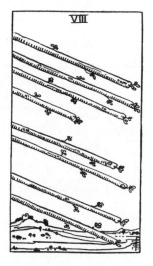 

_____ *within* _____

Looking at these cards next to one another in this order, it appears to me that those eight staves are headed right for the man behind his barricade. And it's not like he doesn't expect them. He's been wounded before, and he's ready for someone to attack him again, though he's left a space open, hoping for the Connection he is also wary of.

Because he expects an attack, he may perceive any judgment or criticism as directed at him. But as my mother used to say, don't take things so personally. Perhaps what's coming at him is not about him at all, but about someone else projecting onto him their own issues or needs, or their desire to control a situation. Of course, Intimate Relationships being what they are, we often choose partners whose projections lock onto our own feelings of vulnerability, the emotions that trigger us into unconscious reaction. Having the Humility to understand it's not about you is relationship judo; it enables you to sidestep an attack and use its energy to turn it around. Not to attack the other, but to create a space where you can discern what's really going on.

Once again, Humility doesn't mean being a doormat. But it does mean dropping your defensiveness to listen for what's going on underneath so that you can discover a deeper emotional truth.

Because we're in the world of Atzilut and because the Eight of Wands suggests there's a revelation coming from above, it's possible to read the figure in the Nine of Wands as someone who has been wounded by his faith community or organized religion in some way so that he doesn't trust his own spiritual instincts (which is one way the Eight of Wands manifests in this pair). He can't hear the quiet inner voice because he is too hurt and defensive. For some, it's hard to separate this inner voice from the introjected voice of organized religion, making it suspect. Also consider the prophet Jonah, who didn't ask for a revelation and didn't want to deliver the message; this pair could be about one's reluctance to take on a task from the Divine.

This being the suit of Wands, we can also consider that the eight staves hurtling earthward are also the arrows of love. But because we are in the week of Yesod and the Nine of Wands is a card of Yesod, it's possible the wound pictured in the card is one of sexuality, that there was sexual abuse as a child or in an earlier relationship so that even a pure love can be experienced as a threat. It is also possible to see these cards as showing the inner turmoil of having passionate feelings arise that feel dangerous to express. I have read these cards at times as showing someone who is afraid of accepting, revealing, or expressing their sexuality or gender identity because of introjected judgments. Once, when I was reading for a religiously conservative man who I had a sense was closeted about his sexual attraction to men, I pointed out that the staves in the Eight of Wands showed that his sexuality was a gift from above, that his passion was not only sexual, it was also spiritual, and that when he could accept this, he would experience new energy and the ability to let greater love into his life. And that's just what happened.

The combination of these two cards—and the understanding that Hod is related to prophecy—can also suggest someone who experiences great bursts of intuitive knowledge. But like many of the Hebrew prophets, the figure in the Nine of Wands is vilified and attacked for sharing the wisdom he receives and must protect himself and the source of this wisdom. If you're a tarot card reader who experiences just these kinds of intuitive bursts but you live in a community or family where people consider this demonic, you know this dynamic well. Earlier this year, I was reading for a friend at a local diner when the owner came up to us and told us that we had to leave, that the cards were a tool of the devil and that he didn't want us in his restaurant. There was no point arguing. I simply scooped up the cards, paid the check, and we continued at a café around the corner. In New York City, that's easy enough to do. But if you live in a smaller community, you may face social opprobrium for doing this kind of work. As above, though, remember that these are often projections; it's not about you or what you're doing. And if you find a situation where you can leave an opening for the other person to really learn about what you're doing, there's the possibility for growth and a new Relationship.

How many other ways can you see these two cards illustrating the Hod of Yesod dynamic?

Day 40: Hod of Yesod in B'riah

The Eight and Nine of Cups

_____ *within* _____

In the popular dances of Intimacy, we've now arrived at the Emotional Abandonment Two-Step. Like many dances, someone leads and someone follows, except here roles can switch in a moment's notice. The basic steps are these: a "Pursuer" takes one step forward, wanting to get emotionally closer in a Relationship, and a "Defender" takes one step back, keeping the distance between them, then spins the Pursuer, thus deflecting emotions and pushing the Pursuer away. Looks great on a dance floor, but it's an emotional mess. You may have already figured out how I see this in the cards, but it pays to spend some time looking over the details to see how this dynamic can play out in different ways.

Every human being has the conflicting needs for closeness and separation. We all need time together for Intimate Connection with another, and we need time apart for Intimate Connection with ourselves. The problem in many relationships is that the timing for these two needs between partners doesn't always match up. And this is exacerbated by our early wounding, so that when we're not matching up, each partner experiences a kind of panic; one is dealing with the fear of abandonment, while the other is experiencing a fear of being emotionally overwhelmed.

For the time being, let's label the Eight of Cups our Pursuer and the Nine of Cups our Defender. It seems obvious, but remember these roles can and will reverse. However, in heterosexual relationships, often the roles are based on socialized gender expectations, with the perception being that the woman is the emotional pursuer and the man is the defender. This is complicated by the social custom that for initiating Relationship, the man is the pursuer and the woman is the defender. Bearing all this in mind, let's look at the cards.

In the Eight of Cups, we see someone who is walking away. There is a wall of cups separating us from this figure, though there is a gap in the wall, not unlike the gap between the staves in the Nine of Wands. Thus, there is a wall between the figure and you as the viewer. If this wall of cups represents your emotional defenses, the figure in this card was a Pursuer who has given up trying to reach you and is walking away from the Relationship. You may have mounted these defenses because you felt the Pursuer was clingy. But when the Pursuer gives up, even if you're the Defender, you get to feel abandoned, which may well be a replay of an early mother-child dynamic. Meanwhile, because you've mounted such a successful defense, while the Pursuer is leaving, they, he, or she gets to feel emotionally abandoned, and so like Elvis, the Pursuer leaves the building. With the moon blocking the sun in an eclipse, the landscape darkens even as our shadow selves are revealed.

In the Nine of Cups, we have a much more complicated psychology at work. The man on the bench shows that he has the full range of emotional responses available to him; after all, they're on the table behind him. But while you know these emotions are there, he's not sharing them with you. His arms are crossed in front of his heart, and he's seated so that he's physically blocking your way to an emotional goal: he is presenting a classic Defender stance. Someone like this could well be working in a caring profession, where he gets to use his emotions in service of others, like a therapist who uses his emotions within the bounded therapeutic Relationship and then goes home to a partner with whom he doesn't share his own emotions at all. This enables the Defender personality to experience the range of these emotions without being challenged to be vulnerable and let someone in.

In the dynamic that pairs a Pursuer and Defender, most often the partner who seemingly illustrates Humility in Intimacy is the Pursuer, since that person can be emotionally vulnerable and often pays more attention to the emotions and needs of the partner (except for that partner's need for separateness at times). However, when the Pursuer is in a panic over feeling abandoned, all Humility is gone, and the Pursuer's Netzach can rise up to persist in demanding his, her, or their emotional due. Of course, this only further activates the two-step dance, and the Defender steps back even more.

I am sad to say I know the dance steps as both a Pursuer and a Defender, though my more common role is as a Defender.

Day 40: Hod of Yesod in Yetzirah

The Eight and Nine of Swords

_____ *within* _____

In the section above on Cups, I wrote about the Emotional Abandonment Two-Step. Here, we have another variation with our now familiar partners, the Pursuer and Defender. In the Eight of Swords, we have our Defender—someone who is under the illusion that they are trapped in a Relationship, that the partner wants to keep this person tied down. Because the Defender is under this illusion, they are also emotionally shut down. If in a Relationship with someone who is a clingy and extremely jealous Pursuer, the Defender may also feel blindfolded—not allowed to look at other people lest the partner's jealousy is further inflamed.

In such a relationship, the Pursuer would be the figure in the Nine of Swords—feeling isolated and alone. The Pursuer experiences the Defender's withholding of emotional Intimacy as cruelty. And because the Pursuer is afraid of emotional abandonment, this fear distorts that person's view of reality, leading to dark fantasies—perhaps about being cheated on—thus keeping the Pursuer awake at night.

Taking a different angle, the Eight of Swords can also show a passive Pursuer's strategy. In this dynamic, the figure appears to be in need of rescue—which may or may not be true—in order to attract a partner. There is a false Humility in this position in that a person takes on the role of someone who is powerless and vulnerable, when that's really not the case. In this dynamic, the passive Pursuer can simultaneously be a Defender; such a person may not really want to be rescued, but only want to know that someone wants to rescue them. And if rescued, he, she, or they will soon consider the new Relationship the next situation to be rescued from. This really messes with the mind of the Rescuer; it's a kind of gaslighting that will lead the rescuer to feel exactly like the figure in the Nine of Swords, confused and lost in a nightmare.

All in all, these are the kind of situations that, if you realize you're in them, it's immediately time to get out. The interlock between personas here is so strong that it would require years of therapy to get through, if indeed both partners were willing to see their parts in the dynamic. But as the Eight of Swords suggests, this is a willing blindness that protects from Intimacy. It takes a shake-up shock seen in the Major Arcana card The Tower to break out of this self-created prison.

Day 40: Hod of Yesod in Assiyah

The Eight and Nine of Pentacles

_____ *within* _____

> *I have singled out Bezalel the son of Uri the son of Hur, of the tribe of Judah. I have filled him with the Spirit of God, with wisdom, understanding and knowledge concerning every kind of artisanry. He is a master of design, in doing metalwork in gold, silver and bronze; in cutting precious stones to set; in carving wood and in every other craft.*
>
> EXODUS 31:2–5

Bezalel is the artisan in Exodus who is tasked with making the Tabernacle, the priest's clothing, and other holy objects used in the Tent of Meeting. YHVH says of him that he is filled with the Spirit of God—and then names Wisdom and Understanding, the second and third Sephirot, Chokhmah and Binah. What's more, he is also given the quality of Knowledge, which is the mysterious eleventh Sephira that appears in different Sephirotic systems instead of Keter.* For all that,

---

*In these systems, Keter is identical with Ein Sof, and so is above and beyond the Sephirot. Thus, Da'at, Knowledge, becomes the Sephira below Chokhmah and Binah to

Bezalel does not have the reputation ascribed to many creative people: he isn't a prima donna. If he were not named in this section, the artisan who designed all these works would be anonymous. So it's clear that Humility is another one of his many virtues. And looking at the man in the Eight of Pentacles, Bezalel's story comes to mind.

There isn't much of a story, however. His appearance in the Torah does not extend much beyond the leading quote at the top of the section. So of course, he appears in midrashic stories that tell us a little more about him. And one story is kind of a "humble-off" in which Moses, the most humble man in the world, is corrected with great Humility by Bezalel.

> The Holy One, instructed Moses: Go say to Bezalel, "Make a tabernacle, an ark and vessels" (Exodus 31:7–11).
>
> But Moses reversed the order and told Bezalel: "Make an ark, and vessels, and a tabernacle."
>
> Bezalel explained to Moses, respectfully addressing him as "Moses, our teacher" that one should "build the house first and only after that put the vessels in the house—but if I follow your instructions in the order you gave me, where will I put the vessels? Maybe God told you to make a tabernacle, ark and vessels."
>
> Moses said to Bezalel: You knew precisely what God said. You have intuited God's commands just as He stated them, as if you were there.[15]

This is not like any conversation I've had with a contractor doing home renovation. But then, my Relationship with contractors has never been one of Humility in Intimacy. So what am I getting at here? The rabbis noticed this detail—that the order changed in two sections of the text. And they created a story out of it to show how detail-oriented Bezalel was when he was engaged in this holy work. Something that might seem minor to others was something he picked up on as a pos-

---

(cont. from p. 399) harmonize their energies. The Chabad Hasidic sect follows this system, and Chabad is an acronym for these three Sephirot.

sible error, and he was willing to bring it up with tact and Humility. Unlike this writer, who in his Virgo nitpickiness rarely points out errors with Humility. I may learn someday yet.

Bezalel intuitively knew how to speak to Moses with Humility, even though he was speaking from a position of expertise that was Divinely inspired; the rabbis said that he knew the secrets of creation with letters. Despite this, we don't see him imperiously correcting Moses or lording it over his workers.

So when I see the story of Bezalel in this pairing of cards, I see a template for how to have an argument. And when the man in the Eight of Pentacles and the woman in the Nine of Pentacles are discussing the next plantings in the garden, I know that each of them will approach the discussion with respect for the other, with Humility intent on preserving the Intimacy of their Relationship. I know that each of them pays close attention to details—not to trip the other up, but in service of making the Foundation of their Relationship stronger. Because here, it's the angels that are in the details.

Questions for reflection and contemplation: Day 40

1. (Wands) How has wounding in your prior Relationships affected your ability to open to Intimacy? How can you separate your defensive reactions to past hurts from the Relationship in front of you now? How has prior wounding blocked your ability to open to your spirituality or respond to the Divine?

2. (Cups) In your Intimate relationships, how are you a Pursuer? How are you a Defender? Looking at this card pairing, how does it reveal any feelings you may have of abandonment?

3. (Swords) What patterns and negative Relationship dynamics illustrated by these cards do you recognize from your own Relationships? What can you do to free yourself from these dynamics?

4. (Pentacles) When you want to correct someone close to you, what do you usually do or say? What might you do to correct that person with a greater sense of Humility? How would this change the situation or the

result? What are some small things you can do to express Gratitude to your partner? What small details do you notice that if you speak about them could evoke greater Intimacy with your partner?

Day 41: Yesod of Yesod

Desire as the Foundation
for All Spiritual Pursuits

Today is the forty-first day of the Omer, which is five weeks and six days of the Omer.

In *Open to Desire: Embracing a Lust for Life; Insights from Buddhism and Psychotherapy,* psychiatrist and Buddhist teacher Mark Epstein explores the "left-handed path"; that is, the path of sensual desire. Like the Baal Shem Tov, who encouraged his followers to examine desire to its root in order to discover the spark of holiness that animates it, so too Buddhism offers opportunities to make desire a path of self-understanding, turning it into a meditation.[16]

When I returned from my first Vipassana retreat, I felt free of the need to act on compulsive desires for the first time in ten years. And a year later, when those desires begin to pull on me again with greater insistence, I thought I could turn the actions into a meditation. I saw into the nature of my acting out and how it was related to my low self-esteem. If I had stopped there, it would have been a valuable lesson. But I did not, and I was pulled back into and eventually lost in the whirlpool of desire. At least I have good company. As Epstein notes, the unskillful way that spiritual traditions deal with lust has led respected teachers from every tradition—I repeat, every tradition—to fall.[17] Nevertheless, his book recognizes the possibility of using desire instead of being used by it. How it can be the Foundation for all spiritual pursuits.

Certainly, this was the reason Rabbi Akiva argued for the inclusion of the Song of Songs in the Tanakh. The erotic sensuality of the poem is interpreted as the love of YHVH for the People Israel. And as I noted in the chapter on the Tree of Life, sexual relations between a husband and wife on Erev Shabbat are considered to be a theurgic reunification of the YHVH and his Shekinah—the Divine Masculine and Divine Feminine.

There was a reason the rabbis traditionally only taught Kabbalah to married men over the age of forty. Working with the Sephirot can unleash sexual energies—or energies that will be acted on sexually—and they believed one needs a container where these energies could be acted on with consciousness and holy intention.

Yesod is not only the Divine phallus; it is also the Divine birth canal of the world of Creation that we live in, Malchut. And we are literally commanded to mirror this creative act, being told to "be fruitful and multiply."[18] This desire is part of our very nature: the question is how we can use it to consciously work in partnership with the Divine to further the work of Creation without getting lost in lust. And it's a question that is alive for me, since as a single man, the search for a relationship that creates a safe container where Intimacy and Connection are affirmed both spiritually and sexually can easily be diverted into a search to satisfy a more insistent, compulsive, and immediate urge. This is the spiritual tightrope I walk.

Day 41: Yesod of Yesod in the Four Worlds
The Nine of Wands, Cups, Swords, and Pentacles

_____ *within* _____

Look into the nature of desire and there is boundless light.
                                                    PADMASAMBHAVA

Gimme, gimme, that thing called love.
    "GIMME, GIMME," FROM *THOROUGHLY MODERN MILLIE,*
                        LYRICS BY DICK SCANLAN

In the Nine of Wands, this "boundless light" is going to have trouble getting through the stockade of staves, if that is indeed what we're seeing. Because just as in the Seven of Wands, these staves could represent a group lined up in opposition against or trying to tempt our protagonist, hemming him in and trapping him rather than offering him protection. And both of these interpretations can be true at the same time. Any way you look at it, though, reaching out to this man won't be easy. Having been hurt before, he expects to be hurt again. But what's on the other side of the stockade? I don't see any other people massed in the distance and readying an attack. It's only open countryside. The attack he expects may only be in his mind; he has been wounded and traumatized, and this has left him in a defensive crouch. The line of staves may be providing him some sense of protection regardless of how puny a defense they may offer. So the gap in the line of staves could be an opportunity for him to step through his fears and into the freedom on the other side.

In Yesod of Yesod, it's easy to read that his wounding is sexual and that he has withdrawn from Relationships, emotional and sexual, to recover. But the thing about this wounding is that for healing to happen, it must happen in Relationship. And right now, he isn't ready for Intimacy; he doesn't trust. The way he holds the stave in his hands might suggest that he is holding on to his suffering and fear and holding back his own sexuality; there's a trauma he does not know how to heal from. He may get help, but ultimately, he has to let someone through the stockade or he has to step through to freedom on the other side. Only he can do this. And by him, I mean me.

Because we're in the suit of Wands, we're in the world of Atzilut, so I want to mention another way to consider the Nine of Wands—as spiritual wounding by a male-dominated, patriarchal religious institution. Which, again, can simultaneously be sexual wounding. I'm not pointing fingers at any one tradition here; there's a lot of blame to go around. Just as I am writing this, another Buddhist teacher has had to resign from a worldwide organization he founded because of sexual abuse, while the pope has just called for a meeting of bishops to discuss the ongoing abuse scandals roiling the Catholic Church.

If this is a wound you share, recognizing the origin of the wound is one way to start the process of healing Intimacy trauma. Given the prevalence of sexual abuse in religious institutions and the silence around it, many people suffer a deep alienation from their own spiritual nature since their experience has made them feel it is unsafe. And it has made them fearful of their own sexuality. This is where finding one's own path, without giving away spiritual authority, is one way to heal. But because healing happens in Relationship, finding a good and reputable therapist to work with is important, even though trusting a therapist is difficult. I found an amazing therapist whom I worked with for more than twenty years, but it took me an extremely long time to trust him. Finding a group of survivors who support each other can be an important part of the process, because learning to reestablish trust is essential for healing.

Intimacy trauma can result when a person or institution on which a child depends for survival significantly violates that child's trust or sense of well-being, and that betrayal can be physical, sexual, or emotional. Some of the many long-term effects of such a betrayal of trust can include overcompensatory actions, such as a strong drive to succeed as a way of creating a sense of protection, sexual acting out, and substance abuse. Sometimes these things go together, since ultimately, things like financial success do not heal the wounded soul. And we can see the Nine of Cups as an example of overcompensatory success to Intimacy trauma.

Clearly, the man seated before us is successful: his clothing and his body language tell us he has done well in the world. But his arms are crossed over his heart even as his legs are spread wide, suggesting sexual Connection without Intimacy or sexual acting out to distract from difficult emotions. So while one could interpret him as a host welcoming guests, it is a welcome of mixed messages. And as noted earlier, the nine cups arrayed behind him could stand for alcohol abuse or, really, any substance abuse or acting-out behavior (such as treating sexual partners as objects or trophies) that enables him to avoid feeling difficult emotions.

Now, for those of you tarot readers who have been silently arguing with this interpretation of the Nine of Cups or some variations of it so far, remember, these images serve as a kind of Rorschach test: I project onto them and then say what I see. This may or may not tell you something of what might have been going on in Pamela Colman Smith's head, but it certainly reveals things about me. That's what this work is about. It is true that the more classic book interpretations of this card are positive: wishes fulfilled, feelings of emotional satisfaction, and sometimes sensual pleasure. Remember, I am interpreting the cards in light of their Sephirotic correspondences and seeing the shadow side as well as the light, since the goal here is to examine our conscious and unconscious blocks to experiencing more Divine energy and flow in our lives. There are other ways to see these cards, of course, based on your experience. And there are other decks that illustrate these concepts differently. There are decks with no imagery for the Minor Arcana at all, which was the tradition before the advent of the Waite-Smith deck.* I bring this up again at this point because I know that what I am writing about right now can be very triggering for some people; there are some people who go to spiritual communities and books as a way of escaping trauma by using the defense of spiritual bypassing. And it's understandable. If you have any abuse issues in your past or if there are such living issues in your life or the lives of people you love, this is challenging and heartbreaking work.

Someone I care for dearly just this weekend revealed to me that he has been struggling with a difficult substance addiction. It should not have surprised me; I have known for years of his struggles with Intimacy as a result of sexual abuse at a young age. I don't need a government-

---

*Yes, there was the Sola Busca deck, which influenced Pamela Colman Smith, but for all intents and purposes, before the Waite-Smith deck the tradition was overwhelmingly without human situational imagery.

funded study to tell me there's a relationship between Intimacy trauma and addiction, but if this is something outside of your experience, please know that in one recent study of people who are struggling with substance abuse issues, 81 percent of the women and 69 percent of the men in the study reported past physical or sexual abuse or both, starting at a median age of 13 and 11, respectively.[19] As a society, we treat addicts as criminals, when most of the time they are victims who are suffering and using substances to self-medicate.

As I write these words, the #MeToo movement continues to struggle to be taken with the seriousness required for our society to heal. But today I'm only concerned about my friend. Like the man in the Nine of Cups, he appears very welcoming. He does in fact have a big heart, but his drug use means that he has lied to everyone he loves over the last few years. And the Connection between his heart and his sexuality is broken; he is not only a drug addict, but he also is sexually compulsive, reenacting his abuse in ways that only hurt his heart and reinforce his addiction. He was able to hide this from a group of deeply caring and psychologically astute friends. Just as in the Nine of Cups, there was a lot going on under the tablecloth in the card that we can't see. And some of what was under the table for me is that I might have been avoiding the truth about this problem in order to keep the status quo and the limits on the depth of our Intimacy. His addiction enabled me to enjoy just as much Intimacy as I could stand, some of which was really just an illusion of Intimacy.

The universe is an interesting place: just as I came to this, the forty-first day, the day on which these issues are the focus, that's when the truth about this Relationship came out. When you work this path, you have to be prepared for what the Divine sends your way. As I hold the brokenness of my own heart, I have to be willing to inquire into my own responsibility for enabling and what that means for my own Intimacy issues. I am not interested in blaming this person; I only wish for his recovery. While my job is examining how and why I colluded in this situation.

This is the work I am doing this year. And if it resonates for you, I am both sorry and hopeful that what you learn about these issues here will help you become a stronger container for great Intimacy with others and with the Divine.

The Nine of Swords—grief over guilt or grief over betrayal—is waking up to the nightmare of what one's life has become, whether it's the middle of the night or the middle of the day. This wake-up call may ultimately be what's needed: it's hitting bottom and knowing it. Because when you hit bottom, you're at the Foundation. You're ready to stand, see things clearly, and gather your strength to begin the climb back up. If the swords represent a ladder of insight, it means there are a lot of painfully sharp insights ahead as you grab each rung of the ladder. I've lived these nights of swords, grabbing hold of the rungs of both guilt and betrayal as I turned a sharp eye on my actions and then owning how they caused me and others harm.

Those swords can also represent unowned sins—not a word I use much. The word for "sin" in Hebrew is chet (not like the name Chet Atkins, it's like the *ch* in *chutzpah*), and it is a term that comes from archery that means "an arrow that has gone astray or fallen short of the target." And it's not merely that one may have fallen short and done the wrong thing; it's also often that one has missed an opportunity to do a good thing. But if these sins are unowned, something that's been stuffed down and out of one's conscious mind, they will come back to haunt you at night when we feel most alone, sometimes even if there is someone in the bed next to you.

Just as Yesod is about Bonding, Connection, and Intimacy, its shadow side is about breaking bonds, disconnection, alienation, loneliness, and isolation. We can see this isolation in the Nine of Swords, and one way out is to reach out, no matter how hard it seems. One of the tenets of the twelve-step program is that the telephone is a lifeline that can help break isolation. There aren't meetings twenty-four hours a day. But there is always someone who will answer the phone and listen. There is always someone who has been there and is willing to share their experience, strength, and hope—someone who is willing to listen without judgment. I know that when I've been in this dark place, making a call has helped get me through the crisis. And when there hasn't been another person to speak with, I pour all my feelings out in prayer.

Because the Nine of Swords is a card of Relationship and Intimacy, the isolation portrayed is also a reason for grief. This image may speak to a profound loneliness. It could be the image of someone who has been shunned or rejected by her community, whatever the reason. Relationship has been cut off, not with just one person, since the nine swords, just like the nine staves, can also suggest a community of people.

Just as in the Eight of Swords, where the blades can represent pre-conceptions and prejudices, here these nine swords can well be the figure's self-defeating thoughts and stories, so that rather than being rejected by others, the figure in the card is living an introjected story that there's something wrong with them. Being alone has become an emotional habit of protection that may save one from fears of rejection but also prevents one from making deep Connections. This is a place where even the possibility of reaching out of the darkness feels impossible.

Many cards have figures of indeterminate gender, so it's easy for people to project whom they want onto the cards. But with the Nine of Swords, both men and women most often say the figure in the card is female. Perhaps because it's one of the few cards that directly show an intense emotion, which men don't feel is socially appropriate for a man to express. I bring this up now because recently, when I read for a female friend and the Nine of Swords came up, she immediately resonated with it because for all the richness of her life, there is one place where she feels empty. She is one of several women friends who are in their fifties and have never been married. Each of these women is beautiful in her own way, and each offers a great deal to a partner. But each, for some reason, is alone and struggles with deep loneliness. Each has a life rich with friendship. But an Intimate relationship with a man hasn't happened. And as they get older, the men who are "age appropriate" (a phrase I don't like, but that's another story) are only interested in younger women. These men are missing a chance for a mature relationship with someone who has realistic expectations because she has been through life. (Those who know me will laugh at my writing this since, generally, the men I date are younger, and I should take my own advice.) This is not only about a partner but also about the lost opportunity for children. Some of these women work with children as a way to participate in Generativity, so that while these children are not their own, they contribute to the chain of transmission across the generations. Still, there is some grief that cannot be assuaged.

Then there is the great grief of loss—the death of a loved one. Many cultures make sure that those who are grieving such a loss are not alone. And many religions have stories of the afterlife to help the mourner get through. While Judaism has lots of beliefs about an afterlife, from reincarnation to resurrection, none are dogma. And the prayer we recite, the Mourner's Kaddish, is not about the deceased at all. It is in praise of the mystery, a recognition that while we have hope and faith, we just don't know.

Except, of course, some of us believe we do, because of mediumship experiences or perhaps other contacts with those who have passed. After the death of the man who was my partner for ten years, I was sick with grief. A friend of mine who is a bodyworker came over to try to ease my pain with some of the therapies she employs. Now, this man I loved was also a bodyworker. And while she worked on me, something happened: we both felt his presence in the room. Not merely that, she felt his hands guiding hers, and I felt as though he were there working on me. She reached deep into a part of me where some parts of him still lived and released them. When I got up from the table, I felt a peacefulness I had not felt since the moment I learned he was dead. But before that experience, the Nine of Swords captured my emotional state exactly because there is no cut more final than death; even knowing that there is something of him alive in the universe somewhere, it doesn't change the fact that I will never share moments with him again. This is the kind of grief that only heals with time and is never fully gone. But because we all endure such loss, this grief is one way we can Connect with others. If loneliness and/or loss has thrown you into an isolation as dark as the Nine of Swords, reach out to others. Now. Do not be ashamed of your feelings, whatever their origin. We are all filled with a yearning heart that others can help fill and that can be healed with the light of the Divine that shines from the hearts of others.

The woman in the Nine of Pentacles is also alone, though she does not appear to be lonely. She is connected to both her spirituality and her sexuality, since birds can represent both, and it's clear that she is in control of when to open to these energies by the fact that the falcon is hooded on her arm. Her ability to Bond with another creature tells us that she has a kind of empathy that extends beyond the ability to Connect with other people because she is in touch with her own animal instincts.

This woman is comfortable being on her own and has the resources—material and spiritual—to face whatever challenges life throws her way. For while she knows her animal side, she also is dressed in a way that suggests a level of appreciation for the refined, the good things in life. She has spent her life building her Foundation, a strong Base on which to live and enjoy the good life.

It's also clear she is not a pushover; falconry is not for the fainthearted. This means that she knows the aggression living within her own heart and that she knows when and how to direct that energy should she need to. She may be someone who has been through abuse and has worked through the issues so that now she knows how to stand firmly in her power.

In some ways, she may be like the women I wrote about in the Nine of Swords: her success and her power may be off-putting to men who can't match her abilities, and that leaves her alone. The difference here is that she won't settle for someone who isn't her match or who doesn't understand the struggle she has been through. And she has her own creative pursuits that seem to satisfy her.

But this may be the issue. Relationships are rarely between equals. And she may have created a sanctuary from the world of Relationship. There's nothing wrong with this, unless it is a defensive approach. If she believes she will never meet her match, she may have created a life, and a living space, where there is no room for another. She may have other kinds of Relationships that are fulfilling. But the card gives us no evidence of this.

Relationship counselors often say that rather than constantly being on the lookout for a partner, one should tend one's own garden, becoming the partner you want to have, and that this will attract a partner, often when you're not looking and least expect it. I believe this, as long as one isn't staying in the garden full-time. As the John Kander and Fred Ebb song goes, "You gotta ring them bells."

Yes, build your Foundation. Yes, create a sanctuary. But make sure there's room for someone else to join you.

Questions for reflection and contemplation: Day 41

1. (Wands) How would you describe the way you've integrated your sexuality with your spirituality? In what ways do you defend yourself from complete sexual and spiritual Intimacy? How might you free yourself from any defenses that no longer serve your higher self? How can you create your own sense of safety in a spiritually Intimate community?

2. (Cups) What is your experience with compensatory behavior as a way of avoiding feelings and Intimacy? What is your experience with substance abuse as a way of avoiding feelings and Intimacy? How have these issues affected your life and Relationships? What have you done to recover from these issues? What can you do to accept the past and open to others in the present?

3. (Swords) When do you feel most alone, and what do you do to break through feelings of isolation? When you are in the grip of grief, loneliness, or loss, what can you do to help see through any projections or stories you use to keep yourself enslaved to these feelings? If there is a particular story you tell yourself repeatedly when you are overwhelmed with these feelings, examine that story when you aren't in the grip of these emotions to determine whether there is any truth to it. How do you grieve in community? How does or how can your community support you in fully feeling all of your feelings?

4. (Pentacles) What creative pursuits do you engage in to participate in Divine Generativity? How have you made your home a Base that

supports you in your Relationships? How does your home reflect and support your inner Intimacy and your most Intimate relationship with another? In what ways do you use your space as a defense against Intimacy with others or yourself?

Day 42: Malchut of Yesod

Being Fully Present for Relationship

Today is the forty-second day of the Omer, which is six weeks of the Omer.

During the festivals of the pilgrimage the priest used to raise the curtain from the Holy of Holies to show the pilgrims how much their God loved them as they could see in the embrace of the two cherubim.

LOUIS GINZBERG, *THE LEGENDS OF THE JEWS*

It is said that God was present in the space between these intertwined bodies and in particular in the space between their eyes, as their faces were turned toward one another while they were engaged in the act of love.

I have never liked kissing with my eyes closed. I like to look into the eyes of the person I am kissing. And I don't like having sex with my eyes closed; it's not that, as Chauncey Gardiner said in *Being There,* "I like to watch," it's that I want to see and be seen in all my vulnerability and pleasure. I want my partner to feel fully seen. I have always thought that keeping one's eyes closed during a sexual encounter was about shame and made an object out of one's partner.

In the Temple in Jerusalem, the keruvim (or cherubim, as it is most often transliterated) were on top of the Ark of the Covenant, and the high priest would hear God's voice issue from between them. I take this teaching to mean that when we are fully Present for each other in Relationship, in emotional Intimacy, sexual Intimacy, and spiritual Intimacy, that the Divine is not only Present as well but also involved in a threesome that is all about what the act of love creates for a moment—a taste of Divine unity expressed through physical union. When we are fully Present to each other and are able to hold all the energies in a firm Foundation, our true Nobility is revealed. May we all be fully Present for each other in all the ways we love each other, so that the Divine is always Present among and between us.

Day 42: Malchut of Yesod in Atzilut

The Ten and Nine of Wands

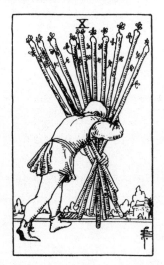 

_____ *within* _____

Wherever you go, there you are. In the Ten of Wands, we see that the man in the Nine of Wands decided to step outside his comfort zone and step through the stockade of staves that served as his defense against Intimacy and Connection. However, the geography cure doesn't work; as you can see, he may have walked through the line of staves, but then he picked them up and bundled them together to bring wherever he's headed next. He may have stepped through the stockade to face his fears, but he hasn't banished them yet. They still take a burdensome toll, and his body language tells us that while he still yearns for relationship, he won't be able to see any possibilities in front of him. And of course, he'll set up the stockade again when he gets to his destination.

If the figure in the Ten of Wands is someone dealing with the emotional burden of abuse, it's something that he has been carrying around for a long time. We can be hopeful that he's headed to the town to seek help. Many abuse victims keep their abuse secret, feeling shame or that they may be to blame, or feeling like damaged goods afterward. So a positive way to consider this pairing is that the figure has come to the end of the abuse cycle and is ready to put this emotional burden down by finally unburdening himself of the secret. Because once victims disclose abuse, they can begin to cope with and heal from their trauma. Of course, healing will not happen overnight—it's a process—but we can see the figure in the Ten of Wands as taking the first steps toward freedom and letting go of this weight.

The author Isabel Radow Kliegman suggests one interpretation of the Ten of Wands as the holding back of sexual libido. And when I think about this in connection to abuse, I recall a time in the nineties when I had a partner who was recovering his memories and finally dealing with the trauma of abuse that had occurred in his childhood. Up to that time, we had had an active and passionate love life. But when he started to deal with this issue in his therapy, any physical Intimacy felt threatening to him. And because I was only just learning about these issues at the time, his withdrawal from physical Intimacy felt like rejection to me, so that I was thrown into my own abandonment issues. Luckily, we both had therapists who understood the situation, so that I learned how to give him the space and time to heal, and he learned how to trust again. When he was ready, we learned how to be fully Present to each other in physical Intimacy anew, so that we were able to experience deeper Connection.

So while, classically, the Ten of Wands is usually read in a negative light, I see the figure in the cards as leaving isolation behind and returning to the possibility of Relationship as represented by the town. And I see that he has come to the point where he recognizes how the abuse has had long-lasting effects that he is now ready to face and deal with. In this way, I see this pairing as a hope for a new beginning.

Day 42: Malchut of Yesod in B'riah

The Ten and Nine of Cups

_____ *within* _____

Ah, the seated man in the Nine of Cups with his arms crossed over his heart; in this pairing, I don't read this body language as defending himself against Intimacy because he is holding the family in the Ten of Cups in his heart. What he is protecting is his love—whether it is for his wife and children or for another family entirely (perhaps memories of his family of origin)—and he is protecting his Bond to this family. And knowing that he has in their love an unshakable Foundation of Connection gives him the ability to share his blessings with others. He holds their Presence in his heart, and he is able to bring his Presence to the guests at his table.

Today we are one week from completing the count, and in this pairing I want to offer another surprising view of the Nine of Cups. Yes, the seated man is awaiting nine guests, which would make him the tenth person. In Jewish practice, you need ten people to hold a public prayer service, and you need a minimum of ten people to read the Torah publicly. Kabbalistically, you need ten people because each of these ten people must embody one of the Sephirot, so that together they create a sacred Bond that embodies the Divine Creator and invokes Its full Presence. So here, the man in the Nine of Cups holds the ten Sephirot in his heart and thus sees all the others as b'tzelem Elohim; that is, he sees all the others as unique expressions of the image of the Divine and sees that their coming together unifies Creation and the Creator.

When we come together in a group of ten to pray, we have an opportunity to raise our consciousness. The prayer service is structured in such a way as to take us through each level of our soul, from the lowest, nefesh in the world of Assiyah, upward to the levels of ruach, neshamah, and chaya, with the possibility of reaching for *yechida,* transcendence of the ego into union with Divine Consciousness. And then we come back down for a landing. Unlike in monastic traditions, for Judaism, this happens in community and requires the communal effort of at least ten people to hold the energy. In fact, the Zohar is the story of just such a community of ten sages led by Rabbi Shimon Bar Yohai. The Zohar follows these men on their journeys as they discuss the secret meanings of the Torah and how to see through the text to the ultimate reality of Ein Sof. And for these ten sages, mystical experiences and revelations occur in a group, not for one person alone, just as all the people received the revelation of the Torah together at Sinai.[20] So yet another way to look at the man in the Nine of Cups is as the leader of a minyan of ten people who is waiting for the other nine to arrive—each of them a strong container, represented by a cup, for the Sephirotic energies he, she, or they are working with.

You could even imagine the seated man as Rabbi Shimon Bar Yohai, the hero of the Zohar and the leader of the circle of ten companions in this epic story, or you could imagine him as the writer of the Zohar, Rabbi Moses de León. Because the Zohar's story of these ten sages from the first century is simultaneously a coded story of ten Kabbalists in medieval Spain, including the writer of the Zohar, Rabbi Moses de León, in their secret mystical search for Divine union. The names of all of the others in this circle of ten men is not fully known, but scholars say there is evidence it included Rabbi Joseph Gikatilla (author of

The Gates of Light) and Rabbi Yosef ben Shalom Ashkenazi.[21]

While I attend a traditional minyan for morning services at my synagogue, I also think of myself as being part of an untraditional minyan that comes together at different times and places. It's a group of spiritual seekers who have known each other and been part of each other's journey for more than twenty-five years. Some of my companions aren't Jewish; I met them in Buddhist circles, or in tarot circles, or at twelve-step meetings. But over the years, we have come together in our spiritual work and supported each other in moments of anguish and in moments of joy.

As we approach the final week, while we have never met, you, dear Reader, have become part of this minyan. You have done much of the work to purify your inner Sephirotic energies and have made yourself a stronger vessel to hold this energy, like the vessels we see on the table in the Nine of Cups.

Day 42: Malchut of Yesod in Yetzirah

The Ten and Nine of Swords

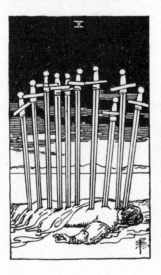 

_____ *within* _____

This is the day and the combination I have dreaded writing about. Just looking at the cards, you know that this is just about the darkest place one can go. And I can't look away or skip this pair: this energy has touched my life and affected many people I love. In particular, I must write about a crisis that brought people together in grief and then fractured many Relationships.

On October 20, 2012, my friend Louis Rispoli was murdered on the street in Queens. It was a violent attack that left him in a coma for five days before he died. He had married his husband, Danyal, as soon as same-gender marriage became legal in New York State; they had been together for more than thirty years. But then one night, he went out for a walk and never returned. The next morning, Danyal frantically called the police to report him missing, only to learn that Lou had been found on the street without an ID and taken to a local hospital, where he was on life support. He had been hit so hard, perhaps with a bat, that half his brain was gone.

For the next five days, there was a line outside his hospital room as people came to support Danyal and be with Lou. Hospital staff asked who he was that so many people were showing up. Lou wasn't famous. But he had touched the lives of thousands of people so that all of them felt they'd had a deep Relationship with him, and they wanted to be present to give their support.

Because they were married and Lou had made all his plans carefully, Danyal had the medical proxy forms that showed Lou would want to be taken off life support. This was a traumatic decision to make, but the right one. Still, the hospital fought Danyal's right to make this decision. I was present at Danyal's side in every meeting with the hospital administrators as they stonewalled and delayed the process of taking Lou off life support, making an emotionally wrenching situation even more difficult. It was only because we knew the local city council member, who called the head of the Health and Hospitals Corporation, that finally the medical bureaucrats relented.

Almost a thousand people from all over the world showed up for his memorial service. You have never heard of Lou, but his great heart and full Presence made an indelible mark on everyone he met. I can't possibly sum up his life, and really, that's not why I am writing about this now. But here, as I work through Counting the Omer,

I can reflect on how this tragedy brought together a community of people in the shared Intimacy of grief and trauma. And then how over time that trauma fractured many of these Relationships. Today, Lou's husband, Danyal, and his family and closest friends are still working through the ongoing trauma years later. This group includes me.

The police investigation did not help. In fact, it helped traumatize people further. Lou was a mentor to his partner's young nephew Alex, who had been struggling to find direction in his life. The police saw Alex as a possible suspect and asked him whether he'd been having sex with Lou. Alex was now not only in pain, he also was deeply outraged that anyone would even think such a thing. Alex also blamed himself for Lou's death, since they had planned to get together that evening and often Alex would join Lou on these late-night walks to talk about his life and goals. He believed that if he hadn't canceled at the last minute, Lou would not have been alone and the attack would never have happened. He didn't tell anyone that he blamed himself, and he tortured himself, replaying the events over and over again in his mind—very much a Nine of Swords experience. In the years following Lou's death, Alex's life spiraled out of control, leaving him disconnected from the support he needed. He threw himself into reckless behavior to avoid his misplaced guilt and anguish, and he became HIV positive.

When I look at the Nine of Swords, I am reminded of all the nights I would speak to Danyal on the phone before we went to sleep or when he'd wake up in the middle of the night shaking with nightmares and overcome with emotional suffering and pain. He too raged against the incompetence of the police investigators. After more than a year of repeatedly answering the same questions that would only retraumatize him, he stopped returning their calls.

With my own emotions on a hair trigger, I found myself raging at people at my workplace and sometimes crying in the middle of the day. My employers had no idea how to handle this, and while therapy helped, I was not a good person to be around. Two months after Lou died, I was fired from my job. I threw myself into an inappropriate Relationship to avoid my feelings. While it provided some comfort and offered positive things for both of us, it ultimately could not serve my partner's or my own higher self as we were both using the Relationship to avoid our own issues.

Even as we came together to support each other, along with many others in Lou's large group of friends, we also fractured as a community, each disappearing into our separate traumas. Danyal was so overwhelmed that he had no strength to help Alex. While he had a core community that was there for him, there were friends who could not remain present for Danyal in his trauma and mourning, so they drifted away over the dark months that followed.

As I write this, it was six years ago. In the crisis, in the moment, we were all fully Present for each other. Over time, each of us has retreated into our private anguish, unable to bear the Intimacy of each other's suffering. After the tragedy of the Ten of Swords, each of us found ourselves figuratively and literally in anguish and alone as in the Nine of Swords. I know that Lou lived his life without regrets, but if there had been one, it would have been that he didn't get to say goodbye. The crowds outside his hospital room and at his memorial were a testament to the fact that he was fully Present for all his relationships; he never left anything that would get in the way of Intimacy unsaid.

Ultimately, we are all alone when we die. I am writing these words on Yom Kippur, a day of repentance that has been called the dress rehearsal for our death. It is one day before the first anniversary of my father's death, and two days before my sixty-sixth birthday. And as these cards tell us, there's no escaping questions of mortality.

We prepare for Yom Kippur by asking the forgiveness of other people for any of the ways we have wronged them because you can't ask for forgiveness from God without seeking it from other people first. The Ten and Nine of Swords, like Yom Kippur, stand as a warning: death can come at any time, and to be prepared, we must be fully Present in all our relationships, so there is no need for forgiveness or regrets when it does come. And when we are faced with traumatic loss, we must be patient and gentle with ourselves and with each other as we struggle with our various ways, skillful and otherwise, of dealing with the pain.

Day 42: Malchut of Yesod in Assiyah

The Ten and Nine of Pentacles

_____ *within* _____

In these two cards, we find ourselves in the enclosed garden and in the agora—the public space often used for a market or assembly in times past. Private and public. We could even consider the woman in both cards to be the same woman, public and private. We can say that the Nine of Pentacles shows she has an appreciation for the finer things in life, which is a nice way of saying that she has expensive taste.

The Ten of Pentacles, though, with its diagram of the Tree of Life hanging unseen in the air by the people in the card, suggests that the Relationships in the card are unconsciously tinged by a concern with the material. And together the pair suggests that the spending habits of the woman in the Nine of Pentacles may in fact be beyond her means, that she has an unconscious relationship with money that isn't entirely Grounded. In her garden, she is alone. In the agora, she isn't connected to the child at her side as she smiles at the man guarding the gate, who does not seem to be returning her gaze. Perhaps she uses her material wealth to create a sanctuary for Divine Connection that she can't maintain when she leaves the garden, so that her principal

Relationship is to the material world and not to other people.

There are few things more Intimate than our relationship to money and how we talk about it in Relationship and how we use or share it in Relationship. One of the taboo questions in our society is asking how much another person earns. And as I've noted in earlier pairings, a couple that has a large difference in their earnings can find this throws their relationship off balance.

Some people hide their wealth because they find it gets in the way of meeting possible partners, only to find that when they reveal their wealth, it opens up other issues. Some people use their money to attract others and then feel used. There's no question that money is a turn-on for many people. Consider the scene in the film *The Wolf of Wall Street,* where the characters played by Leonardo DiCaprio and Margot Robbie have sex on top of a pile of money, literally bringing the material and the physical together.

Together, the Ten and Nine of Pentacles ask us to closely examine our relationship with money, how we use it, and how it affects all our other Relationships, public and private. This pair challenges us to look at the ways we use money as a defense against Intimacy. And to consider the Relationship between our spirituality and our materiality.

Questions for reflection and contemplation: Day 42

1. (Wands) What is your experience of the geography cure? What defenses have you been carrying that have become a burden in your life and that you are now ready to put down? How will you do so?

2. (Cups) Who are the people in your minyan? Consider bringing everyone together to acknowledge this Relationship and consider how important they have been on your journey.

3. (Swords) If you knew you were going to die tomorrow, what have you left unsaid that you need to say to people you are closest with? Whom do you need to forgive? Whom do you need to ask for forgiveness? Who has been Present for you in crisis? Whom have you been Present for?

Whom have you failed in crisis? Who has failed you? What can you do to make amends where appropriate?

4. (Pentacles) In what ways has your Relationship to money affected your Intimate Relationships? In what ways to do you use money as a defense against Intimacy? What do you spend money on that you wouldn't want to tell other people about?

WEEK 7

Malchut

We shall not cease from exploration
And the end of all our exploring
Will be to arrive where we started
And know the place for the first time.
T. S. Eliot, "Little Gidding," *Four Quartets*

WE HAVE COME TO THE FINAL WEEK. And all of the card pairings in the next seven days are combinations that you have seen before, just in a different order, and that makes all the difference. Because this time, we are examining each of the Sephirot in Malchut, the world we live in. And while we have worked with all of these cards before, having done all this work, in this, the final week, we will end where we have started and see the world with new eyes, with new clarity. Because we will see the world we live in from a place of Sovereignty—with a certainty that this is where we belong and with an openness to all its wonders, all the miracles that daily attend us.

The hardest work is behind us. The seventh week is a kind of Sabbath. A time to look back on the last six weeks, on what we have learned and how we have changed. It is a week of integrating all the Sephirotic energies, seeing how they are reflections of the immanence of the Divine, in our final preparation before the fiftieth day, when we open our heart, our mind, and our entire sensorium to an experience of the transcendence of the Divine in our lives and in the world.

Expressing Sovereignty isn't lording things over others; it's rather the opposite. It's a taking of Responsibility for ourselves, our actions, and our feelings, not as blame but as a celebration. Because when you take full Responsibility for yourself, you can give others full Responsibility for themselves. It means stepping out of the roles of victim, rescuer, or persecutor and stepping up to accept our mission of partnership with the Divine to do our unique part in the work of healing the world with a sense of joy. It means acting from a place of Self-Possessed Dignity whatever the world places before us, receiving it all with the knowledge that the whole world (including ourselves) is filled with the Divine Presence.

Day 43: Chesed of Malchut

Directing the Flow with Nobility

Today is the forty-third day of the Omer, which is six weeks and one day of the Omer.

What the world needs now is love, sweet love.

"WHAT THE WORLD NEEDS NOW,"
MUSIC BY BURT BACHARACH, LYRICS BY HAL DAVID

Malchut is the Sephira we think we know the best, because it's the world we live in. But because we see it every day, it's easy to lose sight of the miracle of Divine Flow that fills the world with Love and light at every moment. One of the faces of Malchut is the Shekinah, the feminine Presence of the Divine, and in our prayers, we ask the Shekinah to shelter us in Her wings, surrounding us with her peace.

Malchut receives all the energies from the higher Sephirot, so it is often compared to the moon, which has no light of its own but only reflects the light of the sun. Despite having no light of its own, Malchut represents wholeness because all the other energies merge and are expressed in the world of Malchut. And first among them is Chesed, because, as the Burt Bacharach and Hal David song tells us, the world really needs it. As we are both recipients of Divine Chesed and partners in Creation with the Divine, it's up to us to keep the Flow going.

In the week of Malchut, the week of our inner Nobility, and on this day of Chesed, we look at how we express Love and kindness out of our most authentic selves in all the facets of our lives—with our beloved, with our families, friends, colleagues, supervisors, subordinates, strangers, rivals, enemies . . . everyone. The work of the forty-third day is not unlike the Buddhist metta meditation of Loving-kindness, as discussed way back on Day 6.

Today we experience as much Love as we can take and share as much Love as we can give, from the depth of who we are.

Day 43: Chesed of Malchut in Atzilut
The Four and Ten of Wands

_____ *within* _____

The man in the Ten of Wands has taken on a burden that weighs him down. The staves he has gathered block his view, so he cannot see what is ahead of him. But he isn't even trying to look ahead, since his head is bowed. He sees ahead with an inner view that is motivating him ever forward: he is motivated by Love. So that while it may seem as though he is oppressed (and this is often a reading of the Ten of Wands in divination), he is in fact filled with a Nobility that gives him the strength to bear this burden.

Imagine the man in the Ten of Wands as Moses, climbing down Mount Sinai with the stone tablets of the Ten Commandments. He is motivated by his Love of the people and his Love of God. And he expects to be greeted by a celebration not unlike what we see in the Four of Wands, since the giving of the Torah at Sinai is the marriage of the people to God, with the Torah as the wedding contract.

Yet when Moses arrived with the tablets of the Law, the people were indeed celebrating, but they weren't celebrating what he expected. I remember the first time I came home from a Vipassana retreat; my boyfriend and my roommate were eagerly awaiting my return to hear all about it. I was eager to see them and to share my experience with them. Not only had I experienced profound realizations, I'd also spent a week in the fresh air of the Japanese countryside where at night the silence was total and the sky was filled with stars because there were not even lights from nearby villages. During the day, since most of the retreat was silent, there was also little in the way of aural distraction. I'd eaten only vegetarian fare, so my body was letting go of toxins.

Coming down from this "mountain" setting was a shock. When I opened the door to my apartment, I was overcome by the stench of tobacco. My roommate smoked. And my boyfriend, like many Japanese, smoked like a chimney, even though he was a health professional. I wasn't Moses coming down from the mountain to find the people had betrayed their promise. But I felt the enormity of the distance between the top of the mountain I'd been to in my meditation and life on the ground at home.

The challenge of this day, and of all the days ahead, is to live with the consciousness of the encounter on the mountaintop, to live the changes our work has made in our character with radiance, accepting and directing the Love and Flow we receive, right here in the world of Malchut, the world of our imperfection as it is.

The Four of Wands reminds us that this is the challenge of relationship—to live with all the Love and radical amazement one feels under the chuppah, even as we face the daily Responsibilities of being in relationship.

Day 43: Chesed of Malchut in B'riah

The Four and Ten of Cups

_____ *within* _____

Malchut receives, and Chesed gives. The young man in the Four of Cups sits in meditation and the Flow, well, Flows. He doesn't cling to it. He doesn't push it away. He observes with equanimity and accepts, knowing that like the rainbow in the Ten of Cups, emotions are evanescent, coming and going like the weather. And there is Nobility in this acceptance.

Like the Buddha, he sits in meditation, watching the Flow of emotions, the Flow of time, and the everchanging nature of reality in Malchut. In fourth-century India, some nine hundred years after the Buddha lived, there was a collection of stories called the Panchatantra that supposedly was composed or collected to teach three young princes the virtues necessary to be a good king. It was not a mystical treatise; it focused entirely on ethics. But even the Buddha taught that the foundation for reaching the heights in meditation was having a strong base of *sila,* ethics and moral conduct.

Malchut is often translated as Kingship (and today Queenship), Nobility, Royalty, and, the idea I like best, Sovereignty. Each of us is a Sovereign, and in our examination of our virtues, ethical behavior, and moral conduct over the last weeks, we have learned how best to channel the Flow of Love that the Divine continuously sends our way, and channeling that Flow does not mean just letting the cups line up on the ground in front of us as they come, as in the Four of Cups. It is our job to participate in the Flow by Generously sharing our gifts. And in sharing we also step into a Leadership role that demonstrates to others the path of Generosity.

The family in the Ten of Cups is grateful and takes joy in the blessings they have Received, even though those blessings appear modest. The parents know that blessings do not end with them and that they are a part of the Flow of generations; their children play before them, secure in the knowledge that they are Loved. Just as a Sovereign understands that their Responsibility is not only to today but also to generations to come.

This may be the greatest gift, contributing to the Flow of Love across the generations. While I am not a biological parent, I know that I have made just such a contribution. And I write this book in the hopes that it too will contribute to the ability of readers for generations to come to Receive Love and participate in the Flow.

Day 43: Chesed of Malchut in Yetzirah

The Four and Ten of Swords

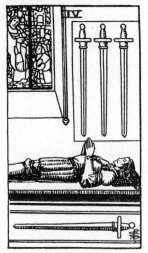 

_____ *within* _____

We first saw this pair on the seventh day, but in the opposite order. For me this reordered combination is about seeing our demons and defenses in meditation and recognizing them without reacting so that we chip away at their power. I noted that like Rasputin, these defenses are hard to kill, if indeed they ever die. But by observing without reaction and from a place of Love and Kindness, we become a Sovereign over them.

We've learned from trying to crack the shell of these klipot, these negative thought patterns and defenses, though, that within them, at the root, is a spark of the Divine that has been severed from its origin. We can think of our neurotic adaptations as klipot—shells that we created to help us cope when we were less able to face the reality of Malchut. This coping mechanism was a kind of retreat of the Self, which was protected by the neurotic habits, defenses, and beliefs we took on until they hardened and hid the Self from us and others.

When we see ourselves with the clarity of Yetzirah and the Loving-kindness of Chesed, we can see through the defenses of the Ten of Swords to the place where the Self has retreated in the Four of Swords. And that place is unsullied, just as the soul we have been given is always pure. This is one of the secrets of Chesed that is within Malchut—a secret hinted at in the stained-glass window of the chapel pictured in the Four of Swords, where the word *pax,* Latin for "peace," appears.

Perhaps in your work over these weeks you have had opportunity to see through your defenses to this place of peace. Perhaps you have learned that when faced with a defense, you're actually seeing a part of yourself that has broken off from wholeness and that by seeing its origin with joy and Love, you help heal your brokenness.

In doing this work, you may have already started to experience this kind of healing. You may feel a sense of freedom from these old patterns. And because you are operating from a place of Love, there is no regret or desire to shut the door on the past because you know that having been in that place you can empathize with and be of benefit to others. This empathy confers on you a kind of Nobility.

Do not despair if you sometimes still feel under the power of these klipot. You have the tools to work with them. The double-bladed sword of insight and Love will ultimately set you free. The tyranny of unconscious neuroses is dead: long live the Sovereign.

Day 43: Chesed of Malchut in Assiyah

The Four and Ten of Pentacles

_____ *within* _____

So here in the week of Sovereignty, I want to note again the crown on top of the head of the man in the Four of Pentacles. And point out that while we can see the entire Tree of Life in the Ten of Pentacles, in the Four of Pentacles, we are in fact seeing a piece of the Tree in the four Pentacles held by the seated man, which represent four Sephirot. This image shows us one Sephira that we have not talked about at all in the Counting of the Omer, since it's not one of the lower seven. Keter, the uppermost Sephira, means "crown," and mapped on the human body, it is placed exactly where we see it in the Four of Pentacles, on top of the seated man's head—revealing his Sovereignty. So rather than go with the interpretation of the card that speaks to miserliness, I want to look at it in this pairing as the King (which in Jewish folklore always refers to God) in the Four of Pentacles giving us a sign—holding up the Sephirot for us to see and reach for. It's a message saying that the material world is not disconnected from the spiritual world, that in fact the blessings of material reality in Malchut all Flow from the Divine Source.

While the people in the Ten of Pentacles seem to be oblivious to the Sephirot shining in the air all around them, today, after all our work, we begin to apprehend the sparkling nature of reality. Seeing things through the eyes of Love, we see that all the world is filled with Royalty and that we are, ourselves, Kings and Queens.

When we embody this Love in Nobility, like the man in the Four of Pentacles, we are holding up a sign, we are modeling for others how to live in the world. And we also help others see through the veil of the material to the star in the pentacle that shines in all of us.

Questions for reflection and contemplation: Day 43

1. (Wands) Think back on times when you have "come down from the mountain" to everyday life. What were your feelings? How did you relate your experience to others? How can you bring or keep the consciousness of the summit to life on the ground?

2. (Cups) How has your relationship to the Flow of blessings changed since you started this practice? Where do you see Flow active in your life? How do you participate in the Flow of blessings?

3. (Swords) What are the defenses that you've worked on most consistently in this practice? What is your experience of their softening? How can you use your experience working with these defenses to help others?

4. (Pentacles) In what ways do you embody Sovereignty? How do you treat your body that demonstrates your understanding that your body is a gift from the Divine? How do you interact with other "bodies" that expresses your understanding that they are both Sovereign and Royal?

Day 44: Gevurah of Malchut

Self-Discipline and Restraint Define Sovereignty

> Today is the forty-fourth day of the Omer,
> which is six weeks and two days of the Omer.

The word *Sovereign,* one of the descriptors for Malchut, has several definitions, including "someone who has supreme power, such as a king or queen." When used to describe a nation, it refers to that nation's autonomy, meaning its independence, that its people are self-governing. The idea of self-governance dovetails perfectly with the Discipline and Restraint that are defining qualities of Gevurah. And in Malchut, Gevurah is essential, since there are so many leaders in the world who believe, and act, as though they have undisputed and supreme power. And when disregard for Law is modeled at the top, you get a lot of people on every level of society who don't believe that the rules apply to them either.

One of the reasons in a democracy that character has always been an important part of a candidate's resume is that we believe that a person's ability to regulate his, her, or their own desires and emotions means this person may be better able to Discern and Judge what the best policies and courses of action are. Restraint in this situation means that this person is able to listen to others and take their ideas and concerns into consideration rather than acting like a monarch with no checks on his, her, or their power.

Here at the forty-fourth day, we are close to the end of this spiritual Discipline. One that you have taken on voluntarily. By doing this work of character refinement and soul cleansing, you are revealing your inner Sovereign. By living the virtues of the Sephirot, rather than trying to impose them on others, you model Leadership.

Day 44: Gevurah of Malchut in Atzilut

The Five and Ten of Wands

 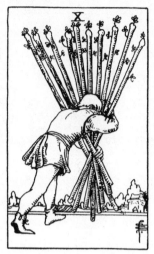

_____ *within* _____

> *Like a city with broken walls is a person without self-control or restraint.*
>
> PROVERBS 25:28

I was watching a panel discussion on a news show recently when the moderator stepped back from his role. As one panelist challenged another, the man who was challenged lost his temper and tried to interrupt the other before she was through. He completely lost Control of his emotions (which is hilarious and sad when you consider that men say that it's women who have no control over their emotions). Then the others all jumped in, interrupting and talking over each other in an attempt to take Control of the discussion and have the last word. I thought of that fracas again when I looked at the Five of Wands today.

The people in the card are fighting over who gets to be the leader, but their very lack of Discipline in themselves demonstrates that none of them is worthy of Leadership. You could think of the man on the left with his staff raised straight up as trying to rally the others and stop the fight. However, like the moderator of the panel discussion that descended into chaos, his attempt to take Control with the force of his personality or some appeal to reason has failed.

We all have areas where our Discipline and Restraint are strong and areas where they're weaker. The fiery nature of Wands as a suit suggests that the first place we look at is our anger, and that's exactly what came up for the hapless panelist. And ultimately, that quality that we have no Control over—whether anger, eating, sex, money, how we use our time—is the thing we become enslaved to. And of course, one goal of the spiritual Discipline of Counting the Omer is to free oneself from the mind-set of slavery, to free ourselves from our inner Egypt. Unfortunately, in this pairing, in the Ten of Wands that is the result we see: slavery. Unable to rule himself, not the Sovereign of his emotions, the man is burdened down by the results of his actions.

In these last days of the count, it's a good time to look at which areas in our life are still in need of better governance and make the commitment to continue that work.

Day 44: Gevurah of Malchut in B'riah

The Five and Ten of Cups

_____ *within* _____

Excessive mourning. Unbridled joy. What do the images in these two cards have to do with each other? The people in both cards are not seeing the full picture and are focused on something that is transitory. What do they have to say to each other? Let's see.

The figure in the Five of Cups has their attention on what is lost, the "spilt milk" of the overturned cups. The figure in the card is so overcome with emotion that the two remaining cups are overlooked. This figure only sees loss, and this is not a true reflection of reality.

The figures in the Ten of Cups have their attention on the rainbow of cups in the sky. They're filled with joy and love. But there is no indication that they understand that their joy is evanescent and, like the rainbow, will disappear as conditions change.

In this way, both cards show how easy it is to get caught up in an emotion, and as the wisdom of the twelve-step world teaches, feelings aren't facts.

The people in the Ten of Cups would tell the figure in the other card to turn around and celebrate what remains. The figure in the Four of Cups would tell the family in the other card that their joy is illusory. Both are right. And both are wrong.

As the wisdom of Solomon tells us, "To every thing there is a season . . . a time to weep and a time to laugh, a time to mourn and a time to dance."[1] And while the great Hasidic teachings tell us our basic orientation should lean toward joy, here in the world of Malchut, where everything is transitory, learning to Govern our emotions—not to repress them, but to know their Limits—is essential. Learning equanimity in the face of change is the middle path, not only of Buddhism but also in Judaism.

Day 44: Gevurah of Malchut in Yetzirah

The Five and Ten of Swords

within

The Restraint that is Gevurah is a virtue in moderation. But this pairing shows us what happens when someone walks away from Responsibility. It is one thing to have humility and to cede or share Authority, but bad actors depend on an appeal to this essential fairness to take advantage of others.

I was on my way home from a Society for Creative Anachronism tournament (before the days of Renaissance fairs, this group held medieval events in full costume, with authentic food, dancing, and duels) with a group of friends, some of whom decided to remain in full costume as we made our way back to the suburban train station to go home. This got the attention of some local teens, who decided to bully us. They shouted insults, they threw bottles, but they kept a distance, since after all, it appeared to them that in the scabbards some of us carried there were real swords. As one of the teens came close enough to throw a punch, one member of our party grabbed his scabbard in a show of defense to scare him off. The teen, sensing that the sword would never be drawn, called him out, saying, "You wouldn't dare use that thing."

My friend, instead of daring him back by saying, "Try me," replied, "I wouldn't dirty the blade."

Very noble. Very witty. Very stupid. It was an admission that the teens could attack us with impunity, and they all immediately did, turning the scene into a melee. Someone in a nearby store called the cops, and with the sound of sirens in the distance, the hooligans dispersed, leaving us a little bloodied. Of course, the police, upon seeing a group of people carrying what looked like serious weaponry, advanced with their guns drawn. Luckily, no one was shot, none of us was arrested, and despite some scrapes, none of us was seriously hurt in the fracas.

When you have Strength, Restraint is called for. But in the face of a bully who does not understand Restraint, it is the height of irresponsibility to hold back. This was the error of the British Prime Minister Neville Chamberlain. And the result of his (and the rest of Europe's) weakness in support of the Sovereignty of Czechoslovakia, Hitler annexed a part of the Czech territory he called the Sudetenland. We will never know what would have happened had the European nations stood together against this aggression, but many historians agree that this demonstrated to Hitler that he could continue on his path of violating agreements with impunity, ultimately leading to World War II.

You can't reason with bullies. They only understand one thing. And when you're unwilling to recognize when it's time to sheathe one's Restraint and unsheathe the sword, the results aren't going to be pretty, as the Ten of Swords shows. It's just as true for individuals as it is for nations; as President Teddy Roosevelt said, "Speak softly, and carry a big stick." And I might add, don't be afraid to use it.

On the intrapsychic level, this pairing asks us once again to consider any ways in which we bully ourselves. To examine if there are any voices we have introjected that cause us to walk away from standing up for ourselves. It also tells us in no uncertain terms that we must remain vigilant and aware of ourselves and our surroundings, whether because of external threats or because of internal defenses that can roar back to life when we let our guard down. This is something I deal with since there are things that can trigger a deep anger in me that can strike out inappropriately. In all these cases, the mental sharpness and Discernment that the suit of Swords and Gevurah represent, vigilance and awareness, are essential. Don't drop your sword.

Day 44: Gevurah of Malchut in Assiyah

The Five and Ten of Pentacles

_____ *within* _____

Malchut is identified with the Shekinah, the Divine Feminine, who has been homeless since the destruction of the Temple in Jerusalem in 70 CE. Additionally, because Malchut has nothing of its own—it only receives the Sephirotic energies from above—it is the Responsibility of a serious Kabbalist to study the origins of poverty, to recognize the Shekinah among the poor, and to support her. The Zohar makes it abundantly clear in many places that it is not possible to have a mystical experience without taking action in the world of Malchut, the material world—in particular, helping the poor with their material needs.[2]

There are those who say that Tikkun Olam as social justice is a recent innovation of people with a political agenda. Those people are looking for an excuse to avoid the Responsibility that the Torah, the Talmud, and the Zohar all agree that we all share. And in this pairing of the Five and Ten of Pentacles, we see the result. As people gather in the marketplace, they have ignored the poor. If I have not been forceful enough in discussing this earlier, I must tell you again that charity is an essential spiritual practice.

This sounds more like a subject for Chesed or Tiferet of Malchut rather than Gevurah of Malchut. So why is it here? Because in this case, we are seeing the shadow of Gevurah in Severity. We are being reminded that the world looks away from the poor and that we must not look away. Jesus said as much himself. And this pair tells us look we must and act we must.

Of course, there is also the inner landscape and how we punish ourselves in the material world to consider. Judaism does not believe this world is an illusion to be transcended. The Divine is immanent in the world, and the Ten of Pentacles shows us this, with the God energy of the Sephirot sparkling unseen in the air around everyone. But there are traditions where one takes a vow of poverty, and sometimes even mortifies the flesh, as a path to the Divine. And because the dominant culture holds some of these values, it's hard not to have them introjected inside us.

When I first moved to the Upper West Side of Manhattan in the 1970s, there were many elderly people who appeared to be living in poverty. There was a man who lived on the streets, wheeling around a shopping wagon that seemed to hold all his worldly possessions. As it turned out, that wagon had a suitcase in it that was filled with cash— more than $100,000. For whatever reason, many of the people I met fit this description: they had stowed away a lot of cash but did not use it to live decently, much less comfortably or extravagantly.

There are many people who are exactly the opposite: they have nothing and spend as though they have everything. But here I am interested in the ways we punish ourselves, whether by being miserly with ourselves or by taking jobs where we underearn, where we live below our potential. Often this is due to some internalized Judgment. And this pairing is telling us to drop it right now.

Questions for reflection and contemplation: Day 44

1. (Wands) Which emotion is the most difficult for you to restrain? Why? In what ways does it rule you? How might you gain better Control of this emotion?

2. (Cups) Between the extremes shown in these cards, where do you fall on the spectrum of optimism versus pessimism? How can you better Ground your optimism or lighten up your pessimism?

3. (Swords) How can you stand up to your inner bully? What is your experience with bullies in your life? What Boundaries do you need to set?

4. (Pentacles) Commit to a regular, Disciplined charity practice. Choose an organization or cause to give to on a regular basis, with either time or money. Are there ways in which you are miserly with yourself? Are you living up to your earning potential? What can you do to change things?

Day 45: Tiferet of Malchut

Leadership Sets an Example through Compassion

Today is the forty-fifth day of the Omer, which is six weeks and three days of the Omer.

The ability to keep one's Heart open (and brokenly whole, holy broken) while remaining Sovereign, the ability to remain Self-Possessed without shutting down one's empathy, these are requirements for one who seeks to Lead through Compassionate action in the world.

On this day, we're looking at two of the Sephirot on the central column, and the healing of the relationship between these Sephirot is meant to reflect the joining of the Messiah with the Shekinah in the repair of the world. Harmony and Balance, two of the facets of Tiferet, are essential qualities for someone who wishes to be a Sovereign of the self. And they are equally essential for someone who wishes to be in a Leadership position in any sphere of life.

Truth, one of the other facets of Tiferet, is not any less essential. One must see the Truth of one's motives as a Leader and the Truth of any situation. And one must be an example of Truth that is lived daily with all those one would Lead. Just as the psalmist asks the Divine to "Lead me in Your truth. . . . And remember Your lovingkindnesses," so too must we lead ourselves and others in Truth and Compassion.[3]

The Hebrew word for "truth" is *emet,* which is spelled with the first, middle, and last letters of the Hebrew alphabet, and this has been interpreted to mean that Truth contains everything: the ultimate Truth leaves nothing out. And because Truth encompasses all, there is no place where Truth can be left out. This makes knowing and speaking Truth another practice that defines Leadership.

Day 45: Tiferet of Malchut in Atzilut
The Six and Ten of Wands

 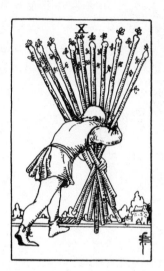

_____ *within* _____

This pairing shows an essential Truth of Leadership. Even as it calls for empathy and Compassion, Leadership is ultimately lonely. It sets the Leader apart as someone who has burdens that cannot be shared. A good Leader knows how to delegate, certainly, but some things can't be passed along to another.

The open Heart of Tiferet in the Leadership of Malchut was on view when President Obama went to Newtown, Connecticut, to meet with the grieving parents of the children murdered at Sandy Hook Elementary School and spoke to the nation not only as the president but also as a father, with tears in his eyes. These are the kind of tears that don't cloud the vision: they help a person see more clearly. These are the kinds of tears that reveal Nobility of spirit.

You can see this same Nobility on display in the letters of condolence that President Lincoln wrote to the parents of soldiers killed in the Civil War. As you read these letters you can feel the weight Lincoln felt; he knew that the decisions he made had serious consequences for the lives of hundreds of thousands of people.

This is the secret of the cross in the Six of Wands: taking on the role of a Leader means you must be willing to feel the pain of others and endure your own suffering even as you make decisions that will be hard for many to bear. The man in the Ten of Wands shows both the burden of the Leader and the burden of those who follow and serve a Leader.

Tiferet is the open Heart that is willing to descend into the world of manifestation that is Malchut: it is the light that descends into the darkness of the world where the light of Divinity is most veiled. And in its Compassion, it brings acceptance when faced with the dark mystery we all face: death.

May we always deserve Leaders who can reflect our highest ideals and our deepest Compassion. And may we all rise to Lead with Truth and Compassion when we are called on.

Day 45: Tiferet of Malchut in B'riah

The Six and Ten of Cups

_____ *within* _____

We have discussed the Six of Cups as possibly showing the betrayal of Trust that leads to a child's loss of innocence. And most often, the locus of that betrayal is the place we see in the Ten of Cups, the family. In Alice Miller's *The Drama of the Gifted Child,* she makes the point that children who are more intelligent and more emotionally sensitive than other children often are hypersensitive to their parents' hopes and expectations for them, so much so that they will lose their connection to themselves, ignoring and locking away their own feelings as they try to fulfill these parental expectations. Often parents of gifted children, in their desire to give their children opportunities they did not have (and they wanted for themselves), push their children into paths that are more a reflection of the parents' needs than the child's needs. And the children, who want to make the parents happy, ignore their own happiness.

This doesn't make the parents bad: they may well be loving parents who are simply blind to their children's inner life. But as the children grow and eventually must deal with the self they locked away, they may discover feelings of anger at the parents because of this.

As we become Sovereign adults, learning to see our parents as human beings who meant well but sometimes failed us means learning to have Compassion for them and for ourselves. We may still feel the effects of childhood wounding that makes Trusting those who love us hard sometimes. This is when it's important to open our Hearts to this wounded child within and to open to the Source of all Blessings so that we may allow ourselves to be loved without being afraid or retraumatized. Feeling Grounded in our Sovereignty and feeling connected to the protection of the Shekinah can help us find our way to the Truth of the loving family we see in the Ten of Cups.

Day 45: Tiferet of Malchut in Yetzirah

The Six and Ten of Swords

 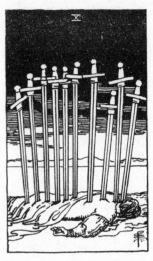

_____ *within* _____

Remember what Amalek did to you on the way when you
came forth out of Egypt.

DEUTERONOMY 25:17

It's our last journey in the precariously Balanced boat in the Six of
Swords. The open Heart of the boatman enables her to hold a space
of peaceful Presence for his passengers. (There I go, switching genders
again.) He holds an awareness of the darkness in the Ten of Swords that
they are leaving behind. He and the passengers in the boat can see the
far shore, just as Moses was granted a view of the Promised Land at the
end of the wanderings of the people.

As we give up old habits and free ourselves of addictions, there
is a period of mourning, and that grief can be for the loss of everything, from the relationships and opportunities lost to addiction to
grief over saying goodbye to the addiction itself. The important thing
is to stay on top of the grief: it can feel as overwhelming as an ocean,
and I hope that your work over the last weeks has helped you ride

the waves in a boat that is Balanced by insight and Compassion for yourself and others along with an awareness that you are held always by the Divine Presence.

It's often true that a habit, a defense, or an addiction began as a strategy to cope with or numb oneself from grief or other difficult emotions. And that as we free ourselves from these old defenses, the grief we tried to avoid can come roaring back—along with a host of other feelings that were being tamped down.

The Ten of Swords tells us that the struggle for freedom is never easy. The Six of Swords teaches us that to stay Balanced we must remember. Even as we journey to the far side and freedom, there are swords in the boat to remind us of what we're escaping. And when we reach the far side, we must still remember because there's always a section of the mind that's ready to convince us that the old way wasn't so bad and that it's okay to slip back into old behavior for just a bit. The yetzer hara is always ready to help us forget the bad and see the bad old days with a rosy glow.

The Torah instructs us to "remember Amalek" even as it also gives us the contradictory instructions to "blot out the memory of Amalek from under heaven. Do not forget!"[4] The Amalekites were a tribe that attacked the former Hebrew slaves as they made their way through the wilderness, who "struck down all the stragglers in [their] rear when [they] were faint and weary."[5] And our yetzer hara, like Amalek, attacks us just as we begin to feel free but are still weak in our determination.

To blot out the memory of Amalek in this situation means we must root out the inclination to fall back as best we can. At the same time, we must not forget, or indeed we will fall back. For only by being aware of our capacity to fall into the traps of the past can we make certain that we stay free of them. Thus, through Compassion for ourselves and for others as we move ahead, we rediscover the Divine gift of our Nobility. By acting with Compassion for others who suffer with defenses or addiction, we help them rediscover their Nobility.

Day 45: Tiferet of Malchut in Assiyah

The Six and Ten of Pentacles

_____ *within* _____

We're in the week of Malchut, the world we live in, the world of action, and we're in the suit of Pentacles, the material world. On the day of Tiferet of Malchut in Assiyah, we are presented with the opportunity to bring the Heart of our spiritual practice into the world by taking action. With this Sephirotic pairing in Assiyah, we recognize that we are partners of the Divine by working to bring Harmony to a world out of Balance. And that's just what we see illustrated in the Six of Pentacles.

We've looked at the Balance scales held by the standing man in this card before, and many interpret its appearance as showing how he Balances and judges how much to give to each of the people before him. Let's consider it a little differently today. Perhaps he carries this Balance so he can remind himself to keep his own Balance. When one acts from the open Heart of Tiferet, it can be easy to lose oneself in the suffering of others.

By keeping his Balance, he maintains his own Sovereignty. By not rushing in to "save" someone else, he respects that person's Sovereignty.

Because he acts from a place of Balanced Compassion, he can see the Tree sparkling in the air in the Ten of Pentacles. He participates in the flow of material blessings in a way that recognizes the Nobility of the people he gives to, as well as his own.

Because we are in the world of the material, today is a day to look at our actions to restore Harmony and Balance economically and in other ways. Are you living beyond your means? Are you paying yourself first with savings? Is your relationship to food balanced: do you eat not only to enjoy but also for the nutrition and health of your body, or do you eat compulsively to avoid feelings? Do you give your body the rest it needs, or do you run on empty? These are the practical questions this pairing suggests in the world of Assiyah. And as we head toward the final day of the Counting, it's a good time to consider what changes you have made over the last few weeks and what changes you still wish to make—and then get started.

Questions for reflection and contemplation: Day 45

1. (Wands) What is your experience of the loneliness of Leadership? What is your experience of the Heartache of Leadership? When you are in a position of Authority, how does it affect your ability to express Compassion?

2. (Cups) What are the ways you felt betrayed by parents and adult Authority figures when you were a child? How have you healed from this? Have you been able to see them with Compassion and forgive them? How can you show Compassion for them without losing your connection to your self?

3. (Swords) Which of your habits, defenses, or addictions is your Amalek—always ready to pounce on you when you're feeling most vulnerable? What are your strategies for protecting yourself and staying free?

4. (Pentacles) Examine where in the areas of money, food, bodily care, and sex you might be out of Balance. What steps can you take today to start restoring the Balance? Write an action plan and commit to it.

Day 46: Netzach of Malchut

The World in a Grain of Sand, Eternity in an Hour

Today is the forty-sixth day of the Omer, which
is six weeks and four days of the Omer.

The great British poet William Blake opened his poem "The Auguries
of Innocence" by writing:

> *To see a World in a Grain of Sand*
> *And a Heaven in a Wild Flower*
> *Hold Infinity in the palm of your hand*
> *And Eternity in an hour.*

Blake captured the essence of the Victory in Divine Presence that is
Netzach of Malchut. It takes Focus to be able to see through the world
we live in into the Queendom of the Shekinah, with all its Nobility. In
these last six weeks and several days, you have Persevered in doing the
work to remove the dross that has covered up your ability to see your
birthright as Royalty and your ability to see the world around you as
the Manifestation of Divinity.

You have faced adversity with Fortitude and the challenges of looking deeply into your unconscious habit patterns with Persistence. You
have Endured the heartache and pain that comes with this work, and
you have come through in Triumph.

We are in the last four days of the Counting, and you have Mastered
much. There is still work to do, though, so be Resolute and Determined
not to waste a moment of the time that is left. As Rabbi Tarfon said,
"The day is short, and the work is great; the laborers are sluggish, and
the reward is much, and the Master of the house is urgent."[6]

Stay focused. Remain resolute. The Victory of Eternity awaits.

Day 46: Netzach of Malchut in Atzilut

The Seven and Ten of Wands

 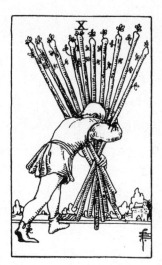

_____ *within* _____

When we look at the Ten of Wands by itself, it's the picture of oppression and hardship. It doesn't appear that we're looking at someone who is Sovereign in any way, but rather someone whose Dignity is not seen by others, or perhaps even himself. But when we consider the Netzach within this image of Malchut, we can imagine that the inner experience of this person trudging toward town and weighed down by his burden of staves is as a Master of Perseverance. Despite their burden, they demonstrate Fortitude and Endurance.

This suggests that rather than being oppressed by an outside force, the figure in the Ten of Wands has taken on this burden willingly, as their Mission. He (she or they) knows it's not an easy job, but understands it as a necessary job that someone has to step up and take Responsibility for. So the figure in the card has made that Commitment.

We all face times when there is a job that falls to us that feels overwhelming and burdensome, but necessary. Calling on one's inner Netzach is the right attitude.

The last eighteen months of my mother's life were a misery for her. Her third surgery for lung cancer was described by the doctor as a success, but the doctor also warned us that the recovery from this last operation would be more difficult and painful than the previous operations. That was an understatement. The nerves in my mother's chest were damaged and traumatized so badly that she was in constant debilitating pain for the next year and a half. She went from being an older woman who still lived with vitality to a shell of herself. The painkillers they gave her were ineffective, so that they constantly upped the dose. If I had taken one dose of all the opioids she took, I'd have slipped into unconsciousness and probably died. They just made her groggy, but they did little for the pain.

As her only relative in any proximity, and of course as her eldest son, it became my Responsibility to manage her care. I traveled to her home several times a week to measure out her meds in containers labeled with days and times, since her twenty-four-hour caregivers were not allowed to do that. I searched for pain specialists who might have some way to give her relief, but every treatment, from injections into the nerves to hypnosis, didn't work. I took her to doctors' appointments and emergency room visits when the pain was unendurable. She was readmitted to the hospital and to rehab six times in her last year and a half.

In her last hospital stay, she contracted the MRSA bacterial infection in her bloodstream through a contaminated intravenous tube, and she spent the next three weeks basically in a coma. Every day I sat by her bedside and swabbed her mouth to keep her lips and tongue from drying out.

I hated the doctors for botching her surgery. I hated the hospital for giving her MRSA. I hated her for getting old. I hated myself for not being able to save her. I wanted to run away. I wanted to skip going some days, and some days I did. The wife of a rabbi who was dying in the next room told me that I was doing a mitzvah. All I could do was cry and rage. But I kept showing up. When she finally regained consciousness, she could barely speak and had become a ghost of herself. Mercifully, she did not live long after that. I had organized my life around her care, and I thought it a mercy for her and a relief for me when she finally died. And while I was sometimes overwhelmed with the burden of her care, it was an honor to be able to try to give back something of the care she had given to me as a child.

My parents were divorced, though they were still close. As I was caring for my mother, my father, also elderly, lived in Florida with his partner and was beginning his descent into the night of Alzheimer's disease. His girlfriend (an odd word for a woman who is ten years my senior) was not obligated to care for him, since they were not married, though they had been living together for ten years. But over the next two years, she stepped up, even as I began to search for a care facility for him because it was too much for her to deal with. Nevertheless, she insisted that he stay at home with her because he'd suffer so much in such a place that he wouldn't live long. It was very hard for her. And a time came when I had to insist she bring in caregivers for support—as much for her relief as for him. I visited as often as I could. It was very hard for her, but she took this on to the end out of her love for him.

All of us are tested by Responsibilities we didn't ask for. We are called to be present as the Divine Presence that lives within all of us withdraws from the bodies of those we love at their death. Making the Commitment to be there for others and following through with Determination and Fortitude while respecting their Dignity is what reveals our inner Nobility.

May we all meet this test with Netzach in Malchut.

Day 46: Netzach of Malchut in B'riah

The Seven and Ten of Cups

_____ *within* _____

With the Seven and Ten of Cups, we're in the world of "pie in the sky," even if those pies are actually cups. This unfocused kind of Netzach leads to an ungrounded experience of Malchut. It's the planning of someone whose retirement plan is a lottery ticket. Not that I don't succumb to buying lottery tickets and fantasizing about winning. I'm even part of a group of colleagues who worked together twenty years ago—none of us work together at the same company today—but who still buy lottery tickets as a group every week.

In fact, a friend of mine once visited me and saw a pile of my lottery tickets in a bowl. Months of lottery tickets I'd never checked. He berated me for not checking and proceeded to go through them all. Not expecting to win, I let them pile up and only check when I'm getting close to the expiration date for the prizes.

Of course, we can look at the unfocused energy of the Seven of Cups as the distractions of our modern age, with people looking at screens on devices and jumping from one site to another searching for some unknown satisfaction, like Tantalus reaching for fruit that always receded to exceed his grasp. This is another negative side of Netzach, which includes the inability to make a Commitment—or even a choice. Today's dating apps have encouraged this consumerist thinking for finding relationships, as the lonely keep swiping left in their endless search for the perfect profile.

So what happens when this negative Netzach is expressed in the world of Malchut? I think about Jeannette Walls's memoir, *The Glass Castle,* in which she tells the story of growing up in a dysfunctional family with a father who always spoke of big plans that were mostly fantasies, as Jeannette and her three siblings end up resorting to dumpster diving for food. When they were small children, she didn't recognize the level of poverty they were living in or the fact that her parents were not very connected to reality. It was only as she grew that she experienced the disconnect between her father's grandiose plans and the situation they'd been living in for years. While they eventually did have a house to live in, there was no indoor plumbing, and her father, continuing to spin fantasies of a grand house, let this minimum of shelter go to complete ruin.

I can see Walls's family in this combination of the Seven and Ten of Cups. You may not have had such an extreme experience as this in your life, but perhaps you know someone whose grandiose plans are based in fantasies, who takes no Responsibility, and who ends up leaving ruin and devastation—both material and emotional—in their wake.

One thing about this path of Counting the Omer: it is Grounded in reality, and this last week is Focused on the world we live in. We are encouraged to see the Divine shining through it, but we are also expected to do our part as partners in completing and healing Creation. There's no room for fantasy here.

Day 46: Netzach of Malchut in Yetzirah
The Seven and Ten of Swords

_____ *within* _____

There's a scene in the film *Monty Python and the Holy Grail* in which a man wheels a cart of corpses through a plague-ridden town, calling out, "Bring out your dead!" And someone shows up carrying what looks like a corpse to load on the cart. Except the person being carried insists, "I'm not dead!"

When I see this pairing of cards and the trickster energy illustrated in the Seven of Swords, I think about this scene: we may think the figure in the Ten of Swords is dead, and he may look dead, but at the most inopportune moment, he'll sit up and insist, "I'm not dead!"

If you've ever had chicken pox as a child, you may encounter this viral trickster energy later in life, because while the immune system eventually does shut down this infection, the virus just hides in the body and can reappear, usually when you've reached an age when your immune system isn't as powerful as it once was. But this time, the virus manifests itself as shingles, a very painful disease indeed, which can leave lasting nerve damage and possibly even lead to blindness.

With this in mind, one way to consider this pair for today is as another warning to stay Focused and aware because our neuroses and addictions, even those that appeared tamed long ago, can come roaring back to life when conditions are right. The lesson here is to know your triggers so that you're ready to meet these submerged urges consciously, with a discriminating intelligence that sees through them and a compassion that recognizes their root. When you're able to do that, no matter how many times these zombie defenses arise, you will be able to Endure their attacks so that you remain Grounded in Nobility.

A last note. A traditional tarot reading of this pair can suggest someone making off with an inheritance. Back in the late eighties, my late friend Lou and his partner, Danyal, hosted a will-writing party for many of their gay male friends. It was the height of the HIV crisis, and we'd seen many gay men die with no will and their estranged families swoop in to take possession of whatever they could while the deceased's partner had no legal rights. So Lou and Danyal called in a bunch of lawyer friends, and we all worked through our estates and our instructions. No one likes to write a will.

No one likes to write a living will or a medical proxy. Who wants to face the reality of their own death? Having been through these experiences, I want to suggest that if you're old enough to read this book, you're old enough to definitely have a will and instructions for a living will. Think about your legacy—what you want to leave loved ones. But more than that, I would like to introduce you to the Jewish custom of writing a *zava'ah,* an ethical will.

Inspired by the Biblical examples of both Jacob and Moses sharing teachings and blessings before they died, Jews have been writing ethical wills for centuries. This document is a true gift to one's spiritual heirs, giving them your words of love and wisdom and rooting them in a tradition going back generations. Today this custom has spread beyond Judaism. And it's not only a gift to your spiritual heirs; writing such a document is a kind of meditation on your death and what you hope to leave behind in people's memories, so it is also a gift to give yourself.

Day 46: Netzach of Malchut in Assiyah

The Seven and Ten of Pentacles

_____ *within* _____

There was a time when meadow, grove, and stream,
The earth, and every common sight,
To me did seem
Apparelled in celestial light,
The glory and the freshness of a dream.
It is not now as it hath been of yore; —
Turn wheresoe'er I may,
By night or day.

> *The things which I have seen I now can see no more.*
> WILLIAM WORDSWORTH, "ODE: INTIMATIONS
> OF IMMORTALITY FROM RECOLLECTIONS
> OF EARLY CHILDHOOD"

Along with William Blake, the poets of the romantic era saw the Divine in nature and, indeed, in "every common sight." But they also lived at the dawning of the Industrial Revolution. Many of them felt that their ability to see the "celestial light" would not Endure: it was as though the new plagues of air and water pollution from the factories were further obscuring the veiled Divine nature of reality.

Indeed, there has always been a prejudice that the best place to be able to see through the veil of Nature to the Divine Presence is in natural settings, as opposed to cities. And that's what we see in today's pairing of the Seven and Ten of Pentacles. There's a split between those who can see the Divine within and those who can't, and it's the difference between someone who lives and works with Nature and people who are in a town.

But the truth is, the Divine Presence, the Shekinah, is always present and visible for those with practiced and open eyes. And in the Seven of Pentacles, we have a reflection of your Persistent work on this path over the last forty-six days. I hope, as for the man tilling the soil in this image, that your work is bearing fruit and that you feel lighter and freer than you did seven weeks ago. But there is still some work to do in this Endurance race to the fiftieth day. Perhaps you have been rewarded for your hard work by seeing more of the "celestial light" of the Divine Kingdom that is implicate within all reality, whether in natural settings or in the center of a city. And since this is a day of Netzach, keep it up!

Questions for reflection and contemplation: Day 46

1. (Wands) When have you been called on to demonstrate Netzach within Malchut in your relationships? In what ways did it test you?

2. (Cups) When you set a big goal for yourself, what practices or disciplines do you use to make sure you Persevere in reaching that goal?

What have been your experiences doing this—when you succeeded and when you failed?

3. (Swords) What are the triggers for your zombie defenses? When you find yourself triggered, what do you do to Persevere in your course and not get overwhelmed? Begin the process of writing an ethical will today if you don't have one. And if you don't have a legal will, start the process of making one today.

4. (Pentacles) Practice seeing the "celestial light" in every activity and encounter you have today. At the end of the day, journal about your experience.

Day 47: Hod of Malchut

Balancing the Openness of Humility with Sovereignty

Today is the forty-seventh day of the Omer, which is six weeks and five days of the Omer.

In the week of Malchut, after the work of the previous weeks, there is a settling into the Sovereignty of the Self that is neither a withdrawal from the world and relationship nor a sense of superiority for having done the work.

This is the exquisite balance of independent Authority without ego. This is Sovereignty without will but resting within Divine Will. On this day of Hod in Malchut, there is Appreciation and Gratitude for everyone who has helped you along the way, including the Divine, which called you to this path. It's a day to recognize and give thanks for this practice, knowing what the gift of this discipline has given in the last forty-six days.

In twelve-step programs, the fourth step requires taking a "fearless moral inventory." One of the interesting things about this step is that instructions to do the inventory include considering one's gifts, one's talents, one's good qualities, and one's moral uprightness. Many of us, however, in false Humility (or perhaps more accurately, low self-esteem) would run to the other side, listing faults, defects, and moral failings only. The confessional aspect of this step is very important, and one has to look at the wreckage an addiction has wrought in one's life and take Responsibility for it. But solely focusing on one's failings ignores the true virtues one has to be Grateful for.

This facet of the fourth step is about true Humility, accepting one's good judgment and one's Dignity with an awareness that these are some of the gifts one has received from the Divine and expressing Gratitude for these gifts. In many ways, this day, Hod of Malchut, captures this element of the step.

Day 47: Hod of Malchut in Atzilut

The Eight and Ten of Wands

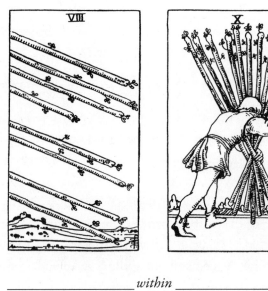

_____ *within* _____

> *Cast your burden on the Lord and He will sustain you; He will never let the righteous stumble.*
>
> PSALMS 55:23

More than one prophet of the Tanakh referred to the gift of prophecy as a burden. Jonah even tried to run from the command of YHVH that he prophesy their destruction to the people of Nineveh. And can you blame him? Nobody likes a killjoy. The messages of prophets such as Jonah, Habakkuk, and Jeremiah are not exactly the words people want to hear. And when people don't like the message, history shows us that they don't treat the messenger very well.

I bring this up today with this pairing of the Eight and Ten of Wands because the Eight of Wands, corresponding to the Sephira of Hod, carries with it the meaning of the ability to prophesy. It suggests that one's ego is healthy enough to get out of the way in order to receive the message YHVH is sending. And like a bolt from heaven, the eight staves hurtling toward the earth carry a prophetic message, and they're clearly all headed in the same direction to reach one person in particular. If you're someone who connects with these Divine radio waves, you know that when a broadcast comes in, it can be a bit of a shock. If you do divination with tarot, you may have these bolts from heaven regularly. And you know that when you get certain kinds of information, unlike Jeremiah, who wasn't afraid of causing a stir with his words, diplomacy and a sensitivity to the emotional state of one's client is essential.

This is one reason I prefer to use the cards for consultative counseling and my own inner work, rather than doing divinatory readings for people. My experience is that being open to receive information and then calibrating the best way to deliver that information can be exhausting. Like the figure in the Ten of Wands, you have to carry this message to people with an awareness that your information may not be welcome.

One of the effects of doing this work of Counting the Omer, though, is an opening of these prophetic channels within. Doing a Sephirotic spring cleaning means you're more open to messages from the Divine. After all, one goal of this work is to be able to receive your own personal revelation on the fiftieth day. Over these last seven weeks, we've been doing the work to strengthen your spiritual muscles. So that unlike the figure in the Ten of Wands, you'll be strong enough to receive and carry your message. As you grow stronger in righteousness, you'll be able to carry this burden without stumbling or falling: YHVH will sustain you.

Day 47: Hod of Malchut in B'riah

The Eight and Ten of Cups

_____ *within* _____

In this pair of images, we can see one of the big differences between Judaism and Buddhism (as well as Christianity). They show the path of the monastic, who is often a celibate ascetic, as opposed to the path of the householder. I first encountered the word *householder* when I began studying and practicing Buddhist meditation. Because while the Buddha favored the monastic path, a path of leaving the world behind, he believed it was possible, if much more difficult, for a layperson who had family and business obligations to attain enlightenment. Because some traditional Christian paths are dualistic, some Christians believe we live in a fallen world that needs to be transcended, so that avoiding pleasures (and sometimes scourging the flesh) will save you.

Judaism takes the opposite approach. Jews see the world as a blessing, a gift from the Divine, and believe that the commandments in the Torah teach us to sanctify the physical world. Sexual relations, properly sanctified, are joyous and not a reason to feel dirty or guilty. Taking pleasure in food, wine, natural beauty . . . these are all Divine gifts, and the Jewish response is to say a blessing before enjoying these gifts. We are encouraged by Wordsworth to see the "splendor in the grass, glory in the flower." The Baal Shem Tov taught people to serve YHVH with joy.

It may sound as if I have a preference here. I do not. I understand that there are many paths to enlightenment, though scourging and painful asceticism are not my paths. On Vipassana retreats, meditators live like monks, and I have found this helpful in quieting the mind to go deep within. In fact, it was on my first such retreat that I experienced the "splendor in the grass." What I object to are paths that vilify the physical world of Malchut.

Turn away from the world to explore the inner depths like the figure in the Eight of Cups. Or celebrate the world as the Divine Presence made manifest by participating in the life of a householder, as in the Ten of Cups. Choose your path. Or like so many today who have the opportunity to go on a retreat for ten days, a month, or more, then to return to daily life, explore both. Or stay in the world and practice the self-denial or abstention of the Lenten practice to explore your own willfulness and desire.* You'll learn which path speaks more clearly to your soul. But no matter which path you take, the One that sustains all reality will be with you all along the way.

---

*The origin of this practice is an imitation of Christ's forty-day fast in the desert, a practice that some scholars think he took on as a member of one of the very few ascetic sects within Judaism, the Essenes.

Day 47: Hod of Malchut in Yetzirah

The Eight and Ten of Swords

_____ *within* _____

> *How is she become as a widow! She that was great among the nations, And a princess among the provinces, How is she become a slave!*
>
> LAMENTATIONS 1:1

The book of Lamentations is read in synagogues in its entirety once a year, on the anniversary of the destruction of the Temple in Jerusalem by the army of Nebuchadnezzar II in 586 BCE. It is a harrowing account of more than the destruction of the central place of worship for the Jewish people; the city of Jerusalem also had been under siege and was destroyed. The writer of Lamentations pulls no punches in describing the violence visited on the people. He (or she, we don't really know, though Jeremiah gets the credit) describes people starving and dying in the streets, women and children cut down by enemy soldiers, and people taken away in slavery. What was once a Sovereign nation became a vassal state. The "she" in the quote above refers to the city of Jerusalem. And looking at the Eight and Ten of Swords, you can easily see why Lamentations came to mind.

In the ancient world, when a nation was conquered, its religion usually disappeared as the victors enforced the worship of their own gods (and often kings) on the vanquished people. The Jews were (and are) a stubborn people; rather than accept foreign gods as stronger than YHVH, they reinterpreted their defeat as the result of their failing to live up to the contract they'd made with the Divine by straying from the commandments. As you probably realize, I don't believe in a deity with a personality who intervenes in human history and uses one people to punish another. But I understand the need for such a belief: it gives meaning to suffering, and it provides a reason for the unreasonable and serves to keep the belief in that god strong and those people together.

What does this mean for us today in the light of this card pairing? The qualities of Hod of Malchut can be read as Humility in Sovereignty, and in the suit of Swords, I see this as a warning about the shadow side of this pair on several levels. On the macroscale, I interpret this as showing us the result of tribalism and religious triumphalism, which are filled with pride and a sense of superiority over others. Religious triumphalism is often exemplified by people who believe that "God is on our side" in a conflict (or not on our side, as above), though which god obviously changes, depending on whether we're talking about the Islamic conquests across the Middle East, North Africa, and Europe in the seventh century; European colonialism across the globe; or the Jewish concept of being the "chosen people."

In *When Religion Becomes Evil: Five Warning Signs* by Charles Kimball, two of the warning signs speak to the image of the Eight of Swords: blindness to other groups' strengths and people's inability to see the morality of their own group's actions.[7] Today, from Islamic fundamentalists to Christian dominionists, Hindu nationalists, and contemporary Jewish zealots, we are surrounded by people who believe that because they have "God on their side" they can do no wrong and that others can do no right. There are even Buddhist monks in places such as Myanmar busy inciting anti-Islamic violence!

On the personal level, I can say that I grew up believing that Jews are smarter than other people. Mind you, I had lots of Christian friends who were much smarter than I was and lots of Jewish friends who certainly weren't the sharpest tools in the shed. But it was part of the atmosphere I grew up with. And it was a semiconscious prejudice I had to recognize and root out as an adult.

Then there's my experience in the grab-bag world of the New Age. I've noticed in myself, and in others, a sense of superiority, as though because we are aware of other levels of reality and go deeper than the literal meaning of sacred writings, we're better than those poor benighted souls who follow an exoteric path. And this is true in many esoteric circles.

This creates separation rather than connection. It's the violence of pride that denies the full humanity of others. And I have often been guilty of it. But when you know what happens when this is taken to extremes, you have to check yourself.

Day 47: Hod of Malchut in Assiyah

The Eight and Ten of Pentacles

_____ *within* _____

An excellent thing is the study of the Torah combined with
some worldly occupation, for the labor demanded by them

both makes sin to be forgotten. All study of the Torah without
work must in the end be futile and become the cause of sin.
PIRKEI AVOT 2:2, *THE STANDARD PRAYER BOOK*

Buddhist monks are, well, monks; they don't have jobs. Catholic priests have a vocation; they're priests full-time for the most part. Rabbis, well, many of the sages of the Talmud had occupations. Because Judaism sees the world as an aspect of the Divine, work can be holy. And as the quote from Rabban Gamliel above suggests, the sages believed that devoting oneself full time to Torah study was to remove oneself from the world, which would not help heal the world in Tikkun Olam.

In the United States, when people first meet each other, one of the first questions they ask is what the other's occupation is. It's one way we judge people, since jobs carry social status or stigma, depending on what the job is. In Europe they think this custom is both rude and shallow. And based on Americans' judgments of certain jobs, the sages of the Talmud would be seen to have very low status jobs indeed.

Hillel chopped wood. Abba Shaul was a gravedigger. Rabbi Yochanan Hasandlar was a shoemaker. Rabbi Yosi ben Chalafta was a tanner, which, oddly enough, was the occupation of my great grandfather Wilhelm Horn, even though he was also the head of the local yeshiva. In fact, the Talmud says that being a tanner is one of the occupations the world can't do without, though it is also considered an unfortunate job to have because of the noxious chemicals and odors associated with the work.

It was important to the rabbis that one's work was not something that resulted in a haughty kind of pride. One can take pride in a job well done, but becoming arrogant because one is good at a job was considered sinful.

All these were jobs that helped encourage an attitude of Humility, just as we see in the Humble workman at his bench in the Eight of Pentacles. The message of this card is respect for this kind of work and for people who work at humble occupations. And for your self-respect if this is what you do. There are people in retail service positions all across the country who have advanced degrees in one subject or another but can't find work in their field. Nevertheless, they need work, and the work they're doing is needed. And there is no shame in this; their work is worthy of respect. We all live in the world of Malchut; the Ten of Pentacles is the agora, a public marketplace, and the Sephirot are all there, shining in the air for those with eyes to see.

In this consideration of work, we can derive some principles for the kind of work to be engaged in. I spend many years wrestling internally with my work in advertising since the industry offers much temptation for dishonesty. And the Talmud is very clear that jobs that tempt one to be dishonest or immoral are not jobs for someone on this path. The rabbis also wanted whatever work one did to give enough time and leave one with enough energy for the Torah study that is the other half of the equation in the quote above.

As we come near the end of this forty-nine-day path, it's essential to remember that the work we do in the world is not separate from this path. And that our work and our path must inform and enrich each other and the world.

Questions for reflection and contemplation: Day 47

1. (Wands) If you do divination work or counseling work, what are your practices to keep your channel open? What are your practices to cleanse and reenergize after doing this work? If you don't do this kind of work, what are your experiences with messages or information that comes from the Divine?

2. (Cups) Which path have you taken on your inner journey: celebrating the world as a blessing or seeing the world as a temptation to be transcended? If you have taken elements from both paths, how do you balance these beliefs? If you have chosen one path, why that one and not the other?

3. (Swords) Were you brought up to believe that "God is on your side" in your tradition of birth? If so, what do you believe now, and why? What are your beliefs around the idea of a Deity that acts in history on behalf of particular peoples? Why?

4. (Pentacles) How does your spiritual path inform your professional or occupational path and vice versa? Is there any way in which you feel your work conflicts with your spiritual path? If so, how? What can you do to bring them more in alignment?

Day 48: Yesod of Malchut

The Foundation of Nobility

Today is the forty-eighth day of the Omer,
which is six weeks and six days of the Omer.

You shall raise up ruined foundations. . . . And you shall be called "Repairer. . . ."

ISAIAH 58:12

In the image of the Tree of Life that appears in the frontispiece of *The Gates of Light,* a man, often identified as Rabbi Isaac the Blind, reaches out to take hold of the Tree at exactly the point of the path between Yesod and Malchut. This is the place where all the power and energy from above flows down into the world of Creation that we live in, so the ability to take hold of the Tree at this point means that one has indeed opened a clear channel to all the higher Sephirot and that one has created a strong Foundation in one's life that enables one to Connect to all this energy without being consumed by it.

Doing the work of all the previous days was in preparation for this penultimate day of the count. Tomorrow, in Malchut of Malchut, we will be ready to receive. But today, in Yesod of Malchut, we are still working to clear whatever complexes we can in this last Channel so that when all the energy from above flows into Malchut tomorrow, we will be in a place of peace; that is, we will have achieved Connected Sovereignty so that we can be fully Present to receive the Divine Presence as it Manifests in the world around us and within us. Doing this work is indeed restoring the Foundations laid long ago and creating an inner Tikkun, reuniting our fragmented selves and effecting a theurgic reunification, creating

Tikkun Olam, healing the world by bringing together YHVH and the Shekinah, the Divine Masculine and Divine Feminine.

Let's see how the cards instruct us in restoring the Foundation.

Day 48: Yesod of Malchut in Atzilut

The Nine and Ten of Wands

_____ *within* _____

> *When I think my foot is slipping, your mercy, O LORD,*
> *supports me.*
>
> PSALMS 94:18

It is time to take the step out from behind the stockade of staves in the Nine of Wands. You have faced inner demons and old Intimacy woundings, and having seen them in the light of the Divine, you know they have no power over you. You can see that there is no danger on the other side and that it's time to return to society and Relationship, so in the Ten of Wands, you gather up the staves and return, trudging a path back to the town in the distance.

Even as we take those steps out from behind our defenses to open to new Relationship and healing, it doesn't mean that there isn't fear or worry. But having done the work and having touched the energy of the Sephirot above, you've opened the gates of the faithfulness of YHVH, so that even if your steps feel tentative or heavy at first, you know you are supported by the One.

And you know that the Divine Presence is present in all your relationships, so that you are supported there as well. Having this support gives you a strong Foundation, so that you don't need to hide behind a stockade of staves: you have the confidence that your Sovereignty is secure.

Make these words from the Psalms your mantra for the day as you go about your daily affairs, so that every time you go out or from one place to another, these words are present in your mind. Allow yourself to feel the support; allow yourself to feel held lovingly by the One that holds all Creation.

Day 48: Yesod of Malchut in B'riah

The Nine and Ten of Cups

_____ *within* _____

Last week, looking at the Nine of Cups, I suggested a new way of seeing the man seated in front of the table—as the tenth man, waiting for the other nine to come to a minyan, a prayer service. And in particular, I suggested we see him as Rabbi Shimon Bar Yohai, the master teacher in the Zohar, waiting for his companions before they begin preparations for the revelation of Shavuot by studying the Torah together. The custom of studying the Torah from midnight to dawn is referred to as "adorning the bride"; that is, preparing the Shekinah for Her joining with her Divine Lover YHVH in the hieros gamos at dawn.

One of those adornments is the rainbow, which is said to become visible to meditators practicing the Ma'aseh Merkavah, the Chariot meditations, when they have a vision of the Shekinah. And in both the Nine and Ten of Cups, we have images of the bow.

In the Nine of Cups, the table lined with cups is a visual echo of the rainbow in the sky in the next card, a hint that the majesty of the earthly rainbow is but a pale reflection of the glory of the rainbow of the Shekinah.

In the Ten of Cups, we see the rainbow in the sky, with a Divine vision of the ten Sephirot sending their flow of energy into the world of Malchut. It is the rainbow following the Divine union that births the world. And it is reflected in the union of the married couple figured in the card and their children playing at their feet.

The world is filled with blessings that are here for us to enjoy—from good food and drink with companionship on the spiritual quest to joining together of the flesh to continue the flow of blessings in the world.

Thinking about this pair brings to mind my first love: Bill and I fell in love because we were reading the same book, and when we started talking about it together it was as though we were opening to each other's souls. So the description of reading the Torah with others as both spiritual and erotic makes perfect sense to me.

Here in this pair, the sexuality of Yesod is Connected to, and sublimated in, Torah study. As I've noted before, traditionally, sexuality is acted on in sacred ritual and within sacred boundaries with one's partner as part of the commandment to continue the work of creation. Of course, I define this sacred Generativity not only as heterosexual couples bringing children into the world but also as anyone bringing new ideas, creativity, and new things into the world to better the lives of all. We receive blessings, and we are expected to keep the flow going. I hope in writing this book I am doing my part.

Day 48: Yesod of Malchut in Yetzirah

The Nine and Ten of Swords

 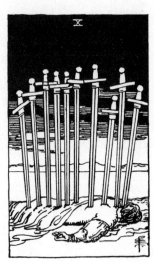

_____ *within* _____

Seen mythologically, the destruction of the Temple in Jerusalem by the Romans in 70 CE is understood by the Jewish mystics as a rupture between the Divine Masculine and the Divine Feminine, a divorce between YHVH and his Shekinah. And in this myth, the Shekinah goes into exile with the People Israel. The Jewish liturgical calendar recognizes this with the observance of Tisha B'Av, the day when it is said the Temple was destroyed—both the first time in 586 BCE by the Babylonians and then later by the Romans. And the Kabbalists were attuned to the cycles of mourning as well as the times of celebration.

Certainly, when the Temple went up in flames, during centuries of pogroms, and then when eight million vanished into smoke over Europe, Jews have asked: Where has God gone? Why has he abandoned us? The last words of one famous rabbi speak for so many of us in our spiritual bereavement: *"Eli, Eli lema sabachthani?"* (My God, my God, why have you Forsaken me?).[8]

Tony Kushner evokes a similar bereavement, speaking for all Creation in his play *Angels in America: A Gay Fantasia on National Themes,* where even the angels are grieving and overcome with desolation because God has abandoned them and heaven to go they know not where.[9]

Where has God gone? The question as most people pose it does not concern me, since it starts from the assumption there is a deity with a personality who intervenes in history, and I don't believe in such a deity. But I do believe that there is the urge of consciousness to know itself and that this is the ultimate hidden level in the implicate order, the Ein Sof, if you will. That which cannot be described but can be touched with our minds and felt within our bodies. And sometimes even those who have had an experience of reaching this place can feel like they can't find their way back there again. And thus, they feel abandoned, cut off, and in deep grief over this lost Connection.

This is how I see the Nine of Swords on this, the penultimate day of the count. The severed Connection to the Divine that leaves us feeling profoundly alone, bereft, and bereaved. Sometimes this is a response to external events, like the very human yet inhumane actions that have led to genocides, mass shootings, and other tragedies that shock us out of the slumber of daily consciousness and lead us to ask questions that cannot be answered.

Sometimes this grief is an inner response to a change in the perception of reality. I remember a man who volunteered to help at meditation retreats constantly; he did this because his experience of meditation took him to places of deep bliss that he mistook for the ultimate goal and because he wanted to help others. His teachers warned him that his experience was simply one more example of phenomena that are subject to change, and this was so. Because the day came when the blissful states disappeared, and he then found himself facing pain, boredom, anger, lust, and a whole host of other emotions in his sitting. But the emotion he experienced most strongly was the feeling expressed in the Nine of Swords. He felt cut off from the Divine and in deep grief. He had become attached to the blissful states that were merely mutable phenomena. He had told himself a story that these states were a reward for how good a person he was. So when they disappeared, he believed he was being punished. Because this was a Buddhist meditation camp, the story he formed for himself was that he was being punished for something he'd done in a former life and that when he'd "done his time," the blissful states would return.

I can't say whether his story accurately reflected reality. I do know that we all do this. Our hearts open and close to the Divine, like flowers open and close for the sun, independent of what we consciously want. And we tell ourselves stories about why.

I know that once, many years ago, when I had done something I considered truly sinful, I felt cut off from the Divine. I don't believe there was a deity with a personality in a heaven telling some ministering angel to go down and close the spiritual gates for me. But I do believe that something inside me closed my ability to perceive the Divine in every moment, that simply by walking so far off the path of righteousness, I had created my own inner darkness so that I felt the grief of the figure in the Nine of Swords.

In fact, I believe that one can walk so far off the path and do things that are so grievous that it feels as if one has murdered one's own soul. This is what I see in the Ten of Swords.

Except the soul doesn't die, and you can't kill it. But it can feel like that. And when you come to this place of desolation, these two cards are where you are. Today, just as we are about to open to the vastness of Ein Sof in the hopes of touching that place where we feel at one with the universe, it's important to be reminded that we are still living in the world of phenomena and that states of consciousness come and go. We may recognize in this pair a place we've been in the past, and it's possible it's a place we'll see again. More importantly, because we're in Yesod of Malchut, we may know someone who is in this place. And your experience can be of great value to someone in this place. Reach out to that person without expectations of results, only love. And as E. M. Forster said, "Only connect."

Day 48: Yesod of Malchut in Assiyah

The Nine and Ten of Pentacles

_____ *within* _____

I will be ever present in your midst.

LEVITICUS 26:12

Our last pair for Bonding in Nobility brings us to our last visit with the woman in her garden in the Nine of Pentacles. With the garden as a metaphor for both her body and soul, we know she has done the work; her channels are open to the divine, and her Foundation in the mindful and sacred expression of her sexuality is solid. So that when she is in her literal garden, she is the mistress of it all.

When she goes out into the world, regardless of the awareness of the people around her, she is aware of the Divine Presence ever in our midst. She can see the sparkling nature of reality hinted at in the Ten of Pentacles.

Because she is alone, though, there is a question of whether her Sovereignty is such that it prevents her from Bonding; it's entirely possible that other people sense her inner Nobility and, not feeling equal to her strength, never get close enough for an Intimate Relationship. This is one of the difficulties of walking this path. Often people who work deeply on their own spirituality and psychological development find it hard to meet a partner who has done work that is as deep. It's one reason I have never restricted my search for a partner to any one particular path; I just want to know that a person is on a path and actively walking it. So much the better if it's a path we walk together. But ultimately, we come to a place on the path where we must face our demons and our deities alone. The woman in the Nine of Pentacles is ready to face them but may not be ready to face another person, and most often that's where we find our demons and deities.

That said, when you're on this path and you meet someone who sees reality as it is—who sees its sparkling nature even as the dog pees on the side of the city gate—it's a beautiful moment, whether it leads to a long-term relationship that's both physically and spiritually Intimate or not. Because it's a moment of true Intimacy, of recognizing each other's souls. And such an experience nourishes the heart and waters the garden.

Questions for reflection and contemplation: Day 48

1. (Wands) Use the words from Psalm 94:18 as your mantra for the day: "When I think my foot is slipping, your mercy, O LORD, supports me." Repeat it silently in your mind every time you stand up to go from one place to another. At the end of the day, journal about your experience.

2. (Cups) What is your experience regarding studying text together in a spiritual community and with another person in particular? Describe how you experience your Nobility and the Nobility of others in this Relationship.

3. (Swords) Remember a time when you felt cut off from the Divine. What happened that led to this feeling? What happened when it shifted and you reconnected? Whom do you know who might be in such a dark place now? Is there any way your experience can be of service to that person?

4. (Pentacles) How have your spiritual search and your journey on your path affected your Relationships and your search for Intimate Relationship? What are the ways your work on your soul is reflected in the ways you care for your body?

Day 49: Malchut of Malchut

Living in Integrity Is True Sovereignty

> Today is the forty-ninth day of the Omer, which is seven weeks of the Omer.

Seven weeks ago, you decided to take a path out of slavery and into freedom. And it wasn't an easy path. But you have reached a place that's more than just freedom: you are Royalty. A King or Queen, true Sovereign of your self. And with Sovereignty comes Responsibility, not only to yourself but also to others. Because as you have grown stronger in your ability to hold Divine light, you are called on to share that light with others. To serve as a beacon for those on the path behind you.

You may feel a new reservoir of confidence and clarity in who you are and what unique gifts you bring to the world. You may feel a quiet and simple joy that suffuses every moment and every interaction. Remember to bring this confidence, clarity, and joy to the places within where growth was harder, and be sure to let go of any disappointment for whatever you are not ready to do yet. Because, of course, while the Counting the Omer is done for this year, the journey does not end here. But today is a day to look back over the past seven weeks and reflect on how you have grown. On the ways in which you have become more open. How your love has grown stronger. How your discernment has become clearer. How your compassion has deepened. The ways in which your endurance has increased. How your humility has become healthier. And how your ability to be intimate with yourself, others, and the Divine has been enlarged.

There's an expression Jews use when someone has done a good service for themselves and others: *yasher koach*. It's most often translated as "go from strength to strength," meaning that may the strength you've demonstrated in your good work and deeds grow ever stronger. So to you, dear reader and companion on this path, I say, "Yasher koach!"

Day 49: Malchut of Malchut in the Four Worlds

The Ten of Wands, Cups, Swords, and Pentacles

_____ *within* _____

The place on which you stand is holy ground.

EXODUS 3:5

In the Ten of Wands, we have reached the end of the journey: it's time to put down anything that isn't yours or that doesn't serve your higher purpose. It's time to be sure that the Responsibilities you take on will be healthy and in service of your growth and of Tikkun Olam.

Regarding the rainbow in the Ten of Cups, in the last seven weeks, you will have no doubt experienced the full spectrum of emotions, and this is a gift. Those who are depressed live a muted experience, where emotions feel muffled if they are felt at all. You have been given the gift of feeling. Feel deeply, that you might know yourself in your heart and that you might share the joy and sadness of others.

The image on the Ten of Swords reminds us to continue to use our insight so that we might not fall prey to illusory fears or desires and that we might not allow old defenses to rise up to try to seize control over our higher self. And it reminds us that our time is short: use it wisely.

Last, the Ten of Pentacles is your reminder of the words YHVH spoke to Moses from the burning bush: "The place on which you stand is holy ground." This is true wherever you stand. The image of the Sephirot shining in the air in this card tells us that there are hidden sparks everywhere for you to reveal and raise up. Now that you are no longer enslaved, it's time to free the light, helping to restore the light of Creation and increase the ability of the universe to know itself. This is your partnership with the Divine, and in celebrating the holiness of wholeness, the enlightenment of Integrity, you reveal your true Nobility. You are taking on the sacred Responsibility of raising these sparks in your daily life, so that having counted the last forty-nine days, from this day forward you will know how to make every day count.

Questions for reflection and contemplation: Day 49

Sit quietly before your journal for a moment, receiving all the energies of the Sephirot. Then write your responses to the prompts that follow:

> Look back over the last seven weeks, and review all the ways in which you have grown.
>
> Remember those who were there for you along the way: name them, and hold them in your heart with love.
>
> Say goodbye to those complexes that may have been useful at one time but had become obstacles in your path forward. Thank them for when they were helpful, and say goodbye.
>
> Think about the responsibilities you want to take on in the work of Tikkun Olam that will become a practice for the rest of your life. What are the practices that will support your moving forward?

Remember to say blessings of gratitude and presence each moment you have a chance to raise the sparks.

Pentecost

Day 50: The Gates Are Always Open

The enlightened will shine like the radiance of the sky.

DANIEL 12:3

I arise at midnight to praise You.

PSALMS 119:62

REMEMBER BACK ON THE FIRST DAY, when we first looked at the knight meditating in the chapel on his Night Vigil in the Four of Swords? This will be your Night Vigil. The difference is that the knight was alone, but the Jewish custom is that this vigil, the Tikkun, is done with other people in community. Yes, you can do it alone. And if you have followed this practice at the same time other people around the world are doing it so that you reach this day together, you have the benefit of the morphic field of energy that will help you along. You are entering mythic time: just as Passover is a reexperiencing of the freedom from bondage in Egypt, so this day is a reexperiencing of the receiving of the Torah at Mt. Sinai. It is not only our ancestors who received the Torah, it also is every one of us now. Tradition says that the Torah is always being given and that it's only a question of being able to tune in to the channel. The work of Counting the Omer was about clearing the static so you can receive this channel clearly.

If you can observe this Tikkun in a group of ten people, all the better to hold the energy of the ten Sephirot. If you can observe this Tikkun in a group of fewer than ten people, the Divine Presence will still be among you. And if this is something you are only able to do alone, keep a space in your heart for all those whom you love so that they are also present with you; their energy will hold you as you hold them, and you will effect the "arousal from below," opening a channel to Divine energy.

INTERPRETATION AS REVELATION

For the ten companions of the Zohar, the act of studying and interpreting verses from the Tanakh is what opened them to revelation. And so the tradition is to take short selections from each of the five books of Moses, always including the verses from Exodus 19–23, which recount the encounter of the people with YHVH.

Each hour of the night, a different text is read aloud, with everyone contributing to and building on previous interpretations. Texts include selections from the books of the Prophets and the Writings, and always include the book of Ruth, sometimes the entire book, for reasons that are better for you to discover on your own when you do it. Other sacred texts are also often included, with selections from the Zohar.

As previously noted, for the Kabbalists, reading and interpreting these texts is known as "adorning the bride," preparing the Shekinah to be reunited with YHVH in the Divine Marriage.

Of course, this is not the most traditional book about this practice, and I have been present when texts from other traditions were also read and studied. I am a big believer in bringing in contemporary midrash, and I think there can be no better addition to the texts read and studied on this evening than the short section titled, "What I Heard at Sinai" in Andrew Ramer's compelling and enchanting collection *Torah Told Different: Stories for A Pan/Poly/Post-Denominational World.* Or poems by Marge Piercy. The guiding principle for finding texts is that they should open you to a sense of wonder and to the Divine in every other person and throughout all Creation. They should surprise you and challenge you to be bigger.

These study sessions are not about reaching conclusions; they are about learning to live in the questions and learning to hold the tension of all the multiple interpretations, recognizing them all as an expression of the Divine. Think of this as a group-created Zen koan that despite the intellectual quality of study ultimately bypasses the intellect to unlock the gates of enlightenment, unifying the Divine Masculine and Divine Feminine within you. And connecting you to a spiritually intimate community of seekers who all see through to the Divinity of each other's essence.

UNDER THE WINGS OF THE SHEKINAH, ON WINGS OF SONG

Between text study sessions (and strong coffee with light snacks and dairy foods), there is often song. Sometimes prayers, most often the wordless melodies called *niggunim.* These acapella repetitive songs can go on for quite a while, creating a meditative state that unlocks the heart. You can find many traditional melodies online. They are easy to learn and share. Some of these melodies were originated by great Hasidic masters, and the Hasidim believe that when you sing a *niggun* from such a rabbi, the energy of his soul enters the room. Some of these tunes are very rousing and are sung with clapping to keep time, so that as the night goes on, this rouses your soul to greater heights. There are melodies handed down from the Baal Shem Tov, so that if you sing them, it is believed that the energy of his soul will appear to assist you.

If you are on your own, there are niggunim that have a slower tempo that are designed to create the deep meditative state known as *devekut,* aligning you with the Divine vibrations that surround and suffuse us all the time. You can find all these varieties of niggunim online, on YouTube, where you can learn them easily. Listen to them until you find a melody that speaks to your soul and make that niggun the one you work with most deeply. There are some sessions where those assembled spend one of the text study hours in song only.

There are some niggun chants that do have words, often from sacred texts, simply repeated, like a mantra. Rabbi Shefa Gold is a master of finding such texts and melodies that speak to the soul.

After a niggun, move seamlessly into silent meditation, listening within for the still, small voice.

THE FIRE AND THE ROSE ARE ONE: CREATING A BEAUTIFUL SPACE

You may recall that in medieval churches at Pentecost, sometimes red rose petals were dropped from the ceiling to recall the "tongues of flame" that came to rest on Christ's followers who were gathered in the same room as the Last Supper on Pentecost following his Crucifixion. Interestingly enough, in synagogues on the night of the Tikkun, rose petals are scattered through the sanctuary, as well as other flowers and greenery.

There is also the custom of decorating with papercut silhouettes of symbols like the Magen David, crowns, the tablets of the ten commandments, and the Torah scroll. Of course, on your own, you may wish to use symbols from the tarot deck, including the symbols of the four suits.

It's not so much what you use to decorate; it's about creating a beautiful space to help set the intention. So go where your heart leads you, knowing that the space you are adorning is adorning the bride.

THE BREEZES AT DAWN HAVE SECRETS TO TELL YOU

If you are able to go all night, the last reading is from the prophet Hosea, verses 2:21–22, to be spoken aloud at dawn, sealing the sacred marriage within.

> *I will betroth you unto Me forever;*
> *I will betroth you in righteousness, and in justice,*
> *And in lovingkindness, and in compassion.*
> *And I will betroth you unto Me in faithfulness;*
> *And you shall know YHVH.*

But if you aren't able to go all night, let these be the last words on your lips before you go to sleep, to seal the Divine union within you and to recognize the radical unity of all Creation. So that when you wake up, you wake up.

One last thing, as if you haven't already read this enough times over the course of this book, is that another custom on the fiftieth day is to give charity in gratitude for the blessings you have received. Keep the flow going.

Meditation Instructions

EACH DAY, THERE IS A MEDITATION you can do to open the gates of that day's Sephirotic energies. Remember, you are not praying to a Sephira, but to the Source of all blessing.

Begin by reciting aloud a prayer adapted from I Chronicles 29:10–13. These verses were a central text in the Zohar because they name the lower seven Sephirot.

> *To You, Holy One, is the greatness, and the power, the compassion and the glory, the truth and the victory: for all that is in heaven and earth is Yours; Yours, Source of All Blessing, is the foundation, the kingdom, and the sovereignty over all.*

After this prayer, you will begin by "invoking" the Sephira of the week. Once you have silently repeated this prayer several times, sit silently, noticing any change in the quality of the light around you, any sensations of energy in a field that surrounds and envelops you. You are not so much calling down energy as opening your sensorium to the already existing Divinity in its many facets that enfold and suffuse you.

When you apprehend this energy of the week, then invoke the Sephira of the day, within the Sephira of the week. Again, sit silently and notice how the energy shifts.

Sit with this energy for a few minutes, letting it flow freely around and through you, scanning your body. If you feel any places where the energy is blocked within you, don't force it. Simply watch with love, compassion, and acceptance for a moment and then move on. Spend some more time each day with the parts of the body that correspond to that Sephirotic combination. On days where the weekly and daily Sephirot are the same, substitute qualities or key words for the name of the Sephira to consciously access those qualities.

When you are done, say the word of the sealing prayer of gratitude that follows.

Inviting the Sephirotic Energy In and Sealing It with Prayer

Your [Sephira of the week] is ever before me.
And I walk continually in Your [Sephira of the day].
May my words of thanksgiving be heard, may my deeds of thanksgiving follow my words, and may I walk in integrity with the Source of All Blessings ever before me.

Glossary

addithana: The Buddhist practice of resolute determination.

Adonai: This word is usually translated as LORD, an appellation for God, and is how the Divine Name YHVH is pronounced when spoken aloud.

aleph: The first letter of the Hebrew alphabet.

Am Y'Israel chai: It literally means "the people of Israel live," though historically, before there was a modern nation of Israel, it referred solely to the Jewish people. It was sometimes translated as "the nation of Israel lives" before the establishment of the modern state, and again, referred to the Jewish people.

Amalek: A term for the tribe of Amalekites, descendants of Jacob's brother Esau, who attacked the Israelites as they made their way through the wilderness.

anicca: The Buddhist concept of impermanence.

Arahatas: In Buddhism, one who has gained full enlightenment and has achieved Nirvana.

Assiyah: The world of Action in Kabbalah. In tarot, it corresponds to the suit of Pentacles.

Atzilut: The world of Emanation in Kabbalah. In tarot, it corresponds to the suit of Wands.

Ayin: Nothingness. The nothingness that existed before Creation.

Baal, Baalim (plural): An honorific title and also the name of a Semitic god. As an honorific, it means "master." The plural, Baalim, refers to the multiple gods worshipped by the Semitic tribes in the ancient Near East.

Baal HaTanya: Rabbi Shneur Zalman of Liadi, the founder of Lubavitch Hasidism and the author of the Tanya.

Baal Shem Tov: Rabbi Israel ben Eliezer, a charismatic rabbi who was the founder of Hasidism.

Binah: The third Sephira, Understanding.

bittul: Nullification. Refers to the extinguishing of the ego self, self-lessness, which is achieved in deep meditation.

B'riah: The world of Creation in Kabbalah. In tarot, it corresponds to the suit of Cups.

B'rit Milah: Ritual circumcision.

b'tzelem Elohim: The image of God, used to describe humanity; that is, that we are made in the image of God.

Chabad: The Lubavitch sect of Hasidism, which takes its name from the acronym of Chokhmah, Binah, and Da'at.

chai: This means "life" in Hebrew and is written with the letters chet and yod. Because Hebrew letters are also numbers, chet and yod can be read as the number 18. The common toast in Hebrew is "l'chaim," which means "to life!"

chaver: Hebrew for "friend."

chaya: One of the levels of the soul, corresponding to the world of Emanation, or Atzilut; it is the life essence within each person.

chet: The eighth letter of the Hebrew alphabet, also read numerically as the number 8.

chet: Sin.

Chokhmah: The second Sephira, Wisdom.

chuppah: A canopy beneath which Jewish wedding ceremonies take place.

chutzpah: Audacity, cheekiness, boldness, nerve.

Da'at: A hidden eleventh Sephira. It means "knowledge."

devekut: Deep meditative state attained during Jewish prayer. Usually translated as "clinging" or "cleaving."

Ehyeh Asher Ehyeh: The Divine name that Moses was told by YHVH to tell the people when they asked who sent him. It means, "I will be what I will be."

Ein Sof: The Infinite One: one of the names of God in Kabbalistic texts.

El: Both a title, God, and a name, God. Commonly used throughout ancient Near Eastern religions.

El Shaddai: One of the names of God in the Hebrew Bible; it can be translated variously as God of the Mountain or Almighty God. There is scholarship that suggests it means God with Breasts, and refers to the Divine Feminine.

Elohim: Plural of El. In the Hebrew Bible, it refers both to multiple deities and to a name of the Hebrew God in the singular.

Elohim Gibor: Almighty God. Gibor is related to Gevurah.

Elohim Tzevaot: The God of hosts.

emet: Truth.

Erev Shabbat: Friday night. In Judaism, the day begins at sunset, so that the Sabbath begins at sunset on Friday night. Erev Shavuot is the evening on which the day of the holiday of Shavuot begins.

Etz Chaim: Tree of Life. In the liturgy, it refers to the Torah. In Genesis, it refers to one of the trees Adam and Eve were forbidden to eat from. In Kabbalah, it is the symbol or diagram that explains the nature of God and shows the movement of Divine energy as it manifests in Creation.

ganbare: From the Japanese verb *ganbaru,* meaning "to persevere."

Gedulah: Another word for Chesed, Loving-kindness. The fourth Sephira.

Gevurah: The fifth Sephira. Awe, Judgment, Limitation.

Gilgul, Gilgul Neshamot: Wheel. Also, the Jewish belief in the cycle of the reincarnation of souls as taught in Kabbalistic texts and as taught by Rabbi Isaac Luria.

haftorah: Readings from the books of the Prophets that follow the Torah reading on Shabbat. It has become the custom in many communities for the haftorah to be read by a bar mitzvah or bat mitzvah at his or her respective ritual, either with or without the reading of the Torah portion.

halakha: From the Hebrew verb "to go" or "to walk." It refers to the body of Jewish law, based on the commandments in the Torah.

HaShem: The Name. One of the names of God.

Hasidism: A Jewish spiritual movement founded by the Baal Shem Tov in the eighteenth century and noted for the importance of joy in religious life.

hevruta: the act of studying Jewish sacred texts in pairs or in a small group.

HinJu: A Jewish person who also observes Hindu practices.

Hod: The eighth Sephira. Humility, Gratitude.

hoda'ah: Gratitude, thankfulness.

Imma Ila'ah: The Higher Mother. This refers to the Sephira of Binah.

Itaruta Dile'eyla: Arousal from above.

Itaruta Diletata: Arousal from below.

JuBu: Jewish Buddhist.

Kabbalah: The body of Jewish esoteric teachings, both written (the Sefer Yetzirah, the Sefer Bahir, the Zohar, etc.) and oral. From the verb *to receive,* it is the "received tradition."

karōshi: Japanese, meaning "death by overwork."

kavvanah: From the Hebrew for "direction," it is usually used to mean conscious intention in prayer or prayerful action.

Keter: Crown. The first Sephira.

ketubah: A Jewish ritual wedding contract

keyn yehi ratzon: Hebrew for "may it be Your will."

kineahora: An exclamation to ward off the evil eye.

kli, klipot (plural): Shells, husks. The remains of the structure that held the first Sephirot, which broke because they were too rigid. Hidden in these shells are broken-off parts of the Divine light, to be restored by human acts of Tikkun Olam.

Lamed-Vavnik: One of thirty-six hidden saints, or righteous people, that Jewish folklore says exist in every generation.

Lubavitch: Most often refers to the Chabad sect of Hasidism, which was founded in the village of Lubavitch. (At the time, it was part of the Polish-Lithuanian Commonwealth, though now it sits within the Russian border.)

Ma'aseh Merkavah: The name of a Jewish mystical text, possibly from the early medieval period, that teaches how to ascend to the heavens through meditations on the sacred names of the Divine. Literally, "the work of the chariot."

Magen David: The shield of David. It refers to the six-pointed star that has become a common symbol for the Jewish religion.

Major Arcana: The twenty-two cards of the tarot deck that correspond to the twenty-two letters of the Hebrew alphabet.

mazel tov: Used to say "good luck" or "congratulations." It comes from the Hebrew, literally meaning "under a good constellation."

middot: Virtues.

midrash: A style of biblical exegesis or interpretation. Often used to describe literary interpretations of biblical stories in the Jewish tradition that fill in the gaps in these stories.

Minor Arcana: The fifty-six suit cards of the tarot deck.

Mishkan: The Tabernacle, the portable shrine that was built and then carried by the Israelites during their forty years in the wilderness. It was where the Ark of the Covenant was kept.

Mishnah: From the Hebrew for "repetition," it is the first written collection of rabbinic decisions, from the third century CE, and is the first section of the Talmud.

Mitzrayim: The Hebrew name for Egypt. It means "the narrow straits" or "the narrow place."

mono no aware: The Japanese aesthetic based on the Buddhist teaching of the transience of all things. It means "beautiful sadness of things."

nefesh: One of the four kinds of souls.

nes: Miracle.

Netzach: The seventh Sephira. Endurance, Victory.

niggun, niggunim (plural): Wordless melodies sung as meditative chants to open the heart and activate the yearning of the soul for the Divine.

olam: World or universe. It can also refer to a period of time, such as an eon. Because of this ambiguity, it is sometimes translated as the Einsteinian phrase "space-time" or "time and space."

omer: An ancient Israelite measure for dry goods such as grain. The exact measure is in dispute, but it was probably somewhere between 5.5 and 6.5 pounds.

Or Ein Sof: The light of the Infinite One. Another name for the Divine.

Pachad: Another name for the fifth Sephira, Gevurah. It means "fear."

Pali: The language of the Buddha.

Pardes: An acronym for the four levels of the exegesis or interpretation of the Torah: Peshat, the exoteric, or literal meaning; Remez, the allegorical meaning; Derash, the meaning derived from analogous stories or situations; Sod, the esoteric, or hidden meaning. The word *pardes* means "orchard" or "garden" in Hebrew, and it is related to the English word *paradise*.

Parsha: The weekly Torah section chanted aloud in the synagogue on Shabbat and during morning services on Mondays and Thursdays. There are fifty-four weekly readings over the course of the year.

Pentecost: The Jewish holiday of Shavuot (Hebrew for "weeks") was called Pentecost (meaning fifty days) in the Septuagint, the Torah as translated into Greek by Hellenized Jewish communities. Celebrated fifty days after the second day of Passover, it was an agricultural holiday that developed into a celebration of revelation—of receiving the Torah at Mt. Sinai. Christianity built on this tradition, with it becoming a holiday commemorating the revelation of the descent of the Holy Spirit on the Apostles.

Pesach: Hebrew for the Passover holiday.

Peshat: One of the four levels of traditional Jewish biblical exegesis—the literal, direct, surface level of the text.

Pirkei Avot: Hebrew for Chapters of the Fathers, and often translated as Wisdom of the Elders, it is a compilation of ethical teachings and sayings of rabbis of the period from about 200 BCE to 200 CE.

pseudepigrapha: Works that have been falsely attributed to a figure of the past. The Zohar, which was published by Rabbi Moses de León in the thirteenth century, was ascribed to Rabbi Shimon bar Yochai, who lived in the second century CE, though most scholars agree that it was written by Rabbi Moses de León.

Qabalah: The common spelling by occultists of the Western spiritual tradition for studies deriving from Judaic Kabbalah in order to distinguish it from the original Judaic tradition.

rachamim: Hebrew for "compassion." From *rechem* meaning "womb." Another name for the sixth Sephira, Tiferet.

Rambam: Acronym that refers to Rabbi Moses ben Maimon, also known as Maimonides.

Ratzon: Hebrew for "will." It most often refers to the prime will of the Divine that led to Creation.

Rosh Hashanah: Hebrew for Head of the Year. The new year holiday that starts the ten-day period of the "high holidays," also known as the "days of awe," that end with Yom Kippur.

Ruach HaKodesh: The Holy Spirit.

Samsara: Buddhist concept of the cyclical nature of reality, the mundane existence we are born into again and again until we reach Nirvana.

Seder Hishtalshelut: The order of descent of the Sephirot from world to world in a chain of "trees of life" leading from Ein Sof down to the world of manifestation.

Sefer Yetzirah: The Book of Formation, one of the earliest Kabbalistic texts in the Jewish tradition, attributed to the patriarch Abraham (see Pseudepigrapha entry), though scholars believe it was written some time between the second century BCE and the sixth century CE.

Sephirot: Hebrew for "emanations." It refers to the ten attributes of the Divine personality emanating from the Infinite. They serve as channels of energy through which the Infinite becomes known within the finite world. It is etymologically related to the Hebrew words for "counting," "book," and "sapphire."

Shabbat: The seventh day of the week. In Jewish mythology, the final day of Creation, on which God rested from the work of creating the universe.

shalom bayit: Hebrew for "peace in the home."

Shamayim: Hebrew for "heavens" (plural).

Shavuot: Hebrew for "weeks." The holiday celebrated seven weeks after Passover. Originally an agricultural holiday celebrated at the Temple in Jerusalem, it developed into a Kabbalistic celebration of the receiving of the Torah at Mt. Sinai fifty days after the Israelites left Egypt.

shedu: A demon. From the Sumerian, and in that language, it referred to a Mesopotamian deity that had the body of a lion or a bull, the wings of an eagle, and the head of a human.

shefa: Hebrew for "flow" or "abundance."

Shekinah: The Indwelling Presence of the Divine in the world—God as immanent. In Jewish mythology, it is expressed also as the feminine presence of YHVH who went into exile with the people after the destruction of the Temple in the first century CE, although because YHVH is One, the Shekinah is not really separate: it's only our experience of the Shekinah that is separate. It is also a name for the tenth Sephira, Malkut.

shiviti: An illustration made up of words, often from the Psalms, that is used as an object of meditation or contemplation. It means, "I have placed" in Hebrew and comes from Psalms 16:8: "I have placed YHVH always before me."

Sh'ma: Hebrew for "listen" or "hear." It is the first word of the proclamation of Divine unity (God as both transcendent and immanent) at the center of Jewish worship services and daily prayers: "Hear O Israel, YHVH is our God, YHVH is One."

Shulchan Aruch: The most widely accepted compilation of Jewish law, authored by the noted Kabbalist Joseph Karo in the sixteenth century.

sila: From the Sanskrit. The Buddhist path of ethics and moral conduct.

simcha: Joy. An occasion for joy. The attitude with which all Jews are encouraged to live their lives.

Sitra Achra: Hebrew for the Other Side, referring to evil or impure spiritual forces.

Sogetsu: One of the three major schools of traditional Japanese flower arranging. It is the most modern.

Talmud: The collection of writings from the postbiblical period that recorded the oral tradition that included debates over Jewish law as well as lore. Written down over a period between 200 CE and 500 CE, it records decisions known in the oral tradition from earlier rabbinic periods. There are in fact two Talmuds: one written in Babylonia and the other in Jerusalem.

Tanakh: An acronym for the Hebrew Bible, which includes the Torah (the Five Books of Moses), the Nevi'im (Prophets), and the Ketuvim (the Writings, which includes books such as the Psalms and the Song of Songs).

tefila: Hebrew for "prayer."

Tetragrammaton: The four-letter name of the Divine, YHVH – *yod, hey, vuv, hey*. It is written without vowels and considered to be unpronounceable. When read aloud most Jews read it as Adonai (LORD) or HaShem (the Name), and many Kabbalists will read it as Havayah (the Name of Being). In the Temple period, it was only said aloud once a year by the high priest, during Yom Kippur. It is thought to come from the Hebrew verb "to be," and some people think of it as "Is/Was/Will Be."

Tiferet: The sixth Sephira. Hebrew for "adornment," it is translated as Beauty, Truth, Balance, Harmony, and Compassion.

Tikkun Leil Shavuot: The Kabbalistic practice of staying up all night through to dawn from before the start of Shavuot to study sacred texts in order to "repair" the oversleeping of the Israelites on the day they were to receive the Torah at Mt. Sinai. And by staying up all night in study, one awakens to revelation.

Tikkun Olam: Hebrew for Repair of the World. From a Kabbalistic perspective, any action that helps reunify the Divine is a Tikkun Olam. Fulfilling the mitzvot (commandments) is essential to this practice. Today, in Jewish social justice settings, it refers to social action that furthers the spread of justice and equality.

to'e'vah: Hebrew term translated most frequently as "abomination" but is perhaps more accurately translated as "taboo," in that it refers to an act that is ritually prohibited.

Torah: The Five Books of Moses. The word *torah* has a range of meanings, including "teaching" and "law."

Torah Nistar: Refers to the hidden meaning of the Torah, its esoteric meaning.

t'shuvah: Hebrew for "return." It carries the meaning of "repentance," but includes a sense of a reconciling return to innocence.

Tzimtzum: The paradoxical concept that the Omnipresent Divine withdrew Its Godself to leave space for Creation that is filled with the Divine. Another way to describe the veiling of the Divine within Creation.

Via Lucis: Latin for the Way of Light. It is a Christian meditation practice that centers on the Resurrection appearances of Jesus Christ. It is a recent development, in reaction to the Via Crucis, the Stations of the Cross, which focuses attention on the torture of Christ on his way to the Crucifixion.

Via Negativa: A theological way of thinking about the Divine in which the only way It can be described is by negation, as in: It's not that. It takes the position that the Divine is beyond our language or our conceptual or our perceptual abilities, and as such, any attempt to describe It cannot be correct.

Vipassana: From Pali, the language of the Buddha. It literally means "insight" or "seeing clearly." In the Buddhist tradition, it refers to one of the Buddha's meditation techniques that give practitioners insight into the true nature of reality.

wa: Japanese for "harmony."

Yechida: The highest level of the soul, always in contact and connected to the Divine.

Yesod: The ninth Sephira, Foundation.

yetzer hara: Hebrew for "the inclination to do evil."

yetzer hatov: Hebrew for "the inclination to do good."

Yetzirah: One of the four Kabbalistic worlds, the world of Formation. In the tarot deck, it corresponds to the suit of Swords.

YHVH: See Tetragrammaton.

yod: The tenth letter of the Hebrew alphabet. It also signifies the number 10.

yoducha: Hebrew for "[they] will give thanks. . . ."

Yom Hillula: The anniversary of the death of a sage or saintly person, observed as a celebration.

Yom Kippur: Hebrew for Day of Atonement. It is considered the holiest day on the liturgical calendar.

zava'ah: An ethical will, written with the intention of passing down wisdom and values from one generation to another.

Zohar: Hebrew for "radiance." Also the name of the book considered to be the most important Kabbalistic text, written by Rabbi Moses de León in thirteenth-century Spain.

A Note about
God Language

JEWS DO NOT PRONOUNCE the four-letter name of God, transliterated as YHVH. With no vowels in the name, it's unclear exactly
how to pronounce the name. Historically, it is believed that only the
high priest at the Temple knew this pronunciation, and he only used
it one day a year, during Yom Kippur, when he would enter the Holy
of Holies. When Jews see these four letters in a text, they substitute a
title, Adonai, which roughly translates as LORD. Or sometimes they say
HaShem, which simply means the Name. Christians have often translated this name as Jehovah or Yahweh. However, by adding vowels, you
fix the meaning in Hebrew; without vowels, these letters, which are the
letters for the verb *to be,* can be roughly translated as "Is/Was/Will Be."
In other words, the Eternal.

In this book, I try not to use the word God very much. Like
Adonai, it's not a name; it's a descriptive title. Orthodox Jews don't
even write the word, preferring to leave out the vowel, just as in the
Hebrew, to avoid taking the name in vain, writing it as G-d. I rather
like a variation that I've seen, which uses either a question mark or an
exclamation point: G?d or G!d. Personally, though, I'd prefer using an
interrobang: G‽d.

Because the Jewish understanding of Ein Sof is that It is beyond gender, I do my best not to use a gender pronoun, though in Judaism, there
are gendered faces of the deity, with the understanding that the Shekinah
is the feminine face of the One. That said, when quoting old sources, I

leave the gendered pronouns in. Just as for many years when reading old prayer books, I became adept at seeing one word and reading another.

In the myths of some other peoples, there are many gods. In the Tanakh, there are many words, names, and titles used to describe this One Being that essentially cannot be described because It cannot be contained by language.

One of the most important Jewish prayers, the Kaddish, speaks to the problem of the inability of language to describe something beyond language by simultaneously praising YHVH with words while recognizing that none of these words of praise can possibly express the ineffable.

> Blessed, praised and glorified, exalted, extolled and honored, magnified and lauded be the name of the Holy One, blessed be He; though he be high above all the blessings and hymns, praises and consolations, which are uttered in the world; and say ye, Amen.[1]

So you'll have noticed that I prefer to use words that speak to the qualities we associate with the Deity: the Source, the Holy One, the Compassionate One, the Divine. These words are also inadequate. Still, I prefer to use many words that speak to qualities and characteristics that give voice to our varied experiences of the Divine rather than the words God or Lord, which can carry childish or medieval hierarchical associations. This practice is hardly radical; it is what you will find in translations from Hebrew in the *siddur* (prayer book) of the Jewish Reconstructionist movement, and many of these names you will find in the Hebrew Bible itself. HaRachaman, the Compassionate One, is just such a traditional name. The Kabbalists use many names for the Deity, and they assigned some of these names that appear in Torah to each of the Sephirot. There are many complicated meditative techniques taught by Kabbalists based on permutations of the names of the Deity. If this is something you want to explore, start by reading Aryeh Kaplan's translation of the Sefer Yetzirah, *Sefer Yetzirah: The Book of Creation.*

All this is to say, don't get hung up on a name. When I'm quoting a sacred text, Jewish or Christian, I use the words used by the translator of that particular text. In your own prayers, use what feels natural and comfortable to you. Or use something that feels uncomfortable so that it takes you out of the illusion that you know Who or What it is that you're addressing.

Notes

EPIGRAPHS

Rav Abraham Isaac Kook, Sefer Orot Hakodesh 1:268.

Campbell, *Inner Reaches of Outer Space,* xx.

KABBALAH, TAROT CARDS, AND COUNTING THE OMER—WHAT'S THIS ALL ABOUT?

1. Leviticus 23:15–16. Unless otherwise noted, all quotes from the Hebrew Bible, the Tanakh, are taken from the 1917 Jewish Publication Society version of The Holy Scriptures, According to the Masoretic Text: A New Translation. The text has been edited by the author to remove archaic language and syntax that is unclear to the modern ear, or to better convey the meaning of the text.

2. Singer, *Standard Prayer Book,* Ethics of the Fathers (Pirkei Avot) 1:1.

3. Westcott, *Sepher Yetzirah.*

4. Levine and Brettler, *Jewish Annotated New Testament,* Acts 2: 1-6. Unless otherwise noted, all New Testament scripture quotes are from this edition, which uses the text of the New Revised Standard Version Bible.

5. Joel 2:28.

6. See Acts 2:17–18.

7. Roberts, "Celebrating Easter for Fifty Days."

8. For this story of another example of revelation on the eve of Pentecost see, Alkabetz, "Shavuot Night in Salonika."

9. Ariel, *Kabbalah,* 211–12.

10. Dan, *Early Kabbalah,* 34.

11. Place, *Tarot.*

12. See more at Tilles, "Kabbalah? Cabala? Qabala?"

13. Decker, Depaulis and Dummett, *Wicked Pack of Cards.*

THE TREE OF LIFE

1. Michaelson, "An Introduction to the Kabbalah Part 8."
2. Pirkei Avot 4:1. All quotes from the Pirkei Avot, unless otherwise noted, are from the *Standard Prayer Book,* by Simeon Singer, 1915.
3. Forster, *Howards End,* 214.
4. To learn more about complexity theory and consciousness, see the lectures of Dr. Neil Theise on YouTube.
5. Heschel, *God in Search of Man,* 172.
6. Sameth, "Is God Transgender?"
7. Kukla, "Classical Jewish Terms."
8. See Husband, *World in Play.*
9. Decker, Depaulis, and Dummett, *Wicked Pack of Cards,* 72.
10. See Katz, *Magician's Kabbalah.*
11. Place, *Tarot,* 184.
12. Pollack, *Rachel Pollack's Tarot Wisdom,* 321.
13. See Ginzberg, *Legends of the Jews.*

WEEK I. CHESED

1. Psalms 23:5, King James Version.
2. Confessions of St. Augustine XI:13.
3. Alchin, "Knighthood Ceremony."
4. Swarupananda, *Srimad-Bhagavad-Gita,* 2:17–21.
5. Exodus 14:11–12.
6. Kliegman, *Tarot and the Tree of Life,* 92.
7. John 15:1–5.
8. Hanes, "Singles Nation."
9. Luke 17:21, note f.

WEEK 2. GEVURAH

1. Deuteronomy 21:18–21.
2. UNHCR, "Figures at a Glance."
3. U.S. Department of State, "Refugee Admission Statistics."
4. Deuteronomy 10:19.
5. Matthew 25:35, 25:40.
6. Pirkei Avot, 2:21
7. I Kings 19:11–13.
8. See Rabbi Sholom DovBer's commentary in the article "Parshat Lech Lecha In-Depth" on the Chabad website.

9. *New York Times,* "Popular New Idol."

10. *Alcoholics Anonymous: The Big Book,* 59.

11. Frankl, *Man's Search for Meaning.*

12. Leviticus 19:16.

13. Genesis 1:27.

14. Exodus 18:18.

15. Deuteronomy 30:12-14.

WEEK 3. TIFERET

1. See I Kings 3:16–28.

2. Green, *Radical Judaism,* 35–36.

3. Singer, *Standard Prayer Book,* 6.

4. Ecclesiastes 1:18.

5. De Ropp, *Master Game.*

6. DeMille, *Martha,* 264.

7. Pirkei Avot, 2:21.

8. I Corinthians 13:11.

9. See Horner, *Minor Anthologies of the Pali Canon,* 22.

10. Dass and Bush, *Compassion in Action.*

WEEK 4. NETZACH

1. Shōwa, "Imperial Rescript on Surrender."

2. I Corinthians 13.

3. Hyde, *Trickster Makes This World.*

4. Exodus 2:11–14.

5. Luke 9:62.

6. *Alcoholics Anonymous: The Big Book,* 59.

7. Numbers 12:6.

8. Numbers 12:8.

9. Numbers 12:3.

10. Babylonian Talmud, Megilla 28a.

11. Genesis 28:16.

12. Numbers 13:33, 14:1.

13. Song of Songs 6:1–2.

14. Exodus 4:13.

15. Babylonian Talmud, Yevamot 65.

16. Singer, *Standard Prayer Book,* 64.

17. Numbers 14:21–23.

18. Decker, *Esoteric Tarot,* 257.

19. *Alcoholics Anonymous: The Big Book,* 83.

WEEK 5. HOD

1. Singer, *Standard Prayer Book,* 91.

2. Kantrowitz, *Counting the Omer,* 149.

3. Psalms 23:5, King James Version.

4. Jebb et al., "Happiness, Income Satiation, and Turning Points."

5. On the Forbes website, search on "Quotes Lily Tomlin."

6. Buber, *Hasidism and Modern Man,* 98.

7. Csikszentmihalyi, *Flow,* 2.

8. Sagan, *Demon-Haunted World,* 29.

9. On the Wikiquote website, search on "Tertullian."

10. On the Wikipedia website, search on "Kalama Sutta."

11. Agrimson and Taft, "Spiritual Crisis."

12. Rūmī and Barks, *Essential Rumi,* 36.

13. Kolbert, *Sixth Extinction.*

14. Leviticus 26:3–5.

15. Ezray, "Va'era."

16. Sen, *Glorious Thoughts of Gandhi,* 50.

17. Pirkei Avot 1:14.

18. Gandhi, *Quintessence of Gandhi.*

19. Sherwin and Cohen, *Creating an Ethical Jewish Life,* 92.

20. On the Wikiquote website, search on "Thomas Edison."

21. Jones et al., *Immigration and Concerns.*

22. Mathews, "Victim Identity."

23. See Cameron, *Artist's Way.*

24. Exodus 34:29.

25. Numbers 12:3.

26. Sacks, *Dignity of Difference.*

27. See Buber, *I And Thou.*

28. Shulman, *Kabbalistic Healing,* 73.

29. See Hammer and Feit, *Omer Counter of Biblical Women,* 8.

WEEK 6. YESOD

1. See Babylonian Talmud, Bava Batra 99a.

2. Jami, "Yusuf and Zulaikha."

3. On the National Sexual Violence Resource Center (NSVRC) website, search on "Statistics."

4. II Samuel 13:15.

5. Wikipedia website, "People v. Turner."

6. Hosea 2:15.

7. Hosea 14:2, 14:5.

8. Pirkei Avot 3:3.

9. Hankins, Hoekstra, and Skiba, "Ticket to Easy Street?"

10. Exodus 24:7

11. Shakespeare, *Midsummer Night's Dream,* I. I. 233.

12. Matthew 7:4.

13. Song of Songs 8:13.

14. Proverbs 9:8–9.

15. Ginzberg, *Legends of the Jews.*

16. Epstein, *Open to Desire,* 10–11.

17. Epstein, *Open to Desire,* 12.

18. Genesis 9:7.

19. Liebschutz et al., "Relationship between Sexual and Physical Abuse."

20. See Hellner-Eshed, *River Flows from Eden,* 4.

21. Hellner-Eshed, *River Flows from Eden,* 18.

WEEK 7. MALCHUT

1. Ecclesiastes 3:1-4.

2. Hellner-Eshed, *River Flows from Eden.*

3. Psalms 25:5–6, King James Version, adapted.

4. Deuteronomy 25:19.

5. Deuteronomy 25:18.

6. Pirkei Avot 2:20.

7. Kimball, *When Religion Becomes Evil.*

8. Matthew 27:46.

9. Kushner, *Angels in America,* 195–96.

A NOTE ABOUT GOD LANGUAGE

1. Singer, *Standard Prayer Book,* 195.

Bibliography

Agrimson, Laurie B., and Lois B. Taft. "Spiritual Crisis: A Concept Analysis." *Journal of Advanced Nursing* 65, no. 2 (November 27, 2008): 454–61.

Alchin, Linda. "Knighthood Ceremony." Webpage. Retrieved May 1, 2019 from the Medieval Life and Times website.

Alcoholics Anonymous: The Big Book. 4th ed. New York: Alcoholics Anonymous World Services, Inc., 2001.

Alkabetz, Shlomo HaLevi. "Shavuot Night in Salonika." Chabad website. Search on article title.

Amberstone, Wald, and Ruth Ann Amberstone. *The Secret Language of Tarot.* San Francisco: Red Wheel/Weiser, 2008.

Ariel, David S. *Kabbalah: The Mystic Quest in Judaism.* Lanham, Md.: Rowman & Littlefield, 2006.

Bailey, Nathan. *The New Universal Etymological English Dictionary: Containing an Additional Collection of Words (Not in the First Volume) with Their Explications and Etymologies . . . Also an Explication of Hard and Technical Words or Terms, in All Arts and Sciences . . . Illustrated with Some Hundred Cuts . . . Likewise a Collection and Explanation of Words and Phrases Used in Our Ancient Charters, Statutes, Writs . . . to Which Is Added, a Dictionary of Cant Words.* Vol. II. London: Printed for W. Johnston, 1760.

Ben-Dov, Yoav. *Tarot: The Open Reading.* CreateSpace, 2013.

Blake, William. *The Portable Blake.* New York: The Viking Press, 1968.

Buber, Martin. *Hasidism and Modern Man.* Translated by Maurice S. Friedman. Princeton, N.J.: Princeton University Press, 2016.

Buber, Martin. *I and Thou.* Translated by Walter Kaufmann. New York: Touchstone, 1996.

Buber, Martin. *The Way of Man, According to the Teaching of Hasidism.* Secaucus, N.J.: Carol Publishing Group, 1998.

Buxbaum, Yitzhak. *Jewish Spiritual Practices.* Northvale, N.J.: J. Aronson, 1994.

Cameron, Julia. *The Artist's Way: A Spiritual Path to Higher Creativity.* New York: Tarcher/Peregree, 1992.

Campbell, Joseph. *The Inner Reaches of Outer Space: Metaphor as Myth and as Religion.* Novato, Calif.: New World Library, 2012.

Case, Paul Foster. *The Tarot: A Key to the Wisdom of the Ages; The Classic Guide.* New York: Jeremy P. Tarcher/Penguin, 2006.

Cirlot, Juan Eduardo. *A Dictionary of Symbols.* Translated by Jack Sage. London: Routledge and Paul, 1962.

Cooper, J. C. *An Illustrated Encyclopaedia of Traditional Symbols.* London: Thames and Hudson, 1978.

Csikszentmihalyi, Mihaly. *Flow: The Psychology of Optimal Experience.* New York: HarperCollins, 2008.

cummings, e.e. *100 Selected Poems by e.e. cummings.* New York: Grove Press, 1954.

Dan, Joseph, ed. *The Early Kabbalah.* Translated by Ronald C. Kiener. New York: Paulist, 1986.

Dass, Ram, and Mirabai Bush. *Compassion in Action: Setting Out on the Path of Service.* New York: Bell Tower, 1995.

Decker, Ronald. *The Esoteric Tarot: Ancient Sources Rediscovered in Hermeticism and Cabala.* Wheaton, Ill.: Quest—Theosophical House, 2013.

Decker, Ronald, Thierry Depaulis, and Michael Dummett. *A Wicked Pack of Cards: The Origins of the Occult Tarot.* New York: St. Martin's, 1996.

DeMille, Agnes. *Martha: The Life and Work of Martha Graham.* New York: Random House, 1991.

De Ropp, Robert S. *The Master Game: Pathways to Higher Consciousness beyond the Drug Experience.* New York: Dell, 1981.

Dubov, Nissan Dovid. "The Four Worlds: Kabbalah, Chassidism and Jewish Mysticism." Chabad.org website.

Eliot, T. S. *Four Quartets.* San Diego, Calif.: Harvest Books/Harcourt, Brace & World, 1971.

Epstein, Mark. *Open to Desire: Embracing a Lust for Life; Insights from Buddhism and Psychotherapy.* New York: Gotham Books, 2005.

Ezray, Nat. "Va'era—Seeing and Creating Miracles." Beth Jacob RWC website, January 28, 2017.

Falcon, Ted. *A Journey of Awakening: 49 Steps from Enslavement to Freedom; A Guide for Using the Kabbalistic Tree of Life in Jewish Meditation.* Seattle, Wash.: Skynear, 1999.

Feldman, Ron H. *Fundamentals of Jewish Mysticism and Kabbalah.* Freedom, Calif.: Crossing, 1999.

Fiebig, Johannes, and Evelin Bürger. *The Ultimate Guide to the Rider Waite Tarot.* Edited by Barbara Moore. Woodbury, Minn.: Llewellyn Publications, 2014.

Fine, Lawrence. *Safed Spirituality: Rules of Mystical Piety, the Beginning of Wisdom.* New York: Paulist, 1984.

Forster, E. M. *Howards End.* New York: A. A. Knopf, 1921.

Frankl, Viktor E. *Man's Search for Meaning.* Boston: Beacon, 2006.

Gad, Irene. *Tarot and Individuation: A Jungian Study of Correspondences with Cabala, Alchemy, and the Chakras.* Berwick, Maine: Nicolas-Hays, 2004.

Gandhi, M. K. *The Quintessence of Gandhi in His Own Words.* Edited by Shakti Batra. New Delhi, India: Madhu Muskan, 1984.

Gikatilla, Joseph. *The Gates of Light.* Translated by Avi Weinstein. San Francisco: HarperCollins, 1994.

Gillespie, Gerald. *The Kabbalah's Twelve Step Spiritual Method to End Your Addiction.* New York: SPI Books, 1997.

Ginzberg, Louis. *The Legends of the Jews.* Philadelphia, Pa.: Jewish Publication Society, 1909.

Goldfeder, Gavriel. *The 50th Gate: A Spirited Walk through the Counting of the Omer: 49 Steps to Being a Better Human.* Boulder, Colo.: Kehillath Aish Kodesh, 2010.

Graham, Sasha. *Llewellyn's Complete Book of the Rider-Waite-Smith Tarot: A Journey through the History, Meaning, and Use of the World's Most Famous Deck.* Woodbury, Minn.: Llewellyn Worldwide, Ltd., 2018.

Green, Andrea. *Kabbalah and Tarot: A Step-up Guide for Everyone.* Amazon Digital Services, 2015. Kindle e-book.

Green, Arthur. *Ehyeh: A Kabbalah for Tomorrow.* Woodstock, Vt.: Jewish Lights Publishing, 2003.

Green, Arthur. *A Guide to the Zohar.* Stanford, Calif.: Stanford University Press, 2004.

Green, Arthur. *Radical Judaism: Rethinking God and Tradition.* New Haven, Conn.: Yale University Press, 2010.

Haber, Yaacov, and D. N. Sedley. *Sefiros: Spiritual Refinement through Counting the Omer.* Jerusalem: Torah Lab, 2009.

Hammer, Rabbi Jill, and Shir Yaakov Feit. *Omer Counter of Biblical Women.* New York: Romemu, 2012.

Hanes, Stephanie. "Singles Nation: Why So Many Americans Are Unmarried." *Christian Science Monitor* website, June 14, 2015.

Hankins, Scott, Mark Hoekstra, and Paige Marta Skiba. "The Ticket to Easy

Street? The Financial Consequences of Winning the Lottery." *Review of Economics and Statistics* 93, no. 3 (August 2011): 961–69.

Harlow, Rabbi Jules. *Siddur Sim Shalom.* New York: The Rabbinical Assembly, 1989.

Hellner-Eshed, Melila. *A River Flows from Eden: The Language of Mystical Experience in the Zohar.* Translated by Nathan Wolski. Stanford, Calif.: Stanford University Press, 2011.

Heschel, Abraham Joshua. *God in Search of Man: A Philosophy of Judaism.* New York: Straus & Giroux, 1983.

Hoeller, Stephan A. *The Fool's Pilgrimage: Kabbalistic Meditations on the Tarot.* Wheaton, Ill.: Quest/Theosophical Publishing House, 2004.

Hoffman, Edward. *The Heavenly Ladder: The Jewish Guide for Inner Growth.* San Francisco: HarperCollins, 1985.

Hoffman, Edward. *The Kabbalah Deck: Pathway to the Soul.* San Francisco: Chronicle, 2000.

Horner, I. B. *The Minor Anthologies of the Pali Canon.* Lancaster, Pa.: Pali Text Society, 2007.

Husband, Timothy. *The World in Play: Luxury Cards 1430–1540.* New York: Metropolitan Museum of Art, 2015.

Hyde, Lewis. *Trickster Makes This World: Mischief, Myth, and Art.* New York: Farrar, Straus & Giroux, 2010.

Jacobson, Simon. *A Spiritual Guide to the Counting of the Omer: Forty-Nine Steps to Personal Refinement According to the Jewish Tradition; The Forty-Nine Days of Sefirah.* New York: Vaad Hanochos Hatmimim, 1996.

Jami. "Yusuf and Zulaikha." Edited by Charles F. Horne. Public domain version available on the Scribd website.

Jaron, Gary M. *The Qabalah Gates of Light: The Occult Qabalah Reconstructed.* Charleston, S.C.: CreateSpace, 2018.

Jay. "The Ten Sefirot: Characteristics." The Learn Kabbalah website.

Jebb, Andrew, Louis Tay, Ed Diener, and Sigehiro Oishi. "Happiness, Income Satiation, and Turning Points around the World." *Nature Human Behaviour* 2 (January 8, 2018): 33–38.

Jones, Robert P., Daniel Cox, E. J. Dionne Jr., William A. Galston, Betsy Cooper, and Rachel Lienesch. *How Immigration and Concerns about Cultural Changes Are Shaping the 2016 Election: Findings from the 2016 PRRI/Brookings Immigration Survey.* Public Religion Research Institute, 2016.

Kantrowitz, Min. *Counting the Omer: A Kabbalistic Meditation Guide.* Santa Fe, N.Mex.: Gaon, 2010.

Kaplan, Aryeh. *Sefer Yetzirah: The Book of Creation.* York Beach, Maine: Samuel Weiser Publishing, 1997.

Katz, Marcus. *The Magician's Kabbalah: Kabbalah as an Initiatory Path Illustrated by Tarot.* Keswick, England: Forge, 2015.

Katz, Marcus, and Tali Goodwin. *Secrets of the Waite-Smith Tarot: The True Story of the World's Most Popular Tarot: With Previously Unseen Photography & Text from Waite & Smith.* Woodbury, Minn.: Llewellyn Publications, 2015.

Kimball, Charles. *When Religion Becomes Evil: Five Warning Signs.* San Francisco: HarperOne, 2008.

Kliegman, Isabel Radow. *Tarot and the Tree of Life: Finding Everyday Wisdom in the Minor Arcana.* Wheaton, Ill.: Theosophical Publishing House, 1997.

Kolbert, Elizabeth. *The Sixth Extinction: An Unnatural History.* New York: Bloomsbury, 2015.

Krafchow, Dovid. *Kabbalistic Tarot: Hebraic Wisdom in the Major and Minor Arcana.* Rochester, Vt.: Inner Traditions, 2005. Print.

Kravitz, Leonard, and Kerry M. Olitzky, eds. and trans. *Pirke Avot: A Modern Commentary on Jewish Ethics.* UAHC Press, 1993.

Kukla, Elliott. "Classical Jewish Terms for Gender Diversity." TransTorah website, available as an online document on the "Resources" page.

Kula, Irwin, with Linda Loewenthal. *Yearnings: Embracing the Sacred Messiness of Life.* New York: Hyperion, 2006.

Kushner, Tony. *Angels in America: A Gay Fantasia on National Themes.* New York: Theatre Communications Group, 2004.

Levine, Amy-Jill, and Marc Zvi Brettler, eds. *The Jewish Annotated New Testament, New Revised Standard Version Bible Translation.* New York: Oxford University Press, 2011.

Levy, Yael. *Journey through the Wilderness: A Mindfulness Approach to the Ancient Jewish Practice of Counting the Omer.* Philadelphia: Rabbi Yael Levy, 2012.

Lew, Alan. *This Is Real and You Are Completely Unprepared: The Days of Awe as a Journey of Transformation.* New York: Back Bay Books/Little, Brown and Company, 2018.

Lieber, David L., and Jules Harlow, eds. *Etz Hayim: Torah and Commentary.* Philadelphia: Jewish Publication Society, 2001.

Liebes, Yehuda. *Studies in the Zohar.* Albany: State University of New York Press, 1993.

Liebschutz, Jane, Jacqueline B. Savetsky, Richard Saitz, Nicholas J. Horton, Christine Lloyd-Travaglini, and Jeffrey H. Samet. "The Relationship between Sexual and Physical Abuse and Substance Abuse Consequences." *Journal of Substance Abuse Treatment* 22, no. 3 (January 2002): 121–28.

Mathews, Andrea. "The Victim Identity." *Psychology Today* website, February 24, 2011.

Matt, Daniel C. *The Essential Kabbalah: The Heart of Jewish Mysticism.* New York: HarperCollins, 1995.

Matt, Daniel Chanan. *The Zohar.* Vol. 1. Stanford, Calif.: Stanford University Press, 2004.

Matt, Daniel Chanan. *Zohar: The Book of Enlightenment.* New York: Paulist, 1983.

Maxwell, John C., and Jim Dornan. *Becoming a Person of Influence: Talent Is Never Enough.* Nashville, Tenn.: T. Nelson Publishers, 2007.

Michaelson, Jay. "An Introduction to the Kabbalah Part 8: What Are the Sefirot?" Huffington Post website. Posted April 5, 2010 and last updated November 17, 2011.

———. *God in Your Body: Kabbalah, Mindfulness, and Embodied Spiritual Practice.* Woodstock, Vt.: Jewish Lights Publishing, 2007.

Miller, Alice. *The Drama of the Gifted Child: The Search for the True Self.* New York: BasicBooks, 2008.

Moorehead, Kate. *Resurrecting Easter: Meditations for the Great 50 Days.* New York: Morehouse, 2013.

Müller, F. Max, and Jack Maguire. *Dhammapada: Annotated & Explained.* Woodstock, Vt.: SkyLight Paths Publishing, 2002.

Nasios, Angelo. *Tarot: Unlocking the Arcana.* Atglen, Pa.: Shiffler, 2016.

New York Times. "Popular New Idol Rises in Bavaria," November 21, 1922.

Nichols, Sallie. *Jung and Tarot: An Archetypal Journey.* New York: Samuel Weiser Publishing, 1980.

Oliver, Mary. *New and Selected Poems.* Boston: Beacon, 2006.

Place, Robert M. *The Tarot: History, Symbolism, and Divination.* New York: Tarcher Penguin, 2005.

Pollack, Rachel. *The Kabbalah Tree: A Journey of Balance and Growth.* St. Paul, Minn.: Llewellyn Worldwide, 2004.

Pollack, Rachel. *Rachel Pollack's Tarot Wisdom: Spiritual Teachings and Deeper Meanings.* Woodbury, Minn.: Llewellyn Publications, 2008.

Ramer, Andrew. *Torah Told Different: Stories for a Pan/Poly/Post-Denominational World.* Eugene, Ore.: Resource Publications, 2016.

Roberts, Mark D. "Celebrating Easter for Fifty Days." Online PDF document. Institute for Faith and Learning at Baylor University, 2014.

Rūmī, Jalāl al-Dīn, and Coleman Barks, trans. *The Essential Rumi*. New York: HarperCollins, 2004.

Sacks, Jonathan. *The Dignity of Difference: How to Avoid the Clash of Civilizations*. New York: Continuum, 2007.

Sagan, Carl. *The Demon-Haunted World: Science as a Candle in the Dark*. New York: Ballantine Books, 1997.

Sambhava, Padma. *The Tibetan Book of the Dead, as Popularly Known in the West: Known in Tibet as The Great Book of Natural Liberation through Understanding in the Between*. Translated by Robert A. F. Thurman. New York: Bantam, 1994.

Sameth, Rabbi Mark. "Is God Transgender?" *New York Times* opinion page, August 12, 2016.

Schapira, Kalonymus Kalman. *Conscious Community: A Guide to Inner Work*. Translated by Andrea Cohen-Kiener and Yosef Grodsky. Northvale, N.J.: Jason Aronson, Inc., 1996.

Schwartz, Howard. *Gabriel's Palace: Jewish Mystical Tales*. New York: Oxford University Press, 1993.

Schwartz, Howard. *Tree of Souls: The Mythology of Judaism*. Oxford: Oxford University Press, 2004.

Sen, N. B. *Glorious Thoughts of Gandhi: Being a Treasury of about Ten Thousand Valuable and Inspiring Thoughts of Mahatma Gandhi, Classified under Four Hundred Subjects*. Delhi, India: New Book Society of India, 1965.

Shapiro, Rami M. *Wisdom of the Jewish Sages: A Modern Reading of Pirke Avot*. New York: Bell Tower, 1995.

Shapiro, Rabbi Rami M., trans. and annotation. *Tanya, the Masterpiece of Hasidic Wisdom: Selections Annotated & Explained*. Woodstock, Vt.: SkyLight Paths Publishing, 2010.

Sherwin, Byron L., and Seymour J. Cohen. *Creating an Ethical Jewish Life: A Practical Introduction to Classic Teachings on How to Be a Jew*. Woodstock, Vt.: Jewish Lights Publishing, 2001.

Shōwa, Emperor, "Imperial Rescript on Surrender." Translated by Hirakawa Tadaichi. Available on the Wikisource website.

Shulman, Jason. *Kabbalistic Healing: A Path to an Awakened Soul*. Rochester, Vt.: Inner Traditions, 2004.

Shulman, Jason. "Society of Souls." Available on the website for A Society of Souls: The School for Nondual Healing and Awakening.

Singer, Simeon. *The Standard Prayer Book: Authorized English Translation by the Rev. S. Singer.* Cincinatti, Ohio: Bloch Publishing Company, 1915.

Strassfeld, Michael, Betsy Platkin Teutsch, and Arnold M. Eisen. *The Jewish Holidays: A Guide and Commentary.* New York: Harper & Row, 1985.

Swarupananda, Swami, trans. and commentary. *Srimad-Bhagavad-Gita.* The 1909 edition is available at the Sacred Texts website.

Theise, Neil D. "Kabbalah And Complexity: Two Routes to One Reality." PDF file. No longer available.

Theise, Neil D., and Menas C. Kafatos. "Fundamental Awareness: A Framework for Integrating Science, Philosophy and Metaphysics." *Communicative and Integrative Biology* 9, no. 3 (May–June 2016): e1155010, doi: 10.1080/19420889.2016.1155010.

Tilles, Yerachmiel. "Kabbalah? Cabala? Qabalah?" Chabad website.

Tobias, Andrew (under the pseudonym John Reid). *The Best Little Boy in the World.* New York: Ballantine, 1998.

Tresidder, Jack. *Dictionary of Symbols: An Illustrated Guide to Traditional Images, Icons, and Emblems.* San Francisco: Chronicle, 1998.

UNHCR: The UN Refugee Agency website. "Figures at a Glance." This is the website for the Office of the United Nations High Commissioner for Refugees.

Unterman, Alan. *Dictionary of Jewish Lore and Legend.* London: Thames and Hudson, 1991.

U.S. Department of State website, "Refugee Admission Statistics: FY 2007–2015 Archive.

Waite, Arthur E., and Pamela Colman Smith. "Universal Waite Tarot Deck." U.S. Games Systems, Inc.

Walls, Jeannette. *The Glass Castle: A Memoir.* New York: Scribner, an Imprint of Simon & Schuster, Inc., 2017.

Wen, Benebell. *Holistic Tarot: An Integrative Approach to Using Tarot for Personal Growth.* Berkeley, Calif.: North Atlantic Books, 2015.

Westcott, W. Wynn. *Sepher Yetzirah and the Thirty-Two Paths of Wisdom.* Wheaton, Ill.: Theosophical Publishing Society, 1893.

Whitehouse, Maggy. *Total Kabbalah: Bring Balance and Happiness into Your Life.* San Francisco: Chronicle, 2008.

Windle, Susan. *Through the Gates: A Practice for Counting the Omer.* Charleston, S.C.: CreateSpace Independent, 2013.

Acknowledgments

IF THE PRACTICE OF COUNTING THE OMER has taught me anything, it's that humility and gratitude are foundation practices. And if writing the book has taught me anything, it's that it would never have been possible without the learning, inspiration, and support I received from a community of extraordinary people.

I wish to thank my teacher and friend Eileen Allman, Ph.D., who encouraged me to take the study of tarot as seriously as the Renaissance texts we studied together. Mrs. Marilyn Tribus, who found me wandering lost in the hallways of Canarsie High School and who made a place for me in a class I wasn't registered for, saving my life in the process. And Joan Glaser, who saw, knew, and held a place in her heart.

Over the years, there have been many members of my hevra—fellow seekers, companions who have joined me on different parts of the journey and whose love, support, and fearless, insightful truth telling are gifts beyond the measure of recognition in a list. The limits of my words cannot express my debt of gratitude to these, my friends and family-of-choice: Sherry Kohn, Marion Solomon, Timothy David Cassidy, Anne Hoff, Steven Sashen, Susan Mayginnes, Deirdre Boyle, Cantor Caitlin Bromberg, Rafi Bromberg, Julie Otsuka, Dylan Leiner, Wayne Cato, Robert Dvorkin, Katherine Kurs, Andrea Schwartz, Irene Weisberg, William Swann, Jeff French Segall, Ricki Lulov Segall, Philip Baisely, Roberta Kiss, Louise Santelices, George Perlov, Mark Segal, Jon Jensen, Alejandro Morales, Neil Patrick Connelly, Judy Kamilhor, Robert Chang, Jordan Stein, Gregg and Martha Fox, Steven Lemoncello, Stan Magnan, John Chiafalo, Christopher Yohmei Blasdel,

Mika Kimula, Andrew Ramer, Laura Simms, Perry Brass, Danyal Lawson, Masayuki Ozawa, Eric Gabriel Lehman, Ian Young, Maic Asti, Annie Schmidt, Jim Fouratt, Michael Knowles, Alan Gomberg, Daniel Neudell, Ronald Sternberg, Mari Makinami, Hiroshi and Wakiko Komazawa, Andrew Achsen, Nara Sangster Fuchs, Dr. Neil Theise, Jackie Haught, Jackie Rudin, Kiyoshi Eguchi, Steven Pascal, Josh Baran, Ilene Malakoff, Colin Glaum, Scott Ryan, Larry Durst, Rachel Marie Morillo, Ben Ellentuck.

My rabbis: Rabbi Marcelo Bronstein, Rabbi Rolando Matalon, Rabbi Felicia Sol, Rabbi Jay Michaelson, Rabbi Amichai Lau-Lavie, Rabbi Tamar Crystal, Rabbi David Ingber, Rabbi Dianne Cohler-Esses, Rabbi Judd Kruger Levingston, Rabbi Marshall T. Meyer, z"l, Rabbi Zalman Schachter-Shalomi, z"l.

My guides: Maxson McDowell, Joenine Roberts, Gay and Kathlyn Hendricks, Jason Shulman.

My tarot hevra: Ferol Humphrey, Abraham Bae, Stacy Creamer, Timothy Liu, Joe Schippa, Scott Martin, Susan Lynx, Angelo Nasios, Sasha Graham, Heather Mendel, Benebell Wen, Ruth and Wald Amberstone, and the crew at the Tarot School, The OTTERS and the many friends I've made at The Readers Studio.

Special thanks to Rachel Pollack, Mary K. Greer, Rabbi Jill Hammer, and Alyssa Gluf, all of whom gave generously of their time to read early drafts of this book and shared their insights and corrections. Any mistakes that remain here are all mine.

My family: Joseph and Hannah Horn, Irving and Frances Horn, Frances Watson, Robert Horn, Richard and Mary Horn, Megan Horn, Hattie Rosenthal Roth Wexler, Helene Figman, Barbara Zemel, and Alfred, Siegfried, and Harriet Horn.

The men I have loved, whose learning informs me every day and whose memory lives in my heart: William David Agress, Stanley Obey, Glenn Denis, Felix Lindicy, Gary Payne, Gilbert Mark Sprague, Louis Rispoli. And the incomparable and inimitable Hiroshi Aoki.

For pushing me to do it, Jacob Dannett.

My courageous brothers and sisters of the Gay Liberation Front,

Gay Youth, the Gay Activist Alliance, Identity House and NewFest.

Last, thanks to my lawyer, Sheila Levine, and of course, Jon Graham, Jeanie Levitan, Jennie Marx, and Jeffrey Robert Lindholm, along with the whole team at Inner Traditions, who believed in this project and helped me bring it to fruition.

Index

Abraham, tent open on four sides, 35, 48, 217

abuse, 64, 415

Acceptance Prayer, 160–61

addiction, 24, 47–48, 52, 82, 136, 154–55, 197, 203. *See also* twelve-step process

addithana, 193

Adonai, 499

"adorning the bride," 482

afterlife, 410

Akiva, Rabbi, 402

alcoholism, 86

Amalek, 446–47

amends, making, 299, 301

Amidah, 155n

Angels in America, 473–74

anicca, 116

anxiety, and Counting the Omer, 14

apprentice, and master, 80–81

Ark of the Covenant, 353–54

Armstrong, Neil, 21

arousal, 349

artisan, 399–401

Ashkenazi, Rabbi Yosef ben Shalom, 418

Assiyah, defined, 28–29

attention, 59

Atzilut, defined, 27–28

author. *See* Horn, Mark (author)

Awe, 294, 295. *See also* Gevurah

Azriel of Girona, Rabbi, 9, 30

Baal Shem Tov, 106–7, 150, 290, 356, 463, 483

Balance, 19–20, 24, 61, 66–67, 119–20, 157–58, 178

Beauty, 20, 112–13, 116, 160. *See also* Tiferet

Being There, 413

belief, 8, 53, 69, 99, 190–91, 196, 275, 295–96

Best Little Boy in the World syndrome, 300–301

betrayal, 143–44, 301, 365, 387–88

Bezalel, 399–401

Bhagavad Gita, 51

Binah, 18

bittul, 324

Blake, William, 450

blessing, 281
nontraditional version, 43

Bohm, David, 27

Bonding, 23–24, 260, 345. *See also* Yesod

Boundaries, 109, 125–26, 232–34, 358–59

B'riah, defined, 28–29

B'riatic Defense, 115

"Bring out your dead!," 455

Brooks, Mel, 86

Buber, Martin, 327–28
Buddha, 37, 297
Buddhism, xii–xiii, 37, 89
  and belief, 296
  Judaism and, 462–63
bullying, 438–39

Cabala tradition, 10, 62, 207. *See also*
  Kabbalah
Caesar, Julius, 151–52
Caleb, 278
cancer, story of author's mother,
  451–53
chakras, 88
Chamberlain, Neville, 439
charity, 66–67, 164–65
  principles of, 164–65
Charleston church incident, 312–13
chaver, 374
cheating, 387–88
cherubim, 413–14
Chesed
  defined, 18–19, 49
  Loving-kindness and, 18–19
  negative side, 19
  week of Counting the Omer, 46–99
Chesed of Chesed, 46–53
Chesed of Gevurah, 101–8
Chesed of Hod, 283–93
Chesed of Malchut, 426–33
Chesed of Netzach, 216–26
Chesed of Tiferet, 156–65
Chesed of Yesod, 346–58
chet, 408
childhood, 64, 67, 95, 160, 170, 190,
  194–95, 216, 275, 409–10
children, gifted, 445
Chögyam Trungpa, Rinpoche, 331
Chokhmah, defined, 18
Christmas Carol, A (Dickens), 112
Church of the Holy Sepulchre, 140

commandments, observation of, 303,
  366
Commitment, 248–49, 371–72, 381–82
communities, and LGBTQ, 367–68
companion, in study, 44, 374, 380
Compassion, 117–19, 187, 237. *See also*
  Tiferet
  limits of, 206–7
  Tiferet and, 20–21
Compassion in Action, 207, 209–10
Compassion in Action (Ram Dass), 207
complaint, 274
Connection, 138, 139. *See also* Yesod
  Yesod and, 23–25
Conscious Community (Shapira), 162
Conscious Loving (Hendricks), 370
Counting the Omer. *See also under*
  individual topics
  biblical commandment and, 3–4
  different ways to perform, 38–40
  group practice, 43–45
  as living tradition, 1–2
  purpose/goal of, 1, 302
  requires counting days and weeks, 38
  results from, 2
  timing of, 8–9
craftsman, 320–21
Creating, 182
Creativity, 223–24, 231
crisis, spiritual, 297
Crown, 17
Crucifixion, 62
cup, shape of, 103
Cups, 29, 42

daily practice, how to follow the,
  38–45
Dalai Lama, 174–75
Daniel 12:3, 481
Danyal, 419–21
Day of Atonement, 343

Days (of Counting of the Omer). *See* listing in Table of Contents, pages xv-ix

Days of Awe, 294–95

death, 50, 96, 410, 419–21

Decker, Ronald, 33–34, 143–44, 317

Defender, 395–97, 398

defensiveness, 69–70, 261–63, 431

DeMille, Agnes, 185

depression, 87–88

de Ropp, Robert, 180

Desire, 379–80, 402–3

Deuteronomy 25:17, 446

Dickinson, Emily, 197

Dignity, 98

Diogenes, 377

Discipline, 54, 56, 112–13, 227–28

discriminating intelligence, 96, 105, 171–72, 288–90. *See also* Swords

divination, 255–56

Divine Presence, visibility of, 457–58

"Don't Stop," 359

DovBer, Rabbi Sholom, 132

Do What You Love, 224–25

Drama of the Gifted Child (Miller), 445

dreams, 253–55

Dynamic Balance, 61, 156–59

Eastertide, 7

Eckford, Elizabeth, 271–72

Edison, Thomas, 314–15, 316–17

eighteen (number), 178

Eight of Cups, 76–77, 131–32, 190–91, 252–56, 285–86, 296–97, 305–6, 315–17, 323–26, 330–31, 338–41, 395–97, 462–63

Eight of Pentacles, 80–81, 194–95, 258–60, 291–93, 300–301, 310–12, 319–21, 323–26, 333–35, 342–44, 399–402, 466–69

Eight of Swords, 77–78, 133–34,

192–93, 256–57, 288–90, 298–99, 307–9, 317–19, 323–26, 331–33, 341–42, 397–98, 464–66

Eight of Wands, 75, 129–31, 188–89, 251–52, 284–85, 295–96, 303–5, 314–15, 323–26, 328–29, 336–38, 392–94, 460–61

Ein Sof, 17, 499

Eli, 279

Elijah, 130

Eliot, T. S., 425

Emotional Abandonment Two-Step, 395–98

emotions, 29, 95, 99, 182, 186, 202–3, 396–97

    feeling painful, 64, 67, 89, 91

Endurance, 121–22, 181–82, 227–28, 236, 312–13. *See also* Netzach

    Netzach and, 215–16

    two kinds, 246

enemies, 71

Enemy of the People, An (Ibsen), 122

Enough Is as Good as a Feast, 285–86

enslavement, 52–53, 85, 123, 233–34, 381–82

Epstein, Mark, 402

Erev Shavuot, 302

Esoteric Tarot, The (Decker), 317

ethical will, 456–57

Etteila, 31–32, 34, 81

Exodus, 3:5, 479

Ezray, Rabbi Nat, 306

farmer, 225, 244, 320–21

fasting story, 227–28

father

    author's father, 234–35

    role as, 194–95

fearless moral inventory, 459

feathers story, 144

femininity, 220–21, 332, 354, 358

Fire Island, 294

Five of Cups, 57–58, 103–4, 108, 111, 114–16, 123, 131–32, 141, 150–51, 169, 230–32, 296–97, 362–64, 436–37

Five of Pentacles, 60, 106–7, 112, 119–20, 126, 135–37, 145, 152–55, 172–73, 234–36, 300–301, 366–69, 440–42

Five of Swords, 58–59, 104–5, 108, 111–12, 117, 124–25, 133–34, 142–44, 151, 171–72, 232–34, 298–99, 364–66, 438–39

Five of Wands, 55, 102–3, 108, 111, 113–14, 121–22, 129–31, 139, 148, 167–68, 228–30, 295–96, 360–62, 435–36

flood, 94

Flow, 347–49, 349–52, 429–30

Flow (Csikszentmihalyi), 291

flower arranging, 110–11

Forbidden Planet, The, 289

Forster, E. M., 25, 475

Forty, in Jewish tradition, 391

forty-nine days, 1–5, 15, 37

Foundation. *See also* Yesod
Yesod and, 23–25, 345–46

Four of Cups, 47–53, 48–49, 57, 76, 85–86, 94–95, 103–4, 159–60, 219–21, 285–86, 349–52, 429–30

Four of Pentacles, 47–53, 52–53, 59–60, 72–73, 80–81, 89–91, 97–99, 106–7, 163–64, 224–26, 291–93, 355–58, 432–33

Four of Swords, 47–53, 49–52, 58, 77–78, 87–89, 95–96, 104–5, 161, 163, 221–24, 288–90, 353–54, 430–32

Four of Wands, 35, 47–53, 48, 69–70, 75, 83–84, 93, 102, 157, 217–18, 284–85, 347–49, 427–28

four worlds, 26–31

Four Yorkshiremen, 319

Frankl, Viktor E., 137

ganbare, 215

Gandhi, Mahatma, 312–13

garden, 268–70, 333

Gates of Light, 150, 153–55, 343–44, 366, 368, 469, 481–82
Sephirot and Divine Light, 12–15

Gates of Light, The (Gikatilla), 33, 153, 279, 320

gay issues, xi. *See also* LGBTQ issues
Best Little Boy in the World syndrome, 300–301
gay marriage, 348
gay relationships, 220–21, 332–33, 363–64, 372–73
transcending defensiveness, 69–70

Gébelin, Court de, 31–32

Gedulah, 19

Gevurah, 19–20, 54
negative side, 20
week of Counting the Omer, 100–155

Gevurah of Chesed, 54–61

Gevurah of Gevurah, 108–12

Gevurah of Hod, 294–301

Gevurah of Malchut, 433–42

Gevurah of Netzach, 227–36

Gevurah of Tiferet, 166–74

Gevurah of Yesod, 358–69

Gikatilla, Joseph, 33–34, 417–18

Ginzberg, Louis, 413

Glass Castle, The (Walls), 454

Glory. *See also* Hod
Hod and, 22–23

glow, 322–23

God. *See also* Ein Sof
beliefs about, 190–91
forsaken by, 473–75
God language, 499–501
voice of, 12

Goenka, S. N., 58
gold, 73
Gold, Rabbi Shefa, 483
Golden Dawn, 32–33
Gospel of Thomas, 163
gossip, 144
Gratitude, 283
Green, Rabbi Arthur, 175
grief, 202–3

HaKana, Rabbi Nechunya Ben, 257
halaka, 127
happiness, 146, 180
    and earnings, 286–87
Harmony, 156, 178. *See also* Tiferet
    Japanese concept of, 377–78
heart, open, 67, 70, 141, 164
Hendricks, Gay and Kathlyn, 77, 141,
    370
Henry V (Shakespeare), 188–89
hevruta, defined, 44
Hidden Saints, 346
hillula, 322
Hirohito, Emperor, 215
Hitler, Adolf, 439
hitting bottom, 203, 408
Hod
    defined, 22–23
    as Glory or Splendor, 22–23, 74, 282
    as Gratitude, 283
    negative side, 23
    Surrender and, 74
    week of Counting the Omer, 282–344
hoda'ah, 282
Hod of Chesed, 74–82
Hod of Gevurah, 128–38
Hod of Hod, 321–26
Hod of Malchut, 459–69
Hod of Netzach, 249–60
Hod of Tiferet, 187–96
Hod of Yesod, 391–402

holiness of creation, 90
Holocaust, 134, 178–79
holy ground, 479–80
Holy Spirit, 6–7, 255
homeless people, 106–7, 145–46
Horn, Mark (author)
    author's father, 234–35
    author's mother (cancer account),
        451–53
    his introduction to tarot, Counting
        the Omer, etc., xi–xiv
    leaving and returning to Judaism, xi–xiv
Hosea, 365
    2:21-22, 484–85
Humility, 76–77, 78–79, 188–89,
        284–85, 287, 293, 295, 323–26.
    See also Hod
    Compassion in, 310–11
    creates space, 333–34
    Endurance in, 312–13
    extremes of, 256–57
    false, 309
    and knowledge, 391–92
    Leadership and, 304–5
    perceived as weakness, 329
    Strength in, 314–15
Hungry Ghost, 261

I-It Relationship, 327, 330
India visit, 309
Inside Out, 168
interpretation, and revelation, 482–83
Intimate Relationship, 370. *See also*
        Relationship
Isaac the Blind, Rabbi, 9, 469
Isaiah, 58:12, 469
isolation, 331–33
Israelites, ancient, 242. *See also* Moses
    Bezalel story, 399–401
    breaking the covenant, 365–66
    Commitment to enslavement, 381–82

and complaint, 272–73
and destruction of Temple, 464–65
enslavement of, 233–34
fitness to enter Promised land,
    277–78
freedom from Egypt, 47
and I-Thou, 328
Marriage to the Deity, 348
and process of Counting the Omer, 1
and Promised Land scouts, 267
worshipping golden calf, 391
Itaruta Diletata, 349
I-Thou Relationship, 327–29

Jacob, vision of, 266–67
Japan
    Endurance in, 215–16
    Harmony in, 377–78
Jeremiah, 461
Jerusalem, 464
Jesus, 248, 386
Jewish liturgical calendar, 294–95
Jonah, 393, 460–61
Joseph, 24, 253, 355–57
Joshua, 278
joy, 437
Judaism. *See also under individual topics*
    Buddhism and, 462–63
    history of, 161–62
Judgment, 105, 166
Justice, 125

Kabbalah
    defined, 9
    goal of, 12
    goal of Kabbalistic work, 280
    origins of, 3–5
    tarot and, 10–11, 31–37
    and Western occultism, 10–11
Kaddish, 500
kanji, 128

Kantrowitz, Rabbi Min, 282
Kaplan, Aryeh, 500
karōshi, 212
kavanath, 38
Keats, John, 334
"Keep Your Eyes on the Prize," 247–48
Keter, 17, 432
key words, 40–42, 128–29
kineahora, 93
king, with high walls, 106–7
Kingdom/Kingship. *See also* Malchut
    Malchut and, 25–26, 92
King of the Hill, 180
Kliegman, Isabel Radow, 64, 415
klipot, 116
knight, 65, 288
    Night Vigil and, 49–51, 58, 71, 96
Kook, Rav Abraham Isaac, 12
Krishna, 51
Kushner, Tony, 473–74

Lag B'Omer, 321–22
Lamed-Vavniks, 346
Lamentations, 1:1, 464
Leadership, 56, 273–74, 322, 337, 344
    burdens of, 443–44
    Humility and, 304–5
left-handed path, 402
León, Rabbi Moses de, 9–10, 322, 417
Levi, Eliphas, 32
Levi, Rabbi Joshua ben, 98
Leviticus, 26:12, 476
LGBTQ issues, 263. *See also* gay issues
    communities that welcome, 367–68
    movement, 218
    ordaining gay and lesbian rabbis,
        127, 140
Limits, 169–70
Lincoln, Abraham, 444
Little Rock Nine, 271–72
loneliness, 409–11

Loop of Awareness, 141–42
Love. *See also* Chesed; Relationship
    Chesed and, 18–19
    Endurance and, 219–21
    Love wins, 217
    Saul of Tarsus on, 216–17
Loving-kindness, 46–47, 89. *See also*
    Chesed
    Chesed and, 18–19
Luria, Rabbi Isaac, 322
lying, 369–71

Ma'ashe Merkavah, 472
Madonna, 97–98
Magen David, 178
Maimonides, eight principles of
    charity, 164–65
Major Arcana, 31–33
Malchut, 90–91, 426
    defined, 25–26
    and Kingdom/Kingship, 25–26, 92
    week of Counting the Omer, 425–80
Malchut of Chesed, 92–99
Malchut of Gevurah, 147–55
Malchut of Hod, 335–44
Malchut of Malchut, 478–80
Malchut of Netzach, 271–81
Malchut of Tiferet, 206–14
Malchut of Yesod, 413–24
manual labor, 291–92
maps, 30
Marshall Plan, 237
master, v. apprentice, 80–81
master key, 150
Mastery. *See also* Netzach
    Netzach and, 21–22
Mazel tov!, 270
meditation, 43, 88–89, 96, 124, 130–31,
        192–93
    and ethics, 429
    instructions for daily, 486–87

Mellet, Comte de, 32
Messiah, 21, 98–99
Messianic Consciousness, 280
#MeToo, 407
Meyer, z"l, Rabbi Marshall T., 368
mezuzah, 154
midrash, 48
Minor Arcana, 33–36
    Sephirot and, 13, 36
minyan, 44, 418
miracles, 276, 306
Mishnah, 4
Mitchell, Joni, 269
money, 422–23
mono no aware, 116, 174
Morris dancers, 167
Moses, 36, 55–56, 153, 267, 428
    and Bezalel, 400–401
    complaint of, 272–73
    and Jethro, 149
    killing of Egyptian overseer, 242, 254
    radiant face of, 322

Nachman of Breslov, Rabbi, 278, 350–52
negative capability, 334
nes, 306
Netzach
    defined, 21–22
    endurance and, 68
    Mastery and, 21–22
    week of Counting the Omer, 215–81
Netzach of Gevurah, 121–28
Netzach of Hod, 312–21
Netzach of Malchut, 450–69
Netzach of Netzach, 246–49
Netzach of Tiferet, 178–86
Netzach of Yesod, 381–90
Netzack of Chesed, 68–73
New Age, 466
niggunim, 483–84
Night Vigil, 49, 58, 89, 96, 481

Nine of Cups, 85–87, 141–42, 199–200,
    264–66, 330–31, 349–52, 362–64,
    373–75, 384–86, 395–97, 403–13,
    416–18, 471–72
Nine of Pentacles, 89–91, 145, 204–5,
    268–71, 333–35, 355–58, 366–69,
    378–80, 388–90, 399–402, 403–13,
    422–24, 476–77
Nine of Swords, 87–89, 142–43, 201–4,
    266–68, 331–33, 353–54, 364–66,
    376–78, 386–88, 397–98, 403–13,
    418–21, 473–75
Nine of Wands, 83–85, 139, 198–99,
    261–63, 328–29, 347–49, 360–62,
    371–73, 382–83, 392–94, 403–13,
    414–16, 470–71

Obama, Barack, 443
Object Relations, 170
olamim, 26
Omer. *See also* Counting the Omer
    defined, 3–4
Omer calendar, 16
"Only connect!," 25, 475
Open to Desire (Epstein), 402
Oresteia, The, 242–43
Organization, 111
orgasm, 75–76
Osho, 183
overwork, 212

Padmasambhava, 404
Panchatantra, 429
Papus, 34
Passover, 481
Pentacles, 29, 97
Pentecost, 481–85
    Christian adoption of, 5–7
    Jewish and Christian traditions of, 3
Perachya, Joshua ben, 374
Perfection, 113

Perseverance, 239–40. *See also*
    Endurance
Peshat, 243
Peter, 6–7
Phillips, Captain Richard, 63
Picasso, 223–24
pockets, two pockets teaching, 92
poor, the, 106–7, 145–46, 440–41
possibilities, endlessness of, 275–76
Potiphar, 355–56
potter/pottery, 80–81, 103–4
poverty consciousness, 173
practice, daily, 38–45
prayer, 486–87
    at end of Torah service, 340–41
    nontraditional version, 43
    for peace, 292–93
    service, 416–18
prayer vigil
    Christian, 7
    Tikkun prayer vigil, 8–9
prediction, 255–56
projections, 384–86
prophecy, 253–54, 460–61
Proverbs, 435
Psalms, 460
    Psalm 23, 103
    Psalm 67, 177
    Psalms 94:18, 470
    Psalms 119:62, 481
Pursuer, 395–97, 398

Qabalah, 10. *See also* Kabbalah
questions for reflection
    on acceptance, 301
    on Balance, 178, 449
    on betrayal, 226, 301, 449
    on body understanding, 433
    on Boundaries, 173–74, 368–69
    on bullying, 442
    on charity, 442

on community, 357
on Compassion, 67–68, 186, 214, 245
on complaint, 281
on correcting others, 401–2
on criticism, 107–8
on defensiveness, 73, 259, 401, 433, 459
on Divine Connection, 271
on emotions, 99, 441
on Endurance, 186, 226, 249, 321
on finances, 99, 226
on goals, 321, 458–59
on honoring the planet, 344
on Humility, 259, 293, 311–12,
    334–35, 344
on Intimacy, 91–92, 423–24
on isolation, 412
on larger causes, 195–96
on listening, 326
on loneliness, 449
on loss/victimization, 137–38
on Love, 53–54, 60–61, 73, 82,
    107–8, 226
on mercy, 477
on Relationships, 271, 281, 335,
    357–58, 368–69, 380, 390, 401,
    411–12
on Responsibility, 155
on seeing "celestial light," 459
on sexuality, 412
on sharing, 260
on spiritual paths, 468–69, 477
on standing up for yourself, 301
on staying open, 146–47
on Strength, 127–28
on Structure, 112, 120
on study, 380, 477
on taking care of yourself, 344
on therapy, 468
on victimhood, 321
reviewing the Counting the Omer
    process, 480

Rachamim, 161
racial discrimination, 307–9, 312–13
Radical Judaism (Green), 175
rainbow, 94–95, 275, 472, 479
Ram Dass, 207
Ramer, Andrew, 482
rape, 359
rape culture, 360–62
rat race, 286
reading tarot cards, 189, 255–56
reciprocity, 378–79
refugees, 117–19
Relationship, 87, 90–91, 382–83,
    398–401. *See also* Intimate
    Relationship; sexuality
  and Endurance, 389–90
  and Heart Connection, 202–3
  ideal of, 270
  I-Thou, 327–29
  and personal goals, 264–66
religion, limitations of, 465–66
renunciation, 76
Responsibility, 94, 148–49
  sharing, 208–9
Restraint, 109–10, 435–36
revelation, interpretation as,
    482–83
rigidity, 109–10
Rispoli, Louis, death of, 419–21
Robin Hood, 241–42
roles, 372–73
Roman coin story, 147
Roof, Dylann, 312–13
Roosevelt, Teddy, 439
Rooster Prince story, 350–52
Ruach HaKodesh, 255
rules of engagement, 139–41

Sacks, Rabbi Jonathan, 324
Safat Emet, 302
Sagan, Carl, 294

Saul of Tarsus, 216–17
Schacther-Shalomi, z"l, Rabbi Zalman, 197
Schindler, Oskar, 299
secrets, 376
Sefer Yetzirah, 4, 500
self-improvement, 137
Sephirot, 16, 131–32
    arrangement of, 12–13
    and corresponding Minor Arcana, *13*
    defined, 12–14
    forty-nine combinations of, 15–16
    individually described, 16–26
    Minor Arcana and, 36
    origins of, 4–5, 12, 132
    top three and lower seven, 15
Seven of Cups, 70, 123, 181–82,
        219–21, 230–32, 239–40, 247–49,
        252–56, 264–66, 274–76, 315–17,
        384–86, 453–55
Seven of Pentacles, 72–73, 126–27,
        184–85, 224–26, 234–36,
        243–45, 247–49, 258–60, 268–71,
        279–81, 319–21, 388–90, 457–59
Seven of Swords, 71, 124–25, 183–84,
        221–24, 232–34, 241–43, 247–49,
        256–57, 266–68, 277–78, 317–19,
        386–88, 455–57
Seven of Wands, 69–70, 121–22,
        217–18, 228–30, 238–39, 247–49,
        251–52, 261–63, 273–74, 314–15,
        382–83, 451–53
sexuality, 197, 268–71, 337. *See also*
    Relationship
    and betrayal, 365
    Boundaries and, 358–61
    sublimation of, 90–91
    Yesod and, 23–24, 88
shalom, 389
shalom bayit, 276
Shapira, Rebbe Kalonymus Kalman, 162

Shavuot, 5
Shekinah, 341–42, 426, 473, 499
    and Malchut, 440
Shemini Atzeret, 343
Sh'ma, 154
Shulamit, 389
Shulman, Jason, 115, 336
siddur, 500
simcha, 265
Simcha, Rabbi Bunem, and the two
        pockets, 92
singing, in Tikkun, 483
singleness, 363–64, 408
Six of Cups, 64, 114–16, 123, 159–60,
        169, 176, 181, 190–91, 199–200,
        209–11, 239–40, 305–6, 373–75,
        444–45
Six of Pentacles, 66–67, 119–20, 163–64,
        172–73, 177, 184–85, 194–95,
        204–5, 213–14, 243–45, 310–12,
        378–80, 448–49
Six of Swords, 65–66, 117–18, 161,
        163, 171–72, 176–77, 183–84,
        192–93, 201–4, 211–12, 241–43,
        307–9, 376–78, 446–47
Six of Wands, 62–63, 113–14, 157–58,
        167–68, 175, 179–80, 188,
        198–99, 208–9, 238–39, 303–5,
        371–73, 443–44
Sixth Great Extinction, 302–3
slavery. *See* enslavement
Sleep of Reason, The (Goya), 289
Smith, Pamela Colman, 33–36, 153n,
        406
social loner, 200
Society for Creative Anachronism, 438
Society of Souls, A, 336
Solomon, King, 32, 166, 389
Song of Songs, 389, 402
soul, four levels of, 30
Soulforce Equality Riders, 127, 129

Sovereign, defined, 434
Sovereignty, 425–26, 429–30
speaking in tongues, 6–7
spiritual discipline, 227
spiritual materialism, 331
spiritual practice, 227
Splendor, 282. *See also* Hod
    Hod and, 22–23
still, small voice, 130
stone that was rejected, 367
Strength. *See also* Gevurah
    Gevurah and, 19–20
Structural inequality, 120
Structure, 54, 57, 111–12, 120, 147,
    149. *See also* Gevurah
study, 44, 374–75, 380
support, 470–71
Surrender, 74, 133–34, 282, 295. *See
    also* Hod
    to a Higher Power, 250
Swords, 50

Tanakh, 269
Tarfon, Rabbi, 127, 186
tarot. *See also* Counting the Omer
    history, 31–36
    Kabbalah and, 10–11
tarot cards, 31–34
    divination and prediction with,
        255–56
    key words and, 40–42
    reading, 189, 255–56
    using in Counting the Omer,
        38–40
tarot decks, 31–36
    having one's own, 42
teacher, 374–75
tea story (Zen), 324
Temple, destruction of, 473
Ten of Cups, 94–95, 150–51, 209–11,
    274–76, 338–41, 416–18, 429–30,

436–37, 444–45, 453–55, 462–63,
    471–72, 479–80
Ten of Pentacles, 97–99, 152–55,
    213–14, 279–81, 342–44, 422–24,
    432–33, 440–42, 448–49, 457–59,
    466–69, 476–77, 479–80
Ten of Swords, 95–96, 151, 211–12,
    277–78, 341–42, 418–21, 430–32,
    438–39, 446–47, 455–57, 464–66,
    473–75, 479–80
Ten of Wands, 93–94, 148, 208–9,
    272–74, 336–38, 414–16, 427–28,
    435–36, 443–44, 451–53, 460–61,
    470–71, 479–80
ten people, 416–17
Tertullian, 295–96
therapy, 98, 384–86
thirty-six, significance of, 346
Tiananmen Square protests, 299
Tiferet, 16, 24, 61–62, 67, 116, 156
    Beauty and Truth and, 20–21
    defined, 20–21
    week of Counting the Omer, 156–214
Tiferet of Chesed, 61–68
Tiferet of Gevurah, 112–20
Tiferet of Hod, 302–12
Tiferet of Malchut, 442–49
Tiferet of Netzach, 237–45
Tiferet of Tiferet, 174–78
Tiferet of Yesod, 369–80
Tikkun, on Day 50, 481–85
Tikkun Leil Shavuot, 8–9, 44
Tikkun Olam, 28–29, 60, 94, 440,
    467, 470
    creating space for, 484
Tissot, James Jacques Joseph, 353
Tobias, Andrew, 300
"To every thing there is a season," 437
Torah, 4–5, 100
    study of, 466–67, 482–83
Torah Told Different (Ramer), 482

traitor, 233

transgression, 257

trauma, intimacy trauma, 404–7

Tree of Life, 12–15, 340, 343, 432, 469. *See also* Sephirot

trickster, 223

Truth, 442–43
  v. lying, 369–71

t'shuvah, 278

Turner, Brock, 361

turning, 348–49

twelve-step process, 132, 203–4, 249–50
  first three steps, 135–36
  fourth step, 459
  ninth step, 280
  and study, 374–75

typewriters, collecting, 339–40

Tzadikim Nistarim, 346

tzedakah, 164–65

Tzimtzum, 100

Understanding, Binah and, 18

Upper Limits Problem, 77, 278

Via Lucis, 7

victimization, 136–37, 299, 318–19, 321
  competitive victimhood, 318–19
  victim identity, 318–19

vine, 90

Vipassana meditation, 193

visions, 253–54

wa, 377–78

Waite, Arthur Edward, 32–34

Waite-Smith deck, 34–36

walls, 217

warrior's path, 51

Weather Underground, 242

Weeks (of Counting the Omer)
  Pentecost, 481–85
  Week 1: Chesed, 46–99

Week 2: Gevurah, 100–155

Week 3: Tiferet, 156–214

Week 4: Netzach, 215–81

Week 5: Hod, 282–344

Week 6: Yesod, 345–424

Week 7: Malchut, 425–80

We Shall Overcome, 246–47

"What the World Needs Now," 426

When Religion Becomes Evil (Kimball), 465

white-knuckling, 249

wholeness, 389

Will, 17

will, writing one's, 456–57

Wisdom, Chokhmah and, 18

witness, 187

Wolf of Wall Street, The, 423

"Woodstock," 269

Wordsworth, William, 457–58, 463

work, 466–69

World in a Grain of Sand, 450

worlds, four, 26–31

writing, creative, 182

yasher koach, 478

Yearning, 379–80, 389

yechida, 417

Yesod
  addiction and, 82
  and Bonding, 197, 345
  Connection and, 23–25, 82–83
  dark side of, 260–61
  defined, 23–25
  Foundation and, 23–25, 345–46
  negative side, 24–25
  week of Counting the Omer, 345–424

Yesod of Chesed, 82–92

Yesod of Gevurah, 138–47

Yesod of Hod, 327–35

Yesod of Malchut, 469–77

Yesod of Netzach, 260–71

Yesod of Tiferet, 196–206
Yesod of Yesod, 402–13
Yetzirah, defined, 28–29
YHVH, 30–31, 130
    on breaking the covenant, 365, 366
    and God language, 499–501
    sustaining power of, 460–61
    and vision, 253

yoducha, 177
Yohai, Rabbi Shimon Bar, 417, 471–72
Yom Kippur, 343
"Yusuf and Zulaikha," 355

zava'ah, 456–57
Zohar, 9–10, 31, 322, 417
Zulaikha, 355–57